POSTAL INDISCRETIONS

POSTAL

... nowe mieszkanie).

... dobrze o tym — zawsze

... i byśmy w jakikol-

... choćby myślami. Mys-

... iji przekonanie,

... gdzieś daleko mamy szczerych i oddanych

przyjaciół. Takich przyjaciół ma Pan w nas.

Jeszcze raz życzymy Panu najserdeczniej szczęś-

liwej drogi, zdobycia odpoczynku po prze-

życiach kontynentu i oczekując od Pana

parę słów z tej i tamtej strony morza

całujemy Pana bardzo serdecznie

Tadeusz i Tuśka Borowscy

[Zakrzym 1. 6. 47 [

Warszawa
Filtrowa 73 m. 37.

INDISCRETIONS

THE CORRESPONDENCE OF

TADEUSZ BOROWSKI

Edited by Tadeusz Drewnowski

Translated from the Polish by Alicia Nitecki

Northwestern University Press

Northwestern University Press
www.nupress.northwestern.edu

Photographs courtesy of the family of Anatol Girs

Printed in the United States of America

10 9 8 7 6 5 4 3 2 1

ISBN 978-0-8101-2960-3

The Library of Congress has cataloged the original, hardcover edition as follows:

Borowski, Tadeusz, 1922–1951.
    [Niedyskrecje pocztowe. English]
    Postal indiscretions : the correspondence of Tadeusz Borowski / edited by
Tadeusz Drewnowski ; translated from the Polish by Alicia Nitecki.
        p. cm.
    Includes bibliographical references and index.
    ISBN-13: 978-0-8101-2203-1 (cloth : alk. paper)
    ISBN-10: 0-8101-2203-0 (cloth : alk. paper)
    1. Borowski, Tadeusz, 1922–1951—Correspondence. 2. Authors, Polish—20th century—
Correspondence. 3. Holocaust survivors—Poland—Correspondence. I. Drewnowski, Tadeusz.
II. Nitecki, Alicia, 1942– III. Title.
PG7158.B613Z48 2007
891.8'517—dc22
[B]
                                                                2007012850

THIS TRANSLATION IS DEDICATED TO THE MEMORY OF ANATOL GIRS.

CONTENTS

TRANSLATOR'S PREFACE

Tadeusz Borowski's four Auschwitz stories "This Way for the Gas, Ladies and Gentlemen," "A Day at Harmenz," "The People Who Walked On," and "Auschwitz, Our Home (A Letter)" are internationally regarded as among the best literature on the Holocaust, but erroneous beliefs are often held about the author's own circumstances immediately after the war (for example, that he spent two years in a displaced persons' camp) and about the stories' place in his literary canon. They are often said to be his later work, written in Warsaw after his return from Germany.

In fact, the four stories are Borowski's first prose, written by him in Munich in the summer and fall of 1945, with two other former prisoners of Auschwitz, Janusz Nel Siedlecki and Krystyn Olszewski, for a book entitled *Byliśmy w Oświęcimiu* (*We Were in Auschwitz*). The stories, as he tells Mieczysław Grydzewski, Maria Rundo's uncle, in one of these letters, were written "to order." The "order" came from forty-year-old Anatol Girs, the preeminent Polish graphic artist and pub-lisher, who had been brought to Auschwitz from Warsaw during the Uprising and transported from there to Dautmergen and then Dachau-Allach—a man Borowski describes in this correspondence as being "like a hero out of Chesterton," and to whom Maria Borowska writes in a postscript to one of her husband's letters, "I am fully aware . . . how much he [Tadeusz] developed both morally and intellectually under your care in Munich." (She repeated this to me over the telephone the year before she died, saying "Ah, yes, Girs had an enormous moral and intellectual influence on Borowski.")

The fatherly, mentoring relationship Girs had with Borowski and the other two young men can clearly be seen in their correspondence with each other here. On receiving a copy of *Pożegnanie z Marią* (*Farewell to Maria*) and *Kamienny świat* (*The World of Stone*) from Borowski inscribed "To Pan Anatol, the stories you made me write," for example, Girs thanks him but says, "I had no hand in the making of *Pożegnanie*. The books that I would have projected would cer-tainly have been written differently." He adds, "You use the titles 'Actor,' 'Singer,'

etc. Even though it is not a clear giving of surnames, some of this gossip was not worth writing about."

In his preface to the 1958 reissue in Poland of *We Were in Auschwitz,* Olszewski calls Girs the "fourth author . . . the initiator of the literary and publishing endeavor. . . . On his initiative in the first months of freedom we embarked on joint work on a cycle of Auschwitz stories." The handwritten dedication in the copy Olszewski sent to Girs reads, "For you Tolek, who are the father of this book."

The circumstances under which the book came into being are recounted in Tadeusz Drewnowski's 1962 biography of Borowski, *Ucieczka z kamiennego świata* (*Escape from the World of Stone*) and in Andrzej Klossowski's *Anatol Girs—artysta książki* (*Anatol Girs—Artist of the Book*). On hearing his young friends talking about Auschwitz in the displaced persons' camp in Freimann, and watching Nel Siedlecki writing down his camp memories, Drewnowski writes that Girs "proposed the idea that the three young men put together a collectively written book, or rather a cycle of books, about the camps." Girs's original intention had been to follow the Auschwitz book with one about the other camps the authors had been in and one about the displaced persons' camp.

Girs not only suggested the writing of the book, but also made the conditions to do so possible when he received permission from the Polish Red Cross Committee in London to establish a family tracing service in Munich, and for the three men to work for him there. They were allowed to leave the Freimann camp (where, as Borowski describes in some of these letters, conditions were less than favorable) and were allocated their own apartment in which, after each day's work at the tracing service, they worked on the stories. Borowski, who Drewnowski says had "bridled" at the very idea of the book, did so reluctantly. "A criminal act" on his part, he says in one letter; an "embarrassing" side of his life, in another. By early November 1945, the galleys were being prepared. By early 1946 the book was in press.

The moral perspective in Borowski's stories has often been repudiated—as it was by the editors of *Twórczość* (*Creative Work*) when, in 1946, they published "A Day at Harmenz" and "This Way for the Gas" (under Olszewski's name, and under its original title "The Sosnowiec-Będzin Transport")—or seen as an example of his "nihilism." But that same moral perspective is present in Olszewski's and Nel Siedlecki's stories as well.

In their preface to the book, they write: "Confinement in the camp, destitution, torture, and death in the gas chamber are not heroism, are not even

anything positive. It was defeat, the almost immediate abandonment of ideological principles. . . . We stress this strongly because myths and legends will arise on both sides. We did not fight for the concept of nation in the camp, nor for the inner restructuring of man; we fought for a bowl of soup, for a place to sleep, for women, for gold and watches from the transports . . . we often renounced our humanity because we wanted to survive."

Their mutual aim in the book, as Olszewski writes in his 1958 preface, was "by using our own experiences, against a backdrop of events we had personally lived through or witnessed, to portray the effect of the workings of the mechanisms of a concentration camp on the psyche and morality of the prisoner."

To this end, all three authors, not just Borowski, who has often been praised for doing so, set their stories in the places they had actually worked—Borowski, for example, did work on the ramp at Auschwitz on one single day and was part of the Harmenz Kommando, Drewnowski says in his biography. Nel Siedlecki did work in the Gypsy camp, as Borowski writes here, and so on; and all of them use their own names and first-person narrators. The idea to do so came from Girs, whose biographer, Andrzej Klossowski, quotes him as claiming full responsibility for it in approving the work as its publisher, and, as Klossowski correctly stresses, "the real question is less whose idea it was, and more, what it was hoped would be gained by it." He goes on to say that Girs answers this question best, quoting him as saying (in a letter to Drewnowski on March 30, 1969), " 'They' is always someone, not us, society. But 'I' reaches everyone. Everyone feels a shared responsibility."

The less than flattering portrayal of human behavior in the camp was, in fact, not some kind of psychological flaw in Borowski, but a deliberate literary device to show to the fullest possible extent the evil of fascism. In a letter to Wanda Leopold on June 23, 1948, speaking about Adolf Rudnicki's stories, Borowski writes, "Adolf thinks that the best cure for fascism is to show the beauty of those dying as a result of it (through this, he obscures the very mechanism of fascism— if people were like this, how could what happened have been possible?)."

It is my hope that this translation of the Borowski correspondence, a correspondence that provides a fascinating picture of literary life and endeavor in the immediate postwar period in Poland, will lead some among his English-speaking audience to a reevaluation of his work.

NOTE TO THE READER ON POLISH NAMES

Maria Rundo was known to acquaintances and friends by the sobriquet Tuśka.

Short forms of Polish first names:
Anatol—Tolek
Barbara—Basia, Baśka
Bożenna—Bożenka
Edmund—Mundek
Juliusz—Julek
Lesław—Leszek
Mieczysław—Mietek
Stanisław—Staszek
Tadeusz—Tadek, Tadzio
Wilhelm—Wilek
Witold—Witek
Władysław—Władek
Wojciech—Wojtek
Zofia—Zosia, Zosieńka

I have chosen to retain the Polish "Pan" (Mr.) and "Pani" (Miss or Mrs.) in front of first names because the form indicates acquaintance or deference to age, rather than friendship, which is indicated by use of the first name only.

POSTAL INDISCRETIONS

Sors immanis
et inanis,
rota tu volubilis,
status malus . . .

Fate—monstrous
and empty,
you whirling wheel,
you are malevolent.

Carl Orff, *Carmina Burana*

INTRODUCTION
Tadeusz Drewnowski

The more certain we are that the twentieth century suffered from an epidemic of totalitarianisms, the more meaningful the life and writings of Tadeusz Borowski become, having been conducted during the twentieth century's period of greatest darkness. The endurance of his literary standing testifies to this. I have not met up with any group of literary critics, or experts on postwar literature, or even communities of readers, for whom his person and his writings do not occupy a prominent place in, or even a position at the forefront of, their literary consciousness. At the same time, it is impossible not to notice that this literature owes its survival, or its rise, almost exclusively to itself and—the spirit of the time.

In Poland, Borowski's work survives on the basis of the considered opinion of a couple of outstanding writers and several critics and, to an even greater degree perhaps, on the basis of its undoubted position in the world. It is thanks to this, I believe, that it still finds itself on school reading lists and has even—as the second of that generation after Krzysztof Kamil Baczyński's poetry—become part of the National Library series (Różewicz still does not have a volume there). Borowski, therefore, has become a classic, but a most forsaken and neglected classic.

He does not have his own collected works other than the (unworthy of the name) *Utwory zebrane* [*Collected Works*] of 1954, and his works in circulation are reprinted in various textual versions. His work has, it is true, entered the National Library, but with a disregard for the fundamental principle that figures in its rules: authorized text. Even though Borowski was not wealthy and died very young, that the papers of this important cultural figure have not been gathered and edited is a shame, not to mention that there is no anthology of criticism of his work, or any other associated activities. Let the fact that in Warsaw, in the center of cultural life, an unknown volume of his poems has been discovered after fifty-two years serve as an alarm signal for this neglect!

Attacks on the writer, though not as persistent as they were until recently, have not abated. A young scholar, Sławomir Buryła, recently recorded anew

in *Pamiętnik Literacki* [*Literary Journal*] ("Na antypodach tradycji literackiej. Wokol 'sprawy Borowskiego'" ["In the Antipodes of Literary Tradition: In the 'Case of Borowski'"], no. 4, 1998) the great resonance and faltering arguments of Borowski's critics. He arrived, as well, at the apt conclusion that from the beginning to this day the dragged-out "case of Borowski" had a common denominator. Writing that found itself at the antipodes of Polish literary traditions by being antiheroic, antimartyrological, antimoralistic, laical, provocative, derisory, and so on, was subject to successive prosecution, provoked successive battles. Certainly, the essential distance between Borowski's writings and tradition was the main cause of never-ending complaints and attacks. But there was something else, too. The historical circumstances under which these fights were carried out meant that protecting tradition took on the character of grieving. And that the final argument—the breakdown, the fall of Borowski—exacerbated this grieving. This matter cannot be ignored—anyway, after nearly half a century, there is no reason to do so.

The end of the twentieth century and, even more, the historic change in Poland have prompted us to balance and integrate the literary scene and the writers' community, and demand the creation of new perspectives and new categories. And in Poland there is no lack of such efforts, if only in discussions about the synthesizing category of modernism and attempts to apply it. Out of this need for balance arises also the previously mentioned essay by Buryła striving for a new attitude toward Borowski. In order to see the past in a more synthesizing and revealing manner, however, one needs not just new ideas and new categories. One needs also a deepening of knowledge, in other words, to bring new facts, new phenomena to light, and over the past ten years in Poland quite a number have emerged and continue to emerge. Apart from the enrichment which the reassessment of the literary scene and the rescinding of censorship have provided, recent years have also brought a spate of personal, intimate writings from a bygone period: memoirs, autobiographies, personal diaries, epistolography. The totalitarian, or authoritarian, press in various countries pushed many subjects into silence, or into the sphere of private writing. It was almost a sign of "times when"—as Jerzy Stempowski, probably our most outstanding letter writer, put it subtly—"not everything was suitable for publication and when the writer had to find other rewards for making black marks on paper than a reader would have provided."

As soon as Polish writing was free, there appeared, together with many personal diaries, a whole epistolographic archipelago. The archives of the Paris

Kultura [*Culture*] alone have so far provided nine volumes of correspondence, mainly editorial, but also semiprivate (for example, Giedroyc, Gombrowicz, Bobkowski, Wańkowicz). And on top of that, various collections of letters are circulating, such as those between Maria Dąbrowska and Jerzy Stempowski, and between Dąbrowska and Anna Kowalska, and the like, which await publication. Also, Czesław Miłosz's correspondence with friends and fellow writers entitled *Zaraz po wojnie* [*Right After the War*] and, in the volume *Legendy nowoczesności* [*Legends of Modernity*], his essay-letters exchanged with Jerzy Andrzejewski by private mail between Żoliborz and Mokotow during the occupation. To this new archipelago belongs also the concentration camp national and international correspondence of Tadeusz Borowski from the years 1943 through 1951, which is presented here.

I came upon Borowski's letters years ago while writing *Ucieczka z kamiennego świata* [*Escape from the World of Stone*], and that book owes much to them. Maria Borowska made available to me a collection saved by the author of letters from people valuable to him for various reasons. On top of that, in the first ten years after his death, three selections of his correspondence appeared in journals: in Wanda Leopold's essay on the fifth anniversary of his death in *Nowa Kultura* [*New Culture*], 1956, no. 28; on the tenth anniversary, the largest selection of his camp and Munich letters in *Twórczość* 8 [*Creative Work* 8] (1943), compiled by Felicia Małek (I have only just now learned, and, what's more interesting, *Twórczość*'s editors have learned, that one of their addressees hiding behind the pseudonym Małek was Zofia Świdwińska-Krzyżanowska); as well as Stanisław Marczak-Oborski's selection of letters to Borowski, which I had commissioned and which were published in *Polityka* 52 [*Politics* 52] (1961). These selections of Borowski's correspondence were so fascinating that I decided to take a serious interest in them.

The collection presented so many years later does not resemble the starting point. First, it has increased threefold in relation to the writer's collection. Second, those selections printed in the press and published in fragments, not to say shreds (this latter term refers to the first and third selections), have been restored, as far as possible, to their integral form (if there are exceptions to this here, it is a result of either lacking the original letter or desiring to avoid repetitions). Third, in 1997, I placed an author's query in *Gazeta Wyborcza, Życie Warszawy, Tygodnik Powszechny,* and *Polityka,* but it did not yield great results, so I expanded it by targeting individuals, which proved more effective. The greatest gain, however, came through my last approach—a search through archives. The

archives I consulted had long amassed writers' papers; now, however, it came to organizing and authenticating them. Letters not acquired through personal connections flowed out of institutions (the National Library, the Literature Museum in Warsaw, the Emigration Archives in Toruń). Through these methods, the store of Borowski's correspondence was greatly enriched and also, which is of great importance to their value, in large part assumed again the form of dialogue. I did not use all the letters out of the acquired collection, not wanting its profile to become too diffuse (I mostly picked through the letters of Anatol Girs and S. Wygodzki).

Thanks to the increase in size of the correspondence, not only have individual connections emerged, but also, as a result of the role that Borowski played during and directly after the war, broader generational contacts are revealed. Just as Miłosz's *Zaraz po wojnie* is a collection of the correspondence of the middle-aged generation of the time, so Borowski's collection has become, thanks to these acquisitions, a collection of the correspondence of the younger generation, which came to literature during the war or immediately afterward. It is, at the moment, the only testament of this kind to that generation. Perhaps others will be found in other areas: in Różewicz perhaps, or Herbert, or perhaps Herling-Grudziński? In any case, a new file has been opened.

Borowski had no illusions about the nature of the real subject matter of the period and of his own experiences, nor about the consequences that airing them publicly would bring. When his acquaintance, Halina Laskowska, wishing to publish his poems in England in 1945, asked the poet for his autobiography, he sent the texts, but without personal information.

"Autobiographical sketch?" he writes from Munich on February 22, 1946:

> Dear Pani Halina! What would I write in it beyond what is in the foreword to my book, which I will endeavor to send to you in final form? That fifteen years before the war those closest to me had a ground-level tour of all the prisons and camps of the north and Asia? That the beginning of my upbringing was a Soviet school? Or, that for a good stretch I never had a family life because either Father was sitting in Murmansk, or Mother was in Siberia, or I was in a boarding school, on my own, or in a camp? Or, that during the war I had friends in the National Confederation, and in the People's Guard, at the university, and in the forest? That I was arrested . . . and that I saw the death of a million people—literally, not metaphorically? That I don't want to return, that I'm fighting with myself and that I will sacrifice poetry for love?

Even against the backdrop of Poland and the backdrop of the period, Borowski's life was an exceptional conglomeration of threatening and uncensored subjects, pushed, at the time, out of existence and out of mind—horrifying some, exciting others, and, above all, endangering him. In his autobiography, Poland's experiences in Eastern and Western Europe join with back-breaking personal events that demanded to be told, and which became his literary canvas. The first manifestation of that writing was precisely the personal correspondence, which moved with difficulty between the two young people, when Tadeusz was on the *Pfleger's* course in old Auschwitz. I am speaking, of course, about "Auschwitz, Our Home (A Letter)," composed of the lovers' letters (about her letters, he wrote from there: "I sometimes receive letters from Tuśka. And what letters!"), in which they asked about one another, in which they found one another.

But, unfortunately, the originals of that internal camp correspondence have fallen by the wayside, although his fiancée was amazed how faithfully it was remembered in his work. Borowski's prison and camp letters to his mother, on the other hand, survived in total, written on official forms, in a foreign, still poorly known, language, and so, at the beginning, in a stranger's hand, and stamped by the Gestapo censors. Can there be better examples of the fine art of writing letters in our period? The most worn-out phrases are used, and between sentences of substantive and banal information there sparkle camp observations and amazingly mature flashes of worldly insight. Beneath the sky of Auschwitz, the son who is barely of age writes: "When human work matters nothing, when all criteria of worth fail, and that which is eternal perishes, only the names of our friends and loved ones are left us of humanity." (May 7, 1944)

Under changing circumstances, in Munich, and after his return to Poland, Borowski's correspondence does not cease being a string of postal indiscretions. It manifests itself in two forms: as literature and as factography or discourse, in other words, as a source of cognition. The letters to Maria Rundo, in particular, are literary letters through and through, often encompassing pages that he didn't have time to write down in his large cycle of stories. The letters to friends stand out as modern epistolary art: letter-memoirs, letter-essays, or letter-repartee. And travel letters? Right to his first impressions of Berlin, which he did not explore the first time he was in Germany.

Literary merit does not belong only to the main hero. It isn't seemly to keep pointing to it in the letters of famous literati and outstanding humanist-scholars, of whom there is no shortage here. I was also struck by it in his fiancée's correspondence. Her letters from Sweden, discovered by some miracle in the archives

of the London *Wiadomości* [*News*], and of which, in truth, only a few samples appear here, create a truly moving impression. Though awkwardly written (I had to edit them), artistry and suggestiveness are also found in the letters from America by the graphic artist Anatol Girs. This collection of correspondence stirs the imagination. One can read it as a novel in many voices about a genial young man thrown into the cruel twentieth century.

It is harder to characterize this collection as a fascinating source of knowledge about the period, about the still puzzling fate of the writer, and finally about his passion—literature. From this point of view, this is an inexhaustible collection, rich in treasures for the interested and for students of the priceless and eternal—in innumerable, eyewitness accounts. A testament, it seems, of primary significance. Here, I can point only to a few of its features.

It asks, for example, for a more clear-sighted treatment of the youthful adventures of the eccentric—for occupation times—Essentialist Club, to which are tied the beginnings of Borowski's poetry. The young Poznań scholar, Justyna Szczęsna, has joined the ranks of those pursuing such an undertaking, and in her book *Tadeusz Borowski—Poet* (Poznań, 2000), has, in Borowski's totally apocalyptic vision, also observed a utopia of "the times of Saturn," a cult of scholarship and poetry, friendship and love. As the correspondents testify, this cult spread among the young despite sharp political divisions, and to accuse them of antipatriotism on this account, as *Sztuka i Naród* [*Art and the Nation*] did in their treatment of Borowski, was inappropriate. The Essentialists took up arms no less than others. The group established itself with the clandestine journal *Droga* [*The Road*], their most mature cultural undertaking, which they also attempted to pick up after the war—but to no avail.

In general, the concept of generational unity (despite internal divisions), and its difference from that of the older generation, emerges clearly here. It was apparent already during the occupation, especially in relation to those who had something to do with them personally, as did Karol Irzykowski[1] and Czesław Miłosz. It was even more apparent after the war in relations with Stefan Żółkiewski, who regarded their pre-mature, wartime independence as an anomaly, and wished them to ally themselves with *Kuźnica* [*The Forge*], and with Kazimierz Wyka, who underrated their literary individuality (except in the case of Baczyński). The generational unity, though not encompassing the entire decimated generation, takes precedence, after the war, over internal conflicts of occupation days, and makes for a common philosophy based on experiences in the resistance movement and for a confrontation with the problematics of, as it was then called,

the "people's democracy" (the journals *Pokolenie* [*Generation*] and *Nurt* [*The Current*]). How this youth is manipulated and led into socialist realism—in a word, how a pernicious operation is undertaken—can be seen here as plainly as in the palm of one's hand. And how it differentiates itself anew amid these manipulations.

But it is not only these collective problems that manifest themselves differently in this collection—but also the fate of Borowski himself and of his art. For quite a long time in Munich, anticipating meeting his beloved, Borowski stands, as he writes, "at an open door." Open toward France, where he goes in search of kindred ideas. Open toward America, to where his Munich publisher and friend Girs tries to tempt him. And open to literary emigration. As chance would have it, Borowski, meanwhile—apart from contacts with military journals—establishes, for personal reasons, direct correspondence with Mieczysław Grydzewski. Thanks to this, both the volume of poetry *Imiona nurtu* [*The Names of the Current*] and one of the stories from *We Were in Auschwitz* (it is not known which) reach Grydzewski's hands at the same time as they reach those of the editor of *Tygodnik Powszechny* [*Universal Weekly*], Jerzy Turowicz, and of the editor of *Twórczość,* Wyka. And they provoke no reaction. It is true that at the time Grydzewski's *Wiadomości* had been shut down by British censors; it was replaced, however, by anthologies of incoming texts. I am ready to perceive in this one of the important, if not most important, reasons why Borowski decided to return to Poland. Because, contrary to what he writes, his literary mission determined this dramatic step. He traveled to where he could transmit his experiences and find his audience.

Equally startling is the question of his throwing poetry over in favor of prose. In the margin of "Rozmowa z przyjacielem" ["Conversation with a Friend"] (*Gazeta Wyborcza*, no. 191, 1999), Marek Zaleski correctly observed that it had to be seen in the light of the later discussion about "poetry after Auschwitz." For Borowski, from the beginning, was one of the admirers of *Skamander,*[2] and much evidence of this can be found in this volume. Even in his Auschwitz poems, he was unable to free himself of their poetics—something for which Różewicz obsessively called in "Elegia na powrót umarłych poetów" ["Elegy for the Return of Dead Poets"], opposing in his own poetry their smooth, decorative verse. Borowski was able to do so only when Girs demanded from him (and his colleagues) the memoirs *We Were in Auschwitz.* There, he found a model for Auschwitz prose, and substantiated it in numerous commentaries. And so, in our literature (before an international discussion erupts on this subject), Różewicz,

a partisan, never in Auschwitz, became the pioneer of "poetry after Auschwitz," while to Borowski falls the discovery of "prose after Auschwitz." It comes very easily to him, as though he were born to it. "So-called prose is very easy," he writes in a wry, cavalier manner in a letter to his fiancée after his return to Poland, "and depends on remembering things one's observed and putting them together into a whole. . . . My story . . . is being read as the best piece of postwar prose since its subject is the very hackneyed camp theme, but the outcomes of the theme completely wanton." Observation and mischievousness . . . I believe that these letters reveal much about Borowski's style, which still, it seems, has not been fully examined.

But most relevant of all is something else. This collection of correspondence allows us a close look at the disposition, behavior, and character of Tadeusz Borowski over the course of almost his entire adult life—from coming of age to early death. The more attentive reader will not fail to see the lability, one might say swings, in his inner state, feelings, moods, and the development of complexes—an overly rigid superego and exceedingly high expectations of self, which quickly turn into an inferiority complex or sense of worthlessness—in his case closely tied to his literary calling and talent. Morbid states, now depressive, now euphoric, maniacal. One cannot help but connect this—even though all such diagnoses are risky—with the last part of his life and his death, which are often turned against him.

Before I go on to this, an apparently trivial matter arises, but one very closely tied to the last period of Borowski's life. In the biographical note on Borowski, I write that, after the attack in Szczecin on his creative work, he intended to take off to America. I vividly recall his telling me this. I attributed this idea to Girs, but today, in reading his letters from America, I see that he could not have suggested this, because he barely had enough to eat in America himself. Naturally, there remains the chance of a stipend (after the Block rejected the Marshall Plan, America offered Poland a wide set of opportunities in this regard). Why am I going on about this issue? Because I am interested whether Borowski was defending himself against this attack, or whether he had a sense of self-defense such as Różewicz manifested when, not allowed to take up a stipend to France, he ran away from socialist realism, leaving Kraków to go first to Hungary, then to Gliwitz. Facts are facts: Różewicz chose to emigrate to Gliwitz, Borowski went to the front line—Berlin.

Borowski's stay in Berlin was at the peak period of the intensification of the cold war, at the main phase of the conflict over Berlin (during Borowski's stay,

the Russians' siege of West Berlin ended, as did the Americans' air patrols over the Soviet zone, but they turned into conflict across the whole of Germany: the creation of the FRG by the three Western powers, to which Stalin responded not only with the creation of the GDR but with threatening demonstrations of force). In his meager letters from there, Borowski uses Newspeak for the first time (even his wife is afraid to write about local gossip). A letter from a friend in Poland makes one realize what was going on at the time: "For how many days did we not move from the radio: what's happening in Berlin?" (W. Woroszyłski, October 16, 1949). The world was a hair's breadth from war. Politics pushed every other argument aside. Borowski suddenly found himself facing a fundamental choice: either/or, and experiences during the war determine on which side he stands. He who had opposed moral, social, political absolutism and had smashed national and literary stereotypes, succumbs to political Manichaeism. And as an "extremist," as Wyka described him, draws the most far-reaching conclusions from his political stance. The postcard of the city hall in Leipzig, where, as he stressed, Luther fought for his heresy, indicates in what an almost mystical state he performs his attack on literature in the newly created *Rozmowy* [*Conversations*] and condemns himself as a writer. This madness does not go away after his return to Poland. Those close to him do not recognize him.

After returning from Germany, he engaged in a series of suicide attempts. In a letter to a friend, he once described the mechanism of these breakdowns: "Sometimes it seems it would be good to leave the field of battle before one commits some kind of compromise" (October 2, 1946). The point to which he had now arrived was no longer "some kind of compromise." For a person of such a degree of awareness and sensitivity, it was simply a betrayal of his faith, of his calling, a betrayal of the self. Borowski did not retreat from that which had, for a long time. persecuted him . . .

My hope is that this collection of correspondence reaches Borowski's faithful readers and those who don't know him well, since it contains the highest and closest that remains of him. My hope is also that this collection—with possible supplements and corrections—will become one of the volumes of Borowski's collected writings, which, in his case, should also look astereotypical.

I.

FEBRUARY 25, 1943–AUGUST 12, 1944

PAWIAK AND AUSCHWITZ

"Your son who is now of age . . ."

1. FEBRUARY 26, 1943

[from Pawiak, Warsaw; prison card, written in pencil in German in a strange hand, almost unreadable today][1]

To Frau Teofila Borowska, 2 Smolna St., Apt. 18

Dear Mom,

I've been here since yesterday. Am well. Please send me a two kilogram food parcel once a month through the Seventh Police Commissariat, Krochmalna St. In addition, I also request a package of clothing and a blanket, pillow, sheets, towel, soap, toothbrush. I can only write once a month. You can write to me more often in German. Don't worry about me. Regards to Father. Kisses,

Your Tadeusz Borowski

2. MARCH 26, 1943

[from Pawiak; in German]

Dear Mom,

Thank you from the bottom of my heart for both packages, and in April please send me a package (more fat, a bit of sugar, saccharine, a little piece of meat, everything in a sack or a carton) and one special package for the Easter holidays. Let it be a better one! I received the postcards of 2/6 and 3/12, thank you.

Am well. Send me a Bible, as small a format as possible. I am working in the garden, just as though I were home. Are you all well? How is Brother's health? He needs to keep getting treatment. If there isn't the money for it, sell some of my things. If the packages are too costly, then send me less. How does the accommodation situation look at the State Office? I would like you to finally get a better apartment. Kiss Father and Brother and all my friends. Kisses to you, my Mom, I send all best wishes for Easter. Think about me,

Tadeusz

3. APRIL 26, 1943

[*from Pawiak; in German*]

Dear Mom,

I don't know how to thank you for the packages. I want to really thank you. I was sad that we weren't all sitting together at the Easter table; I shared the eggs with my companions, and that's how we celebrated. The cake was wonderful—it all got eaten with great joy, the cheesecake in particular was excellent. Don't worry about me: I'm healthy and that's the most important thing. Don't worry about my things either; if you like, sell what there is to sell. Be as concerned about Tuśka as you are about me. Worse that you are not writing to me. I received only one letter of 3/31. [*The following sentence was added interlinearly.*] A moment ago I received the letter of 4/16, thanks. The Bible's here and the other things too. A letter from home gives great joy. Mom, I marvel that you send me such packages, but don't know what you have to eat.

Your Tadeusz

4. JUNE 20, 1943, AUSCHWITZ

[*in German; all letters from Auschwitz are stamped "inspected," geprüft, with a censor's number—KL Auschwitz*]

To Frau Teofila Borowska, Apt. 18, 2 Smolna St., Warsaw

Mom,

Thanks to you all. Yesterday I received the letter of 6/10. I haven't received the money yet, perhaps at the next mail call. I can receive money monthly and, please, send some again. To date, I've received 8 packages.

If you can, please send more, and more often. Send me more well-baked bread, sliced and whole, a bit of fat and sugar, marmalade and artificial honey, if they're well wrapped, best of all in cans. Add to each package 1–2 pieces of wrapped soap and 2 black shoe polishes. On top of that, send me frequent packages of onion and garlic, they're good and I like them very much. Naturally, a list of contents with the number and date of the package. I thank my friends for helping you. Tell them I won't forget them. Brotherly greetings to you, Julek. You now have to work for both of us in order to help our parents . . .

Tadeusz

5. MAY 30, 1943, AUSCHWITZ

Dear Mom,

Thanks from the bottom of my heart for the letter of 5/25, which I picked up yesterday. I received the package of 5/21 on Friday 5/28. In the packages, send me only food and a piece of good soap. If my friends and acquaintances want to, they can also send me packages, with, e.g., fruit, onion, marmalade, or cakes and sweets. You, yourself, send me onion, fat, bread—crackers, as before, and saccharin. The packages must include an exact list of contents. Send me also kielbasa and butter. In the final analysis, send me whatever, and as much as, you are able, and preferably as often as you wrote in the letter. Don't worry about me, I am completely healthy and feel fine. Write to me more often about what's going on at home and send me postage stamps. Put my things away. Give my regards to all my acquaintances and friends.[2] Kisses to Father and Julek. Kisses to you, Mom.

Your son,

T.B.

Send me a letter with Tuśka's photograph.

6. JULY 5, 1943, AUSCHWITZ

Dear Mom,

I received the letters of 6/16 and 6/29. I am glad that my friends are helping you. For Tuśka I always enclose lots of good feelings. Has she written now?[3] The boiled eggs were, unfortunately, rotten. Send fresh ones, well packed, not boiled ones. They arrive here in good condition. As of now, I've received 13 packages, I receive everything you send me. My sincere thanks to Zosia Świdwińska, who sent me a beautiful package. Send bigger packages and as often as possible. There cannot be any liquids, medicines, or money in the packages. More dried bread, also loaves of bread, as much fat as you can. Apart from that, what's important to me are whole packages of onion, garlic, and other vegetables. 40 marks a month is enough money. I feel well, have a good appetite. Very many thanks for the packages, and I await the next. I know that you send me as much as you are able.

I enclose friendly greetings to my friends. Warm kisses for Father and Julek. I kiss you with all my heart,

Your son,

Tadeusz Borowski

7. NOVEMBER 6, 1943, AUSCHWITZ

Dear Mother,

Thank you for the name-day wishes. You remember how a year ago we sat at the table together. 12/8 is Tuśka's name day, please send her the best, sincerest wishes from me. Everything you send, I receive in perfect condition. The bread isn't moldy. I truly do have enough underwear and clothing. I am well and in a good mood. Don't send money. Please don't worry about me so much. Send packages and don't think about anything else. Warm thanks to Julek, but I never doubted him to be a good brother. Regards to friends. How very much I miss you! But you, Mother, know that my nostalgia and love can be shared. I also know, Mother, how hard things are for you, but it cannot be otherwise.

Heartfelt kisses to you, Father. Brotherly regards to Julek,

Tadeusz Borowski

8. NOVEMBER 21, 1943, AUSCHWITZ

Liebe Eltern, Euer schon volljähriger Sohn grüsset Euch von ganzen Herzen. Er lernt das Leben zu kennen und die Zukunft mit Mut zu begegnen. Ich änderte in mich gar nicht, bin mehr weich und leichtseelig. Vielleicht ist es ein Wiederspruch, aber mit grosser Sehnsucht nach Euch ist es leichter zu leben, weil sie auch Hoffnung auf Heimkehr gibt. Bei uns ist es auch kalt and und oft es regnet, aber das macht überhaupt nichts. Die Nächte sind schon lang geworden und ich denke viel von Euch, von Tuśka, von den Freunden. Ich möchte gern zu meinen Freunden einzeln schreiben, kann aber sie nur gesamt grüssen. Grüss von mir besonders für Staszek und Zofia. Ich weisse, wieviel Mühe Zofia mir offert, um mir zu helfen. Julek, zu Dir nur einige Worte, ich bin dir sehr, sehr, dankbar. Bei mir alles in Ordnung. Gerade zum Geburtstag bekam ich zwei Päkchen (Nebenbei: bis Nr. 40 alles gut gepackt und in grosster Ordnung, Kuchen war extra, Sardinenfische prima, sehr dankbar für die Adressen). Ich bin

gesund, mir fehlt nur das Heim. Vergisst nicht zu Tusia zu ihren Geburstag am 8 XII schreiben. Geduld und Mut wünschen und meine Grüsse übersenden. Ich küsse Euch sehr herzlich, sende Grüsse für Mutter Tuśka's.

Tadeusz Borowski

Dear Parents,

Your son who is now of age sends you all his love. He's learning to know life in order to be able to face the future. I, myself, have not changed at all. I am always indolent and light-minded. This might be a contradiction, but it is easier to live with this great longing for you because it gives one hope of returning home. It is cold here, too, and often rainy, but it doesn't matter. The nights have turned long,[4] so I think a lot about you, about Tuśka, and about friends. I'd very much like to write to them separately; however, I am able only to send collective regards. Particular regards from me to Staszek and Zofia. I know how much trouble Zofia goes through to help me. Julek, just a few words to you: I am very, very grateful to you. Everything is fine with me. On my birthday, I received two packages (an aside: everything in No. 40 was well wrapped and in the best order, the cake was extra special, the sardines first rate, thank you for the addresses). I am well, I just miss home. Don't forget to write to Tuśka for her name day 12/8, wish her patience and courage, and convey my regards to Tuśka's mother.

Tadeusz Borowski

9. JANUARY 1, 1944, AUSCHWITZ

Dear Mom,

On the first day of the New Year, I send you, Father, Brother, Zosia, and all my friends my sincerest expressions of love and hope. Perhaps this year everything will be well. Christmas was truly beautiful for me; and a Christmas tree sparkled here, as well. Right before Christmas I finally received a letter from Tuśka.[5] She writes that, as usual, she doesn't have a lot of money or health, but, in spite of everything, her husband will help her as much as he can. Dear Mom! You can write letters to me twice a month. Everything you send me arrives in the best condition. A small request: the bacon tasted so good. You must kiss Pani Eugenia[6] fondly and wish her everything good: that her loneliness shortly be over, and that those whom she loves return. Warmest kisses to you my beloved, good, full of patience Mother. To Father I send that which his son wishes to send

with the New Year—loving words, and to you, Julek, a request: laugh, drink for the two of us, and always be with our parents—

Tadeusz Borowski

10. JANUARY 23, 1944, AUSCHWITZ

Liebe Mutter, entschuldige, dass meine Briefen so verschiedener Art sind und dass ich bloss von meinen Sorgen und Troste manchmal rede and suche Hilfe bei Dir. Wem aber soll ich meine Unruhe anvertrauen als nicht Dir, Mutter? Deshalb darfst Du nicht denken, dass ich ohne Mut bin. Allgemein braucht man im Leben nicht so viel Mut. Ich weiss sehr wohl, ich hatte Dir besonders im Sommer viel Sorge gemacht, doch immer entdeckt man in sich etwas Kindisches. Wie Du siehst, ist bei mir alles in Ordnung. Brief vom 28 XII erhalten; dem Bronek müsst Du, Mutter, meinen innigsten Beileid ausdrücken: ich weiss, wie ihm schwer ist, so allein zu leben. Julek, zu Deinem 25 Geburgstag sende ich Dir verspätete aber herzliche Wünsche der besten personlichen Glücks. Und sei nicht durch Drang zu Tat verrückt. Nicht das Geschaffene, das DingßMensch ist wichtig. Und wie leicht kann man durch grosse Worte betragen sein! So.— Weisst Du, bei mir ist es volkommen gut, bin nur etwas müde und fürchte mich, dass ich schon niemals derselbe werede als früher. Auch von Tusia bekam ich ein Brief. Es ist Hoffnung, das ihr wird das Leben etwas leichter. Leider, so schreibt Sie, fühlt sie nicht ganz wohl. Ich sende für sie Grüsse. Endlich meinen kleine Sachen: Mutter, gebratene Kohlkraut ist sehr praktisch, also mehr schicken; ausserdem etwas Schuhpaste und möglichst viel Cebion in fast jedem Paket. Für meine Freunde, Zosia, Staszek und die alle, die mich nicht vergessen haben—Grüsse. Herzliche Küsse fur Dich, Mutter, den Vater, und Julek.

Euer Tadeusz Borowski

Dear Mom,

Forgive my letters for being of such various kinds and that I sometimes speak only of my own problems and hopes and seek your help. But in whom am I to confide if not you, Mom? Don't think, because of this, that I lack courage. Life, anyway, doesn't require that much courage. I am well aware that, especially in summer, I caused you a lot of worry,[7] but one keeps on finding something of the child in oneself.

As you see, everything is fine with me. I received the letter of 12/28; give Bronek my sincere condolences, I understand how hard it must be for him to be living alone. Julek, on the occasion of your turning 26, I send you belated but sincere brotherly wishes for personal happiness. Don't go crazy trying to reach certain goals. It's not what one creates, and not a thing—it's man who is the most important. And how easily big words can betray one! Yes.

As you know, all's well with me, I'm just a bit tired and I fear that I will never be the same as before. I received a letter from Tuśka as well. There's some hope that her life will be a tad easier. Unfortunately, as she, herself, writes, she's not feeling completely well. I send her my regards. In closing, some small matters of mine: Mom, the baked cauliflower turns out to be very practical, send more; also, some shoe polish and a fair amount of vitamin C in nearly every package.

To my friends, Zosia, Staszek, and all who haven't forgotten about me— greetings. Warm kisses for you, Mom, Father, and Julek.

Your Tadeusz Borowski

11. FEBRUARY 6, 1944, AUSCHWITZ

Liebe Eltern! Schon fast ein Jahr bin ich vom Hause weg. In diesen Jahr müsste ich die anderen und nicht immer die besten Seiten des Lebens anschauen und alles als gleichgültig and unwichtig nehmen, und meines Denken zu schützen. Ich hatte die lustigsten und schlechsten Erfahrungen gemacht, ich müss mitteilen, das alles ist leichter als man gewöhnlich denkt. Aber Euch brauchte ich davon nicht schreiben. Ihr wisst sehr wohl das Bescheid. Als man zurückkehrt, wird man neues Leben schaffen oder—besser gesagt—altes weiter führen. Deshalb bin ich sehr dankbar, dass est gibt die Leute, die sets un mich denken. Es wird mir leichter, ins Leben zurückkommen. Der Brief von 22 I erhalten. Vom Staszek bekam ich nichts. Die letzten Pakete von Hause waren von 11 I under 18 I datiert. Von Tusia seit lange keinen Brief. Doch ich hoffe, dass ich bald von Sie sowie von Euch einen Brief bekomme. Herzliche Grüsse für Frau Eugenia. Für liebe Zosie herzlicher Küss für gute Worte. Für Staszek: besten Dank für Sorgen um mich. Ist er endlich verlobt? Gott schutze Ihn! Für Dich, Mutter, für Tatusko und Julek—Grüsse

Tadeusz Borowski

Dear Parents,

I've been away from home for almost a year. During that year, I had to look at other, not always the best, sides of life and to accept everything as being of no concern or importance in order to protect my own thoughts. I have had the best and the worst experiences; I have to say that everything is easier than is usually assumed. But I don't need to write this to you. You know very well.[8] When one returns, a new life will be formed or—to put it better—the old one will be resumed. That's why I'm so grateful there are people who go on thinking about me. It will be easier for me to return to life. I received the letter of 1/22. Nothing has arrived from Staszek. The last packages from home were dated 1/11 and 1/18. I haven't had any letter from Tuśka for a long time. I hope, however, to receive a letter from her, as from you, shortly. Warmest regards to Mrs. Eugenia Rundo. Warm kisses to dear Zosia for her good words. For Staszek: warmest thanks for his concern about me. Has he finally got engaged? God help him! To you, Mom, Daddy, and Julek—best wishes,

Tadeusz Borowski

12. FEBRUARY 20, 1944, AUSCHWITZ

Dear Mom,

I received the letter of 2/2 yesterday. I'm grateful for your good words, although I am very aware that not everything with you is quite as good as you say. Unfortunately, your long ongoing help to me is still needed. It makes life easier for me. You, however, Mom, also have other responsibilities: you cannot forget about Father and Julek, since I'm not your only one. It's a bit more practical if you send me packages twice a week; if one vanishes, another comes. They don't have to be so beautiful. I keep thinking about Tuśka. I am grateful for the Broneks' and Regina's[9] regards.

Kisses to you all,

Tadeusz Borowski

13. MARCH 5, 1944, AUSCHWITZ

Dear Mother,

Everything is well with me. I am again receiving packages normally. I ask you very much not to send me such good packages. It causes you too much hardship.

Write more and precisely what is happening with you. I have a little time to think through again everything I did in life. It seems to me at times that I'm not worthy of your love and patience. From time to time, I get letters from Tuśka. You, of course, know her well: she's full of courage and strength just as before. Warmest kisses to you, Mother, and for Father and Julek; give my regards to all my friends.

Your

Tadeusz Borowski

P.S.   Thank you very much for the vitamin C. Forgive me for continually asking for something new. Please send me your photographs. I'd like to see you. Keep sending the vitamin C and, perhaps, something else—Tadeusz

14. UNDATED
[*to his father, unsigned*]

Dear Daddy,

On the occasion of your name day, please accept my sincerest wishes for good health and the fulfillment of our hopes that our life and our work won't have been for nothing. Dear Staszek! For your name day, I send fondest regards and wish you all the best and thank you very warmly for your faithful friendship, which is truly priceless to people. Regards to all our friends. Dear Julek. I received your letter of 3/29 exactly on the evening of Easter. Don't take it amiss that I demand letters from home, but when I don't get them I worry greatly about you all and then I think that things are not right with you. Do you understand me, brother? I am well. I receive everything you send; I'm faring quite well, so that I basically don't need large amounts of assistance. Spring here is very beautiful. There are many friends here, from time to time something good to read,[10] and so one lives in yearning, but not without joy. Warmest kisses, greetings to Mrs. Eugenia Rundo and her family, to Zosia and all my friends.

15. MAY 7, 1944, AUSCHWITZ

Zu Deinem Namenstag, meine teuere u. sehr liebe Zosieńka, sinde ich aller-
herzlichste Wünsche. Zwar schwer ist heute Ruhe finden, doch das, was wir
Glück nennen, liegt vieleicht innern in uns, wenn wir gegen allen Umstände
handeln und unseres Wert behalten. Trotz allem glaube ich alles, was vom Geist
ist, ist ewig und unverdeblich. Als menchliche Arbeit, als Nichts gilt, als alle
Massstabe stürzen um das Ewige verdirbt, sind vielleicht die Namen unserer
Freunde u. Geliebten das Einzige, was uns von der übrigen Menschheit bleibt.
Ich weiss, diese Worte sind nicht froh, verzeihe mir. Ich freue mich sehr, dass Du
besonders ausgezeichnete Schülerin bist, Du müss für uns alle lernen. Immer
hattest Du grosse Kummer um mich, soll ich Dir schreiben, das ist gerade vor
einem Jahr nach Hause geschrieben hatte, hat sich viel bei mir geändert. Es geht
alles gut bei mir. Manchmal bekomme ich Briefe von Tusia, aber was für Briefe!
Sie ist immer dieselben. Ich hoffe, das Du gesund bist. Grüsse von mir alle
unsere Freunde. Ich küsse dich herzlich—Tadeusz

Liebe Mutti, ich bin gesund, alles in Ordnung. Es geht alles gut, ich kümmere
etwas um Euch, und warte mit Ungeduld auf Briefe. Pakete kommen in Ordnung. Ich küsse Dich, den Vater und Julek and danke sehr herzlich für alles.

Tadeusz Borowski

On your name day, my dear and very loved Zosieńka, I send you my very best
wishes. Although it is hard today to find peace, that which we regard as happiness probably, however, lies within us when we act contrary to all circumstances
and retain our own self-worth. In spite of everything, I believe that everything
that comes from the soul is eternal and indestructible. When human work matters nothing, when all criteria of worth fail, and that which is eternal perishes,
only the names of our friends and loved ones can be the one thing that remains
of humanity. I know these are not happy words. Forgive me. I'm happy that you
are a particularly good student, you have to study on our behalf. You were always
very concerned about me; do I have to write that I am truly grateful to you?
Since my first letter, which I wrote home precisely a year ago, much has changed
with me. Everything is going well for me. I sometimes receive letters from Tuśka,
and what letters they are. She is still the same. I hope that you are well. Give all
my friends my regards.

Tadeusz

Dear Mom, I am well, everything is fine. Everything is going well, I worry about you and await letters with impatience. The packages arrive in order. Kisses to you, Father, and Julek, and many thanks for everything.

Tadeusz Borowski

16. MAY 21, 1944, AUSCHWITZ

Dear Mom,

Nothing special with me. As always, I'm generally in good health and well fed. That's why I feel so well. Seriously: don't worry about me, since I am not worried about myself. Summer here in the mountains is wonderful. We're waiting again for a great fall, the time of memories . . . Naturally, I miss everyone . . . From time to time I get letters from Tuśka. One can be proud of how much spiritual strength she has: "I've been thinking a lot of things over, and I feel almost happy." She often writes about you, "you have a very strong mother, Tadeusz." Give her my regards and write to her. I really truly do miss everyone. It's good Julek is home. Everything's fine with you, right?

Tadeusz

17. MAY 29, 1944

[*from Warsaw, from Zofia Świdwińska; from a Polish text prepared for German translation*]

My dearest Tadek,

Thank you for your dear, sweet letter, which moved me and brought me so much joy, and, above all, for steadfastly remembering me. I truly never imagined that after a year's stay in your conditions and difficulties it was possible to think about someone, remember their name day and send such a letter! Warm and sincere hugs and kisses for this, and also that we agree with each other about the things you write. It was always a great joy to me that we had so many thoughts in common. You are right now, too. Just don't lay too many large obligations on me, because I may not live up to them. I am very pleased that you are well and brave, and, above all, that you are holding up so well. It amazes and impresses me. Anyway, your courage always impressed me. My thoughts, and all of our thoughts, are always with you. We often reminisce and talk about you, and

Hanka Bodalska, in particular, helps you a lot. I, myself, unfortunately, can't help you very much. Please when you write to Tuśka give her my best wishes, kisses, and regards. Everything is fine at home. Your parents and Julek are well. They're already working in the garden, and also have a goat and rabbits that they are raising.[11] Everybody: Mother, Father, Julek, and we, your friends, send you our best wishes and very warm kisses. We add to these the fragrance of the most beautiful lilacs and much, much, sun. Your mother sends you packages twice a week. Are you happy with them?

Kisses,

Z.

18. JUNE 4, 1944, AUSCHWITZ

Liebe Mutter, ich bin sehr betrübt, dass ich seit zwei Monaten keinen Brief von Euch erhalte und ahne alles schlechteres. Obwohl ich zu Euch schreibe, als ob es zu Hause "alles in Ordnung" wäre, ist mir sehr schwer, Unruhe und Ungewissenheit zu ertragen. Wenn es Dir möglich is, sollst Du oder einen von meinen Freunden ein Paar Worten zu mir senden. Es war sehr angenehm, alles wissen, was es zu Hause geschiecht. Briefe von Euch waren für mir immer frölichste Lektüre. Niemals gewohne ich mich, dieses Leben als mein eigenes betrachten. Deshalb lebe ich in anderer Welt, obwohl ich schon schönes Stück Zeit hier verbrachte. Doch gilt diese Zeit keinesfalls als verlorene. Habt keine Trost an mich. Alles geht gut/man mochte sagen: vorübergeht/. Man hat Ruhe und Essen genug. Je lauteren sind die Ereignisse, dest stiller ist man und ruhiger. Viele Freunde mach mir stets die Briefe von Tusia; wenn ich sie Dir lesen konnte! Ich küsse Dich sehr berzlich, auch den Vater und Julek. Ich sende beste Grüsse für Tusia, für alle meine Freuden u. Bekannte. Ich danke für die Pakete, die immer im besten Ordnung kommen. Nochmals bitte um Briefe.

Euer Tadeusz Borowski

Dear Mom,

I am very worried because I haven't had a letter from you for two months and am assuming the worst. Even though I am writing to you as though "everything were fine" at home, it is very hard for me to stand this worry and uncertainty. If it is possible, write me a few words or have one of my friends do so. It was very nice to know everything that was going on at home. Your letters were my

best reading materials. I will never get used to regarding life here as my own. That's why I live in a different world, even though I've spent a pretty chunk of time here. In any case, however, I don't regard this time as wasted. Don't worry about me. Everything is going fine (one might say: passing by). One has peace and enough to eat. The louder the circumstances, the quieter and calmer one is. Tuśka's letters give me a lot of joy. If I could just read them to you! Warm kisses to you, and to Father and Julek. I send Tuśka my best regards, and also to my friends and acquaintances. Thank you for the packages, which keep coming in good condition. Again, please send letters.

Your Tadeusz Borowski

19. JUNE 18, 1944, AUSCHWITZ
[*to Zofia Świdwińska*]

Liebe Zosia, ich danke Dir für Deine herzliche Worte, aber glaube mir, es ist alles viel, viel einfacher, als man denkt: man lebt und das ist alles. Ich küsse Dich und sende beste Grüsse füre undere Freunde. Lieber Julek, es tut mir leid, dass Du krank warst. Das war für Dich gewiss sehr schwer. Aber jetzt ist alles schon gut, nicht wahr?

Von Bronek keinen Brief. Kehrt er zurück oder vielleicht vergass er mir yu schreiben? Lass ihn und Regina herzlich grüssen. Es wäre für mich die grosste Freude, wenn es der Frau Eugenia gelingen wurde, Ihre Tochter zu sich zu nehmen. Ich fürchte aber, dass diese Bemühungen umsonst geben. Doch es wäre für sie die hochste Zeit. Wenn man so wie ich von Tag zu Tag lebt, sieht man nicht, wie schnell die Zeit vergeht (no, etwas Geduld muss man auch lernen), aber schon ein schönes Stück Zeit lebt sie weit vom Hause. Sie ist aber ganz zufrieden vom Leben, das ihr immer Freundschaft und auch etwas Liebe gibt. Beste Grüsse füre Fr. Eug. and Ihre ganze Familie. Liebe Mutter, keine Angst: Eier u. Küse immer prima. Wenn Du kanst: denke an Gemüsenpakete. Ich weiss, dass ich Dir immer Sorgen mache, aber das ist schön Dein Schicksal, Mutter, immer am jemanden zu kümmern. Ich küsse Dich, den Vater und Julek.

Euer Tadeusz Borowski

Dear Zosia,

Thank you for your kind words, but believe me everything is much, much simpler than one thinks: one's alive and that's everything. Kisses to you and best

regards to our friends. Dear Julek, I am sorry you have been ill. It must have been very hard for you. But everything's fine at present, yes?

I haven't got a letter from Bronek. Is he coming back, or perhaps he's forgotten to write to me? Be so good as to give him and Regina my regards. My greatest joy would be if Mrs. Rundo could manage to bring her daughter to her[12]—I fear it's effort in vain. Although it would be the highest time. If one lives from day to day as I do, one doesn't see how quickly time passes (well, one also has to learn a little patience)—but she's been living away from home for a chunk of time already. Actually, she's quite pleased with life, which always brings her friendship and a little love. Best wishes to Mrs. Rundo and the whole family.

Dear Mom, don't worry: the eggs and cheese are always excellent. If you are able, think about a parcel with vegetables. I know I'm forever creating problems for you, but it's your fate, Mom, to always worry about someone.

Kisses to you, Father, and Julek,

Your Tadeusz Borowski

20. JULY 2, 1944, AUSCHWITZ

Dear Mother,

What's of greatest interest first: the eggs are amazingly fresh and very much desired, the butter is wonderful, straight from the cow. And the cheese as well. As well as your package, I got one package from Staszek (the eternal problem—he should write my number properly) and one package from the Red Cross in Geneva. I, myself, am, of course, well and cheerful, a normal person who accepts the present as though it were already the past, who is full of hope and not without a future. Thank you for the letter of 6/21. Thank you for your kind words, having a mother like you, could I be any different? I'm happy that Tuśka often sees her husband[13] and is finally happy with life. I enclose the warmest greetings to her, her mother, and Basia. Kisses to you, Father, and Julek. Staszek, my friend, do you recall how exactly two years ago we were getting together? What is Arkadiusz doing? And Mundek? And Piotr?[14] And all the girls, what are their names? Is it all over? Will we ever be so young again? Life truly is short. And is art truly long? To you and your wife, dear Roman, I send best wishes for your happiness. May your life pan out as you would wish! May your wishes be appropriate!

Your Tadeusz Borowski

II.

MAY 1945–MAY 31, 1946

MUNICH
MARIA RUNDO LETTERS

"I will return. And what will be, will be."

MUNICH

Cards and letters
I draft and write,
peer intently
at typewriter keys.

Tadeusz Borowski,
"Korespondencja"
("Correspondence")

1. AUGUST 3, 1945, FREIMANN NEAR MUNICH, CAMP FOR FORMER PRISONERS OF DACHAU

[*to his family*]

My address: Polish Committee, 15 Pienzenauer St., Munich, Bavaria, American Occupation

My dears,

I survived the war. I feel well and am very homesick. I will try to return home as soon as possible. Since August 12, 1944, I have heard nothing about Tuśka. About you, a little from Janusz Walicki.

Much love,

Tadeusz Borowski

P.S.   It doesn't matter that there is, and will be, hunger. You have to manage.

2. SEPTEMBER[?] 5, 1945, MUNICH

[*to Zofia Świdwińska*]

Dear Zosia,

I am sending you cigarettes, I think you'll find them useful. Under separate cover, a small packet of tea and a few little volumes[1] with the request that you distribute them. I'll tell you to whom. It is difficult to send anything more, there's no one through whom to do so.

Best wishes,

Tadeusz Borowski

3. SEPTEMBER 12, 1945, MUNICH

[*to his parents*]

Sender: T. Borowski, Polish Committee, 15 Pienzenauer St., Monachium (Munchen, Munich)

My dears,

I am writing to you blind, not knowing whether, or how, you are living. I expect the worst. After the Uprising, I received a card from Julek, which is how I know

your new (or, perhaps, last) address. I worry about how you managed. I survived this lousy business, albeit under varying conditions. The Americans found me in Dachau. At present, I am in Munich—Polish Committee, 15 Pienzenauer St. where I work . . .

I am planning to come back to Poland, but I'd rather get a letter from you first. Write to me in detail what life is like for you, what the conditions are like in Poland, which of my acquaintances and friends are alive (I very much want to know which of my professors are alive). I will send you a detailed letter as soon as I can (this one is going right away, by hand).

Keep well, I know that everything will be fine.

Mommy, I am extremely grateful to everybody for their help. After all, that's why I'm alive. Don't let either Daddy or Julek lose heart.

I will come as soon as it's possible. Homesickness truly is worse than hunger. Greetings to my friends. Warm kisses,

Tadeusz

Your son

4. SEPTEMBER 13, 1945, GAUTING

[*from Stanisław Wygodzki*]

Dear Pan Tadeusz,

How happy your letter made me! How very pleased I would be to welcome you here. You absolutely must come. I have a pile of poems that I would like to show off (what an unambiguous suggestion!). I am writing a lot, a whole lot, and would like to show these poems to you and to Mr. Dąbrowski. I am often beset with doubts—lead me out of the state of uncertainty. Munich is so close to Gauting. They have just performed an operation[2] on me and in two days I will crawl out of bed. I feel fine, want for nothing except good books and newspapers from Poland, which I fervently request. I await you.

Sincerely,

S. Wygodzki

Perhaps we could organize an authors' evening for ourselves in Munich?

The Road

The road home goes almost forever,
my home is so distant, so far.
I speak of this never to anyone,
leave it to dreams and to night.

The road is long and unending
from Munich, through Augsburg and Linz
on rails, on bridges, on bricks—
links, links, links.

The road is long and arduous
through wind, through frost and snow,
at its end a street without people,
along which I walk like a spy.

I know that no one is left there,
the doors boarded up in an X,
on this road I walk as I used to—
links, links, links.

Stanisław Wygodzki

5. SEPTEMBER 17, 1945, MUNICH

Teofila Borowska, Kotowice near Milanówek (Milanówek Warsaw Line 28), c/o Mrs. Maria Rybicka

Dear Mom,

I am well, after going through several camps, I found myself in Dachau. I am currently working in Munich (Polish Committee). I have absolutely no idea what has happened to you all and I am very uneasy because I expect the worst.

Be sure to write (through the Red Cross or simply through the post) how you are living, what the outlook is for the future. I miss you very much and would like to return as soon as possible; however, I have nothing, absolutely nothing: neither a suit, nor shoes, nor a coat. I need to earn a bit of money, because you must be very hard up, and I wouldn't want to be a burden to you, Mom. I am very worried about Tuśka, I'm afraid that she didn't survive this so terrible winter.

I've been searching for her in vain for a long time. Nearly all of my friends died. But chin up, Moms, things will somehow work out. I'm writing a bit, and maybe something will be published (at Bruckmann's, it's one of the best printing houses). I'll send it, or bring it.

Warm kisses, Moms. Just don't let Daddy and Julek get disheartened.

Tadeusz

6. OCTOBER 6, 1945, MUNICH
[*to Z. Świdwińska*]

Dear Zosia,

If you are alive, read this letter, which, though typed, is written from the heart and out of great concern for you. The Uprising scattered you all across the earth, across so many camps and countries that I don't know who of my friends is alive and who is already on the other side. Wacław [Bojarski] and Andrzej [Trzebiński] perished; Bronek [Wihan], that funny boy who knew how to discreetly and ineffectually sacrifice himself, was shot; Krys [Baczyński], with whose *Wiersze wybrane* [*Selected Poems*] I so much disagreed, and Tadeusz Gajcy, known as Topornicki—"a marvelous Warsaw poet" as the girls from the Home Army who cherish his single volume like a relic call him—both perished. I don't know the whereabouts of Piotr [Słonimski], whose parents died tragically in the Uprising, nor of my dear friend Stanisław Marczak.

I don't know whether my parents are still living in that little village near Warsaw, Kotowice by Milanówek, from where after the Uprising they sent me a letter telling me for the umpteenth time that they had to "organize" their life anew.

The void around me grows ever greater, and I yearn for people who aren't here and experiences that won't return. The letters that I send daily, quite literally to all four corners of the world, get lost, and the people to whom I write remain silent.

I'm writing to you blind, but I truly cannot imagine that you have perished, because that would make no sense, would be particularly cruel and unfair on the part of Fate. I'm writing because you ought to be alive.

Dear Zosia, I would like to tell you how very grateful I am for the letter that you wrote to me in the camp, and for the many other letters that you wrote to me on behalf of my parents. They were letters from another, better world,

one that knew neither boundless hunger—the most ignominious of human feelings because it reduces man to the level of an animal eating scraps, grass, and clay—nor a hatred so corrosive because absolutely powerless; nor fear, the worst fear because it was daily, and completely impotent; nor the disgusting, repulsive death by gas—not for one's country, but simply from wasted flesh, from swollen legs, from boils and phlegmon, from scabies and typhus.

I deluded myself that you would all remain on that other, better side of the world and that I, returning from here, would find you all just as I had left you. I deluded myself, too, into thinking that I would find my own self.

Staszek once wrote me that you had completed your studies very successfully . . . There were, after all, degree ceremonies at that broken university. I even imagine that you are working at the university, writing some important papers about things from a completely fantastical world. You have no idea how happy that makes me (just in case) . . . I will never again apply myself to the honest, beloved field of Polish studies.

I'm writing this letter to you from Munich. But I didn't get from Auschwitz to Munich by the shortest route. I went through several camps, sometimes on foot, sometimes in open cattle wagons, unable to get much sleep, and completely without eating. You probably haven't got the slightest idea how long a person can live without food. I went from near Stuttgart to Dachau in a transport of sick people destined—according both to those of us who went and those who remained behind—for the gas.[3] They didn't gas us. They wanted to shoot us wholesale the day of liberation, but the Americans came a few hours too soon. So they didn't shoot. Then I tried to get better by relying on my own wits: I copied poems for a manic scribbler—it was one of the worst jobs I've ever had in my life—and in this fashion I supplemented my diet. Then they exchanged our prison stripes for SS uniforms and gave us felt boots, which I immediately threw away. I toured Munich, a beautiful city, wandered through the woods, crawling through a hole in the fence each time, because the camp was closely guarded (ostensibly on account of typhus and theft). Finally, I settled at the Polish Information Center, in other words, the Polish Committee in Munich, with a very clearly defined goal in mind: to acquire boots, a decent shirt of my own, civilian clothes, coat, hat . . .

Were it not for tremendous homesickness and uncertainty, life would be tolerable, pleasant even, there are wonderful books, albeit German, beautifully produced (about Greek art with thousands of illustrations; about Grunwald,

French painters, and God knows what else). There are magazines that reach us, though infrequently. I've read the latest poems (with which you are probably not familiar) by Broniewski, who has gone through a deep spiritual and artistic evolution, and Wierszyński, the greatest contemporary Polish poet, whose subject matter is unusually daring and whose form is beautifully finished. The poems about Warsaw by Stanisław Baliński are excellent. His "Poranek warszawski" ["Early Morning in Warsaw"] was once published in *Piesnie Niepodległe* [*Songs of Independence*]. Słonimski's poems still bring Mickiewicz to mind, and the miniatures of the dead Pawlikowska continue to be subtle and very delicate. Lechoń is editing *Tygodnik Polski* [*The Polish Weekly*] in New York, a very interesting paper. He publishes a lot, but very sloppily—to use Prof. Adamczewski's expression. That's why I am happy to have met one of the greatest graphics experts, the great lover of beautiful books [Anatol Girs], the prewar cofounder of Oficyna Warszawska. (Do you remember *Legenda o mastowej sośnie*?[4] It is he who published it.) He is currently publishing my poems for me, a little against my better judgment because they are neither particularly artistic nor intellectual achievements, but it will be without a doubt one of the most beautifully produced volumes of poetry from the war period. I read a few poems in the weekly *Wieś* [*Countryside*] and am in despair. There must be something better out there? I'm very curious about Przyboś's volume *Miejsce na ziemi* [*A Place on Earth*].

Dear Zosia, letters reach us either through the Red Cross, or else someone takes them by hand (as this letter), or else through the mail. I very much depend on hearing something from you. I'd like you to write to me what the conditions are like for studying at the university, what the prevailing atmosphere is, and which of my friends are alive. I wouldn't presume to ask, but if you know anything about my parents let me know, or make them write. I'd like to return as soon as possible, but as you well know, I can't quite . . . I need to know whether I have someone to come back to.

Say hello to all my friends and professors for me, yours affectionately,

P.S. 1   Despite everything—chin up!
P.S. 2   My parents' address was (postcard of October 4, 1944): Juliusz Borowski, Milanówek near Warsaw, Warsaw Line 28, Mrs. Maria Rybicka. The card suggested that my parents were living in Kotowice near Milanówek . . . What's the situation with searching for families through the Polish Red Cross?
P.S. 3   My address: Tadeusz Borowski, Polish Information Center, 15 Pienzenauerstr., Munich; Polski Komitet Monachium Pienzenauerstr. 15.

P.S. 4   You must write and give your address, because, of course, I'd like to send you my book!

P.S. 5 of October 6, 1945   A liaison officer from the Polish Mission is going to Warsaw tomorrow. Since I'm not sure whether the previous letter I sent will reach you, I am sending a copy through him. Nothing has changed for me over these past few days. Just a bit more reading matter and the book in proofs.

7. OCTOBER 16, 1945, MUNICH
[address on back of letter]

Zofia Świdwińska, 27 Francuska St.

Dear Zosia,

Truth to tell, I've already sent you one letter, and three copies of it at that, so I could wait for a reply quite peacefully, but since we are living in rather weird times when it is not clear who is alive and who has already died, one is allowed to commit a small faux pas. And anyway, the current letter is only in two copies.

Just in case you didn't receive my first letter, I am repeating certain relevant matters: I survived, it was awful, but no matter. Then I wandered around a bit looking for Tuśka whom I still have not found. All the Red Crosses over the whole of Europe know me (from letters). I am hanging up posters in search of Tuśka everywhere—like Orlando and his poems in praise of Rosalind. I haven't found any of my friends, and I'm becoming superstitious. Apart from that, I wear SS trousers and am trying to organize civilian clothes. This is taking a terribly long time, because it is being done in an honest way. I am writing a lot. One little volume (I say one, because, if all goes well, there'll be others) I am sending you straight in proof-form, uncorrected and without a cover [the last words are crossed out, and in the margin: "I'm not sending it, because I don't have it any more!"] The only way I can justify and defend myself is that I am a poet and in exile.

So much about me. I'd like you to write me that you are a Ph.D. and working at the university. I'd like to find my parents, they were in Kotowice near Milanówek right after the Uprising and I received a card from there. I'd like to finally learn something definite about our friends and what conditions in Poland are like for studying.

Dear Zosia, sit down at the table immediately, take paper and pen and write

me a very long and detailed letter. And let my other friends at least put their marks in the margin.

Keep well,

Tadeusz Borowski

P.S. of November 7, 1945   Courtesy of Mr. Jerzy Zagórski, I am sending you a copy of the letter of October 16. Forgive that it's dirty, it's from the heart. I'm writing an awful lot of things (Auschwitz stories), not good, but on demand. It might produce some cash and chocolate. Toil away, emigrant poet—but I don't want to be one; the atmosphere doesn't suit me. I will return. And what will be, will be.

Find Tuśka for me. In August 1944, she went to Bergen-Belsen or Ravens-brück. If she's alive and is in Poland, tell her that I still exist. If she got married, it would be best for her to divorce right away, and if she didn't, okay, I'm writing very romantic poems about her. Greetings to Staszek.

Keep well,

Tadeusz

8. MUNICH

[undated, written by hand]

To Jerzy Zagórski, 5a Juliusz Lea St., Apt. 14, Kraków

Dear Jerzy,

You've probably arrived back in Kraków, so listen to the news: Konstanty Ildefons Gałczyński is in Hext or maybe in Lemferden near Hanau, Frankfurt-Mainz, working at the headquarters of the Polish Red Cross; he travels to Paris, is alive, whole, and as healthy as an ox. Girs saw him, talked to him, and informed him about "Poszukiwania." Ildefons it seems is writing, but, Girs, being Girs, forgot to ask what. So tell Natalia not to worry. And my fiancée—in Sweden! I beg you, sit down at the table, pick up a pen, and write to her that I am in Munich, that I'm waiting for a letter from her; perhaps it will reach her more easily coming from you, because here the world is boarded up. Write to the Polish Red Cross in Stockholm, 22 Regiringgatten, Sweden, attn. Maria Rundo, born February 17, 1920, daughter of Jerzy and Eugenia, evacuated from Ravensbrück. Be so good as to give her address to my parents (Stanisław Borowski, Milanówek,

Warsaw Line 28), also to Stanisław Marczak, get him to write to Sweden as well. But perhaps Maria is already in Poland? Write, and I won't wait for my books which are in press, just pack my things.

Will it be possible to publish something? I'm very curious.[5] Forgive me for burdening you with so many of my affairs, but what else can I do?

Heartfelt regards to Maryna and Mirka as well as to the younger generation, the one that allows you to take part in poetry competitions—and to everyone— Christmas greetings,

Tadeusz Borowski

P.S.   Write whether you got in touch with Mrs. Olszewska; Krystyn and Janusz send their kind regards.

9. NOVEMBER 7, 1945
[*from S. Wygodzki*]

Dear Pan Tadeusz,

I hasten to thank you for your letter and little volume [*Imiona nurtu*]. I liked some of the poems very much, others less so, or rather, if I'm to be honest, didn't much understand. I'm not opposed on principle to the avant-garde—though I wouldn't include you among the "radicals"—but the manner of writing as in the poems about the girl is nearer and dearer to me. When I consider that you are 24 years old,[6] I can tell myself that I, an old man, don't understand you young ones.

And now, sensational news: Today, I received a letter from engineer Jan Krukowski (13 Szustra St., Apt. 3) in which he asks about you.[7] I wrote him all I know. What I don't know, you can write to him yourself. The guy is worth a letter. He sends me best wishes from the vice minister for culture and art with an assurance of assistance from the ministry the moment I step into the territories of the republic. Leon Kruczkowski promises me this assistance in the name of Związek Zawodowy Literatów.[8] And so, young man, do we return, or not?

When will I see you here?

Sincerely,

S. Wygodzki

Do you know anything about Jakub Jamiołowski, because Krukowski is asking about him, too?

10. NOVEMBER 7, 1945, MUNICH

[*to Stanisław Kazimierz Marczak, Zakopane*]

From poet Tadeusz to my friend with two names, Kazimierz Stanisław—best wishes!

. . . for being alive, even though I wrote a poem in honor of your death! But it's a friend's duty to do nice, unexpected things. So, please accept my being alive and well as a joyous and unawaited thing too. I know a lot about you and about your thesis on the theater. But why are you ill? Don't keep it up for too long—even though Zakopane is fashionable. Mr. Zagórski sent me his powerful poems and I read them late into the night. How trivial my own poetry seems to me! However, only six months ago I was unable to stand on my feet, and I weighed little more than 35 kilos.

And in two years, I wrote not more than ten poems. So please accept these poems I am sending you with the forbearance due a convalescent. *Imiona nurtu* is not obligatory reading. Written in May and June 1945, they are by way of being a remembering, a flexing of hands and poetic conscience.

Yes, but is that any kind of justification?

* * *

My prison adventures are short: hunger, damp, and bedbugs in Pawiak's cellars, Tuśka's tears when she saw me on Szuch Avenue. Quiet, pregnant, Maria (is it true that she escaped on the way to Majdanek?) and the very badly beaten Czesław [Mankiewicz]—it was only then that I started to like him.[9]

Then there were the touching postcards from home: that the garden was in bloom and that the dog was missing me. And the transport on which I nearly choked to death. I and the whole wagon—a hundred and twenty people. Finally, Auschwitz: work, rain, exhaustion, sickness, parcels, parcels, parcels . . . from home, from friends, from acquaintances, from people I didn't know. Why? How will I repay them?

Never-ending worry about Tuśka, who was on the brink of death. And news from you (wonderful letters, how grateful I am to you)—about Wacek's death, then Andrzej's, about the publication of my little volume. And all of Tuśka's illnesses: angina, flu, lungs, malaria, typhus . . . and the most painful of all—scabies, incessant scabies. That was what winter '43–'44 was like.

Summer of '44 was different. I lay on the bunk for days with Tuśka and a beautiful, simple woman with a bright smile and slender, delicate hands. Perhaps

from "Światło i cień" you'll pick up something of the feeling that overcomes me when I remember her.

Winter '45 was dreadful. Nobody will bring it to light in all its threat. Anyway, what for? Uprising, death of friends, snow, exhaustion, hunger . . .

Then came liberation. For a long time, I still wore prison stripes before they dressed me in an SS uniform. For a long time, I was still hungry.

I've started to learn poetry anew. I long even more for Tuśka. And for Poland.

Here—well, I have a few friends and a huge, lonely apartment. Many books from medieval and classical times. Art, stories, legends. Boxing gloves on the wall, and a ticket to a rather silly cabaret in my pocket.

I am writing. They published *Imiona* for me, a little volume which in proof form already irritated me. They're waiting for a second, Auschwitz stories, which may appear already this year in some fantastical binding. I want to publish "Noc zza oceanu" ["Night from Across the Ocean"], poems with peace as their problematic, however, they've not yet been written. I'm thinking about "Pokolenie" ["Generation"], a cycle of poems.

* * *

I don't know, can't imagine, what you look like, what you're writing, what you're doing. I know about Andrzej [Gwiżdż]. Why? Nothing about Zosia [Świdwińska], although I've written a few letters. My family was in Kotowice, near Milanówek, after the Uprising. Write to my brother: Juliusz Borowski, Milanówek near Warsaw, Warsaw Line 28, c/o Maria Rybicka. Tell them to write to me: through England, through the Polish Red Cross in Paris, by telegram through Switzerland, because it is not permitted to write directly.

Do something for me: try to find Tuśka in Poland, find out whether she's alive. Her personal details: Maria Berta Rundo, born February 17, 1920, in Warsaw, 16 Chmielna St., Warsaw, mother's name Eugenia. Auschwitz 43 558. She probably went from there in August 1944 to Bergen-Belsen near Hanover. Tell her, if she's alive, that I exist. That I will return at her slightest summons leaving everything behind: writing, stories, promises . . .

Give my regards to Hanka Bojarska, although I don't know her, I have a lot of sympathy for her,[10] and Trzebiński's little sister,[11] Edmund,[12] Arkadiusz,[13] and everybody else who is still alive. Write about the dead and the living.

Write to me. I think that Mr. Zagórski will be able to bring me a letter from you. And poems, poems. Yours and other people's that came out during and after the war.

Sit down at the table, pick up a pen and paper. In faraway, hateful Munich I await a letter from you.

And keep well, Staszek.

Tadeusz Borowski

Write to the Repatriation Mission: Major Łazarski, 15 Pienzenauerstr. St., Munich (attn. Tad. Bor. Committee Tracing Department).

Private address (don't write there): on the right, 22 Brucknerstr. #2, Munich.

11. ZAKOPANE, NOVEMBER 19, 1945

[Sender: Stanisław Marczak-Oborski, "Szopęnówka." Jagiellońska Street, Zakopane, Poland. Envelope with eagle and the seal of the Special Commissar for Assistance to Prisoners of German Concentration and Labor Camps, Kraków office.]

[Addressed in English in the original, as follows:] Citizen Tadeusz Borowski, Polish Red Cross, Subdelegation for Bavaria. Frankenstr. Obermenzing, Munich, Deutschland. (For Polish Committee, Tracing, 15 Pienzenauerstr.)

Tadeusz! Beloved old pal!

You can't imagine what enormous joy I felt on receiving news from Zosia Świdwińska that you had been found. I don't know what you are thinking these days, but not for a single moment have I stopped regarding you as my closest and most beloved friend. Zosia writes that you are planning to come back to Poland in the immediate future. What a joy that would be to the Essentialist family!!!! After the Uprising, I was taken prisoner-of-war; the moment the Red Army arrived, I made it back to Poland on foot. I regarded it as a duty, and I'm happy I did so. Living conditions in Poland are not at all easy, but we finally manage somehow. Cultural life in full swing! Because of a shortage of paper hardly any books come out, but around 20 literary and artistic journals exist, some of a really high level. Julian Krzyżanowski is editing a serious monthly, *Nauka i Sztuka [Science and Art]*. The journals have a socialist, Communist, humanist, or Catholic bent. Masses of theaters and some performances are far better than prewar ones. Szyfman is opening the Teatr Polski [Polish Theater] in Warsaw in December (imagine—he survived!). My sister is a major bigwig on theater at the Ministry of Culture and Art. Anyway, I'm probably writing these details to you unnecessarily, because you know them from the press.

And now as to the Essentialists![14] Mundek Kujawski and Andrew Gwiżdż[15] are studying law and living in the Academic House in Warsaw. Mundek was in a camp—he had pneumonia and typhus, but made it through and is blossoming now. The "Kujawianka" survived. Piotr [Słonimski] is studying medicine, he lost his parents in the Uprising.

Krystyna Jurasz lost her younger sister in the Uprising, lives in Poznań but frequently stops by Warsaw. Zosia Świdwińska is in Warsaw, she was in a camp—she'll write to you herself, I'm sure. Wanda Leopold lost her husband and little daughter, is working at the Baltic Institute in Toruń. Olga Peczenko[16] is at the Academy of Fine Arts in Kraków, unfortunately I have had no news of Arkadiusz Żurawski since the Uprising. Maria (Czesław's [Mankiewicz] friend) is alive, I saw her in Kraków. Czesław and Jurek Kreutz are back from Oranienburg, and Jurek's wife from Ravensbrück.[17] Jurek was emcee in some cabaret, he's also studying musicology. Berti (he married in Spring '44!) is in Łódź. Tadeusz Sołtan hasn't returned from P.O.W. camp yet. His wife perished in the Uprising. Ewa Pohoska with whom I founded and ran the clandestine literary journal *Droga* was executed by firing squad in March 1944.[18] Of our coworkers, these also perished: Krzysztof Baczyński and his wife (I made peace and buddied around with them) and Karol Lipiński, editor of *Płomień* (*The Flame*). Almost the entire *Sztuka i Naród* group died. Wacek Bojarski (married to my sister) mortally wounded during the action at the Copernicus statue in May 1943, died in hospital. Andrzej Trzebiński shot during the public execution on Nowy Świat in the autumn of 1943. Topornicki [Gajcy], Chmura [Stroiński], Mencel perished in the Uprising. The war didn't spare us, Tadeusz! Bronek Wihan was arrested right before the Uprising, I don't know what happened to him.

And now about the Polish studies students. Borowy, Krzyżanowski, Suchodolski, Szmydt are alive and lecturing. Of that group, only Wiwatowski,[19] perhaps, perished. Stefan Świerzewski is a professor at the *gimnazjum*. Ala Karpowicz is going into a convent, Marysia Szmydt married her Bodz.

I got tuberculosis in the camp and returned to Poland with holes in my lungs. I've been licking my wounds in Zakopane for nigh on a year. There's some hope that in a couple of months or so I'll be able to go back to normal work in Warsaw. News of Tuśka came from Sweden; she wrote to her mother. Your family (I haven't seen them since the Uprising) is apparently writing letters to you. Tadeusz! Reconstruct your poems quickly! All your manuscripts were with me and went up in flames along with my entire apartment, library, and archives. Naturally,

of course, a couple of copies of *Gdziekolwiek ziemia* survived. Even before the Uprising, I tried to disseminate them as much as possible and a lot of people read those poems—from Andrzejewski, through Staff to Zawieyski. Under the *Droga* imprimatur in February 1944, appeared your "Arkusz poetycky" ["Poetic Sheet"] made up of the "Na Zewnątrz noc" ["Outside, Night"] erotica. This also survived, as did the printed poems "Pieśń dla przyjacioł" ["Song for Friends"] and "Modlitwa o nieśmiertelność" ["Prayer for Immortality"]. I know a handful of epigrams by heart: "Modlitwę poety" ["Poet's Prayer"], "Pieśń Horacjańska" ["Horation Song"], "Początek ewangelii" ["The Beginning of the Gospels"], "Modlitwa do św. Weroniki" ["Prayer to St. Veronica"]. I don't, however, have "Pożegnanie Skaryszewskiej" ["Farewell to Skaryszewska"], nor "Ballada o esenc-jastach" ["Ballad about the Essentialists"], nor "Spacer z Porfirionem" ["A Walk with Porphyry"]. Sometime in the autumn of 1943, I organized a retrospective of your work in sculptor Karny's beautiful studio. The program included my critical sketch about your lyrics, and a broad selection of your poems rendered by Elżbieta Barszczewska and Marian Wyrzykowski.

I've tried to give you a handful of information. If you're not planning to return over the next few weeks, write to me about what you want to know, and I'll reply straight away. I shall await news from you with great impatience—how you're feeling, what mood you're in. I trust that we shall soon be able to fall into each other's arms.

Yours most affectionately,

Staszek

P.S.   Your companion from Pawiak, the actor Jaksztas, is alive and performing.

12. UNDATED, 5/7 ROZBRAT ST., WARSAW

[*undated; to Mrs. Teofila Borowska*]

Dear Mom,

I received Julek's letter of October. I'm sorry that I can't offer to help you at the moment. There are problems with communications and things taken by hand disappear. I have Tuśka's letter of October and card of November 5. She's getting settled in Sweden, worked in a hospital, was to study in Lund. You probably have a letter from her. I sent her address to Zosia. I have absolutely no idea how to meet with her, perhaps she has some thoughts. As for me, I live in

a state of constant expectation—now for a letter from home, now for a letter from Tuśka. Conditions are very good; albeit chaotically, I am improving myself "culturally" with the help of operas, concerts, and theaters. There is absolutely no Polish literature. Of course, problems with food or housing are nonexistent. Nevertheless, it's all stopgap and waiting for Tuśka to make up her mind . . . I'm sending the little book of poems. It's published very nicely. The camp stories are in press. I might put together a second volume of poems that I have. It would be good if I could get my poems from before the camp (would copies be possible?). I'd publish them before returning. I've been thinking about a cycle of Horation poems, but it would be incomplete without those others. I'm very homesick, Mom. It's been three years, after all, since I left home. I was supposed to come back for dinner. Ah, well.

Write and tell me what kind of circumstances you are living in, and how I can help. I expect, Moms, that, as before, you are sewing, and have the whole house on your head. Why is Daddy in Olsztyn? Julek, I am writing a longer letter to you. Don't worry. It's not good that you were sick, it is hard to get better under present conditions. Belated, but very sincere, birthday greetings. Yes, yes, Brother, we're getting old . . .

Fond kisses to you all,

The prodigal son in the wilderness

P.S.   What's with Regina? Her father asks about her. He's in Nuremberg. What's with Bronek Wihan? Did he perish after all?

13. DECEMBER 31, 1945, GAUTING

[*from S. Wygodzki*]

Dear Pan Tadeusz,

By coincidence, I am writing this letter on the last day of this, and of my 38th, year. It's sad that I had to live so many years in order to think the way I do in these poems that I am sending. How weak we are! There is no joy, even that love which has now appeared is sad. Of what use is it to me? I must now find affection for a young woman who doesn't care that I am many years older than she is, that I am incurably ill and no longer capable of hard work. She came here a few months ago, not knowing me, in order to bring greetings from my niece in Warsaw, stayed half an hour, only to return several weeks later having made

up her mind to stay by me. She lives far from here and visits me every once in a while, but she's going to return to Warsaw with me to a very difficult life. All this is hard for me, but requests that she leave haven't helped, and I can't say to my-self: Somehow it'll work out. You will understand me. It is hard to get involved with a woman after having poisoned my wife and own daughter.[20]

Thank you for the newspapers. I'd previously read that note about Władek [Broniewski], but the authors don't understand that it discredits them. He was with them until November, after all, and the fact that he's a drunk is neither new nor unusual. Anyway, I wrote to him. I owe the most beautiful years of my youth to him, Standeg, and Wat.[21] You, Sir, were then four years old.

I'm sending 33 poems on numbered pages, at least this is the arrangement I've thought up, but I don't know whether or not it's the right one. My first volume was arranged by Jasieński, the next two by Kruczkowski,[22] this one—with your help—I'll gladly change, if you find a need to alter the sequence.

In my unprofessional estimate, the volume will take two and a half quires of paper. If one or two poems would be needed to make up this quantity, they could be added, because as I've already mentioned, I have poems set apart for a second volume and I think I'll be able to fish out two of the same tone as the ones I am sending. From page 12 on, one could add the heading, "Poems About My Daughter." I ask you to read them and give me your honest opinion—but be polite!

I'd like to know from Mr. Girs what the cost of the printing would be, pro-vided, of course, that he wanted to take the job on. As I've already mentioned, I'd regard it as an honor if an outstanding artist such as he would undertake the job. Not insignificant (for my colleagues in Poland) will be the gloss which I would like to have at the end, namely, that apart from the poems on pages 13 and 31, which were composed in Auschwitz in 1943, I wrote the remainder in hospital in the second half of 1945. I believe that this explanation is relevant, as far as the setting in which I remain from the moment of gaining freedom is concerned. Thank you for thinking of me, and I am happy in your happiness at finding the woman dear to you and gaining news about your family. You have no idea how afraid I am of being a "civilian" again. I'd think about all this differently if I were in good health. They advise me to take it easy and not work hard or I'll have a relapse. Unfortunately, now that it is no longer necessary, I am to be a recidivist again, because where will I find a quiet life and be able to take it easy? Ah, that Gryphius, an excellent poet of the first half of the 17th century, born in Głogów in our Silesia. A bit like Janicki and Villon, but without elegance and without

roguery—a tragic poet. Not surprising since he saw the Thirty Years' War and knew how to think.[23] I'd like to see thinking but happy people today.

I shall await news from you impatiently. If the costs will suit, not the capacity, but the contents, of my colleagues' pockets, we'll bring the thing to fruition. On the occasion of the New Year, I wish you . . .

Best regards,

S. Wygodzki

[*postscript*]

Title of the volume: *Pamiętnik miłosci* [*Journal of Love*]

First page: For My Dead

Page 40, poem entitled "Wiek" ("Age"): Do you remember how it goes in "Ojcu zadżumionych" ["To the Father of the Plague-Stricken"]: tiny kid or small child? Can this be determined? Do you perhaps have Słowacki?[24]

[*added in pencil:*] Please pay attention to punctuation.

14. JANUARY 19, 1946, MUNICH
[*to Mieczysław Grydzewski, London*]

Dear Sir,

I am making haste to use your address sent to me by Tuśka, and am taking the liberty of enclosing a letter to her with the request that you forward it to her address (Anna Zboromirska, Kristl, Folkhögskolan, Box 79, Fönköping, Sweden, for Maria Rundo). This address is from a letter of 10/27/1945 which I received only yesterday.

If it wouldn't be too much trouble for you, I would ask that you send her a telegram saying that I am still in Munich and that I am waiting for her, because it's possible that she learned from Poland that I intend to return.

I would be enormously grateful to you, Sir, if you would be willing to correspond with me and help us get in touch with one another.

Very respectfully yours,

Tadeusz Borowski

15. JANUARY 27, 1946, GAUTING
[*from S. Wygodzki*]

Dear Pan Tadeusz,

It is hard for me to collect myself after our conversation. We discussed so many things, but I think that we devoted the greatest amount of time to "other," but such close, matters, namely the poems of Baliński[25] and Broniewski. We spoke least about our own concerns, and most about our love—poetry. It comes back to me now that at one point you and Krystyn expressed something like amazement that I write so much, that I already "have" a second volume, and Krystyn tried to explain to me that "it's six years later, of course," and that's why there's so much that's good (?!). And I almost had to justify this scribbling of mine! I have so much time, after all, and so many unreconciled things of which I cannot let go! I can't get away from those whom I held dear and I keep being unsure whether my daughter isn't actually wandering alone and hungry across the ruins of Warsaw. And if not my daughter, then, in so many towns, hungry, lonely children are sure to be wandering, and I, who lack breath, write this defective letter into the night and truly weep. I still delude myself that if we tell people that someone who's been dead "for six years repeats the motion of leaving, running, fleeing, jumping"[26] that people won't want to murder any more because "we'll remain forever frozen to the wall in this formation, to our knees in chilly water, on our eyelids rubble falling." You see Munich every day, and I know that over time one's perceptions blunt, but on me that town, with its gray-green tones, made a terrible impression. When will we see not germans, americans, poles, jews (I'm deliberately writing in lower-case), but what we so much need—people diligently tending to small matters! Have you ever reflected on the fact that writing is a moral problem, a disturbing one, which doesn't leave one in peace? Let's not use the word "mission," let's not talk about conscience—if we endure, it will be only for that single moment when we write about a person who is suffering. And you see, I'm in a situation where I don't at all need to place this burden on myself. I'm stuck in this matter. When I come out of it, I'll stop writing.

I'm sending you several poems written in the last month. Do they support the theory that to write a lot means to write badly?

Please give my regards to that childishly confused lady, to serious-as-ever Krystyn Olszewski, and you, Sir, jovial youth, please accept my respects.

Perhaps you could drop by here? We'll spend the night, we won't infect you with Koch's bacterium,[27] and chat.

S. Wygodzki

I'm waiting to hear from Mr. Girs, of course. Perhaps we could organize a writers' evening? Krystyn, that W. [?], Borowski, and I. What do you think?

16. FEBRUARY 2, 1946, MUNICH

[*to Halszka Bodalska, Łódź, 133 Piotrkowska St., 3rd floor, Polish Press Agency*]

Dear Pani Halszka,

Sincere thanks for thinking of me. I received your letter of mid-December and am replying immediately "courtesy of" as we say here. I am typing and making several copies. I am sending them by various routes. It should arrive.

I owe you, and all my friends, a deep debt of gratitude for help with life in the camp. Thank you.

I immediately wrote to your sister, of course. The letter should arrive because the post works well on the whole, albeit slowly. I've asked her to write back and when I get a letter from her, I will write to you again.

The news about our "group" made me very happy. I received Zosia's (two) letters and immediately replied; I don't know whether she got them, because she hasn't written to me. I'm sending them again "courtesy of" just in case. (I'm reading a bit of literature from the Thirty Years' War and am noticing many similarities between the periods: from mental pigheadedness, mass migrations, and photogenic rubble, all the way through to special messengers who are sent off with news.)

I truly admire Zosia. She has the enormous (and so rare) allure of the good human being.

It comes as no surprise to me that she's working wholeheartedly, she's Zosia after all! I know that she was in a camp. It's hard for me to imagine her anywhere other than among books. I'm interested in her work on Krasiński. Of the problems of Polish romanticism, the Pancras problem[28] is the most relevant for us today. It is finally an issue of the supremacy of one of two commandments: either the Christian "don't kill" or the Marxist "don't exploit" and of subordinating all the other "less" important ones to it. I'm curious how Zosia managed

with his "difficult" doubt-provoking artistry? (Difficult because unfashionable, discontinued, and little known. We have so little intellectual poetry!) Is Zosia's work only in Polish studies? Because I hear (and sometimes read) that the principles of sociological-historical criticism are gaining more and more of a following. The issue is very compelling, not very common among us (Boy[29] made a start—as usual), worthy of the West. You must admit, for example, what a graceful work: Mickiewicz (the one from *Trybuna Ludu* [*Tribune of the People*]) as a socialist—having brought him out of provincial gentry (the déclassé intelligentsia) throws him into the arms of utopian socialism (I read some of his articles: they're as far removed from human nature as the epistles of St. Peter). Or: to strip Słowacki[30] of his "democratic" halo. *Anhelli?*[31] certainly. *Beniowski*[32]— Democracy as a means of artistic contrast with the descendants of Adam sounded nice in octaves. But *Król Duch* [*King Spirit*]—that fascist poem? And his "Führerprinzip?" I regret not having a broader range of literature by me, it could be most entertaining. There's only Pasek,[33] him I read with passion because he's very amusing, especially where the king chases Lubomirski across Poland. I'm writing all this in jest, but there are two serious things here: that I am interested in Zosia's work and that I have something to read.

I am very pleased that Stefan received his M.A. Please give him my sincere congratulations. It's a surprise to me that Ala [Karpowicz] is studying. So she's not going into the convent? They wrote me she was. If I could, I would dissuade her—from the convent, of course. I think it must be terribly cold there. If you should meet Marysia Szmydt, please convey to her and her mother my best wishes. I am truly sorry not to be studying, I would undoubtedly argue with her about sonnets. From the point of view of the above said criticism. How did it come down to sonnets? "The gendarme carries Mickiewicz from place to place across the stretches of the empire," (that's Boy), he's carried to Crimea and what does he write?—sonnets! Everything's fine till now, apart from the salon form, which is perhaps not appropriate for a poet in prison. And we look: is there an echo of prison in them, a rebellious shout, an admonition about human dignity? No! There's "description" and Byronic grief. "I sailed into the dry stretches of ocean."[34] Excuse me, but where's the gendarme? Please believe me when I say that some parts of Germany (Dresden, Württemberg, the Alps, for example) are as beautiful as the landscapes in the novels of bygone centuries. But when we walked across them in prison stripes, we did not extol the beauty of this country. The beauty of an enemy land? We developed our own criteria for beauty: the most beautiful city? Frankfurt reduced to rubble. And in sonnets the poet praises

beauty as though he were completely free. Reality—next to the poet stands a gendarme, . . . an alien hierarchy which doesn't see in him a poet, not even a teacher from Kowno, but simply a dangerous revolutionary. Anyway, . . . we contemporary Europeans are very sensitive on the issue of distribution of bread and freedom (on account of their shortage) and we make greater demands on writers. We would consider it gauche if Kossak-Szczucka after a two-year stay in Birkenau were to write her impression of Beskida. (On the other hand, for me they are unforgettable[35]—how changeable the shapes of the earth can be!) What I'm writing is, of course, only effective barbarism.

What subject have you chosen for your work? I'm very interested. Also Romanticism? We are, of course, clearly experiencing its crisis: Mysticism is going bankrupt, being chased out of poetry, up with Positivism! It would be interesting to compare Positivist novellas to the contemporary American "short story": the same "Positivist" point, the same style (colloquial language, heroes from the masses); fantasy, Benet, for example, is very close to Prus;[36] in others it smacks of the grotesque (for example, the general's conversation with a mule-driver, a wife who is a witch). They have the flavor of primitivism like old copies of *Tygodnik Ilustrowany* [*Illustrated Weekly*].

I'm writing this because it seems we are going to experience a renaissance of Positivism. Prus is becoming the greatest Polish writer, Sienkiewicz is being put to the side, and Żeromski is distinctively getting smaller. It would be worth brushing up on Konopnicka and probably on Dygasiński.[37] I read *Gody życia* [*The Feast of Life*]—the section on hunting is very strong. In any event, this change in taste (social conditions!) testifies to the disappearance among us of any kind of understanding of pathos. Western Europe's reaction to the war and the camp is interesting: it speaks with the cultured man's distaste (and vulgarity) about hunger and lice as though these were not common concerns. May Balzac and Flaubert take vengeance on them.

I'm very curious about the shape of contemporary Polish poetry—they scare me when they say that there's nothing there except Imagism. Miłosz is writing a lot apparently.

I'm working at the Polish Red Cross here. As I've said, I'm not studying. Worse—I'm writing. I've already committed one criminal act, the camp stories are in press, they are trying to persuade me to do a second volume of poems. But, since I'm writing little and badly (nothing surprising in that), I'm not in a rush. I would bring out my former poems, the ones from before the camp, if I had them. It's not a great shame that I don't. Apart from that, officially, I am

searching for missing people; we bring out a central Polish Red Cross bulletin, my friends amuse themselves by publishing postage stamps which have brought the Polish Red Cross a mass of money. We have a series of further ventures in mind.

Of the literati: Melchior Wańkowicz is unbelievably fat and tells everyone about Monte Cassino, which he conquered (cane in hand, since it was uphill), and Gałczyński whose wife was worried about him is in the Polish Red Cross, Lemforde near Osnabruck.

Another address: *Defilada* [*Defilade*] (a journal of the 1st Panzers) P.40/OS Polish Forces BAOR (British Army of the Rhine), Germany. Please give both these addresses to: Jerzy Zagórski, 5 Juliusz Lea, Apt. 14, Kraków. I wrote there several times but without confirmation.

That's it for me here. I stand as though at an open door. I'm waiting for a letter from Sweden, for letters from home. If it is not too difficult for you and other of my friends, please write. I still consider myself a member of the group and that my rights to an exchange of thoughts have not expired.

Please give my best regards to Professor Krzyżanowski and all the other professors.

Sincerely,

Tadeusz Borowski

If Zosia has some time, please let her write to me. We have bought up a mass of books here for the university (art, architecture, etc.) which we will send. I'll try to send at the same time my volume—it's a crime (Stanisław Marczak will probably kill me), but nicely produced.

17. FEBRUARY 5, 1946, MUNICH
[*to Zofia Świdwińska*]

Dearest Zosieńka,

How very pleased I was to receive both of your letters! How good that you exist, that you survived, and that you've remained the way you were! It's bad that you were in a camp, that atmosphere is never good for people. You write very little about yourself, but H. Bodalska wrote me more. If my heartfelt admiration for you and your work doesn't offend you (not studying or working myself, perhaps I don't have a right to it), accept it, because it is sincere.

I'm interested in your work on Krasiński, since it's still a war thing. For me, the Pancras problem is the most relevant of the problems of Polish Romanticism. And the questions of the poet's artistry (. . . intellectual poetry, etc.) is also tantalizing. What are you pursuing now?

Sincere thanks for news about my parents. I received Julek's letter (addressed in your hand), you probably know the contents. I'll try to write separately to my parents. I'd like to ask you, Zosia, to write to Tuśka. I received a letter from her in October; she's full of optimism, as Tuśka always is when she writes to me (her letters from the women's camp where she was lying totally ill were wonderful "Tadeusz, there's nothing the matter with me," she wrote, "I'm as healthy as an ox, I'm just . . . in hospital").

If I don't write as well now as I used to, it's not my fault. The camp has an effect, one has to learn the simplest things afresh, even writing. As to me, in brief: I overrated my own strength. It's increasingly difficult for me to live here despite ever better conditions, the so-called material ones. My famous little volume (*Imiona nurtu*) (I sent the proofs to Staszek) finally came out at the end of November.

The graphic work is on a level, two-toned print, etc., anyway, I bragged about it in every letter. Today, however, I'm less enthusiastically inclined toward it. It offends me with its eclecticism, artistic indecisiveness—a typical "selection of poems" and not the best at that. Nevertheless, I'm sending it to you and asking your indulgence. It is to bring me (and this is important, because it's the first honorarium in my life) three thousand marks; translated into everyday things this means either 300 best seats at the opera, or two good wristwatches, or 30 thousand journeys by tram (with transfers, can you imagine how much I'm going to ride?), or, finally, four years' worth of rent for the four-room apartment with bathroom, which we have taken from Hitlerites. For a while, I seriously considered a good suit and tie, but since these things never stick to me, I have to make do with the opera. I'm also sending you the poem in which I killed off Staszek.[38] Please let him forgive me because it was for the Polish Red Cross. It hurt no one, and its sale made several hundred thousand marks. The camp stories are in press. I've written two to which I will admit, a few I'd like to pass over in silence. The thing is an unfortunate mix of encyclopedia, symphony, proclamation, and anecdote. The very titles—"With a Baedeker Among the Wires," "I Don't Recommend Getting Sick," "This Way to the Gas, Ladies and Gentlemen"—say a lot. I'm sorry they were my idea. I wrote for various reasons: first, that it could be published; two, so as to show (though in a few fragments)

everyday camp life and to strip man of so-called martyrdom; and finally, because evil was not the work of one side. The book (written by three of us) is very raw and full of glitches (you know, I've forgotten my mother tongue), contrary to fashion there are practically no SS men in it, nor too many wires in the night. Anyway, I'll try to send it to you immediately. They're promising it will be ready in a month.

I've already sent the corrected proofs (200 pages) back. This is one side of my life, maybe the most embarrassing. The second—those ties, coats, and shoes. Don't fall for it, Zosia! As in the old days, I have an amazing striped tie, and, as before, I don't clean my shoes. In truth, my colleagues from the camps who are now holding various "functions" are strongly urging me to buy or steal something, but I won't be persuaded. For some time, I've been making use of culture. It's amazing how I've got into music these past few months. The excellent philharmonic orchestra here performs great concerts practically every day which are always well attended. Mozart, Beethoven, lots of foreign French and Russian composers. I've been to the theater a few times, Thornton Wilder's *Our Town* and Shakespeare's *A Comedy of Errors* are playing. You remember what a great stir Wilder made in Warsaw before the war? What's left of him today is a specifically American sense of humor (e.g., aural scenery without visual scenery); this lack of scenery in dramatic scenes (the cemetery) is very funny. Imagine for yourself, a man in profound, very realistic mourning, who in the depths of grief bends over a woman sitting in a chair (his wife's grave) and pretends to place nonexistent flowers at her feet. This very novelistic play is typically "American." I'm reading a bit of this literature now (very difficult because it's in English) and I am finding many similarities with our Positivism. The technique of the novellas (the famous "short story") is just about the same, apart, perhaps, from the culminating point. I cannot study (truth to tell, there is a university here, but I have had absolutely enough of German literature, during the summer I skimmed whole mountains of minor writings), and not having too much talent for English, I resort to reading. I'm reading a lot about the art of my beloved Middle Ages, I've been looking for *Carmina Burana,* but haven't been able to get it. There's practically no trade in books, except, perhaps, among those in the know . . . But I've not been let in on the secrets of the black market.

I've become thoroughly familiar with Dürer and have profited a great deal from Wölfflin's theory of art. I've discovered very interesting things about antiquity; I'm immersing myself in the history of the "fall" of the Empire. We don't know how to think in proportions, but there is a greater distance between

Augustus and Marcus Aurelius than between Napoleon and—Hitler! What's more, they say that Nero was not a good emperor. He rebuilt a scandalously neglected Rome, lifted the death penalty for prisoners of war, and—music. He apparently composed quite well. In any case, antiquity had the same cult of antiquity as we do, and learned from Plato, Marathon, and Demosthenes. And the free development of thought constrained them as it did us in a certain era . . . As a warning to all of today's rhetoricians, it's worth thinking deeply about its role at the time. In addition: statistics show that from Nero to Aurelius, 200 Christians died martyrs' deaths . . . Happy times.

I take no part in emigrant life. The worst kind of politics in full bloom. One doesn't say Poland, but "Warsaw." Someone goes into the service of "Warsaw," someone has escaped from the "Warsawites," there are "Warsaw" opinions, "Warsaw" money, etc. A single expression for describing the emigrant position hasn't yet arisen. The government in "London" isn't popular, so its name is not used. Along with this, a rampant cult of heroes (Monte Cassino!), looting, robbery, etc., are common among us.

The services Poland rendered are mentioned at every step by people who on closer inspection turn out to have been on the Volkslist[39] or worse. They look askance at anyone who wants to do anything. The Americans are unbelievably civilized and forbearing. They're talked about a lot. But—over a period of two months in summer, the community in Freimann in Munich (plus or minus 6 thousand people) stole about 10 thousand requisitioned sheep. It's not surprising that they locked the camp and imposed a quarantine. A bitter story of emigrant life is taking shape, all the more painful because the Germans are exploiting our behavior extremely skillfully and making themselves look very good by contrast with us. I think that our pretension to Western civilization is only the delusion of a group of intellectuals. I write about this with bitterness, because I'm resigned to my own resources, not wanting to engage in dirty dealings nor to loot for one's country. The Germans have left us a love of public life and boundless mendacity. Any slaughtered cow is a great act of patriotism, any misappropriation of a hundred marks cries out for a Grunwald medal. We are living in strange times, Zosia! We have lost everything: a sense of the value of things and thoughts. We are told how much to charge for goods and what to believe in. It seems to me that we are in the midst of a terrible ideological void. There's no point taking American idealism seriously, it's the age of the man of the street about whom Wallace dreams and of the president's "four freedoms,"[40] a utopia of thoughts without hierarchy, a goal, not a path. The most interesting,

perhaps decisive, things for our era are happening beyond Europe: the unification and emancipation of China (four hundred million! several thousand [years] of unbroken cultural tradition! a country never beaten culturally!) as well as the liberation of India. Do you know that, after the States, India is the largest creditor in the world? True to their ideology, they are not picking up arms, but nonetheless, England will leave. If one could know what will come out of today's chaos, it would be easier to live!

Forgive me for writing all this to you. Don't retort that this is rubbish that doesn't concern those of us living on the rubble of a world reconstructing itself, that the problems of freedom and bread are closer to us. The world, you see, is always being born through its deeds and people are always full of hope. But the new man will not emerge out of Europe.

Anyway, it's hard for me to write about personal matters. With every passing day I grow ever more uneasy, as though I were neglecting my obligations. I know how disloyal this is to you and it torments me not a little. You see, the entire summer and autumn, I looked for Tuśka because I regarded it my duty. Wrongly so, perhaps, I don't know. Szuch Avenue and Auschwitz brought us closer together than anything else.

Last winter was very hard on me. I was unbelievably concerned about her. Now, I don't know, I really don't know. Tuśka writes that she's staying. Her uncle is trying for a stipend in Lund for her. Sweden is a very beautiful country. But I could always snap my fingers and do what's easiest for me. It's hard for me to decide what I should do. What is loyalty to her? To myself? Because if I stay (I can't imagine life here), I will never write anything good: I never learned abstract poetry; our era hurts too much to write poems about the setting of the moon, and I will write nothing against Poland ("Warsaw" they say, here). Because poetry is like money: it's not worth the same amount everywhere. And a written poem is not an honest poem everywhere.

Perhaps this sounds funny and pretentious, I don't know; you must forgive me, because I don't know how to weigh words. If I give all this up (and I'd give it up gladly), Tuśka will bear me a grudge. I wrote her that I would not return without her.

But if she comes back with me, and we are unable to manage, she'll blame me. Not for anything in the world would I want her to have hardship in life because of me. She went through enough hell in Birkenau to last her for the rest of her life. On the other hand, I know that it is very hard at home. I wouldn't want my coming back to be problematic for them. I wouldn't want to be a burden

for them, but I doubt it would be possible to avoid being so, at least in the first months, despite Jerzy Zagórski's promises (outdated by now). Dear Zosia, I truly dream of starting to study in our former atmosphere. I think that I'd be able to make up for the years in the camp and the year in emigration.

I yearn for good literature, to write something decent. I have a hundred ideas a day, but my hands fail me here, for whom? For what? I sometimes read *Odrodzenie* [*Rebirth*] and various literary supplements that reach us. How one would like to stir up a few dunderheads!

Please don't think I'm afraid about conditions or anything like that. After all, many things which to normal people seemed normal, to me were exotic. Family life (ask my mother how many years we were together), a corner for books, light, quiet in the apartment. So now that the exotic is the norm, I'd feel like a fish in water.

As you see, Zosia, I'm writing somewhat chaotically, but that's exactly how I am living: with these thoughts and chaotically. If this should offend you or seem inappropriate, accept it as a fact of daily life. I'd like to live through this period of my life as fast as possible. Despite the people with whom I associate. They are like heroes out of Chesterton, people who totally incorporate certain moral principles into their daily lives. They try to help others and make up as best they can for the bad reputation the Poles have. But how can I help it? This missionary-educational work absolutely does not speak to me. I have no faith in the millions that we have made for the Polish Red Cross, the diapers, medicines, and apples. Searching for missing persons and reuniting scattered families bores me. As does persuading thieves not to steal, and swindlers to stop politicizing. But these Chesterton heroes have faith in me and count on me. I'd willingly run away without saying good-bye, leaving them to the manuscripts and proofs.

So, if it's not too much trouble, write to me, Zosia. Regards to the professors. Warmest greetings to your mother.

Most sincerely yours, stay well, Zosia.

Tadeusz Borowski

18. FEBRUARY 6, 1946, MUNICH
[*to Zofia Świdwińska*]

T. Borowski, Polish Committee, Tracing Service for Missing Persons, 15 Pienzauern St., Munich

Dear Zosia,

I'm taking the opportunity of sending you postage stamps issued by the Polish Red Cross Committee.[41] Here in Germany, they're being fought over and their market value exceeds the face value many times. Michel's catalog is due out soon (it's the philatelists' official bibliography), these stamps are going to figure in it as the only stamps from a concentration camp. Their value will increase even more then. I've no idea whether they will be useful to you; I'm sending them just in case. If they turn out to have some value, write and I'll send you more.

Best wishes,
Tadeusz Borowski

19. FEBRUARY 15, 1946
[*from Tadeusz Sołtan*]

6 Jahn St., Quakenbrück (Kreis Cloppenburg)

Dear Tadzio!

It was with great joy that I received from Mr. Ptakowski the news that you are alive and currently working at the Polish Red Cross Committee in Munich. Unfortunately, I don't have the time at the moment to write at great length, because my informer is going back early tomorrow morning. During the coming week, I will try to send you a longer, more extensive letter.

Fate drove me through the Warsaw Uprising to Germany. After a year of imprisonment and longer wanderings, I have landed up for the moment in Quakenbrück, at the editorial offices of *Defilada*. I have very skimpy information about our friends. What I can report is not very happy. Staszek Marczak, who took an active role in the Uprising, is now in Poland. He is seriously ill with tuberculosis. His condition is apparently hopeless. He's writing a longer piece about the theater. Halszka is also in Poland. I recently wrote about the tragic fate of the editors of *Sztuka i Naród* in *Defilada* ("There were four of them . . .") About the rest, I have no news. My life has been quite dramatic and interesting.

I'll give details in my letter. I shall await your "writing" and for you to send your little volume as well as newer, current poems with permission to print them in the journal. I would like you to pay attention to the materials for publishing a book by one of my friends from the Uprising, which I am to send to Mr. Ptakowski. Pay attention to form and the proofreading of the edition!

Times are changing and life's roads have taken a strange turn. I'm counting, however, that perhaps we shall meet again with our "Essentialist" greeting.

Sincerely,

Tadeusz Sołtan

20. FEBRUARY 20, 1946, GAUTING
[*from S. Wygodzki*]

Dear Pan Tadeusz,

My letter, or rather, attempt to discuss your creative work,[42] is going to be incomplete if only for the reason that I am somewhat all of a dither after the "journeys" I've recently undertaken. On Sunday—Munich, where I saw a film about Ehrlich, and now I am back from Feldafing where I spent two whole days. I am sleepy, I can't sleep in a strange bed, and I went about the matter of a suit and coat, rather like you to Murnau (did you go?). I'm writing, however, so as not to put it off any longer, because on Friday I am going by car for three days to Garmisch, to see this universally praised wonder.

While I was reading, I filled a huge sheet of paper with comments, noted down titles, but now that I'm about to write it's going to be hard for me to put this all together into some coherent whole. From "Początek ewangelii" ["The Beginning of the Gospel"], I noted down the following titles of poems which I liked enormously: 1) "Początek ewangelii," 2) "Zapis" ["Notation"], 3) "Kontemplacja" ["Contemplation"], 4) "Poeta emigracyjny" ["Émigré poet"], 5) "Liryk 53" ["Lyric 53"], 6) "Stracona jest noc bez wiersza" ["Lost Is a Night Without a Poem"], 7) "Modlitwa do św. Szymona Słupnika" ["Prayer to St. Simon Slupnik"], 8) "Kuszeniw św. Ildefonsa" ["Temptation of St. Ildefons"], 9) "Bajka o lisie" ["Story about a Fox"], 10) "Legenda o św. Janie" ["Legend of St. John"], 11) "Życiorys obozowy" ["Camp Biography"], 12) "Dary demokratyczne" ["Democratic Gifts"] (even though I don't agree with the ideological treatment of the subject, the poem has enormous fluency), 13) "Po wojnie" ["After the War"], 14) "Ale sądze" ["But I Think"], 15) "Piosenka dla Ziuty" ["Song for Ziuta"], 16)

"Kotlet, wiersz" ["A Cutlet, a Poem"], 17) "Dialog o żonie" ["Dialogue About a Wife"], 18) "Lepsze w łapie" ["Better in the Paw"]. In "Work in Progress,"[43] I'm struck by the very serious moment in the narrative, a reverie, one of those narrated reveries, a very difficult type, where the narrative flows into the lyrical, but the conversation with the self does not become egotistical prating. The best (in my opinion): 1) "Jabłonie stały przy drodze" ["Apple Trees Stood by the Road"], 2) "Do X w Londynie" ["To X in London"], 3) "Do X we Włoszech" ["To X in Italy"], but, what's most important—the general "reserved" tone, the color of these poems.

About the cycle "Światło i cień" ["Light and Shadow"], I can only say that it is unspeakably beautiful. I don't know poems like this, or, more precisely, don't know such sublimely beautiful poetry. I'm not looking for analogies, one might find some here or there—in whom wouldn't we find such a moment? One's struck by maturity of expression, gravity, and what is particularly appealing to my taste, the lack of description for description's sake and the very beautiful projection of the inner state onto the external world. Of a different type, "piosenka o pomocy amerykańskiej" ["Song About American Help"] is very successful (I'm "discussing" poems according to the order of reading, hence I'm discussing diametrically different poems in a single—as I might put it—breath). I single out "Droga do Tipperary" ["Road to Tipperary"] as a whole. Very beautiful poems in "Z pamiętnika" ["From a Diary"] with the exception of the last one, which seems to me to deviate from the preceding poems. The whole of "Noc zza oceanu" is beautiful. Not everything in "Szkice inteligenckie" ["Intelligentsia's Sketches"] was to my taste. The best probably "Życiorys dobrego Niemca" ["Biography of a Good German"] and (?) "O Adasiu" ["About Adaś"]. I think that you treated "Wieczór w Monachium" ["Evening in Munich"] too lightly, that more, and something other, might have been wrested from this poem. I liked "Cztery wolności" ["The Four Freedoms"], but I've read better poems of yours. The "raw cabbage stumps" in poem xxx, the third from the last (fourth line in the first verse) grated on me, because, obviously, we "cook soup" from raw cabbage stumps and not cooked ones. Wouldn't "out of cabbagey green stumps" be better? The last poem in this cycle contains too many allusions to a certain acquaintance of yours for me not to thank you in his name. A very beautiful poem and if I may be so bold as to ask you to send it to me (I didn't want to transcribe it without your permission), I would be most grateful.[44]

The most beautiful, however, is the sketch, essay, study (?), I don't know what to call it, "O poezji i poecie" ["About Poetry and the Poet"] as well as "Pokolenie,"

with which I was enamored. I would also like to have this essay and also this poem. I would like to write these poems myself. They are beautiful. On the other hand, you treated the photomontage "Koniec Wojny"[45] too lightly. It could have been dramatized more rapaciously. I imagine it this way: on the German woman's feet—your girl's shoes; the tot kicking in the pram—and the pram belonged to my daughter; the "democratic functionary MG"—wearing your coat on his back. The last verse, splendidly written—outstrips with its aura the others. In "Ksiądze z dnia wigilii" ["Book of Christmas Eve"]—the best in my opinion: "Do towarzysza więźnia" ["To a Fellow Prisoner"], "Niebo października" ["October Sky"] as well as the introductory poem. "Kolęda dla ludzi prostych" ["Carol for Simple People"] is beautiful, and "Modlitwy norymberskie" ["Nuremberg Prayers"] is also excellent, lighter in kind, but nonetheless splendidly done and very wise. You have at least three volumes ready. I would collect the epigrams together with the Nuremberg prayers in one, the rest in two different books, which shouldn't be published here—strictly from a practical point of view, apart from a little resonance, which is not a very important matter. I received a letter from Poland: they pay very well for every bit of trivia, one can live well for quite some time from a published book. (I sent a dozen or so poems.) Would it not be worth thinking in practical terms about getting money for these poems, which, in turn, would allow you to study in peace, and continue writing in peace? Anyway, one writes for someone (one exception: a stay in hospital) and if you return, a moment of cheering will be needed, which we will probably not have here. I'm interested in what you think of my conclusions.

What's with our case? Is it possible to rush it? I would like, would very much like, to get out of here in spring, and to return to Poland in summer. Before we leave for Biber (March 11 we are getting married before a justice of the peace in Feldafing) shortly after getting married, I'd like to know, to see rather, at least the first proofs. If you experience any difficulties, please write to me openly about them. If I am thinking about publishing this book here, it's because I want to leave something about Poland to all those Jews who lost everything under Hitlerian occupation and, hungry and stupefied, are now seeking a Promised Land that doesn't exist.

Those Auschwitz sketches (we need to talk extensively about them, your Céline-esque manner[46] puts me off) I have kept for [unreadable] and if you have to have them, I'll return them immediately, all right?

I'm going to Garmisch for three days. I will be back on Monday, and leave here again on March 10 for Feldafing, from where I may go back again to Garmisch

with my wife for about a week. I have a room and good board reserved there. I await news from you with, I might say, impatience. Is my book going to be printed at Bruckmann's under Mr. Girs's eye?

Sincerely,

S.W.

21. FEBRUARY 2, 1946
[*from Tadeusz Sołtan*]

Dear Tadzio,

After the card sent through Mr. Jerzy Ptakowski, I am now writing the announced longer letter. I was, of course, inordinately pleased by the news that you had survived the KZ hell and are currently working in the Munich community. I am very sorry, however, that such a great distance divides us and I can't relate my historic vicissitudes to you in person, and that we cannot conduct a long Essentialist-émigré conversation. There is so much to tell and discuss. Because it's a great joy here, on foreign soil, to be able to meet a friend and club companion from occupation years. I never liked great, exploitative pathos, but at the news that you, you old rotter, were alive and prospering quite well in this foreign land, I drank half a flask of whisky by myself and raised beautiful and lofty toasts in praise of poetry and friendship. The news that you had added a second (after *Gdziekolwiek ziemia*) volume to your posthumous collected works also fills me with emotion. In any event, I don't know whether you know that it is actually the third volume. In January 1944, as a supplement to the clandestine literary journal *Droga* there appeared in mimeograph, with nice graphic work, your poetic folio. (Poetic folio by the author of *Gdziekolwiek ziemia*—as the caption read). The folio was prepared and compiled by Staszek Marczak who, in addition, placed several other of your poems in *Droga*. The same publishers also put out a poetic folio by the late Krzysztof Baczyński who fell during the battle in Wola during the Warsaw Uprising.[47] Staszek himself also took part in the Uprising as a lance corporal, taking part, among other things, in the famous capture of the PAST[48] building on Zielna Street. His house on Ceglana Street in ruins. The last time I saw him was the day before I was taken prisoner of war. He was in an old, navy-blue police coat, in a bitter, somewhat grim, mood, and was considering whether to go to prisoner-of-war camp as a soldier, or with the civilian population. After liberation, I searched for him to no avail in Germany. I only

recently received news that he is alive and in Poland. His sister is also with him. His lungs are apparently seriously infected. His condition is apparently grave. He's writing a larger work about theater. I haven't, however, found his name in the Polish journals that reach me. I'm currently trying to get more detailed information and his address. When I wrote to my mother, who lives in Warsaw, I asked her to find Staszek and Halszka. I want to make direct contact with them at all cost. My wife, Alina, perished from an aerial bomb in mid-September 1944, under the rubble of our house on Czerniakowska Street. I've already mentioned the tragic death under the German occupation of the editors of *Naród i Sztuka* [*sic*] Wacek Bojarski and Andrzej Trzebiński (Stanisław Łomień). I devoted a sketch to them, a reminiscence, in *Defilada* (No. 6 of this year). Topornicki (Tadeusz Gajcy) who was recently representative of the highest class of poetry, superior even to Krzysztof Baczyński, and who had published two wonderful collections of poems, fell to artillery fire in the Old Town together with his friend, the gifted lyricist, Chmura (Zdzisław Stroiński). On Marszałkowska Street fell one of the closest of my recent friends, Wojtek Mencel, who during the Uprising was finishing his interesting play about St. Francis of Assisi. This list of losses is tragic. Especially for me. One after the other, I lost the people closest to me, to whom I was bound not only by personal friendship, but also by strong and deep intellectual ties. Only you and Staszek are left. So understand my great joy when Ptakowski made it known to me that you were alive. About the worthy Essentialists, our noble friends, I know virtually nothing: Piotr, Andrzej, Mundek Kreutz, whether they are alive, what is with them . . . These past years without you were no longer so colorful, even though the club hymn from Piotr's pen, "We Are Essentialists," did ring out more than once. Last New Year's Eve, a new Essentialist song came into being whose refrain best expresses the atmosphere of those evenings and nights: "Hey, Essentialists, the noose will choke you," and the toast: "So for the last time let's drink to the noose." And we drank. As I'm reminiscing, I have to ask this rhetorical question: when are we going to sing together again, and drink to good friendship once more and to that snippet of poetry which will suffice for the entire pathos of super-patriotic feelings? I often sip the "water of life" here with the most exasperating alcoholic, the greatest and involuntary bigamist and buffoon, Konstanty Ildefons Gałczyński. There is no Porphyry's Ass, Tower of Hildegard, or Helicon's trumpet No. 6 in our "Kwaczymość,"[49] there is only foul, rainy weather and a foreign, noisy wind. And there is a terrible, wearisome yearning for Poland, for native mud, for packed Warsaw trams, and for the people around us to be speaking only Polish. Do you ever yearn for that

wooden hut on Skaryszewska Street? I'm not prone to nostalgic tears, but this is so . . . goddammit, blast!

After the Warsaw Uprising, I went through a not long, but very difficult period in prison. Barracks of the prisoner-of-war camp in nightmarish Sandbostel, work under bombardment in Hamburg, penal "Kommando," long evacuation march. Freedom found me in a camp in Schleswig. I suffered from serious heart problems. As soon as I managed to pull through and was on the mend, I acquired by my own wits a rotary press, a copier, and started to publish a journal with the characteristic title *Powrót* [*Return*]. In April, I moved to the small island of Sylt, near the Danish border, where a large Polish community, military and civilian, had been organized. I set up a small publishing house there. A daily bulletin, a weekly with nice graphics, which I put together almost single-handedly with local events. I even brought out, as a private publication, an interesting little book of poetry by a colleague of mine from the Uprising, Marek Gordon, entitled *Cudzy Chleb* [*Other People's Bread*]. At times too journalistic, careless, perhaps, as well, but good, clean lyrics. In April, I also married for the second time. I am incurable. I struck it quite well, however. My wife is a pleasant, cultured woman who surrounds me with solicitous care. So I am almost fine.

For a few weeks now, I am working for the weekly of the First Panzer Division, *Defilada*. This also, however, is a transitory period. I am writing quite a lot, depending on the paper's current needs. Mainly reportage, columns, for a generally educated audience, prefaces sometimes. I have quite broad contacts with Polish journalists and publishers abroad. As to my personal plans for the near future, they are not finally crystallized. The new reality in Poland, as you can easily imagine, attracts me a great deal. On the other hand, however, many factors decidedly repel me. I know that I would, despite everything, have quite a lot of possibilities for creative work in Poland at present, it's difficult for me, however, to give up certain convictions and feelings. To a large extent, it's a question of inner integrity. In any event, I don't intend to proclaim forever my entry into the new "great emigration." After mulling over a series of issues, it's entirely possible that I will decide to return, speedily even, to Poland, having thrown off all unnecessary anxieties and scruples. My mother urges me to return. I don't know how you intend to decide your fate, I assume, however, that you will not renounce taking up the fight and discussion about the program for new culture and art in today's Poland. We would then certainly find ourselves side by side again. I shall wait for a longer reply from you with precise details about your experiences and plans for the future. I would very much appreciate your sending

me your book as well as some recent poems, especially ones suitable to be published in the paper. *Gdziekolwiek ziemia* went up in flames, I think, in the ruins of my parents' house on Żoliborz. I am very interested in how and what you are writing now. My writing in the last period in Poland was mainly essays in the area of cultural and artistic theory.

All the materials, and there were a lot of them, unfortunately went up in flames, as far as I know, during the Uprising. Now it's come down to ordinary journalistic labor! . . .

Dear Tadek, I am counting on your reply, and a speedy one at that, because I don't know where fate may take me again. Write to me, if you know anything, about our mutual colleagues and friends. Send me your book and poems as well as anything that you might want to publish. If you are going to send a reply before 3/2 of the current year, address it to me—6 Jahnstr., 23 Quakenbrück; if you are going to reply after that date, then write to: Westerlánd 24, Sylt Polnische Hauptquartier—"Belvedere," to my attention.

I greet you again with the Essentialist greeting. Live, old man, and write! Yours very affectionately,

Your truly devoted

Tadeusz Pereświet-Sołtan

22. FEBRUARY 22, 1946, MUNICH

[*to Tadeusz Sołtan*]

Dear Tadzio,

How wonderful that you are alive! What happened to you over these few years? With you and our friends? And with poetry?

About me, brother, you know. Pawiak, Szucha Avenue, Auschwitz. Normal business . . . I survived the camp with parcels and luck. Summer of '43 I was ill and thought about poems that I would write if I'd had paper and pencil and— wasn't in the camp. Summer '44, I spent whole days on the bunk with Tuśka. Our girls in the camp were magnificent, Tadziu.

Then there were less interesting things; rain, mud, a different camp, hunger, etc. Enough that I went to Dachau on a transport of *muzulmen*.[50] Then, "noc zza oceanu," a summer of emigration, poems . . .

I wrote, Tadzio, a lot and the most various things. In the camp, a couple of poems for friends. In prison, I inscribed a poem into a Bible for a boy who was

supposed to go free, a poem "Do towarzysza więźnia" ["To a fellow prisoner"]. This boy died in Auschwitz in the same bed on which, a day after him, I came to lie on with typhus.[51] *Imiona nurtu,* that book that I published in Munich, is a very unobligatory collection of poems, and an old collection at that—from April when I didn't yet have either poems, nor could I walk or think very well. You'll find "Pieśń," "Spacer z Porfirionem" (if you see Gałczyński, his wife from Kraków is looking for him, she's at the Zagórskis', 5a Jul. Lea, Apt. 14), a few good and a few unnecessary poems. Anyway, read them and judge for yourself. In addition, I'm sending you a few other poems, neither new nor relevant ones, truth to tell. If they'll be useful to you—use them.

I'm thinking of a volume, *Pokolenie,* and I'm still thinking about "psałterz poety Tadeusza" ["Poet Tadeusz's Psalter"], but I don't have prayers from before the camp, I don't remember a word. What or when I will publish, I don't know. I could put together a selection of poems, but still don't have a decent whole or cycle.

It's hard to have, anyway. I don't know about you, Tadzio, but it's hard for me to collect myself. Two years outside of life, and outside of oneself, have an effect. In truth, the whole of Europe fell apart around me. One saw the corpses of friends and enemies, ate stolen bread, carried heavy loads. In fact, Tadzio, life's roads take strange turns. Tuśka went through all the depths of the war and is alive, but Ewa [Pohoska] who read poetry so beautifully, was shot by firing squad. And we are alive, exist, write to each other. I still can't take in, not that we are alive, but that they perished. Wacek [Bojarski], Andrzej [Trzebiński], Krysztof [Kamil Baczyński], [Tadeusz] Gajcy. I knew the details about Wacek already in the camp. It surely must have been an unnecessary, reckless death? That garland?

Andrzej—he was an impetuous boy . . .

I got a letter from Staszek from Zakopane. He's optimistic about his illness, is thinking about returning to Warsaw when he's better. He wrote about himself, about his *Droga* and about my poems that he published as a chapbook. I know he's writing something about the theater, and his sister is a bigwig on theaters. Unfortunately, at that time in October, I was unable to offer him any help. I wanted to send him something, but there aren't dependable people. Zosia Świdwińska from the university wrote to me as well. She's doing a doctorate.

I'm not thinking to return, even though the atmosphere of life here irritates me a great deal. Tuśka is so affected by the nightmare of the camp that she wants to live without worry and fear. I am going to try to arrange things for her here.

Tuśka is now in Sweden. It is very difficult for me to come to an understanding with her . . .

I remember practically no poem from before the camp. Not a single hexameter, not a single prayer. Not a single wedding song, practically nothing of the epigrams, not even ballads about the Essentialists—nothing. If you remember anything, write it down and send it to me. I will be truly very grateful. Everything Staszek had was burned and there is no hope of retrieving either the manuscripts or the printed versions. If it were possible to get *Gdziekolwiek ziemia* or "Na zewnątrz noc" they would be nicely published for me. In *Imiona nurtu* you'll find three poems from the cycle "Światło i cień," written on the last day, or, rather, the last night, in the camp. I'd like to make something in the form of a diary of love, obviously about slightly different issues than just love.

I nearly forgot: together with two friends, I wrote a book of camp stories, infused with the sad spirit of Céline, and it is being printed. It'll be an encyclopedia, proclamation, symphony, and anecdote about Auschwitz. I admit to two of the stories, the rest I'd rather fob off on others.

That's it about me.

I'd very much like to invite you here, or to pay you a visit? What do you think?

What are you reading? What new poems do you have? Lechoń published "Aria z kurantem" ["Aria with Chimes"], Wierzyński, Baliński, also. In Poland, Przyboś and Miłosz, "Ocalenia" ["Salvation"]. Write to me if you should need some books, I can get something from the Germans. And if you have some good books—send them.

Affectionately,

I'm waiting for a letter,

Tadeusz Borowski

23. FEBRUARY 22, 1946, MUNICH
[*to Halina Laskowska*]

Dear Pani Halina,

Sincere thanks for the letters which I received from you through Miss [. . .]

Please forgive me, Pani Halina, for imposing on your patience and taking up your time with burdensome correspondence. It is sometimes difficult for two people in the space of a single room to understand each other, never mind across a continent.

Mr. and Mrs. Zagórski were with me at the end of October. They left for Poland in mid-November of last year. They promised to come to see me again in the middle of March, I received word that they were planning to. Perhaps they will bring some literature from the period of war, because I asked them to, and they promised. Everything of Staszek Marczak's was burned: the entire library, all his and my poems (which he was taking care of after my arrest), probably all the materials from *Droga*. Some things published by others survived, but nothing in longhand. I don't know who has Trzebiński's diary, I know his first books and regard them as very characteristic of a certain period. Anyway, I wrote to Poland about various manuscripts that could be published very nicely (nicely means in respectable form graphically), but have not yet received a reply. . . .

It's possible that Tadeusz Sołtan may remember some poems (maybe you know him, a dear friend of Staszek's and mine, excellent reciter, good philosopher, and probably editor of some journal propagating cooperation, currently he's on the editorial board of the First Panzer's *Defilada*); I am writing to him with the request that he immediately send to your address any poems he owns or remembers.

In any case, if I receive anything, I will send it to you. Trzebiński's "Uderzenie" ["The Strike"] was published in *Orzeł Biały* [*White Eagle*], as was "Ballada o Koziej Górze" ["The Ballad of Goat Mountain"] which, at Jerzy Zagórski's suggestion, I sent to Italy.

As for me: unfortunately, I have no prose except for a few longish camp stories infused with the sad spirit of Céline. These are already collected into a book which should come out in print in a while. It's difficult for me to send something from this because the publisher has the moral copyright. I will attempt to write something, if there's a need, and will send it along as soon as I finish translating for the Polish Red Cross. I am compiling a periodical for Poles out of English monthlies put out in German by the Military Government. In future issues we will run Polish items providing we get permission and approved [*sic*].

Autobiographical sketch? Dear Pani Halina! What would I write in it beyond what is in the foreword to my book, which I will endeavor to send to you in final form? That fifteen years before the war those closest to me had a ground-level tour of all the prisons and camps of the north and Asia? That the beginning of my upbringing was a Soviet school? Or, that for a good stretch I never had a family life because either Father was sitting in Murmansk, or Mother was in Siberia, or I was in a boarding school, on my own, or in a camp? Or, that during the war I had friends in the National Confederation, and in the People's Guard, at the

university, and in the forest? That I was arrested . . . and that I saw the death of a million people—literally, not metaphorically? That I don't want to return, that I'm fighting with myself and that I will sacrifice poetry for love?

Why would I write this? In order to endanger some and repel others? My entire genealogy—colored and deadly boring—is in the foreword to *Imiona nurtu*. If you would allow me to, however, I will send you a few other poems to read. If they appear to be better or "different" from those others, please send them out into the world.

Forgive me for going on about myself—it's a fault of autobiography.

What news do you have from home? And from Brwinow? During your stay on the continent, did you see Zbyszek? Please write to me. Our friends' worries are our worries, after all, aren't they?

Sincerely,

[*unsigned*]

I am enclosing a separate letter for the beautiful young lady Tula.[52] She gave me the address of the Polish Red Cross in London. Why should the letter accrue weeks worth of officialdom by lying in one of many pigeonholes? And one other thing, a fresh problem: you wrote to me about the possibility of bringing people from Sweden to Germany. What kind of possibility? Through whom must one do this? [. . .] My friends are supposed to go to Sweden to fetch those close to them and her. I don't know whether it will work out.

24. MARCH 10, 1946, MUNICH
[*to Mieczysław Grydzewski, London*]

Dear Sir,

Thank you very much for your letter, which I received a few days ago. I have made contact with Tuśka, although letters travel for months as usual.

I am trying to bring her to Germany, to me. It is very important to us to be together. At present, I am managing my life well and will earn enough to support us both. In any case, it will be necessary to leave Sweden. I don't think I'm making a mistake attempting to bring her to me. At present they are arranging this for me in Frankfurt; perhaps UNRRA and Polish War Relief intervention will succeed.

As to me: I am twenty-four years old, come from Zhitomirz, came to Poland in 1932 in an exchange of political prisoners; I got to know Tuśka at university

(we were studying Polish together under Krzyżanowski). I had certain scholarly and literary ambitions. In 1942, I published a book of poetry, "Gdziekolwiek ziemia" (incidentally, not counting anthologies, the first book of poetry published in Poland during the war).[53] In '43–'44 a second book consisting of personal poems was published for me in the literary journal *Droga*. Some poems were also printed in the underground press after our arrest (in February '43, exactly two months before our wedding).

In the camp, it varied. Summer 1944, I spent on a bunk with Tuśka, adding one more to the many paradoxes of camp life: a pastoral. In any case, after liberation I had to learn to look at, and react to, a normal world again.

It seems to me, that I haven't wasted the year in emigration. In April, I prepared for publication some poems written in the meantime and some remembered ones. I am taking the liberty of sending this book to you. I continue to work with Girs of the Oficyna Warszawska, at present at the Polish Red Cross. By publishing Dachau Concentration Camp postage stamps, he contributed large sums of money to the Red Cross. Four tons of medicines (a thousand ampoules of penicillin among them) were sent to Poland. A few books (art history, reproductions, architecture, etc.) are waiting to be sent. Unfortunately, they are afraid to accept them, suspecting us of fascist tendencies. People's thoughts move in strange ways!

The book about the camp, infused with the sad spirit of Céline, is already in proofs. It should leave the printing house sometime in May. There is nothing artistic about it, since it was written in haste and to order. I am sending you one of the stories as a sample of no worth.

Would it be too difficult for you to send me the page proofs of your anthology?[54] Among the reading matter in many languages which one picks up indiscriminately here, the rarest thing is a Polish book, never mind a volume of poems!

Best regards,

Tadeusz Borowski

P.S.   If you will permit, I shall use you as an intermediary in my correspondence with Tuśka. She should know, because I wrote her this several times, that we are not going back. She mustn't worry.

25. MARCH 10, 1946
[*from T. Sołtan*]

Dearest Tadeusz,

For me, your letter was one more proof of the endurance of friendships forged in the difficult time of war and terror. Throughout all the experiences and curses, the thread of attachment whose basis is the togetherness of surviving a moral test, which our creative work was under conspiratorial conditions during the period of occupation, remains whole. The atmosphere of night-long Essentialist discussions, poetic dawns in smoke-filled rooms, and that real understanding born of a tight circle of words and gestures, tight circle of friendship, wafted to me again from your letter. Because I don't hesitate to call our mutual relationship by the great and respectful term "friendship," which is sometimes bandied around too easily. After receiving your letter, I can state with complete certainty that the Essentialist knot did not grow loose through the long years of separation, its worth is all the richer for the store of experiences confirming it. I'd like to write all this very simply, without unnecessary pathos and commentary, which are so hard to rid oneself of. In any event, not many words are needed. I hope that you understand accurately and well my thoughts and feelings at the moment of writing to you, poet friend and Essentialist. At this moment I feel an inner need for loyalty to club traditions, even though my relation to them, on the surface, is so uncertain and impermanent.

The news that Staszek's condition isn't threatening, and that he, himself, is of good mind, pleased me enormously. A fragment of your poem, so relevant for us today, comes back to me now: "Staszek, my friend, ever more bygone days have passed . . ." Unfortunately, I don't remember anything of that rich Essentialist creative work, ballads, songs, and epigrams. And just odd phrases from your "Pieśń," master, alchemist, and mage. That's nothing. More than once I drank all by myself in honor of our former good nights on Skaryszewska Street. Your "Spacer z Porfirionem" in your volume brought many occasions to mind, thank you very sincerely for sending it to me, and for the dear dedication. In the new works, you return to former echoes and reminiscences, but you are acquiring now a very individual and beautiful poetic expression. (The shades of our friends should thank you for the simple, ordinary, tragic nature of "Umarli poeci" ["The Dead Poets"]. The verse account of your community work is very individual, especially in those words of Staszek's.[55] How good it is that he was found beneath the ruins of this war. I printed two of your poems in *Defilada:* "Moja modlitwa"

["My Prayer"] and the excellent, despite the journalism, "Odezwa" ["Response"]. Unfortunately, the journal doesn't give honorariums, so I have nothing to send you. I'm sending you a copy. *Defilada* may, possibly, place something else of your work, perhaps some reprint from your chapbook. If you are able to send some other materials, which we strongly ask you to do, send them to: The Editors, *Defilada*, 6 Jahnstr. (23), Quakenbrück.

The thought that we will probably not see each other very soon makes me sad. As you've probably been able to deduce from my letter, even though I haven't written it outright, I have decided to return to Poland. A difficult and responsible decision. For many who knew me and worked with me lately this will come as a great surprise and grounds for accusations of betraying ideals of patriotic steadfastness. It's the result, however, of deep internal considerations, based on fundamental motives of more than a sentimental-personal nature. The psychological atmosphere of the new "great emigration" will become unbearable and, undoubtedly, expose many to an "exiles without a homeland" complex, despite, and in spite, of all cut off from the current of a creative, social-cultural life. One of the fundamental points on the basis of which this decision is made has to be a reply to the question: "Has the time of national metaphysics passed, the time of emotions, easy pathos which was the justification for ordinary cowardice once?" Because if this time is still in existence then, perhaps, it might be worth starting to sell oneself on the black market of European culture.

I don't know which road you will choose; remember, however, that you must always justify it with the purity of your poetry. I'd like to believe that the time separating us from the moment when we will again be on the same barricades won't be long. Letters to Tuśka, the news of whom truly cheered me a great deal, you can send to Sweden and through my friends in Quakenbrück. I doubt, however, that it will hasten their arrival. My address in Quakenbrück and to Second Lieutenant Krystyn Wojcicki. I have a major request. My departure from Lubbeck will probably be around 3/22, so I'd like you immediately after receiving this letter to send a telegram to me giving me Staszek's address in Zakopane, and also, if you know it, Halszka's address in Warsaw. It is very important to me because I would like to establish contact with them as soon as I get there and attempt to help them. Apart from that, state briefly whether you agree to have some of your poems, which I am taking with me, reprinted in Polish journals. Telegram "dringend" to: "Pereświet Sołtan, Tadeusz, (24) Westerland (Sylt), Poln. Hauptquartier "Belvedere." To Poland, send the letters to my name and the address: Pius XI Street, apt. 38, Warsaw, where my mother is currently living.

I hope that I will be able to raise the Essentialist Easter toast together with Staszek. And we will certainly think of you in distant Munich. And wait. Kostia Gałczyński has said good-bye "forever" for the nth time, and gone off again for some "wedding" of his. . . . Here we have the mud of the end of a German winter, and I'm returning to a Polish spring. Very affectionately yours, former "Mage" of the great Essentialism.

Your Tadeusz

26. MARCH 23, 1946, JORDANBAD

[*from Irena and S. Wygodzki*]

My dearest Tadeusz,

I came, I saw, but didn't conquer. Bewitchingly beautiful landscape. Beautiful forest, avenue as in Dersławic along which Raphael and Helena de Wilt walked,[56] meadows fragrant as in our Beskida, and, coming out of the station, it smelled of a Polish cowshed and that was very nice. I have set myself up very well, have peace and am more than happy. You'll come here Tadeusz, I am ready for your arrival, just let us know when you are planning to come, especially because that lady about whom my wife told you is expecting you. May I bother you? Could you, perhaps, send through the mail, under separate cover, a few newspapers from Poland and local ones? And perhaps a copy of that "Auschwitz," because I left the first one to Dr. Szor and I would like to introduce you before you arrive. And you forgot, or else don't want to give me, that poem about the poet "from Będzin or (?)" as well as the sketch about poetry. Perhaps you'll send them? I'm waiting for news and am very affectionately

Your S.

If you want to have a rest and spend your time well—come!
We're awaiting you!

Keep well, Irena[57]

27. APRIL 7, 1946, MUNICH
[*letter written in English, to Zofia Świdwińska*]

My dear Zoo,

a few days ego I received your third letter from October 26th. Excuse me, please, that I'm answering your letter in English; it's necessary according to the rules of the censorship. You know, I'm heartly thankful to you personally for all you for yuour kindly letters and I think much of you. I hope that soon I shall thank you personally for all you have done for me.

Maybe, I was too long out of the our country and home to rely upon anybody's help after my return; neverthelles I want to go back. Before—I suppose—I shall go on a journey to Paris and perhaps to Bruxelles to see the Western Europe. After this travel I'll go back to you and try to establish myself and if I'll have the luck—other men I love.

The book of the concentration camp lay in the printing-house continuelly. Also the UNRRA Monthly news for Poles (I had translated near all the articles by Dewey, McLeish etc. and short stories by Poe, Hemingway and O. Henry. Also the next Tracing Magazin for Polish Red Cross (about 150 pages including ten thou-sands names of the missing persons) I suppose that I haven't dissipate the emigrant year, although I handn't done so much I ought to do.

You know yourself—East, West, home is best—if you have one!

I wish you all best—

Yours,

Tadeusz

Don't [be] angry, if mistakes—this language is rather difficult for me.

28. APRIL 8, 1946
[*to Stanisław Marczak-Oborski*]

Dear Staszek,

I sent letters in your direction many times—it was like throwing stones into water. But it's not your fault: letters travel practically for years and it is hard to conduct conversations across continents.

I don't know what or whom I shall find in Poland. I'm returning toward the

end of April or the beginning of May. I still want to be in Paris and Brussels to see what is worth remembering and to buy a few French poets.

I'm still waiting for my Auschwitz stories to appear and the UNNRA monthly for Poles which I edited.[58] I'm falling apart in the print shop.

I have a few odds and ends in my briefcase—poems and sketches for stories. I don't know whether they will be in tune with the season. I'm reading a lot of American literature—in a very difficult and almost incomprehensible to me language. Some of it stays. I've translated a few stories of Poe's, Hemingway's, and O. Henry's for the above magazine or monthly.

Stacks of books—I fear that they'll remain here. It's not allowed to take American things—police order. What stupidity!

I'm very interested about your work in the area of theater and those letters from Zakopane about which I read in *Odrodzenie*.

I am hoping that you will get completely better in the Zakopane climate.

I'm very grateful to you for the letter of October. Don't take it amiss that I'm not writing much. I no longer feel like doing anything.

Your Tadeusz Borowski

29. APRIL 24, 1946, PARIS

[*to Z. Świdwińska*]

Dear Zosieńka,

For the past few days I've been wandering around Paris with the nonchalant mien of a parvenue. People in uniform (even of the Polish Red Cross Committee) are held in high esteem and go to museums for free—a belated tribute to militarism. Paris, of course, is beautiful and exotic by the Seine, and on the narrow little streets of Place Clichy, Notre Dame, and on the Trocadero near the Eiffel Tower. There was no war in Paris, the only recollections are the Resistance films (very bad, by the way, and very jingoistic) and two German tanks by the entrance to the military museum. And the Louvre being closed, as well, perhaps. A mad jealousy grabs me when I look at the buildings by the Seine drowning in verdure, at the Etoilles with the unruined Arc de Triomph, at Napoleon's grave, massive and cheerful. The norms of war were different here than at home. Here, the Gestapo man in the films is like Laurel and Hardy, and the French laugh at him out loud. And in the whole of Paris I saw seven tablets for those who

had died for their country. What a happy country that got itself out of the war so easily with Pétain! Because, too, every Frenchman has something of Colas Breugnon in him, a lot of cheerfulness and amicability. And always feels whole. Bitterness and envy apart, however, it's a wonderful country: it knows how to regenerate itself. Very expensive (a good dinner costs 200–400 francs, that means nearly two dollars), true, the girls walk around in clogs, true, but these are always Parisian clogs. Apropos fashion: on the lapel some kind of big dog out of majolica or some other unexpected colorful accent, hair piled unusually high, but not from the back to the front now, but normally. Red hair is fashionable, as is a dyed sepia color. You can recommend this fashion to someone you don't like, I'll take long-distance responsibility for it.

A slew of books, even the Polish Bookstore has the latest. I bought Miłosz's *Ocalenie* and Wyka's *Twórczość*, but I'm a bit too tired to read them properly. I was struck by the abundance of classicism and symbolism in general in *Twórczość*. The flight from ordinary, contemporary realism testifies to the unresolved complexes and fears in writers, to their organic flaw, to Daltonism. Gajcy's poems reminded me of my old poems—and cheered me up.

So, a slew of books. The most interesting thing from the perspective of a bookshop window is probably Romain Rolland's *Peguy*, finished in 1944. It is the last work of a great writer about the great tutor to whom he owes much more than to anyone else. A mass of poetry, inaccessible to me because of the foreign language. Mostly, in any case, collected editions of prewar greats: Aragon, Cocteau, Jacob, etc. Russian things are fashionable, the unfailing Mayakovsky obviously.

Dear Zosia, I want to thank you as sincerely as I know how for the letters that I periodically get only from you. You know, I seem to be living at a crossroads. A person's biggest mistake, truly, is to allow people to forget him. And I am very grateful to you for continuing to remember me . . . I've had it. I went to Paris to have a break. My situation is such that—in practice, without making purchases—I don't need to worry about money. Well, that's nothing. I have so totally had it.

Because of that, after I return I will most probably pack what I have and go to Poland. I've had enough of wandering around the world and wasting time and myself. I should still be able—I think—to learn something and write something.

I'm very curious to know what's happening with you. I sent you my poems

(several times, to be on the safe side) and a few odds and ends through people. I don't know whether you got them (cigarettes, e.g.?) because people can never be trusted.

Write me (at the Munich address) what you are doing and what you are writing, or rather what you're working on now. I very much envy you sitting among books. I've convinced myself that neither being alone between four walls nor wandering the earth are good for me. It's almost making me ill.

How is Staszek? I've read that he's writing letters from Zakopane for *Odrodzenie*. How is he feeling about his lungs? Tadek Sołtan went to Poland, I gave him your address because he asked for addresses of friends. You don't mind, do you?

I have had only one letter from my parents, a very terse one. How are they managing? Unfortunately, when I return it will be without dollars. I didn't know how to make money either on the black, or the white, market. I just know a little English (for private use and for translation). The only letters from Poland are from you. Dear God, how grateful I am to you, Zosia.

Give my best to everyone.

Affectionately,

Tadeusz Borowski

Ah, and you are going to have to supplement my Polish studies education, all right?

30. APRIL 25, 1946, PARIS
[*to his father*]

Dear Daddy,

It's with quite a heavy heart that I write to you, because I'm still here, outside Poland. After almost a year of sitting in Munich, I took off for a few days in the West, I would like to go to Brussels . . .

If that disappoints me . . . I'll pack what I have (not much, unfortunately, because I didn't know how to collect dollars) and arrive as one more problem for you. I'm very afraid of that, burdening you. Here, in the so-called West, life is soft: so far, I've managed well and, on the whole, don't owe anybody anything, I am very careful about that because such debts are the most burdensome . . . I've really had enough of wasting time and pseudo-social work, consisting of writing

on a machine, driving to printers, etc. I'd like to be studying. I think that will be possible in Poland. Anyway—to be honest—I'm very homesick and that makes my life hard.

It would be good if you'd write to me at my Munich address. Write, if you remember it, in Russian because of censorship (the four "occupation" languages are permissible). Through all those Polish Red Cross Committees and Missions it takes months before one gets the letter. I've only had one letter from you, anyway (from Julek). I get letters from Zosia very often . . . The dear girl remembers about me. I've had one letter from Staszek. I'm writing to him separately.

I would very much like it, Dear Ones, if you'd write to me. And for you to forgive my wandering the earth for three years. The good in this evil is that one gets to know the world. I've read a lot of American literature. That world is completely unknown to us and waits for its Columbus. I wrote a little, was published a little, a little went to waste, as is usual when one has nobody to write for nor a reason to write. But it's not important. Write to me about yourselves at last.

Love and kisses to Momsy, Julek, and you, Daddy,

Your Tadeusz

31. APRIL 28, 1946, LYON
[*to S. Marczak-Oborski; postcard*]

Hey, friend,

I'm at the Lyon Fair. I'm living at a pork butcher's and his daughter's. What a wonderful thing—the bourgeoisie! And the wine! It's a pity I have a weak head—for wine, and for the daughter.

Tadeusz Borowski

32. APRIL 28, 1946, LYON

[*to Z. Świdwińska; postcard*]

Zosia,

Greetings from the Lyon Fair. What a dingy town, this Lyon! And how cheap dates are here! I'm going to the Mediterranean Sea!

Tadeusz Borowski

33. APRIL 30, 1946, NICE

[*to Z. Świdwińska; postcard*]

Dear Zosia,

So much sun here! Wonderful, magical vacation.

Sincerely,

Tadeusz Borowski

34. APRIL 31 [*SIC*], 1946, NICE

[*to S. Marczak-Oborski; postcard*]

Sun in Nice. And palms. The gypsy girls on the photo—authentic. Affectionately! I've become a snob (out with the bourgeoisie). Tadeusz

35. MAY 2, 1946, PARIS

[*to S. Marczak-Oborski*]

My dear Staszek, friend of Essentialist nights!

Here I am writing a letter to you from Paris. On the right, behind the five walls of the Hotel by the Les Invalides Station, lies a wide, green square ending at a golden cupola guarded by rusty cannons of the Old Army and two captured "Panthers" covered with red mud. Beneath the golden cupola, in a floor scooped out like an egg, surrounded with a barrier, rises Napoleon's grave its dimensions in the form of an eight hewn out of marble the color of rust. On the left—on the grating of the hotel's window, socks are drying—poorly washed, out

of laziness—and the high walls of a Parisian courtyard's well rise up. From the bottom of the well rises the eternal gurgling of the academy of trumpet playing on a number six helicon. At the setting of the sun, a doleful journeyman plays on it, puffing out his cheeks and looking dolefully into the bottom of the well in which the sky is reflected.

And so, friend, I am in Paris. Here, Mickiewicz, a teacher from the little town of Kowno, bon vivant of Odessa, steely sectarian and socialist, stands on a teeny column equipped with funny little wings on obscure Alma Square, stretching his hand out toward a policeman in a short cape who, by whistling, regulates the street traffic. Here, Rodin's *Balzac* leans back toward an avenue of dead plane-tree trunks, planted in the middle of a noisy boulevard brushing against Montparnasse. Looking at the green trees of the boulevard, at the restaurant of boulevard painters, at the colorful crowd as though at a sack of garish rags, the bent Balzac has a strange, inscrutable, smile on his face with its empty eye sockets. Looking at his face, the passerby hurrying to a portion of roast fish and salad of veiny herbs will understand more of *The Human Comedy,* which is still going on around him, than will the scholar of literature, wasting his eyes, and a light bulb of the "Osram"[59] variety, over manuscripts.

Here, friend, they are advising on the peace of the world in the Luxembourg palace. Ministers arrived, Mary Pickford and Marlene Dietrich came. All this is going on not far from a four-sided column stolen from Egypt, the Luxor obelisk sticking out on the Place de la Concorde. And on Place de la Republique, beneath a statue that tactfully melts into the darkness, Great Fun has spread out: merry-go-rounds, swings, shooting galleries, and electric wagons on which you ride as on a tank. Here, the boulevards of a hundred bridges by the Seine sway in the green of the flowering chestnut trees, and, amid the greenery, only the cathedral of Notre Dame stands like a shriveled, hardened tree. And when you walk, friend, down a bourgeois street, then, between some bar in whose window sits a tubby cat and two skinny bottles of wine, and a barber's with a day-before-yesterday's *Figaro* in his hand, you'll suddenly come upon a window filled with well-known names: Rimbaud next to Villon, Superveille by Eluard, Valery by Flaubert. Among scribbled flowers, sugary naked girls, and fish skeletons on a cubist plate, you will suddenly discover a strangely familiar name: Braque, Bonnard, Picasso . . .

A newcomer from a dead, hated country, I dipped myself into Paris as into the current of a mountain river. I lived its official life, paying visits with unimpeachable manners to publishers and bohemians and then noisily drinking wine

with them in smoky bistros. I saw exhibitions and varnishing-days, and, with a degree of interest, looked at the work of a certain older man by the Seine who, having placed many splotches on a canvas stretched on an easel, glanced at the spectators, smiled, and, beneath the picture, placed the signature—Matisse. I wandered around cinemas and cabarets, which every honest tourist does. I was in the Palais Goumont with four thousand seats for viewers, and at the Moulin Rouge, where I was extremely bored, was at films about the Resistance and at Laurel and Hardy's of twenty years ago. But, friend, I was also in Paris by night. Treading Parisian pavement (which Mickiewicz pondered over), entered narrow little streets, architectural marvels (Słonimski marveled over them, sometimes also mentioning Warsaw), visited the metro stop at Levallois (Miłosz, with Sherlock Holmes's pipe, asked God's mercy over them), entered the tight streets near the Place Clichy which don't appear on any poetic map of the world. I drank wine with bought girls, and was even in the Allied Troops Theater, because I wear a threadbare uniform that once belonged to an English soldier.

I came, I saw—and I am sad. I still have in my ears the shout of Paris's main streets, the roar of the Seine, black as tar at night, and the rumble of the metro, the underground into which half Paris goes every day. My head still hurts from the aperitifs and countless colorful wines drunk to a mirror. I can still see the fabulously colorful exhibits at the Museum of Captured Art, where Arkadiusz, drunken with vodka, would have found much of his own.

Forgive my unclear and careless writing, friend. Because I am writing you this letter in installments, and in various places. A few days have passed since the time I put the first words on these pages. I left Paris, friend, and went by military train to Lyon, to the Fair and to the daughter of a meat butcher whom I met by chance. I was also in Nice among palms and sea, between a tall girl taken off the street, at the Red Cross where I did not get anything to eat and about which I immediately wrote a lampoon, and an exhibition of paintings at which two sardines cut by the edge of a transparent platter cost one hundred and fifty thousand francs.

I returned too tired to go wandering at night. Paris went crazy on the First of May. I walked in a crowd, shouted in French, shook my fist—and am sad.

Because Paris isn't a sanatorium for people sick with nostalgia. This huge, clamorous, and smiling only unto itself town—is like a poem. Like a memory. A newcomer from a dead, detested country where, among ruined houses, girls walk with blacks through ever-burgeoning greenery, a poet without listeners and without friends, doesn't feel well in Paris.

And having returned from an intellectual feast where sardines, salad, red wine, and Malinowski's "the sexual life of savages" were served; having returned from a house where a wild cat who sticks out her tongue when you scratch her ears and a wild setter understands French; having returned from there to the Hotel by the Les Invalides Station, to Napoleon's grave behind the five walls and to the academy of playing a trumpet, from which comes eternal gurgling, I am lying melancholy on the bed and writing a letter to you on Aragon's book, which I opened at this poem about nostalgia:

Persienne

Persienne   *Persienne*   *Persienne*

Persienne   *Persienne*   *Persienne*

Persienne   *Persienne*   *Persienne*

Persienne?

Sincerely,
Tadeusz Borowski

36. MAY 21, 1946, JORDANLAND
[*from I. and S. Wygodzki*]

My Tadeusz,

Finally! I thought they had locked you up somewhere and that you'd never see Munich again and instead crawl around Paris and beg for a position at the Sorbonne. Bad person! You could have written from abroad, we were seriously worried about you. Bad person! You don't say a word about the promised visit to us. What is this? You're not going to leave without dropping in on us. We have to arrange where to meet, whom you have to visit, you have to take some poems for me, etc. It's beautiful here, but I've come to an impasse. I'm not writing anything, I can't, I read, but superficially, I'm learning English, and thought about an excursion to Bodensee—but with you. We've waited until today. Since you haven't come, we're going for two days on Thursday. Incorrigible one! If you come, and you will, of course, come, we'll go again. *Twórczość* still has not arrived, but I'm waiting patiently. You've probably already read this excerpt but I'm sending it just in case. By chance, I received a copy of *Odrodzenie* from the end of March with my poem and a poem by Ginczanka, very beautiful. They

murdered Zuzanna in Kraków.[60] I envy you Matisse and Picasso. Apparently in Konstanz where we are going it's possible to see French paintings. Write at length and come! You must! Train station: Ummendorf by Biberach. Send a cable! I'm exercising my powers of veto: you will not leave without visiting us.

Kisses, your St.

When you come, bring some smokes, because they don't provide them here.

[Irena's postscript]
Dear Tadek,

Is this a way to treat friends? You'd miss a lot by not visiting us before you go to Poland. Our life goes by peacefully, we often go to the cinema and the theater, but the theater is bad. Write to say when you're coming, we'll expect you. Keep well, Irena.

MARIA RUNDO LETTERS

Close Maria
Living Maria
to everywhere you are
I send birds . . .

Tadeusz Borowski,
"Wołania Marii"
("Calling Out to Maria")

1. JANUARY 21, 1946, MUNICH

Tadeusz Borowski, Polish Red Cross, 7 Frankenstr., Munich-Obermenzing, For Maria Rundo. Mrs. Anna Zboromirska,[1] Kristl, Folkhoqskolan, Fönköping, Sweden [*sic*]

Tuśka!

On Saturday, I got your letter of 10/27 from Sweden. Don't blame that officer who went to marry his fiancée (see how much of the romantic people have in them), just the German Post Office, which with an indifference peculiar to itself makes light of our concerns.

I got the letter on Saturday, today is Tuesday. On Sunday, I sent you a few words other than by mail, on Monday two through the American mail, and today I am writing an extensive, sober, and substantial memorandum, because those letters were packed with emotion. For two days I walked around in a daze, went completely mad, I know your letter by heart now. So we're going to be together, just think! After so many years, after so many camps! And you're going to be my wife! We'll probably have a little night lamp again and conduct long conversations about poems which, of course, I will write for you. Just think, I'll have you by me! And you didn't forget about me! And you survived the camp! And you're the same as before! No, one can go completely mad. And think: your Mendels and Drexlers are sitting under American arrest awaiting the executioner from England, and they hanged my Molows and Endress's long ago, not even far from me in Dachau,[2] but we are alive and you're the same as ever! Tell me is there some mystic strength in love that protects those who love each other? And that we exist as a result of it? I walk around Munich in a state of asphyxiation. The town in a splendid winter, crows on bare trees, people in filled theaters. I walk and the world disappears from my eyes. See, a dry, official card from the Polish Red Cross is one thing. I know the way they operate, I was certain they hadn't informed you, and that you were long gone somewhere else. I wrote, and wrote, and nothing—no reply. Either they never reached you or didn't find you home. I'm writing you this letter Auschwitz-style—in a chain: first to a certain lady somewhere near London, that lady will send the letter to that other one whose address you gave, and that second one will probably be so good as to give it to you. I'm sending a copy to your uncle,[3] I think that's the safest road, and a third to that lady in Paris. At least one should reach you. Anyway, I'll keep sending

until I get a result. Having searched for you half a year through all possible Polish Red Cross Committees, I've learned patience.

Tuśka, my dear, do you remember that Monday when we said good-bye?[4] Already that evening I was on a transport, and after a week's quarantine I went to near Stuttgart to make some factories that were to squeeze butter and oil out of stone. Because our camp[5] was Boy Scout tents on a flowery meadow on the slope of a hill, surrounded by SS-men, first we made traditional horse barracks provided by some German firm out of the tents, and out of the flowery meadow mud of epic proportions into which all the camp authorities together with inspectors (our camp acquired a certain dark fame for an unheard of number of *Totenmeldung*[6] and 70% sick) sank up to their knees. The *muzulman*[7] vanished in the mud without even having time to shout. How it actually was, the poem with the three stars[8] will tell it you best, because I usually talk in verse and it's hard for me to do so in prose. Then we went to Dachau on a transport of *muzulmen*. In open wagons. But since I was born with a silver spoon, thanks to me the entire transport had weather to order for the whole five days—sun the whole time. My friend, a guy almost two meters tall,[9] carried corpses through the wagons, received a loaf of bread a day. We slept unbelievably. They greeted us very hospitably in Dachau—placed us in hospital. Now I, a "student" in the files and a poet, privately received bread (less, because what does a poet mean in a camp as compared to someone who carries corpses!), and, again, we slept unbelievably. Canada[10] came into being when they threw us onto a normal block. Imagine, the block elder was a graphomaniac, had five hundred poems, which I copied onto a typewriter. Masses of grub. But after three days, I couldn't—it truly was graphomania. He respected my decision and did the wisest thing: gave me the machine for my own poems, and stole another for himself. And gave even more grub. The psyche of a man who wants to be a poet has never been studied! Finally the camp became so overcrowded that the SS-men adopted the usual method: some they chased into the fresh air in the mountains and did them to death, and some they left in the camp to kill off at the end. Until one night the Americans started firing over the camp at SS positions, and the SS at American positions. The dialogue of Europe and America. By mistake, the SS hit the camp. A delegation immediately went, and a moment later, again. In the end the Americans discharged a volley and the SS went to the devil—if there's life after death.

In the morning, the Americans came,[11] greeted with ovations. They were dumbfounded when they saw people eating raw potatoes. Americans always

92

were idealists. Then they took care of us with wholehearted sincerity . . . And then I looked for you. By various means. There still was no mail, I sent a load of letters through people in all kinds of directions: home, to the camps in Bergen, Ravensbrück—nothing came of it.

I was very surprised when I caught myself one day looking at all the women I passed on the street, because—what if? Then, I wrote poems that started to be published. I'm thinking of a second volume. We're finishing writing a book about the camp that is to be published in an edition of ten thousand copies. So next: I have made friends with three people from the camp. One is Anatol Girs whose wife is also in Sweden (Malmo), the prewar cofounder of Oficyna Warszawska and publisher of many beautiful books. An interesting character, like a hero out of Chesterton. Imagine, he leads his life according to ideological and moral principles and refuses to deviate from them. He conducts his life in a very original way. For example, he wears SS trousers and says that he'll take them off when he's made a million marks for the Polish Red Cross.

An excellent joke, we all laugh. Today, thanks to him, all the Polish emigrants in Germany are provided with medicines, which are hard to obtain. He's already made "his bit" for the Polish Red Cross. Or: I'll publish your poems, but like never before during the war. He published them—we stared in amazement. The second one is also from Auschwitz, not a publisher but a storekeeper from the Gypsy Camp, so old a number that it has hairs on it, an engineer and very well versed in the world. As they say—an Englishman. It's strange because he really was in England. He returned across ten borders from France to his fiancée in Poland. The third, also from Auschwitz, but neither a publisher nor an engineer, just an unbuilt architect. Finally, me, the laziest and the most carefree. They say I have one failing: I talk so much about you! They already know you through and through, and one thing puzzles them: how could she have put up with him? We worked together at the Polish Committee in Munich looking for lost persons for ourselves and others. We publish bulletins, send out thousands of letters.

We organized our tracings wholesale: we printed 5 thousand tracing cards and send them out to all the offices across the whole of Europe. They curse us everywhere.

Right on your name day I received a card about you from the Polish Red Cross. Without an address. Sweden. That was all. Then came Zosia Świdwińska's very warm and very dear letter. Tempting me to return. Just don't stay away too long, she wrote! Then a letter from my brother, telling me not to worry about them and that I should definitely get in touch with you before coming back.

Very warm and very good. Other than that card, I've had no news from you. I wanted to go, I was desperate. You can't be surprised that it was hard to be in that situation. I wanted to be with you.

If you haven't yet received information, I'm giving you addresses: Rozbrat 5/7, m.13, Father: [Olsztyn] Pocztowa 2 m.6 (and not as I wrote Pocztowa 6), Baśka,[12] Łódź, Wigury 22–8 or Polski Monopol Tytoniowy,[13] Łódź, Kopernika 62, Witold Bielański.

My cycle, *Gdziekolwiek ziemia,* like a few other books, survived. After our arrest, Staszek published the cycle of love lyrics you had on you when the Gestapo arrested you. A few poems were printed, especially from the Horatian odes and epigrams. Not everything exists. Tough. It's better to write a new poem than chase after the old ones. Now: I've published a volume of "emigrant" poems. They're called *Imiona nurtu.* 15 poems with a huge foreword not of my doing and not by me.[14] The poems are very muted in expression like chamber music, the graphic work is marvelous. Italy bought the edition of 3,000 copies printed by the best German firm. Furthermore: we are writing a book about the camp, about two hundred pages. I contribute to it a little, but in a left-handed way. Nevertheless, the book—which, unfortunately, is everything: encyclopedia, sonata pathetique, response, and anecdote—should create a bit of a stir. I wrote two stories for it to which I will admit, and a few other things that I'd willingly foist off on my friends.[15] We're hurrying to finish it, because the proofs of the first hundred pages have arrived. As a social deed, Girs published a series of things that unexpectedly brought the Polish Red Cross money for diapers for illegitimate Polish children, of whom there are many, and for medicines for those with alcohol poisoning. Plans? Very broad ones for publishing. Many, though mostly inferior, poems in my briefcase. Some of them I gave to Jerzy Zagórski to take to Poland. He promised to print them.[16] We'll see. Perhaps there'll still be something in reserve to print here. I'll write new ones when you are with me, because, otherwise, so far I haven't felt like lifting a finger. Actually, I've been living as in a doorway in anticipation, and cannot give myself up wholeheartedly to anything, not to studies on the nature of democracy, nor to learning languages, nor to reading, not even to poetry, which is such a very anemic young lady. I dream about you and put together plans for poems that I will write for you.

Then there's one of Anatol's projects: we are going to a farm in Canada, we'll raise chickens or buffalo, doesn't matter which, and also a small typography shop, gather a few honest people, literati and graphic artists, and we'll send

books out into the world. The plus—far away from people. The minus—far away from people. Question mark—what do you think of this?

At the moment I'm alive and awaiting you. A post-Hitlerite apartment—three rooms, kitchen with gas, bathroom. So-so furniture in the rooms: a tolerable bedroom for the three of us and a living-room decorated at our own expense. Books and skis, electric stove. Material conditions vary. Because, for example, theaters, cinemas, music, etc., first-class seats are notoriously cheap. Food—canned, typical bachelor establishment, you understand. We are too lazy to cook our own meals (two hours a day! how much one can write in that time, or sleep! or go to the cinema!), sometimes we eat communal meals at the office, peas, and more peas—enough to drive you crazy; we swear a lot but we don't cook. Money—of no account. Which means no one counts it. A choice of cinema, opera, theater, usually on a level. I listen to Haydn, Mozart, Beethoven, Debussy, and Stravinsky. I have one failing. My friends say that I don't listen to my friends! Transportation—usually democratic: trams, cars if for a longer distance. Who knows if we won't get our own car? One of us knows how to operate a steering wheel.

But clothes, for example. We're too lazy to seek out the black market. Anyway, for what? I have a black, formerly SS-man's, tie acquired in some storeroom after the end of the war by my friends, an English shirt, boots that they claim are American, trousers of Italian fabric, and a jacket cut in Vienna. It's only my strong individualism that harmoniously unites quarrelsome Europe. And to go out, add a little Tyrolean hat (I ripped off the flowers because they created a great sensation among Munich's Poles) and a Burberry coat as worn by Tuwim's sleuth.[17] I think with some emotion that it would be good for Jurek Kreutz, were he not so thin. Books? I practically know no English, but read American short stories in fits and starts. German marvels about the Middle Ages. Polish books on occasion (Malraux, Céline), a few imported from Italy and England. Newspapers from Poland.

I'm wondering whether I've written you everything about myself and can, with a quiet heart, go on to more important things, you, for example. And so: where are you now and what are you doing? Not in hospital still? If you are at university and have a stipend, what do you plan to do? What are you studying? Because I don't believe they have Polish studies in Sweden. If you have any means, listen: apparently one can go to Sweden on a temporary visa for a week or two, Anatol, who is planning to go to his wife, says. However, the visa has to

come from there. So if you could. If I get the directive, I'll obviously do what is allowed, and what isn't allowed. If you can't—then it depends. For example, my friends say that you must study at the university because at least one of us has to be smart. Anatol adds: you'll get an entry visa and we'll both go, I to my wife, and you to take a wife yourself. Meanwhile, let her study. But Anatol isn't sitting in my skin! Which is just as well, because we wouldn't both fit. Other than that, everybody agrees that I'm getting increasingly weirder without you. I'm thinking: when will this letter reach her? A month, a month and a half? I'll try to send telegrams, that I exist, and am waiting. Which means: I'm patient. I've learned to be. If you decide that you should study, study. If you decide it's not important, come to me, we'll go west from here, or wherever you want. I think we'll manage to get away from here. But do what's most convenient for you. I think we could meet in France, if you are planning to move there.

Whatever you do will be fine.

I think a lot about my parents in Poland and about friends. I thought of going back, but Julek wrote that you were in Sweden and staying there. I now think that we will be able to help them more materially from here and that we'll manage. If sending something were allowed, I could do so now. It isn't. It will regulate itself.

I miss you very much Tuśka. I can't think without you, or do anything. I worry whether you haven't done something foolish on impulse, whether my letter, so belated, will find you somewhere. I think about how long it will take and get overcome by despair. I send them by reasonably good and sure roads, but so what! I'd like to be with you, I'd so very much like to.

It doesn't matter where, and it doesn't matter how. Just think, it's been three years since we last saw each other in freedom! And for three years I was afraid that you'd depart, that you wouldn't be able to endure. I wrote to you from the camp near Stuttgart, but the letter probably never arrived. The entire winter I hadn't the slightest piece of news. I saw the hell of transports on foot. Women who were herded for hundreds of kilometers. It was hard to think about you with tranquillity. I am very happy that things are fine with you, although I know how hard it was. How are the lungs? Really, nothing? Because the fact that you worked in a hospital proves nothing to me. It would be best if you went for a check-up.

You wrote something about women to me. If I understood correctly, you consider me capable et cetera. No, no I'm not. Absolutely not. Most absolutely not. I didn't even try. And anyway, it's not fair to use such arguments. Not fair.

Because I am living like a hermit and my beard is even growing since I only shave from time to time. Why, I reason to my friends, when Tuśka isn't here. So you'll also start to clean your shoes when Tuśka's here? they ask. I'll even start going to the barber regularly, I respond.

Listen, if you've already read this very objective and unemotional, soberly written letter, pick up a pen and piece of paper, sit down and write back through all possible avenues, preferably through your uncle. Ask him to send it via air mail, that would be best. Never through offices—the Polish Red Cross, etc. A waste of paper. It won't get here.

When I get your reply, I'll describe all the curiosities of life here. Side-splitting.

And so: I miss you terribly, more terribly by the day, and I am happy that you exist, and I am changing into waiting. I live as in an open doorway, and am collecting myself like you. I have a great desire to share my thoughts with you—and my self.

Keep well, Tuśka, and write to me.

Tadeusz

(Send your reply to the address on the envelope, and stamp it in the normal way for overseas.)

Forgive the few poems, but how can I not share with you what even others already know?

> *You remember the sun of Oświęcim*
> *and the distant green of meadows lightly*
> *lifted by birds into clouds,*
> *not green now, but celadon-white*
> *in the clouds. Together*
> *we stood, looking into the distance, and feeling*
> *the distant green of meadows and the clouds'*
> *white-celadon as though in us,*
> *as though the hue of distant meadows*
> *was our blood or the pulse*
> *which beats in us, as if the world*
> *only existed through us, and faded not at all*
> *while we exist. I remember*

your smile, as elusive
as the shade of the color of the wind, which
is swayed by a leaf on the cusp
of sun and of shadow, but ever
passes and remains. So you
are, today, for me, across the celadon
of the sky, across the verdure, across the wind,
which sways along with the leaves. You are
my blood and my pulse. I feel you
in every shadow, in every motion
and as you encircle me with light
as with your arms, so I feel the world
as your body, with the whole world
you look in my face and call me . . .[18]

From *Imiona nurtu*

I know you live. How else can
the shadow and light
of distant, cold stars, reflections
of the world's crystal, make sense? The black earth
as usual shines with dew, forests
beyond the horizon, grow dark
as above the sea's blue depths
and the blood pulses as if answering
the rhythm of the waves
of the universal sea which is
at once so close and so distant from me
and which pulsates with your blood.
I feel you live, I know you live.[19]

From the cycle "Światło i cień"

[A third poem, the epigram "Moja Droga" ("My Road"), was included here.[20]]

2. JANUARY 27, 1946, MUNICH

For Maria Rundo, Anna Zboromirska, Kristl, Folkhögkslan, Box 70, Jönköping, Suede

Tuśka,

For a week, I've been sending you masses of letters, unfortunately, instead of to Jönköping to Fönköping because that's how I read the address. The card from the Polish Red Cross set my error straight. You know how happy I am now. I'm very pleased that you are going to be studying, although I don't deceive myself into thinking that your situation is as good as you write it is. That grind in the hospital must have been dreadful, right? Are you already studying? And what, surely not Polish? Do you have things to read? You're not leading a communal, camp life? Terrible nightmare!

About me very briefly: despite good material conditions, lots of publishing opportunities, social work, friends (three), etc., I'm dying of homesickness. I get very warm letters from Zosia Świdwińska and Staszek Marczak—they believe I'll return. They returned in summer already—on foot. My parents: Rozbrat 5/7, apt. 13. Your parents in Łódź: "Monopol"; apart from that, everyone is there, even Czesław and Maria.[21] Life is probably hard for them, but when was life ever easy in Poland? Although I've fulfilled certain obligations (e.g., a second volume of poems ready to be printed), I am definitely not living on permanent ground. I stand at an open door at all times and can slam it shut if I want to. Quite simply: I can whistle at everything and go wherever I want. My plans are totally dependent on you. If you absolutely do not want to return, I'll settle down here; if you return, I'll go back at once. My possibilities "there" are very limited. I don't know whether, for example, I'd have an apartment, actually I do know, I wouldn't, although Jerzy Zagórski (from Wilno) promises me something else—in Kraków. Because, as he said, "I'm not unknown in Poland," a lot could be done. I don't believe it. I have friends here (three), and everything I need, apartment, money, even plans for Canada or America. But that would keep me dreadfully far away from you. I'm not going.

It's hard for me to live without you. I'm writing a bit more calmly now, although from the moment I got your letter I went around in a daze. I don't know how to live. I'm becoming increasingly uptight and doing ever more stupid things.

I'm writing little and very badly. Lots of reasons why. I don't know whether

I'll write better. I simply don't recognize myself. I am afraid you might not recognize me.

I'm afraid to write to tell you to come. Although conditions are good—and can become better—one lives in total isolation from the world, in an unbelievably "degraded condition." One is an isolated individual and nothing more. In addition, it is very hard to get out of Germany into the wider world. I don't want to bring you to this enormous camp. Better for you to be in Sweden. Study and learn a new life. I've tried, but it absolutely doesn't work. I've studied many things: Greek, English, art history, Latin hymns—but never for longer than a month. Didn't work.

They say it's possible to get a temporary visa to travel to Sweden. The visa has to come from you. I'd be extremely pleased if that worked out. Write what I should do. I panic that it'll be very hard for us to meet in life.

* * *

I've been unfaithful to many things in life: my country, my parents, friends, poetry. But of all my feelings, I've been least unfaithful to my love for you.

Tadeusz

Write to me. As much as you can, through all roads. Through your uncle (then air mail). To the address at the top, or to: Tad. Bor. Polish Committee Munich, Pienzenauerstr. 15, Germany.

You know how feverishly I await your letters—Auschwitz style.

Tadeusz

3. MARCH 9, 1946, MUNICH

Maria Rundo, c/o Brown, Siriusgatan 5, Lund, Suede

I've written you a lot of letters. All of them typed and very short except for one, three copies of which I sent out into the world. Perhaps it'll reach you. I've received five letters from you and a card from the Polish Red Cross. This one I'm sending through the kindness of my friend's father who is going to England tomorrow. It should reach you. I'm trying with all my strength for us to be together. I had thought that Girs would go to you. Unfortunately, it can't be done. Under the current state of things, I could easily bring you over from France.

We'll see what Girs manages in Frankfurt where he went on my (our) behalf to UNRRA and the Polish Red Cross.

I had thought we'd go back, Tuśka. But if that doesn't suit you, we won't. We'll try somewhere else. In any event, I'll use all possible means to be with you. I don't want it otherwise. It was your birthday a short while ago, and some anniversary or other of our arrest. I celebrated (your birthday) in a quiet and modest manner, trying, to no avail, to figure out how old you are. Ha!

* * *

I got a letter from your uncle. I'm writing back to him and sending the volume of poems, about which, as he writes, he's "curious"! I'm also sending it to you—a second copy. But the one which I have, which is for you, is still with me.

I'm also writing back to Mrs. Annie Zboromirska. What's with the wedding by proxy?[22]

* * *

Listen, my dear one, enough of this. Let's talk in human terms now, like on Skaryszewska, although half a continent apart. First, however, switch on the night-light, and, as you read these words and poems I'm sending you, imagine that I'm with you. Outside the window, it's the same in the world now as it was then: a world divided by a window frame, filled with the footsteps of soldiers and the screams of people being murdered.

A great wheel of events has opened up for us, and will come back and close only when we are together. This isn't among the words that I entitled "Światło i cień." A strange story: I wrote them one sleepless night in Dachau, a month after liberation.[23]

* * *

I think more than once about the yearning that overwhelms me. I increasingly live through you. There were moments in the camp when you distanced yourself from me and were something completely unconscious, instinctive. But now I increasingly live through you. And am increasingly anxious. A strange thing, I've come to know all the great passions: fear and jealousy, hatred, pain, but always there, at base, were you. And I never thought (never before you, I divide my life into two periods—before you and with you) that love could be such an overwhelming, I might say, unmanly, power. I find it hard to find a better term

for it. I'm writing you this in order to talk to you. I'd gladly say it to you. And I'd again be surprised that you came to me.

* * *

There's a great unease and dislike of people in me. It's hard for me to live because I hate the vulgarities of communal life, military buffoonery, and social hierarchy. I feel as though I'm in the middle of a mad crowd, which, having finished playing a bloody miracle play, is stuck, without knowing why, on the boards of a stage. If only we could manage to get out of this mob into a different, truer world!

* * *

But I'm full of new thoughts. I'd like to write a lot of things, more for us than for other people, because it's not worth it. Actually, I might brag that some of my poems were read through a microphone in Italy, but since they're fascists (as a friend from there puts it, "non-kosher"), let's leave it. Strange people in their own way. They promised to send a few books. We'll see.

So there's a lot to write. I'm not confiding the details of the projects to you, because I'm waiting for you. We'll do it together.

* * *

Ah, one of your letters from November: no. No way am I going into the army. Not for my temperament and not for my feelings of freedom. I tried, made scenes (Can you imagine? Scenes, me?) and ran away having learned what I think about the army—not as a temporary phenomenon, but generally. Anarchist. But since pacifism is in fashion . . .

* * *

I'm occupied with many things. I'm investigating the bases of democracy with real scholarly passion. I've surrounded myself with books and newspapers, am studying the forms of democratic life "in the thick of it" and—am no wiser. A pity because I'd like to write something by way of a vade mecum.[24]

* * *

I'd write you a lot about myself, but it would be better if you saw for yourself. I wander around theaters and cinemas and come off as a fascist.[25] You see, I'm very red—that means democratic. I listen to Beethoven, Mozart, and the proceedings of the Nuremberg Trials. I own bedroom slippers and two ties and one poet

friend who recently married.[26] The sole is coming off the right slipper. It can't be repaired because the shoemaker turned out to be a Hitlerite. My poet friend has tuberculosis, and I've given the ties away. The book about the camp is in third revision. It's going to be bound in concentration camp stripes. A very, very, weak thing. It's a pity it cost me two months' work. Doesn't matter—I'd only have written poems. This way—something useful.

* * *

I'm not studying, even though I could have. Not anymore now, anyway, I have to work. For the past two weeks my work consisted of translating from the English (!) various articles of everyday fodder for Polish consumption, from which will come a hundred-page newspaper.[27] We'll see if the printers manage to do it. Probably not.

* * *

These are my plans: plug away at literature probably. I sent a few poems to Italy, and a few to London, but there, it seems, Pietrkiewicz (yes, yes, the very same)[28] is sitting on them, and nothing can be done about it. Laskowska wrote. I'm trying to send a few things again. We'll see whether Tadek Sołtan places something in *Defilada,* the journal of the First Panzer division. I may send my book to *Tygodnik Polski,* to Lechoń.[29] At the moment, I don't have the opportunity to.

* * *

When we are together, I will tell you some very strange things that I am putting together every evening. I'm not writing about them to you, because I don't know how. I'm also going to describe the simplest things for you, their content keeps changing and they really know how to get to a person!

I also think that I will knock that exhausting and nervous life out of your head. And those with whom you play bridge. Without even looking for it, life is so exhausting that one fears one may stop living.

* * *

Try to come to me through France or UNRRA. I'm trying, too. And send letters through all possible means, best through H. Laskowska because she sends them to me most conscientiously.

* * *

Ah. Turn off the night-light and think about me some more.

Tadeusz

P.S.   Write to my and Girs's address.

4. MARCH 10, 1946, MUNICH
[to Maria Rundo]

Here in Munich, the earth already smells of spring. Soon, it will be a year after liberation, a year of emigration. A year of ups and downs, Tuśka! A lot of letters received from various parts of the world, a lot of people perished, and . . .

E.g., in Freimann, a Polish camp near Munich, immortalized by me in poems, and by Girs in postage stamps.[30] We dressed ourselves in SS uniforms and started forming an army, marching for whole days and singing patriotic, very legionnaire, and very Piłsudski-regime songs. Those imbued with a different spirit—like me, who lay belly-up in the sun learning Greek and reading a tale about Ulenspiegel,[31] or my comrade from Łódź with three surnames who maintained that if those others were responsible for Katyn, then they'd done well. Clearly it had been necessary. In a word, people's craziness takes different forms—those others were stateless and didn't get rations or passes into town, into Munich. We had to leave through a hole in the fence like the ordinary bandit going off to kill one of those ten thousand sheep belonging to the Germans that we in Freimann camp slaughtered. Apart from that, every once in a while we organized various festivities, burned bonfires, and the priest-editor of the local journal *Polska Chrystusowa* [*Christian Poland*] lit with his own hand the bonfire on which cardboard SS men were hanging. We shouted that we wanted living ones, but the editor got very angry with us and said as a symbol, the cardboard ones would suffice. We sang patriotic songs around the bonfire, and the infantry company and the camp police marched briskly stamping their feet. We amused ourselves in this fashion for quite a long time, subject also to instruction from higher authorities: I walk out the gate to the green of a nearby forest, and a higher authority shouts behind me, "Why?"[32] and then, to use a classic expression, it was as if he had a mouthful of hot potatoes.

I say "Why!" And then, in parentheses in Polish, tell him to get off my back. But the Higher Authority gesticulates and a local policeman explains to me that one cannot walk out in just a gym shirt, because it's immoral.

Those were marvelous times, Tuśka! And people so keen to create new hierarchies. Long-forgotten colonels and majors turned up, younger than me, who had once been clerics, lawyers, and doctors. A lively community came into being, although broken by sociopolitical arguments whose common thread was disagreement about Poland's political system, and why there were no potatoes in the soup. And the damned cooks stole, as cooks always do.

I got a real shirt sometime around August, in the above-named Freimann. It was a strange story and I wanted to tell it to you personally, but the temptation is too great. Anyway, I have enough to tell for ten letters and as many years.

For a certain time, I was the gentleman giving food out to people. A transport of Jews from Poland arrived, they'd been somewhere near Pilsen, they wanted them back, they escaped—in a word: an ordinary continental story, a fragment of the migration of nations, and of lice together with those nations. The transport arrives. "How is it in Poland?" I ask, because I'm interested. I'm walking down the corridor, and a woman, like a . . . , you can imagine for yourself. Of Poland, she remembers one thing: the wonderful jokes. Why did she escape? Very simple: her fiancé is in the army, and this fiancé is of nationalist leanings and does not like Jews at all, and she had been on Aryan papers the whole time, but now she wants to get back into her own skin ("Rightly so," I added), and is afraid that when her fiancé finds out . . . Wishing to spare herself a tragedy, she ran away. Ah, romance in the days of the gas chambers! . . . and what the shirt has to do with this is that, shortly afterward, I got material and a certain tailor friend sewed it for me for two packs of cigarettes. Do not treat this as a memoir or excerpts from a diary. I want you to understand my spiritual state, which is the result, and the offshoot, of all the exotic postwar experiences. Because it was written without a rough draft there is in these words a certain carelessness of expression that you must overlook.

I had the opportunity to go to Italy. I didn't go, of course. But I was in Murnau, the notorious center for officers. They gave out American pineapples there, and the products of white civilization long unknown in Europe: toothbrushes, razors, and even chewing gum and powdered eggs with which we sprinkled the beds, because they're good for killing fleas. I'm not writing this for effect, nor am I lying. So, in Murnau, there's a building beneath a bulb. The bulb is a dome in the shape of an onion, and, inside it, one dances and organizes balls. I went once and a drunken officer of the Home Army nearly shot me. That would've been a pity. But, later, we collectively, and with great effort, shoved one of those kids into a cement barrel of fire-extinguisher water. The balance of nature must

be preserved, and whoever disturbs it has to be punished. There are beautiful mountains near Murnau. Brenner (behind Austria) is close by. From a distance, the Alps look like a drawing by Słowacki.

Nevertheless, I ran away from Murnau. I wasn't cut out to be a soldier—didn't go to meetings; didn't salute the leaders; wasn't a "God-and-my-country" type; taking a pile of books, I headed for the fields and lakes, very beautiful in these parts.

My life actually began at the Polish Committee. All the Polish Committees have one characteristic in common: from a distance, the people in them seem to be upright and opaque, close at hand, however, one can see straight through them, and figure out who stole what, and when, and from whom.

It was most entertaining.

Imagine, there's a river here that, edged with beautiful parks and stone banks, flows and runs like mad. You barely slide into the water in one spot, and you emerge half a kilometer farther down.[33] We bathed there until November, but when the first snow fell we gave up. That's when the era of concerts began.

I never thought that opera could be so entertaining! Imagine, *Fidelio*. *Fidelio* is an opera written by Beethoven. One of its overtures is famous.

But it's most outlandish: for the whole first two acts they're in despair over someone whom the governor has illegally locked up in a cellar. In the end, thanks to his wife (one's on the someone's side, not the governor's) the someone is let out of the cellar.[34] And the audience devoured the happenings on the stage with its eyes! I nearly died laughing. Only a year ago they had the same show for free and didn't widen their eyes. And now they're pretending to be moved! They applaud love and sacrifice, and get enraged at the governor! Oh these Germans, when will they learn not to lie? And when will we Poles learn to lie?

Music stands on a high level here. But they don't have theater or cabaret.

They don't know operetta, and when they perform one, it's rubbish. The ruins are very romantic by night. I wrote very laudatory poems in their honor, pagan in spirit, as Mickiewicz might say.

Having written all this to you in a single breath without paying attention to spelling errors and typos, I'm trying to think (!) of something more serious. I'm sending you my notorious volume and am attaching a couple of poems to it.

I wish to brag: I now have a suit and a beautiful shirt. A black one, which I like so much, I have, unfortunately been unable to obtain. Fascist. We await you eagerly, not only I, but also my friends, live under your flag, setting their hopes on the fact that, when you arrive, I'll be livable with, and, even, perhaps, apply

myself to honest literary work. I've set one condition: if she doesn't, I won't, I tell them, I don't need fame but you do need prose.

A desperate Girs has gone to Frankfurt on your, my, and our behalf.

If the Polish Red Cross, UNRRA and the Polish War Relief don't arrange things for us, I'm writing a petition to all the authorities and creating a stink in the press. I know English well enough to slap together a nasty letter. And I've painstakingly compiled a list of the major American and English journals. Our Polish Red Cross is strangely passive. The Jewish Joint Committee arranges these matters without delay. Good people, but they can't help me, because I'm not one of them, and am not planning to go to Eretz—in their language Eretz means the Holy Land.

I think that reading this letter you'll get the impression that I've gone a bit mad. Yes, not completely, but a little. Don't be fooled, Tuśka. I'm as normal as we all are, it's just that I miss you. I do write poems, but rarely. We issue postage stamps. And now, to end this interminable letter, the third in a row, the weirdest tale: have you ever heard of poetry being used as a receipt? Surely not. But one of my poems serves in this way. A beautifully produced little book of two poems—one by my friend—in 50,000 copies—serves as a Polish Red Cross receipt for donations given. *Spiritus flat, ubi vult!*

Listen, don't worry. Things will work out. If not in Germany, then we'll meet in France. But I'm waiting, how I am waiting! May Girs arrange things for me in Frankfurt!

Kisses,

Tadeusz Borowski

Write either to my address or Girs's which I sent you through APO: A. Girs—22412, Polish Red Cross–Clerk, Atted UNRRA HQ US Zone, APO 757 US ARMY, Munich-Pasing, Germany

5. APRIL 23, 1946, PARIS

[*to Maria Rundo*]

Dear Tuśka,

I'm writing from the fifth floor of some obscure little hotel on the Place Les Invalides, not far from Napoleon's tomb and two metro stops. I've been in Paris since Friday and, today, my head is splitting. We've seen to (I'm here with the

invaluable Krystyn who speaks for me, pays for me, and tires himself out for me) a thousand different things. We deposited our luggage for a franc apiece at the station, changed money two francs to the mark (the official rate is 12, but what can you do), we gave the Polish Red Cross our invaluable poems (600 copies) as a "gift" from Munich,[35] we sold Dr. Lam (of the Polish Library in Paris, formerly of Gebethner's)[36] my equally invaluable *Imiona nurtu* (20 copies), mingled with the local Polish community, and, then, gave ourselves up to the charms of Paris. But before that, we went to send you a telegram and to visit Cil Loebel.[37] We send the telegram from some obscure office on St. Germain and Cil Loebel (Krystyn maintains it's Cecil) lives on some floor or other reached by elevator of a modern house. She was just leaving, because it was Saturday (Holy Saturday), but charmed by my flowers they stayed. I'd brought a bunch of some flowers, white probably. I think they were roses. We bought them on a corner from some fat, be-aproned shopkeeper, oh, to hell with it, stall keeper! But that's another story. In Miss Cil's apartment there's a black dog (terrier) and a black cat tied to the wall with a leash. I immediately took the cat off the leash, because it's un-heard of. I didn't touch the telephone. There's a very interesting, tasteful portrait (a little like Witkacki) of Miss Cil above the sofa opposite the window. It's the face of a mature, thinking, "emancipated" woman. Cil, herself, is even more interesting: unbelievably lively (she kept walking around the room and talking, forgetting that it was useless since I can't understand), mannishly dressed, an original mix of vagabond with a distinct womanly charm. She wears trousers and a watch-chain in the pocket. Her hairstyle is most beautiful—it's the best graft-ing of a man's haircut onto a woman's head—creative and bold. Miss Cil has a woman friend, about whom friends I had dispatched to Paris on a regular basis had told me. *Parmi nous:* she has a haircut which goes from back of the head forward, a primly painted face, a majolica figure, and a voice which doesn't know what it wants. She'd been the girlfriend of a certain friend of mine who returned to Poland. I've apparently forgotten how to behave both with intellectuals and statuettes because I didn't say a word the whole time, just stroked the cat, which had crawled on my lap in gratitude, and stuck its tongue out as it purred. As usual, Krystyn saved this dual language conversation. We commandeered your letter to Krystyn and the photograph. And then Krystyn and I went to dinner and, for the fifth time in two days, to the movies.

* * *

Actually, I saw everything in Paris except the Moulin Rouge and the Mickiewicz monument. We got soaked in the rain looking at Notre Dame and the boulevards by the Seine.

On a chilly, windy day we went to the foot of the Eiffel Tower, sunbathed in the Bois du Boulogne, and went to the horse races along with a hundred thousand other people.

We were in all the famous Paris squares, at Napoleon's tomb, at the basilica of Saint Coeur,[38] by the Louvre, Arc de Triomphe, and the obelisk stolen from Egypt. We saw the statue of Joan of Arc and even a taxi—one of those that had saved Paris in 1914. During those few days, my ears were full of the roar of the metro and police whistles, full of music and the stamping of crowds. Munich is dead. Germany is dead. One lives there as on a desert island: without time, without money. This is the old Europe, the one I remember from Warsaw. One is caught in an eddy of unknown activity. For those few days, I dragged Krystyn everywhere into that eddy. We lived the European way. And spent thousands. Because Europe is expensive. Life is expensive. Germany is dead. Costs nothing. But I'd rather live in Paris. Or in Warsaw. I am so tired of Munich!

* * *

This whole year—the Americans came to Dachau on May 1—I did nothing. It was convenient for me to live in a corpse. I lived in camps, ate UNRRA rations, went to the forest to read books, and came down with indefinable nostalgia. I slowly made a career for myself when I became someone in the camp who gives out soup and other things to eat. Then I went to Italy, via Murnau, and got stuck there, sixty kilometers from Munich. I sat in the Polish officers' camp, looked, spat, and returned.

There's much to say about the way I lived in Munich. You've probably got my letters, if they ever reached you. Several times I wanted to chuck everything and return to Poland.

I can no longer sit in one place. This sedentary style of life is driving me to despair. I dream of burying myself in books, in the atmosphere of our set. But this way—truth to tell, I don't know. I've driven my friends to despair. For nearly two months, I've done nothing, absolutely nothing. I edited a periodical for the Polish Red Cross (by edited I mean translated, because they're passages from English) and lay belly-up reading American illustrated magazines. They left me in peace. Anatol, the one who wanted to go to Sweden, thought I was sick. He left me in peace.

* * *

He's a very strange man, that Anatol. He belongs to a sect in Boston, to Christian Science. When I was completely shattered, he gave me their bible to read, written by a certain lady in 1870. It contains all the world's wisdom. Bible, Einstein's theory, and the whole of Marx's *Das Kapital.* But since there were American magazines on the table, I didn't read that bible. And he didn't make me, because the sect doesn't allow it.

Apart from that, he's got a nose for business unusual in a sectarian. And he's friends with me. (He apparently wrote some letters to you about me.)

* * *

But, actually, I live entirely alone, even though with a "group" of friends. I had one very short letter from home, very reserved. Strange people! What do they want from me? How can I help it if I can't think about anything and feel no attachment to anyone?

I get very warm letters on a regular basis from Zofia Świdwińska. Staszek Marczak wrote once, and before he went back to Poland Tadek Sołtan asked me to give you his best regards.

* * *

We're a pair of sick people, you and I. We suffer from some indefinable nostalgia and are weary of the world. But evil doesn't lie in the world, it lies in us. I think it is going to be hard for me to live like this.

* * *

When I was at your friend's, Miss Cil's, she told me a lot about you. The whole time was spent talking about you. And Miss Cil told me that I should write you encouraging words, raise your spirits, etc., because you are a person who falls into despair when things don't go as you think they should. I think this assessment is wrong and stupid (French *l'esprit*), but be it or not, I've never known how to encourage. And now as well, I really don't know what I want. I don't know what you'll think of me, but take into account that I count this past year as part of camp life—I think about it with such loathing. And I am tired even though I've been doing nothing and had a comfortable life.[39] I detest this living on a corpse.

110

I thought it would be easier for me to write to you from Paris. But it's as hard as from Munich. And I feel equally alien here—in this town full of hubbub.

Tadeusz

4/24[*sic*]/1946

6. APRIL 28, 1946, LYON

[*postcard*]

M-lle Maria Rundo, c/o Brown, Siriusgatan 5, Lund, Suede

I'm going to Nice for the day. I'll try to send a letter. Have to be in Munich on 3rd May. Don't know what'll transpire in Paris. Will send letter. Kisses.

Your Tadeusz

7. APRIL 30, 1946, NICE

[*postcard*]

Returning to Paris. Have to go to Munich immediately. Won't be in Belgium. Didn't get a ticket. It's beautiful here—like on not very good colored postcards.

Tadeusz

8. MAY 30, 1946, MUNICH

[*to Maria Rundo*]

I'm very sorry that you misconstrued the language of my letters written in Paris. I went there with the thought of being closer to you and, believe me, I tried to do all I could. The fact that I didn't succeed is, of course, my fault. I didn't know how to look patiently into strangers' faces and listen to the prevarications of people caught up in their own affairs.

If this stupid impatience and childish bitterness, built up through hopeless months, were reflected in my letters—I offer you my apologies. How terribly difficult it is, even for us, to understand one another across the space of half a continent!

Believe me, Tuśka, I have never wished to stand in your way in life. I wanted, selfishly perhaps, for you to be with me, without realizing my own ineptitude in

life, even with people whom I love. I knew it, and was always afraid you would reproach me with it, because I realized how much of your life you were giving to me out of love. If you had difficulties with me when we were together, and if camp life and émigré existence were even harder because of me, don't, if you can help it, bear resentment against me. The knowledge that I've taken away a part of your life, which I can never give back, will be sufficient for me.

Today is my last day in Munich. Tomorrow I'm leaving on a transport to Poland. I don't know how I'll manage or what will become of me. It's of no interest to me! I've also stopped being interested in people I once liked. It's not for them that I'm going.

I very, very much want you to know how you have to live. Of the two of us, at least you must know! Perhaps it will now be easier for you to know. It would be easier for me if I knew you were happy. I love you. Believe me, I love you. I have never longed for you more than now. You can think, and say, about me whatever you want, but I love you. If at any time, in any place, things become hard for you—come. I'll be waiting for you. I'll be waiting for you from the moment I arrive. I know I've broken my promise to you that I'd stay. If you can, understand me. If, however, you find peace somewhere else, forgive me, for God's sake, forgive me. I sometimes think that I'm on the verge of going mad and have only occasional awareness of what I've done.

Tadeusz

Perhaps you'll read me wrong; I'm giving you my addresses—my parents: Olsztyn, ul. 22 Stycznia 2 apt. 6; me: probably Warsaw, Rozbrat 5/7 apt. 13.

[*Editor's Note: Because Maria Rundo did not save her letters to Tadeusz Borowski, I am including, as an exception, eight letters from her ample correspondence with her uncle, Mieczysław Grydzewski—five in this chapter, three in the next.*]

9. AUGUST 9, 1945, JÖNKÖPING

[*Maria Rundo to Mieczysław Grydzewski*]

Dear Mietek,

I am awaiting with impatience the books you sent and am even happier now than before when you sent them to Chmielna Street for me. I am very interested in poetry. My fiancé, so to speak (we both studied Polish together), introduced me to various aspects of poetry, rhyme, rhythm, and so on. He, himself, anyway, right up to the moment of his arrest, wrote a lot, and I have the impression that he had unusual talent. I helped him to run off, on a duplicating machine, a small volume of poems, which later Arct and Szelążek[40] sold to the trustworthy. The volume consisted of ten hexameters on wartime subjects. In my opinion, however, he was most successful at witty, gracefully built intellectual epigrams.

I was basically most drawn to the study of language (historical phonetics in particular). Prof. Doroszewski planned to conduct a series of lectures on Sanskrit, but it didn't come to pass before our arrest. I chose the language of Berent as the topic for my master's thesis. Unfortunately, I didn't manage to do anything on the subject. From the beginning of the war I was preoccupied with work at the university and in the resistance.

In addition, we established a little literary club, "The Essentialists' Club," to which belonged, in addition to students of Polish, a medical student, Piotr Słonimski Junior. I suspect you know him. We were close friends with him since, despite his dissolute habits, he was endowed with wit and above-average intelligence.

We created a colorful life for ourselves, and of a fairly high intellectual level, despite Gestapo activity in Warsaw.

And precisely for this reason, it is hard for me to write to you in any detail about what was happening with our family, since I was home less than I should have been. After September 1939, I saw Wiśka[41] quite often. At Mr. Łobzowski's request, my mother and I lived in your apartment. There were some problems with the family who came to live there after the bombardment, and it was a question of protecting the apartment. Wiśka enrolled at midwifery school. Her fiancé was in Auschwitz. He returned after a few months and then we stopped seeing each other. After the eastern territories were taken by the Russians, Marian[42] got through to Lwów. He was, I think, completing his studies. He visited the family in Warsaw once.

On that occasion, I saw him in fine physical and mental shape. After Lwów was occupied by the Germans, he gave no sign of life. Pan Ludwig[43] was tremendously

upset by this. For two years in Auschwitz, I had no news from Wiśka. Mr. Łobzowski took care of the printing house and had, of course, huge problems with it. Luckily, the Germans closed it down after about a year. They took away all the machines. I must confess that I regarded this as a stroke of good fortune.

I had finally extricated myself from a strange web of psychological-business problems, which I clearly would never have been able to solve. I can't begin to tell you how happy I was when the person of Mrs. Sawiczewska[44] and the complicated social insurance invoices receded into memory. Anyway, Mother and Mr. Łobzowski didn't take these matters much to heart. I know that Mr. Łobzowski had all kinds of financial problems, but he somehow managed. I don't imagine there were any serious changes later, because Mother would have mentioned them in letters to me.

When it comes to the Rundo family, Mother had a tremendous amount to go through during the first years of the war. First, everyone from Łódź took refuge at our house on Chmielna Street. Among them, Paweł[45] and his family. Mother feverishly helped him and Stanisław[46] as much as she could. I looked at this with little enthusiasm, since my family patriotism is not well developed, and I didn't think it proper for Mother to sacrifice herself for them so much. I preferred to help my friends who deserved it more for social reasons. Either out of cowardice or out of detestation of illegality, Stanisław and his wife stayed in Warsaw under their own surnames. Anticipating a catastrophe, I advised them to change their style of life and place of residence a little. They couldn't decide. Summoned one day by the Gestapo, they went of their own free will, and after a several week long stay in Pawiak, vanished without a trace. Wanda Rundo[47] ended up in Pawiak a week after me. With childlike honesty, admitted to being related to me.

By some miracle, she didn't crush me completely. Complications of heredity coupled with basic political issues would not have allowed for such a happy solution as Auschwitz. A few days later, she was shot at the wall of Pawiak. I heard the shots in the night in my cell. I admit that I got nauseous.

It isn't out of selfishness, Mietek, that I wasn't more interested in family. Life was so stormy in Warsaw that family matters seemed secondary to me. Anyway, I consider spiritual ties to be stronger than blood ties. That's how I think, and that's why I haven't decided to return to Poland. This morning, I received a letter from Sergiusz Rapaport, Bolesława's[48] son, who has been in Stockholm for a year. In a few days, he's returning to Poland on a coal ship. He wanted to take me with him. I turned him down, however. I plan to stay in Sweden for a while,

and then go to Paris. I have a friend there who is trying to get a visa for me. I dream of going to Paris. Perhaps I'd be able to study. I know enough French to manage easily for myself. I am aware that after wartime adventures, I will be unhappy leading a quiet, in many respects limited life in Poland. And, anyway, I'm very attached to my friend. I wonder whether you know Madame Balkis, she's a French writer. I don't know to what extent she's popular. It is she who together with her friend are making efforts to bring me to France. I don't know how to tell you how very much I would like to go. I've dreamt for a long time of traveling a little.

In the meantime, I'm working very hard from 7 in the morning till 8 at night,[49] but it's good for my nerves. Only the complete loneliness is sad. I talk to myself all the time, imagine wonderful situations, and it often tires me out. The repetitive physical labor provides me with inner sustenance. Pulling a cart down the long hospital corridor, I pretend I'm making a wonderful journey. The cacti on the windows are the flora of an exotic land. The fauna are the sick I meet on the way, in striped pajamas, frequently unshaved, and making the strangest sounds, incomprehensible to me. I play like a child. I think I'm retarding my development. But it calms my anxiety and terrible melancholy a little. Unhappy are those who censor my letters. Anyway, this letter is becoming irritatingly long, so I'm closing.

Sincerely,

Tuśka

P.S.   Mietek, don't worry yourself about not being able to offer me material assistance, because:

1) I'm managing.

2) I'm only moderately concerned about material things.

3) One can enjoy life even without having money.

Forgive my spelling mistakes and don't imagine that being abroad I've forgotten how to write in Polish. I haven't! Though I'm a student of Polish, I've never been good at spelling.

I'd be very grateful if you could send me some textbook for learning English and an English-Polish dictionary. I once learned a little English and would gladly continue doing so.

10. FEBRUARY 17, 1946, LUND

[*M. Rundo to M. Grydzewski*]

Dear Mietek,

Thank you very, very much for your letter and telegram. I've already sent Tadeusz several letters through various Polish Red Crosses and individuals. I don't have much desire to go to Munich. If, however, the Swedish police give me problems extending my visa, I'll flee to Denmark and try to steal across the German border. That, however, will be the last resort because being arrested by the English for illegally crossing the border doesn't much appeal to me. Anyway, I'm a bit too tired to make a fool of myself like this. I would, however, like to get out of Sweden as fast as possible. A friend of mine is leaving Sweden to go to France and has promised me to arrange the matter of a visa for me in Paris. She'll simply bribe someone into giving me an affidavit that I lived in France before the war. I trust that she'll do everything possible because I've helped her out a lot financially of late. I'm managing splendidly for myself! I work intensively. Earn money by giving Polish lessons.[50] The stipend would have been absolutely sufficient for me, obviously, but I have to think about my friends. If I manage to leave Sweden and set myself up in Paris, I shall burst with pride. I will consider myself the bravest hysteric. Lately, I've been quickly dragging myself out of spiritual torpor and acquiring energy. I don't think about suicide at all. I'm trying to study in a systematic way.[51] The conditions at the university are working out nicely. I've finally received the Gustaw permit to take exams with an impressive stamp in the shape of a rosette.[52] On top of that, the professor of Slavonic languages invited me to take an upper-level seminar that is open only to philosophy students. The Swedes envy me. My professor is trying to persuade me to study Lithuanian (his hobbyhorse), I use lack of time as an excuse to squirm out of it. He's chivalrous to the highest degree. During the Swedish lectures he often explains things to me in Polish. Everything would be fine were it not for the Scandinavian atmosphere, which I find so alien.

I do a little community work. Simply out of decency. I've long lost any liking for community work.

Apropos your love of Racine. The French professor is giving a series of lectures on Racine. Unbelievably boring. The man is totally devoid of any divine spark, summarizes all kinds of books, quotes other people's words, and often yawns himself. I can't imagine such lectures at Warsaw University. Generally speaking, Mietek, the Swedes are poor intellectuals, and as for individualism, it doesn't

exist here. The young people listen to lectures and classes as they would to church sermons. No one here reacts to anything. It's impossible to argue on any subject with anyone. The women are usually heavily made-up and the men colorless. I've got to know them well because I belong to the Polish-Swedish club and have recently even become its secretary. They respond to all my caustic outbursts with a total lack of comprehension. Well, tough, I'm of the Julian Krzyżanowski school and have little regard for mental torpor. Mietek, what about the anthology?[53] I can't wait to get it. I'm making all manner of plans to enlighten the Swedes on the subject of Polish poetry. I don't want them to think that we have our [unreadable] or other such hacks. Thank you for "the sixth column."

I've lately become interested in Koestler.[54] I read some of his shorter pieces in Swedish journals.

Sincerely,

Tuśka

11. FEBRUARY 26, 1946, LUND
[*M. Rundo to M. Grydzewski*]

Dear Mietek, some kind of evil forces are conspiring to destroy me. I've been ill again. A pretty bad flu. It's markedly better now. During the space of five days, I returned to the condition of a "camp *muzulman.*" I'm incredibly weak and thin. The two women for whom I previously worked have taken care of me. Thanks to this, I've got good conditions for the period of convalescence. Marysia Lasocka[55] has shown me a tremendous amount of heart. I've become very close to her. She's an above-average person. I don't know when I'll start functioning normally again. I'm very perverse by nature, so now that I could, with a clear conscience, give myself up to my fate, I've decided not to.

Thank you very much for writing to Tadeusz, Mietek. I must now explain a few things to you, because I don't think you quite understand me. (I don't want you to think me a chit who doesn't know what she wants.) I suspect you're surprised at my lack of enthusiasm about staying in Sweden, and I suspect, too, that you think I should settle down here for longer. It seemed to me before the war, Mietek, that university was my goal in life. Today, I think that it's just an addendum to life. Fate has given me the addendum. Life I haven't yet started, and that's why I'm tossing about impatiently and putting all my energy into leaving here.

To me, studying is like an accompaniment to vodka. Forgive the vulgar comparison.

There are two people inside me. The first from before the war, from freedom, who thinks that in life one should have goals, plans, order. The second, the one with a number, to whom nothing is important, who tries to fill inner emptiness. Unfortunately, the second is closer to me.

Ania once wrote me that you were interested in my views and reasons for my internment. I belonged at one and the same time to a Communist organization[56] and to the ZWZ.[57]

The Communist fighting squad appealed to me, and I liked working at radio communication in the ZWZ.[58] I considered that one had to fight the Germans regardless in what ranks.

Now, of course, I nurture no liking for communism. I've completely lost ideas and good judgment. Don't laugh, but I feel attracted to Christianity. That doesn't mean—God forbid—that I'm attracted to the Catholic Church, oh no!

I do wonder (very primitively), however, why go chasing after any idea, if only one is true. Yes, I am only convinced by Christ's ethic. Christian morality is comprehensible to me and explains everything. Faith in a deity and similar questions, of course, are still dark and alien to me.

I sat for so long in international company in the camp. I observed people in situations in which one normally never sees them. It confirmed my former conviction that there is no such thing as national or racial traits, no differences.

Criminals of all nationalities are simply criminals. Honest people are the same everywhere. Various flowers bloom in various social systems.

I'm convinced that masses of Poles could be made into wonderful Hitlerites, and also that you couldn't make Hitlerites out of some Germans.

I'm a decided cosmopolitan. I feel great in international company. I never feel the lack of socializing with my fellow countrymen, but of Polish books, a Polish word, which to me is the most beautiful and the richest. Because of my attitude toward these things, I suffered a lot of persecution in prison and camp.

Apropos Koestler. There is no way I could read him in English. I've been learning Russian[59] and a little Lithuanian recently (the latter because of my professor). I read Swedish. I may be able to try English in the fall. Right now, I don't have time.

Forgive me for writing so much about myself, Mietek, but I wanted to explain myself a little. I agree that what I am doing here will prove useful to me (Ania thinks so, too). I am convinced, however, that I could do the same thing

somewhere else to better effect, because in a better internal state. Don't condemn me, or, rather, my plans to flee from here, even though right is on your side.

Sincerely,

Tuśka

P.S. I beg you, Mietek, don't suggest in any way to Tadeusz that I can stay patiently and productively here. No, it's deadly here.

12. APRIL 23, 1946, LUND

[*M. Rundo to M. Grydzewski*]

Dear Mietek,

I'm in the depths of despair. I received notification from the Polish Red Cross in Belgium[60] that the ministry refused a visa. This week, Tadeusz is in Paris. If he doesn't manage to come to Sweden for a few days, our situation will be hopeless. I'll never get out of Sweden to Germany. Tadeusz's friend writes telling me to try to get to France and England or Belgium, from where they'll easily be able to get me in. But it proves to be completely impossible. I have no hope of being able to get away from here. I'm having a nervous breakdown. In a few days, it'll be a year of sitting and waiting in Sweden.

I have a Swedish visa until 5/25, and I know that again there'll be arguments and delays. Thank you very much, Mietek, for *Wiadomości* and the books. Forgive this letter being like this, but I am dreadfully crushed.

Sincerely,

Tuśka

13. JUNE 19, 1946, LUND

[*M. Rundo to M. Grydzewski*]

Dear Mietek,

I haven't written for a long time because there have been some fairly sad changes in my life.

Tadeusz has returned to Poland. In his last letter from Munich, he writes that he's completely depressed.

He hopes, of course, that I'll return, too.

I don't know what I'll do, and I admit that I'm not thinking about it at all.

They're advising me here to try to bring him illegally to Sweden. I'm scared of being responsible for an undertaking of this nature. Anyway, my psychological state isn't any better, and I doubt that we'd be able to come to an understanding with each other. I don't think I have the right to drag him out of Poland if I'm not sure myself that I'd be able accompany him in emigration.

Because of the liquidation of [unreadable], the stipend has come to an end. So far, the Swedes show no desire to look after Polish students. Ostensibly, I should start to work on 1 April, but, because my friend from Paris is coming, I plan to spend a few weeks in the countryside with her. At the moment, I have no plans for the future. I am very confused.

Thank you very much for the books and *Wiadomości*. What's with the anthology, Mietek?

Sincerely,

Tuśka

I've changed my address.

III.

JUNE 1946–JUNE 1949

A bitter and biting current

1. JUNE 6, 1946, WARSAW

Sender: Tadeusz Borowski, 5/7 Rozbrat, Apt. 13
Teofila Borowska, 2 22 Stycznia St., Apt. 5

My Dears,

After a couple of mishaps, I'm in Warsaw. Mom, can you come?

I'd like to arrange a few things with the university. Haven't seen anyone yet.

Lots of kisses and I'm very impressed (Mrs. Dąbrowska told me.)

Your

Tadeusz Borowski

2. JULY 10, 1946, ŁÓDŹ

[*from Stefan Żółkiewski;*[1] *on letterhead:*] *Kuźnica,* Socio-Literary Weekly, 96 Piotrowska St., Łódź

Dear Sir,

I realized that I hadn't asked you for some kind of prose for *Kuźnica.* I'm doing so with this letter. Send a story of some kind. At the same time, I'm reminding you about the column on the subject of the "Próg" poets.[2] I'm also asking you to talk to the people from your group—we'd gladly take strong and aggressive reviews of new books from them for *Kuźnica.*

I also think it would be good for you to talk with Piórkowski, Miss Fiszer, Zalewski, Bratny, your group, and with young people close to you and us in Łódź and Kraków, as well as Warsaw—with Czeszka (18 Marszałkowska St., Apt. 19) and Gruszczyński—and for you and Miss Fiszer to gather materials and prepare a whole issue (12 columns) for *Kuźnica.* Such an issue of *Kuźnica* completely devoted to the young—contributing to the journal—could be published regardless of whether or not you would have some kind of journal of your own. Even such a single issue[3] would be a valuable manifestation, interesting from all kinds of points of view. See to it.

This issue would need an introductory article about the vicissitudes of the occupation, changes, and present aims of the various groups of young people appearing in the journal.

This project would have to be coordinated. Just don't let it be written by Bratny, whose judgments have nothing to do with reality except in his neurotic

fantasies. Take care of this so that Miss Fiszer goes where I've opened up opportunities for her.

Sincerely,

S. Żółkiewski

P.S. Write a Jal Kurek review for us!

3. JULY 10, 1946

[*from S. Żółkiewski*]

Be sure to send me no later than 7/23 some story—or segment about the Uprising. I'm counting on it!

Sincerely,

Stefan Żółkiewski

4. JULY 10, 1946

[*to Stanisław Marczak-Oborski*]

Dear Staszek,

I'm sure you're already in your Zakopane, so having greeted your countess and energetically kissed her hands, be so good as to read this letter which contains the substance of a conversation with Citizen Stefan Żółkiewski, the head of *Kuźnica*. He's a fat and full of himself man with a great sense of humor and broad-mindedness, for a Marxist. He wears a green suit, the trousers are a bit too baggy, and the hotel room in which he lives has two beds.

He bought us cherries which I ate myself because Ewa, a well brought-up young lady, didn't touch them out of modesty. First, Citizen-Editor and we ascertained that *Droga* differs in ideological perspective from *Kuźnica* only in so far as there's no question of a similarity in their status.

That undoubtedly means, I said, that we all lean toward Marxism as the clearest, and, possibly boundless, ideology at present, nevertheless, the status of *Kuźnica* in the artistic field is not always dear to us.[4] There isn't room in Poland for two generations, Żółkiewski replied. Our generation is only now coming on the scene, you younger ones as well. I want to enable you to express yourselves. What forms of expression do you regard as most suitable for yourselves?

There are four possibilities. First, to have your own journal under the auspices of some political cooperative that would bind you to journalism and political work, demanding artistic and ideological compromises. And what do you artists care about political work? Creative work is far more important. That, and only that, allows for reconstruction, if that is what one wishes. People teach stories, poems, novels, not introductory articles. On top of that, a journal takes masses of energy and can be ephemeral despite all efforts. Like *Warszawa* or *Wieś,* which are closing down. Even *Kuźnica* gives no profits. If, however, we decide on having our own journal, he'll do everything he can for us to have it.

The second possibility is to be a literary supplement to some journal. Such supplements have only one reason for being—to publish weaker works, aesthetic statements, but not finished works, which today every journal is grateful to have.

The danger is like that of having a journal—little space and political work as well. The third possibility is a page or two of space in *Kuźnica.* There we could print, under the aegis of *Droga,* our own artistic views whose individuality we wished to stress, as well as weaker works. Decent works could be run in *Kuźnica* without being singled out in any way, or else with the footnote, "The *Droga* Group" or whatever. One condition: that we not publish in *Tygodnik Powszechny* or in *Tygodnik Warszawski,* decidedly reactionary papers. The fourth possibility is to work with *Kuźnica* in a normal way, in other words to join that group. Each of these possibilities should be looked at and discussed and Żółkiewski will do all he can for us whatever we decide.

After we'd finished discussing all of this, Bratny and company (Zaleski and Chram) appeared screaming at me for not waiting for them because I'd arranged to meet them elsewhere. It somehow happened. Bratny was at my place the day before the meeting with *Kuźnica,* and, wolfing down endless amounts of pickled eel, which my mother had brought from Olsztyn, nearly made me editor of his "flaming" journal.[5] Chram decidedly has the face of an idiot, and the weirdest facial expressions—those of a man periodically trying to put his face back together. He's so preoccupied with doing this that he doesn't say a thing.[6]

Bratny proposed publishing my stories with Kuthan and added that it would also be good to try in *Wiedza* [*Knowledge*], which he would arrange for me. I replied I wasn't interested because my stories haven't appeared in life yet and so we have to wait. We were supposed after that to go to Płomień, he to sign a contract and me to look at all this. Instead of that Ewa came from Łódź and dragged me to Żółkiewski. A few hours later, Bratny and company came there, too, and Żółkiewski, who previously had been complaining about him at length,

was scathingly polite to him and Bratny kept trying to get out from under his insolent propositions. "I understand and I agree," Bratny said, "that Poland must be, etc. . . ." "But I don't understand and I don't agree!" Żółkiewski shouted. To my sincere amusement, Bratny tried with futility to be *plus catholique que le pape* and, giving up, went on the offensive, declaring that the classicism of the *Kuźnica* poets was undialectical and not Marxist (!) and that he, Bratny, who had written *Dramat w końskiej źrenicy* [*Drama in a Horse's Eye*], rejected by *Kuźnica*, would establish a journal that wouldn't sputter like *Kuźnica*. Then he bemoaned for a long time that *Kuźnica* rejects his creations. Well, replied the gentleman in the green suit thoughtfully, I have no other more objective aesthetic tool than my own taste . . . and as for the journal . . . You see, I spoke earlier with Ewa Fiszer and Borowski and they, as artists, are more careful about not squandering themselves. But you can try . . .

And so on in the same vein. Zalewski and Chram didn't say anything. Zalewski is pale and haggard; he, apparently, isn't back to himself after the hardships of the Partisans. It's because of that, probably, that his stories also lack nerve.

Take from my ramblings (I'm not aiming for succinctness) what's relevant to you and since Żółkiewski is going to be in Warsaw toward the end of April, or maybe before, write me how your energy is (don't squander it needlessly) and what we should tell the editor. Apart from that, he asked me for something to print. Maybe I'll find something, but I'm not in a rush at the moment.

Piotr [Słonimski] is in Warsaw and Jerzy Kreutz, a very handsome and blasé boy, a beloved composer. Piotr cannot get over Dołęga. Barbara had been in Wrocław, came back in a good mood and disheveled. I don't know what or why, because she doesn't say, just laughs—like a goat or silly goose. Anyway, she's attractive. (To cheer you up.)[7]

Hang in there, Staszek, and when they've dug you out of the rubble, write.

Tadeusz Borowski

5. JULY 12, 1946, WARSAW

[*to Maria Rundo*]

Dearest,

How very much I'd like to get even a word from you. I sent you two telegrams and a letter, I don't know what you received. Even worse, I absolutely don't know what you plan to do and whether in our lives we'll meet again. I feel that, if we

don't meet, my life will be wasted. I very much sense your absence, as though I weren't myself. Perhaps you don't believe me. I'll never write anything different. It's hard for me to find objective words that you, perhaps, want. I don't know how.

Everyone—your and my mother, Baśka, my father, all our friends—Maria, Jerzy, Czesław, Piotr, etc., think you should be with me. Don't believe what is being written about Poland—there's a lot of hysteria and unhealthy unease, completely unnecessary. In any case, the platitudes about rebuilding are not simply platitudes. There's rubble, moral as well. Tough—it was war. In Poland, it was the worst manifestation. No, I haven't changed in any way. But I'd like to be honest. I wrote you why I returned. I'll say it again: I think I did the right thing. This country has to be seen to be believed. And that a love for something that we generally called Poland would return. These are shameful matters and perhaps I'm talking about them in platitudes. Forgive me.

I'm studying a bit. I'm writing a bit. At the moment, the situation with literature is as never before: a complete lack of people. I'm trying to do good things. It's hard for me. My financial conditions are good. Baśka is trying to settle in Warsaw. I don't have an apartment at the moment, just a room on Rozbrat. A bit like Skaryszewska, but it will work out. It's a great locum in Olsztyn and Łódź. From the fall I will have something in the city as an assistant to Krzyżanowski. There are masses of positions, and good ones, but I don't want to waste my time. I'd rather write, select, and publish something sometimes. It's the best way [8]—other than you, because you are my dearest, my sweet.

If you can, reply. I would so much like to receive even one word from you!

Tadeusz

6. JULY 15, 1946, WARSAW

Second-Class Citizen Stanisław Marczak-Oborski. Villa Hrabina, Road to Biały, Zakopane
Sender: Good Citizen Tadeusz Borowski, 5 Rozbrat St., Apt. 13, Warsaw

Dear Staszek Marczak,

After writing the previous letter, I got overwhelmed with scruples that my letter was too dry, because I asked neither about your health nor about your conditions, so I'm now trying to make up for this mistake and forgetfulness and

ask you to forgive me, because I was truly shaken up and in a hurry because I might forget everything that the gentleman in the green suit and soft, quiet slippers was saying to the thin as her literary fortune Ewa, and what Ewa said back to him, and that I ate cherries, and that I forgot to go to Bratny's as he'd asked me, so Bratny came this morning at seven and I was still sleeping in women's pajamas, and I had to dress in front of him, which was most unpleasant because the pajama is ripped at the side and now I don't know what Bratny will think though I know that he'll write sometime in a memoir that he saw me in torn women's pajamas and that's why he, Bratny, is a genius and wants to create a literary journal with "flames," and gives me cash that I don't want to take, and asks me about some article, he's lately agreed to only a note, just that I write something, so, at my place on Rozbrat, Bratny, like *Droga,* was at a crossroads. So I told him that I'd write, oh God, not a prayer, but a note that Bór wrote about the Uprising, in other words that article I told you about. But maybe I won't write it, because I don't feel like it. I promised and joy to Bratny. So, how are you feeling, friend, and have you already made contacts? This machine writes well, doesn't it?

All my friends have abandoned me, not even a lame dog drops by, I'm not reading anything and thinking of suicide myself, except I don't yet know how. I'm waiting until they reopen the bridge. I started writing a story, but I won't finish it. Why should I, if I'm to kill myself? I just want you, friend, to preserve for future generations the fruits of my hatred of the world and negative attitude toward it, so be so kind, and I made this point in the first part of my story (there should be a colon here, but I don't have one, just a dash, period, exclamation, and question mark).

"Hey, stop it," I shouted jumping off the parapet. "No fighting, you sons of bitches! The archbishop is going to Holy Mass!" But I don't know whether the point is too forceful, and whether I shouldn't put prelate or canon instead of archbishop, but then it wouldn't be realistic because the archbishop really was on his way to Mass then, only I wasn't jumping off a parapet and I don't know whether I'm being realistic and I'm very concerned about it.[9] It shouldn't matter.

You should write back to me because I am very worried about the lack of letters from you, and don't know whether I'm to write an epitaph, or wait a while. I'm torn two ways because I want to be up-to-date and am lazy. Apart from that, I received a letter from overseas, from a certain very dear lady, our mutual friend, beginning with the words (there should be a colon here, but I haven't got one)

"Dear Pan Tadeusz," so I'm very confused and am seeing that bridge as a truly useful object, there's no more room,

Your friend and admirer,

hero of "A Day at Harmenz," Tadzio

7. NO PLACE OR DATE

[*to Maria Rundo*]

Dear Tuśka,

Forgive me for writing letter after letter to you without being asked to, but I am not able to write anything else at present. I think that this way I will maintain the contact with you that you wish to break off. Anyway, I've given up attempting to understand what is going on inside me. The dominant impression is probably the sense of enormous weariness of myself and apathy. I would like to get away from myself. The worst is the state of anticipation day after day. I'm thinking a lot about my psyche these days, and I'm slowly, but definitely, coming to the conclusion that only for a very short period of my life have I been ethically correct in terms of myself and of other people. I've distanced myself at present from so-called family and friends, and am trying to sum myself up. The conviction is growing in me that I was the cause of unease to people I met, something that demands, perhaps unconsciously, sacrifice. It's a certain type of superstitious faith in human beings, an anachronism at a time when a style of mass thinking and collectivism rules. Anyway, this is only a certain approximation of how things seem to me. I've also discovered a different impression in myself that greatly surprises and in a certain undefined way amuses me, namely the impression that man is actually completely alone. The irony is that this feeling is very commonplace and banal. Unfortunately, it is completely novel and clear when one admits it. There's also an equally banal feeling of unfounded jealousy of others' lives.

It's very amusing that every day I perform a series of so-called normal activities —from eating cucumbers to replying to editors' letters. I never thought that one could be so amusing to oneself and derive so much malicious satisfaction for oneself. I'm trying to take up the least possible space in the psyche and actions of others and am promising myself to pay off all of life's, and so-called moral, debts as fast as possible. At the moment I'm still living on credit and my debts are rising. My parents' love and human friendship weighs heavy on me. I'm doing away

with them quickly. There's a universal method for it—not keep one's promises, and offend other people's sense of self-love, and also waste so-called self-worth. In any case, these methods are mutual.

This last month hasn't been pleasant for me. During this time, I went to my parents whom I haven't seen for three years. I met up with all my friends, other, of course, than those who had perished. I was also in Łódź. It amused me greatly when everyone said that I'd finally be able to put my life in order, as though this was the greatest good for which one had to strive. I talked to a dozen people who wanted to give me money for work of some kind. I left it until later, let's say till fall. I was also foolish enough, however, to commit myself to an assistantship and to writing—to my great dissatisfaction. In any case, I've given up poetry. It's the wisest step I've taken in life. So-called prose is very easy, and depends on remembering things one's observed and putting them together into a whole—the longer, the more entertaining. My story, printed without my knowledge, is being read as the best piece of postwar prose since its subject is a very hackneyed camp theme, but the outcome of the theme completely random. It's a very empty game, which I will not continue. I became convinced in the camp that I did not necessarily have to write in order to live. That once seemed unbelievable to me.

Anyway, many things are unbelievable. I never thought that so-called social life, its range and its spirit, would tire me. In Munich I lived in total detachment and choked, here I've fallen into a vortex of broad-ranging matters and I'm tired, perhaps because I see the sense of these matters. Pride always played a large part in my life. Now, I'm turning it only in a single direction—not to be indebted to anyone. I should be able to manage it. It's very necessary to me because I'd like to be able to take charge of myself. I think about it with a certain impatience.

I apologize for writing all this to you. I think I've only recently arrived at certain conclusions, and that I know more about myself now than I ever have before. I've been sitting over this letter since morning, and I'm under some illusion that I'm speaking to you with difficulty. I probably shouldn't be sending it, but the fact that you may, perhaps, receive it is a certain accomplishment for me. Anyway, I haven't touched on any burning issues of which I was guilty. Exactly a year ago, I lost a very ambitious game started two years earlier. One always loses such things if one acts according to small-minded principles. A year ago, I stayed put out of convenience. I tried several times to mend my game.

I think that I've never known how to impose my desires onto other people, and that I acquiesced too easily. This came back on us since human friendship is very barren.

I've come to another conclusion about myself. I couldn't do this before because I didn't have the so-called background. I've decided that over the past few years I did not grow larger so-called spiritually, nor did I perceive that any so-called good I have in me was left over from Skaryszewska times, that my instincts were amusingly warped. It also turned out that I don't know much.

Many of my auto-suggestions turned out to be unfounded almost to my joy.

This is what I've discovered about myself so far. I'm a little surprised and amused. This defines my stance toward myself. One could add to this, also, that I am waiting for myself [sic]. Because these are matters of importance to me, I'd like to emerge reasonably honestly out of them and without indebtedness.

This seems to me the first thing I should do. I don't think I would know how to take up any position in life, although there were days when I sincerely wished it. My domain was something else, a little faint by contrast with my imaginings, unfortunately.

This letter is probably ethically wrong. If I've given you pain, I apologize, that truly wasn't my intention. Perhaps, however, you should know about me what I think I know myself. I'd like things to be easier for you. Forgive me for asking of you things unpleasing to you, I thought it would be easiest for us to be together. I wanted us to be together as quickly as possible.

I lost a very beautiful game. I think one plays a game like that only once. I would very much like it that when you think that I love you, you also think that I'm not worthy of you.

I'm convinced that I'll derive a benefit from this. I'm still waiting for myself [sic].

Tadeusz

8. JULY 17, 1946, WARSAW
[to S. Marczak-Oborski]

Dear Staszek,

The day before yesterday I received two letters from *Kuźnica* in which, apart from an order for a so-called Uprising story (probably the result of a misunderstanding, since I'm not going to write anything about the Uprising), there's a proposal for the "Droga" group to put together materials that would take up a whole issue of *Kuźnica*. According to the editor's words such a young people's issue could be published independently of our plans to acquire our own journal.

It would be a valuable and interesting manifestation. Because editor Żółkiewski asked me to take up this matter (I don't know by what lights) I think it good for you to know about it, and to write me what you think of it. If you would like to put together such an issue, or to establish closer contact with him, write to him. And let me know what you plan to do in this matter. Bratny is jumping around like a louse on a comb but is establishing that journal. I'm not squirming out of the promised article about Bór. We've decided that it will be put in the "Notes" section.

All the best and I await your invaluable to me pronouncements.

Your Tadeusz

9. JULY 23, 1946, ŁÓDŹ
[*from S. Żółkiewski*]

Dear and respected Sir,

Thank you for the story.[10] It's going into print. What and how I think of it I'll write—as a lover of literature. It's stylistically weaker than those printed in *Twórczość*.[11] As the editor, I'm printing it.

Put together your issue of *Kuźnica*—I'd simply like it to be literary. How to arrange it, decide for yourselves. We'll discuss the completed thing. In any case, I'll give you maximum freedom and decisions.

When? Whenever you want—I'm ready now and, let's say, in September.

Speak with Zalewski and Piórkowski. I've spoken to Zalewski so he knows best what to think.

Find out precisely about Miss Fiszer's problems. Because she also writes unclearly. And I'd like to arrange it for her.

What's going on with you? Why the depression people write me about? What's happened?

Sincerely,

Stefan Żółkiewski

10. JULY 24, 1946, LUND

[*Maria Rundo to Mieczysław Grydzewski*]

Dear Mietek,

For a few weeks now, I've been working in a hospital. I have a night shift in surgery. This work (purely nursing) suits me very well. I even have a bit of time to read at night. I've already learned quite a lot, and, of late, am alone in the department, that means without supervision from a Swedish nurse. The hospital has become a sort of shelter for me. During the day, I feel terrible. Apart from great physical fatigue, I feel hopelessly lost and dejected. At night, on the other hand, I feel fine in every regard. I'm even able to concentrate and have thrown no fits. In any event, I like working at night.

Since Tadeusz is happy being in Poland, I've lost all hope of seeing him again. I'm resigned to it, truly, honestly resigned. I'm only hurt that he regards my position as the result of my indifference to him and of my falling under the influence of "some new friends." In the last letter, he used words worthy of a true poet: "I know that my life will be wasted if you don't return." Of course, I don't resent that he went back, I'm just hurt by his selfishness. I'm more isolated lacking family and friends by whom he's surrounded. And so our roads have parted.

My "Auschwitz" friend from Paris was here for a few weeks. Those were very valuable days. I'm becoming convinced that in friendship one can discover a huge, full, completely full, world. It's just that everything's dismal and painful. I feel strange sometimes, because it's not life, but literature, that nags at me. In life, one doesn't suffer only as in a tragedy. Apparently! I've decided to go to Belgium illegally, Mietek, with three students (they escaped from Kraków to Sweden hidden at the bottom of a ship). I've become friends with them. They treat me like a fourth comrade since they've noticed that I'm not fearful.

If things work out, we'll leave at the end of August on a Swedish ship. They have friends and backers in Belgium, so perhaps we'll get stipends. I'll enroll in nursing school. I need to find absorbing, tiring work that gives moral satisfaction, in order to quiet my weakened spirit. I've decided irrevocably to devote myself to nursing. I neither want to, nor can, live only for myself, or do things for my own amusement. And, in any case, I'll be able to manage in any country as a nurse. That apart, it's also important that on night shifts one can often read. So in the meantime, I'm pulling myself together and attempting to bring this plan to

fruition. At worst, meaning if they don't give us stipends, we'll have to work like we do here, but in a better atmosphere, perhaps. So we have nothing to lose.

It's unbearable in Sweden, and there are no prospects. I'm happy that I've finally met people who've had it with the climate here. My acquaintances scream in horror that I'm setting off for foreign climes in exclusively male company, and tremble for my reputation. I think, however, that whenever I've undertaken various adventures, contrary to society's expectations, they worked out well and so this one will too. I've got lots of further plans for the distant future, but I'm not writing about them, because I've got to undertake one thing first.

I think that if I were a real woman, I would have relieved all my woes at my beloved's bosom and be at peace, but, because I'm more like a man, unease drives me in the other direction, and life is harder. I'm curious, myself, to see how far I will go, what will happen along the way, and where I will finish up.

Sincerely,

Tuśka

Many thanks for the books, and, most of all, for *Wiadomości*. *Wiadomości* opens the eyes of a rat like me from the back alleys of Scandinavia to the world.

Mietek, I very much do not like Sweden. Very much. Why after the Lager did I end up here as though for further penance?

11. JULY 24, 1946, ZAKOPANE
[*from S. Marczak-Oborski*]

Dear "Droga,"

It's good that you both wanted to write me an account of conversations at Cecora. As a result, I created a more or less complete picture for myself, and only then rested my head on my hand and marveled. Well! Simple conclusion is that one has to make the most of Citizen Żłk.'s "sincere desire." The most realistic of all ideas he threw out seems to me the "page in *Kuźnica*." The whole stumbling block is what he understands by this, how liberally would he want to treat us, and to what extent would we be independent? I already more or less have "in mind" the first issue. There would be certain issues to discuss in connection with it, and that's why I would like to see you. And so: first—the leading article. There are three possibilities: A) reprint the leading article of "Road" without changes;

B) rewrite it and update the same leading article with certain surnames and examples; C) give up on the form of this kind of article and say our piece in works of a purely literary character as, e.g., Tadeusz's "O poezji i poecie" ["About Poetry and the Poet"] or my "O rozumieniu" ["On Understanding"].[12]

Second: prose. I'm thinking of reprinting Ewa Grochowska's "Granice" ["Borders"] or one of Kowalewski's short stories. (Kott took two for *Kuźnica*—they could be withdrawn and given to us.)

Three: Kimbo[13] ought to write an anti-Kapist[14] epithet of some kind. Does he have something like this? Could he do something in a short time? What might he have at his disposal? Tadeusz Kantor enthusiastically agreed to collaborate. He'll write about theater. Mieczysław Porębski has a free-wheeling essay at *Kuźnica:* "On the fastidiousness of the profane," which we would take. And you, Ewa, do you have anything on literary criticism? Something about that must be in there from the start.

Poetry. I've secured the collaboration of a young, very talented (in Bieńkowski's, my, and the Kraków "arbitrator's" opinion) poet, Kazimierz Mikulski, whom we will discover (he hasn't been published yet). Wirpsza has agreed to collaborate (not as *Droga* but as a freelance collaborator). I'd willingly write an overview of Włodek's[15] Kraków group, Warsaw's Próg, and possibly Bratny's group. But, perhaps, not for the first issue.

It seems from all this that we need to see each other. I've no cash at the moment, but expect to have within the week. So I'd go out into the world. The question is: should I go directly to Łódź to meet you both, and to make final arrangements with Żółkiewski (we'd already have to have the materials, if not all, a lot, at least). Or, should I come to Warsaw first and talk over this and the other with you? Tell me immediately how things stand by express mail. I'll telegraph you about my possible visit, because I think we need to move quickly.

Tadeusz, in the last *Przekrój* there is a reprint of your poem and a very laudatory mention by Osmańczyk.[16] In the Łódź socialist *Pobudska* [*Awakening*] I found a very reasonable summary of your *Twórczość* story. I'll bring the cutting.

Bratny sent me a letter asking me to collaborate with him on his Uprising issue. I got the letter too late, but didn't intend to anyway.

They suggested I take up the editorship of the Poznań *Życie Literackie,* because Bąk is leaving Poznań. But it's too far away and a bit inconvenient.

Ewa, perhaps you should try to write some review of some volume of poetry that "counts" (e.g., Miłosz, Przyboś, Bieńkowski, Staff, Słonimski, or someone

like that). Is it possible for you to look through the foreign press and find something interesting and striking to translate?

Kisses, hugs, and for God's sake write back quickly.

S. Marczak-Oborski

Ewa! Tadeusz!
Tadeusz! Ewa!
Hugs, hugs.

[on the other side of the second page of the letter, Ewa Fiszer's note:]

July 29, 1946
Tadeusz,
Żłk.'s here. He'll be at my place at 4 P.M.
Be there! Where'd you get to this morning? Ewa

12. JULY 27, 1946, WARSAW
[*to S. Marczak-Oborski*]

Listen Staszek, I'm very pleased that you haven't died yet, because you didn't write back for such a long time that I thought of, and started to, just in case, composing an epithet beginning with the words: "Hey, so one has to, dismal fate" but I didn't finish it because a moment ago I received your letter. Since I haven't met with Ewa yet, and there's a mass of news, I'm writing back by express mail, not the way those of my friends loitering around summer resorts do.

1. As to *Kuźnica,* we should make them a whole *Droga* issue with some kind of journalistic, and not literary, leading article, e.g., about the two generations problem, or about young people (companion to the Żłk–Koźniewski discussion), a literary manifesto somewhere in the middle, don't you think? This issue (we can give it to Żłk. at any time, and we have until September) must be aggressive. It would be good to include Kantor's debate with the Kapists; someone with quick wits and kid gloves should write on Przyboś, Kurek (Janosik), or Miłosz—and reveal their Parnassism, I could try to write about Auschwitz morality (I guarantee you that it will enrage, and provoke, more than one), a story would take up too much space, etc.

Anyway mull it around, that's what you're for, and I'll write what I can for

you. I should add in parentheses that Ż. asked me very insistently for this issue, and I'd like it done (I wanted to write "to do it" but since you, most beloved, are going to do it, I had to write ungrammatically).

2. As to the page in *Kuźnica*. Ż. will give two columns, i.e., two columns under our control with the proviso that these pages would be a repository for possibly weaker things, and mature pieces could go into the rest of the issue with an acknowledgment to *Droga*. I regard this idea to be completely fair (as the English would say) and willingly lean toward it as the sunflower does to the sun (in connection with which I sent *Kuźnica* a little story, a bit of drivel, about the camp, of course).

3. It appears from this that you should collect material and, before seeing Ż., be so KIND as to see us . . . don't you think? I'll throw in a few items from literature and journalism into the materials, together with some American reportage and maybe some Russian, if such things would be useful to you. In any event, I have books to which even professors from *Myśl Współczesna* [*Contemporary Thought*] don't have access. We'll have to go over *Próg* and the others in your letter. Anyway, these are subjects for discussion. We must hurry.

4. The Bratny situation is more or less like this: I promised him one poem for his (Uprising) issue. Not even a stone could have refused, if approached night and day! On the other hand, I am totally opposed to Bratny's suggestion for brotherly collaboration on the journal, light-mindedly forgetting all meeting dates, which practically reduces one to tears. And it's such a good position—six thousand rubles!

At the side, Roentgen—shape without a spine,
and in the stomach—outline of a tapeworm . . .

I have one more meeting with them today, and fear that they'll beat me up. But what should one suffer for, if not literature?

5. As to me, generally, and personally, I am pessimistic. I see no POINT in life, and am very unhappy because of IT and depressed according to EWA's classic definition. I already composed another posthumous poem and burned it immediately because it was a terrible piece of scribble. So much for joy in life! I did not get an apartment for your beautiful sister, which troubles me greatly, they turned them down at the housing office. It's a shame!

6. Under the circumstances, I've begun to write a historical story entitled "Bitwa pod Grunwaldem," but don't know whether I'll finish it, because I don't know what my archbishop, who, as you know, went to Holy Mass, is going to do.

Apropos, in *Rycerz Niepokalanej* [*Knight of the Virgin*], Ziembicki wrote a wonderful article on the entry of Cardinal Hlond. Residents clung to the empty sockets of windows . . . et cetera. One of these days, I'm going to pour a pitcher of cold water on him, to stop him making a fool of himself, though he's so nice, and it's for bread.

> 7. *Terrible heat, not a thought in my head.*
> *Which I wish you, too*
> *and press you to my heart*
> *and your pale forehead*
> *lay on my heart*
> *Your friend most sincere*
> *Borowski Tade*
> *usz*

P.S.   I didn't send this letter because I saw Bratny on Saturday and definitively turned down the honor of joining his Editorial Staff, but would willingly help them with my enlightened advice and good sociological taste. Ewa was intimidated, because that idiot Ziembicki spread a rumor that I, together with him, was under Bratny's command. I was very irritated.

Which I wish you, too, etc. (see above).

13. AUGUST 2, 1946, ŁÓDŹ
[*from S. Żółkiewski*]

Dear Sir,

I owe you a few words about your story, which I only now read with care. It's good, very good. It possesses all the marks of your talent and all of your sharp realism. It has that disquieting harshness that your previous work revealed.

It's new, however, both in atmosphere and, actually, in subject. While in the previous ones there were many Céline-esque provocations, here, rather, there is quiet human ordinariness in all its rawness. Morally indifferent—as Father Pirożyński would not say. But precisely the depiction of that indifference—not evil, not sinister, harmful, malicious, or dogged—but simply the indifference of animals that do not behave morally, but simply purposively, efficiently. You showed, without the pathos and provocativeness of your previous stories, the

hierarchy of values governing the consciousness of a lower than normal human level of material existence. It is precisely the lack of physical threat, prison force within this story—the rather gentle atmosphere of a "successful" day—which depicts all the more forcefully, painfully, and fully the fate of the prisoner of fascism.

I think, however, that you should now, for your own good, break with this topic. Try your strength on completely different material. Write a story about contemporary life: Poland in 1946. Because you stand at risk of repeating yourself.

Your story will run most probably in the next issue. I ask for your continuing collaboration. Please send reviews, notes, and so on.

Sincerely,
Stefan Żółkiewski

14. AUGUST 10, 1946, MUNICH

[*from Anatol Girs*]

[*stamped on the back of the envelope:*] Replies should be directed to: "Repatriate" Administration, 48 Mokotowska Street, Warsaw, through the mission in Frankfurt am Maine, with exact address of the recipient.

Dear Pan Tadeusz,

Today I received your letter dated 7/14.[17] I'm very pleased that you found everything as you expected—good, in other words. It's good that you are going to continue your studies.

"Auschwitz" is finished. I'll send you copies. Opinion abroad is very good.

Janusz and his mother have gone south. Krystyn is still here. You have lost no "great match," simply exchanged it. There is a difference. You exchanged (I write this out of total love and sympathy for both of you) a woman's love for friends, an assistantship, and other values. I received a letter from Tuśka truly full with feelings for you, and despair. Exactly two days before receiving your letter she had managed to obtain papers for you to come to her. She, herself, through Krystyn's efforts during his stay in Belgium as well as others', has the possibility of studying there, that means Belgium. I didn't learn this last directly. That Miss Loda[18] is depressed, I can fully understand and am not very surprised. She placed her affections in the wrong place. That sometimes happens in this fleeting world.

In these circumstances, the woman is always the unluckier one. Love really is eternal, but that which you, my dears, call love, in most cases isn't. They are just fleeting thoughts, more or less successful imaginings about something that we don't wish to earn, but dearly want to possess and not have to care about. True Love, however, outlasts everything and can never exist without reciprocation. It is a Law. It is the greatest treasure that one can have on earth. It's the flower of the fern out of fairy tales, but without its negative sides. Pan Tadeusz, you write that you are bitter. A little. Find yourself. Because what you are seeing is only a caricature of yourself. Just as your imaginings about me are not me at all. Just a poor caricature of man writ large. That which you perhaps sometimes saw clearly is a small, a tiny reflection or echo of true Man—the most beautiful word on earth after the word "God." There is a point to life, even though you sometimes don't see it. But you, like all of us, have eternity before you—to understand and recognize. I apologize for not writing on the machine, but it's broken down a little. Please write often, if, that is, you wish to. If I go further off somewhere I'll give you my new address. I'm going to write frequently to Tuśka, because I feel sorry for her.

Many greetings and with sincere affection,

Girs

15. AUGUST 12, 1946, LUND
[*Maria Rundo to Mieczysław Grydzewski*]

Dear Mietek,

I received word from Stockholm that English stipends have been assigned to Polish students to go to Ireland, Portugal, or Spain. Lasocka and I are applying to go to Ireland. The matter will be settled during the course of the next few days. I think the granting of stipends depends in large part on the Union of Polish Students in Stockholm, and so lecturer Folejewski[19] has an influence on it. I think this ostensibly unrealistic matter (the prospects are a bit too good) has a chance of succeeding.

I would very much like to leave together with her, Lasocka, that is, because she's very close to me (out of kindred spirit, not relationship, of course). It would hurt my heart to leave her in the Germanic country (Sweden really is Germanic), at the end of a career, since it's all over for Poles here.

Just so I don't get burned by the damned authorities before getting the visa.

At times, this unbelievable luck seems impossible to me. The uncertainty is wearing me out. If I manage to leave, I will gain freedom, real freedom, which has to replace even Tadeusz.

I think that at my age freedom is more necessary than love. Tadeusz thinks otherwise, but I think that at some point he'll come to understand the error of his calculations.

Dear Mietek, please don't think my agitation and constant changing of plans odd. I have to leave Sweden, even if on the devil's tail. Sweden has finished me off more than the camp did. In Ireland, I won't feel so penned in. What's more important, I have greater conviction about the English language than Swedish. I learned a little Swedish, but completely by chance. English, however, I shall take up eagerly.

Mietek, don't be angry that I'm burdening you with such a long letter again, but I have to unburden myself. And although I know how little time you have, I am counting on your indulgence.

I got the anthology today and will immediately start reading. I noticed that my favorite Gałczyński poem, "Kuferlin," is in it and Liebert's "Jurgowska Karczma." You've chosen beautifully, Mietek! Lots of Tuwim, that's good!

Sincerely,

Tuśka

16. AUGUST 17, 1946, WARSAW

[*from S. Żółkiewski, postcard*]

Tadeusz Borowski, 5/7 Rozbrat, apt. 13

Dear Sir,

Today, August 17, I am going to Paris. Will return in the first half of September. You, Marczak, and Miss Fiszer see to your issue of *Kuźnica*. Let's float it immediately after my return.

Greetings,

S. Żółkiewski

17. AUGUST 2, 1946

[*to Marczak-Oborski*]

Dear Staszek,

You're not writing to me no doubt out of laziness, which bothers me a lot, I swear, because I'm not feeling good since the road to Sweden is very long and the MSZ (NSZ?)[20] don't know anything yet, and it's hard to tell when they will know. Ewa has gone to Świder, and our commander-in-chief Żółkiewski to Paris to a conference because she can't come to an agreement without him. He'll return sometime mid-September. He asked us to put together the issue, which can be launched right after his return. I discussed the matter with Chram, he'll do anything we want and, if need be, he'll chuck Rozbratny. *Pokolenie*, the social-literary bimonthly journal of the youthful opposition to the regime (faithful to the regime) is in print and available everywhere, so I'm not sending you a copy because it costs 7 zet. There is in it my beautiful, but famous, poem and a series of other less interesting items, all of it, however, on broad sheets and beautiful print, almost Garamond (lies!).

Ah, Ziembicki is offering me fifteen minutes on the radio (poetry) at the beginning of September, what do you suggest I air?

Greetings to your wife, and write.

Tadeusz Borowski

18. AUGUST 28, 1946, ZAKOPANE

Outstanding Citizen Tadeusz Borowski, aesthete, 5 Rozbrat Street, Apt. 13, Warsaw. Sender: Very Outstanding Citizen Stanisław Marczak-Oborski, "Hrabina," Biały Rd, Zakopane.

Tadeusz, dear to my heart!

You unjustly accuse me of laziness in your last epistle neatly written on a typewriter. I have much work and responsibilities here. And so: I started to write a poem. It was going to be a verse rendering of my screenplay: "Między ustami a brzegiem" ["Between Mouth and Bank"], which got burnt in Warsaw. I wrote the first section (background action) and stopped because it wasn't in keeping with the times. I'll certainly go back to it, but sometime later. At present, I'm sitting up to my ears in—a novel set during the Uprising. It's called "Corporal

Buda," and also out of sync with the times, because the hero is a lumpen prole-tariat, and that's not allowed today. But I've brushed that aside and am going on having fun.

Other than that, I wrote letters to the many young scribbler protégés of Żółkiewski's, and am now chortling over their responses. I'm filled with good hope, however, just don't you let me down, Rascal. Write stories, cross things out, revise, add until you've got a gem. Otherwise your prospects look dim, be-cause you'll lose your sweet life in the bloom of your youth to a violent death at the hands of a friend.

Out of habit, I'm publicizing you in Zakopane as well. My wife regards you as the greatest marvel of Pol. Lit. (Polish Literature). I dampen her enthusiasm as best I can.

Pokolenie reached me at the same time as your letter. I consider its level good, but nothing more. There isn't a single striking and interesting position. Graphi-cally, however, it is most impressive, it's almost a shame the journal is literary.

Outside the kitchen windows at "Hrabina," there extends a view of a pictur-esque heap of garbage, not removed since earliest times (probably since sanitary servitude). All manner of carcasses lie in it, and rot at will. So are you surprised that we have all come down with stomach ailments? President Iwaszko[21] had a fever of close to 100 for three days. As soon as the aforesaid Jaroslaw I, The Great, (but is he the Greatest? The Greatest?) recovers, I will pop over to him with your tome.

I gather from your letter that Ewa Fi. has come back from Silesia, her little left breast packed carefully into your poem. Is Baśka B. also in Warsaw now? Why are the Zofia's, the one and the other, not writing to me? Aah? That your depar-ture is being delayed doesn't surprise me at all. It's the normal course of things. I truly hope, however, that with backing like that, the matter will come to frui-tion, and don't worry about it. Give *Kwadrans* [*Quarter of an Hour*], "Nocna elegia" ["Night Elegy"], "Czasy pogardy" ["Times of Contempt"], *Pożegnanie z Marią,* the first and last poem in *Imiona nurtu,* "Odejście poety" ["A Poet's Departure"], "Odezwa" ["Response"], and, perhaps, something from the erotica. On top of that, try to have them give you a second quarter of an hour at some point, for satires and epigrams, because I think it's hard to connect these things. I will be in Warsaw in the middle of September—I'll write again before then. Write as much as you can, too.

Your Staszek

19. SEPTEMBER 10, 1946, MUNICH

[*from Krystyn Olszewski*]

Dear Little Puppy,[22]

It's highest time I penned something to you, particularly since Nel's letter[23] after some lengthy wanderings is only now fit to be sent. It happened like this: Nel wrote it (look at the date), left it on the table, and went out; Dorsz arrived, saw it, read it, and asks if it's about him. "Why, Dorsz, that's offensive!" To this, Nel, because he was slightly embarrassed, responds, "Because that's Dorsz." Then Tolek[24] asks Juliusz[25] in confidence what Dorsz actually looks like. But that's history now, almost two months ago. Then Nel and his mother suddenly left for a health spa for the summer, and I stayed behind in a kitchen with three rooms. I got two letters from them a few days ago, one of them to you, which "Mól" took by mistake. They write that they're very comfortable and are persuading me to go there.

I'm still waiting. I'm staying here until October and in the meantime studying at the famed UNRRA university, architecture, of course. The level's mediocre, but I regret not getting off the tram earlier, because I'd have managed to get two semesters out of the way, and now I don't know whether I'll manage one. Anyway, I feel completely different—you understand. I'm still on very warm terms with Tolek, but no longer official ones. I marvel at *Polonus* and *Goślicki*[26] (this second is finished—a jewel!), and he marvels at my finds. Apropos, you know in that warehouse from which I got those old books then, I found unusually interesting things: old, truly old, architectural handbooks, good graphics and something from your field. If I get the opportunity, I'll send them to you.

Obermenzing received an "affidavit" from some professor Julek knows. And meanwhile the consulate told them that the "contingent for Catholics" had been exhausted. Tolek came back at this with Boston, and he's going to go there himself in ten months time.[27] A good joke. Meanwhile, Czytelnik is offering him the directorship of big publishing houses in Berlin, but he doesn't want it, despite all guarantees. God forbid that he reads this letter . . .

Also, he wrote to Tuśka and received a letter back from her. It isn't true that she doesn't want to know Tadeusz. She wants to very, very much and hopes . . .

So much about Tolek, and now on the subject of *We Were* [*in Auschwitz*] problems are starting. The "Meneliki" enclave (book distributors) wants to skin us alive. As a result, Anatol has suspended sales until such time as one of us takes

144

it up. And word has already spread. Our worthy publisher doesn't want to give me a single copy beyond the author's one, and I can't shake free of prospective buyers. For one uncorrected copy which Franek took from me, all the local dignitaries are standing in line and signing up weeks in advance. Opinion is good on the whole. Some of the more drastic stories arouse reservations, the Gypsy camp one,[28] for example, which "for reasons of national prestige, etc., should not be translated into foreign languages." I've heard comparisons to Remarque. I've not yet seen any reviews, however.

Right now I'm reading Morcinek's *Listy spod morwy* [*Letters from a Mulberry Tree*].[29] The thing is written from a retrospective point of view, in the form of memories arising as a result of various experiences during a rest cure in the French Alps. There's a lack of expression, it doesn't capture the camp in the heat of the moment. It equals in horrors, same ideological stance as ours, but is too quiet in its form. On the other hand, I also see these things somewhat differently now.

It's like looking at a model through half-closed eyes and instead of separate elements and details seeing only the clearer contrasts of darks and lights; memories also break down into separate experiences: these, threatening and tragic, and next to them those from comedy and Canada times; from these, it's as though the smell of a burning human being emanates. It is because of this, perhaps, that when I sometimes read one of our chapters I'm not bored (this analogy comes from the fact that I'm currently drawing plaster figures). And you know what's occurred to me? Maybe someone's already tried; every once in a while, once a year, for example, to write a memoir of the same experience, "the same section," and to compare them at some point and see how the point of view has changed, what's stayed the same, what's gone from memory. Is it possible, however, to write anew each time? Perhaps you'd try?

So, Young Puppy, I have nobody to wake up each morning, nobody to "conceal" myself from, nor "to bristle" at—as somebody once, very accurately, described my bad moods. I'm by myself, it makes me sick, and I remember our walks by the Isar when we debated, excuse me, you talked and I, as usual, listened. You probably now regard that time, oh assistant professor or lecturer, as wasted time, I benefited a great deal from it. Merci, mon vieux. Despite your good advice, I haven't completely stopped dabbling in verse, but since I haven't produced anything interesting, I'm not sending anything; when I do produce, I'll send. It's true that I haven't given you here a little verse from Paris dedicated to you. When you're with my folks, ask for it.

They tell me that you twice found no one home. I'm very sorry, but would ask you to stop by again, because now I'm concerned, and haven't written to them for a long time. And leave your address.

Your announced reportage didn't reach us. I know that you have a bit less time than you did here, but keep in touch from time to time. Write what you are doing, writing, reading, learning, etc. I'm not being polite, I'm truly interested. My sincere regards to your parents and brother, give my regards, too, to all your friends whom I know from your stories, and don't let them be forgotten in your letters.

All the best, dear Tadeusz,
Krystyn

I enclose correspondence to you (I'm not sending back the letters from Poland) and a few photos. Write what I should do with your passport.

20. SEPTEMBER 10, 1946, ZAKOPANE

Sender: Stanisław Marczak-Oborski, 14 Sobieski St., Apt. 13, Kraków
Loyal Citizen Tadeusz Borowski, Polish Writer

Tadek,

Why, you silly monkey, haven't you written to me? I would very much like to know what you are doing, how things are going, and whether you are writing that monumental prose? And what is the gang—bunch—set—the whole lot of them doing? Edmund? Andrzej? Ewa? The Silly Goose? Kiss the last for me very tenderly, and with the appropriate passion.

In Zakopane—a wonderful conference. Zosia Świdwińska, Stefan Świerzewski, Krzyżanower, and Doroszenko are here at present. We've already collectively decided that as soon as we've burned the candle at both ends, we'll start classes.

And either tomorrow or the day after, I'm leaving here. Going to Kraków where I'll stay for 4 or 5 days, and then, Tadek, will rest in your broad, Warsaw arms. I'm sure that you will be waiting for me with a bunch of flowers and a bottle of mad cow's milk. Dixi.

Just so you don't have too quiet a life, I'm burdening you with a certain matter. Go to the bursar's (the cashier's) at the university and take the 600 zł. owed

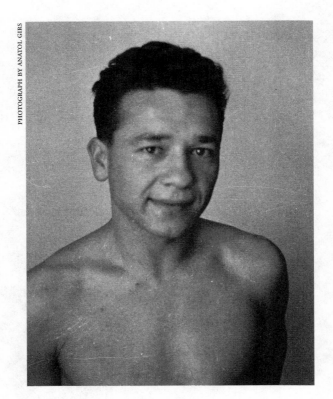

Tadeusz Borowski in his "post-Hitlerite" apartment in Munich, 1946.

Maria Rundo in Lund, Sweden, 1946. Ill and weak, she wrote to her uncle: "Some kind of evil forces are conspiring to destroy me."

Maria Rundo, probably in Warsaw either before or during the war. Borowski called her "full of courage and strength."

Tadeusz and Maria Borowski on a visit to Quedlinburg, Germany, in 1949, accompanied by a translator.

Janusz Nel Siedlecki, an engineer, in Munich, 1946. According to Borowski, he was "very well versed in the world."

Krystyn Olszewski, an (as yet) "unbuilt architect," in Munich, 1946. At the suggestion of Anatol Girs, he and Nel Siedlecki were the coauthors, with Borowski, of We Were in Auschwitz.

The publisher Anatol Girs, whom Borowski described as "an interesting character, like a hero out of Chesterton," in Munich, 1946.

The cover of We Were in Auschwitz, *designed by Anatol Girs, wore prison stripes, and some copies were actually bound in fabric cut from concentration-camp uniforms.*

The title page of We Were in Auschwitz *lists the authors by their camp numbers.*

The cover of Girs's personal copy of Borowski's Imiona nurtu (The Names of the Current), *which Girs published in Munich in 1945.*

This stamp was designed and printed by Girs in postwar Munich for mailings between displaced-persons camps. The American flag flies above the Polish eagle; the letter Z on the eagle is the initial of Girs's wife, Zinaida, for whom he was searching.

A sheet of such stamps from Dachau-Allach. Their appeal to German philatelists was such that Girs, who retained no money from their sale, was able to contribute large sums to the Red Cross. Borowski notes, "Four tons of medicines (a thousand ampoules of penicillin among them) were sent to Poland."

Tadeusz Borowski in Munich, 1946: "It's hard for me to live."

me for assistantship lunches for August. I fear that when I come to Warsaw after the 15th, the cashier's may already be closed and I could lose it, and every little bit counts. What else? Only hugs and hugs.

Your Staszek

Authorization

I authorize comrade Tadeusz Borowski to receive the compensation for my assistantship lunches for the month of August of the current year.

Stanisław Marczak-Oborski

Junior Assistant at Warsaw University

September 10, 1946

21. SEPTEMBER 12, 1946, WROCLAW

Tadeusz Mikulski, the University

Mr. Tadeusz Borowski, 5/7 Rozbrat St., Apt. 13, Warsaw

Dear Mr. Borowski,

Your book and the dedication gave me great joy. I thank you most sincerely for remembering me. Your words on the title page about those funny and heroic times together brought the year 1940 clearly back to mind. About the poems, I will say—if you will allow me—that some of your pages are on the same level as the beautiful graphic work of the volume, and that, surely, means a lot.[30] We sampled your prose here with great relish.

We hope that, thanks to Miss Wanda Leopold,[31] we will also be seeing you in Wrocław very soon. We would like to book a long conversation with you at that time.

For now, please accept my expression of true joy that you have returned, and are in such good form.

T. Mikulski

22. SEPTEMBER 24, 1946, MUNICH

[*from A. Girs*]

Dear Pan Tadeusz,

I have so far received barely a single letter from you, not a lot given your promise to write often. I'm very pleased that you're happy that you went back, and with the work that you received. That is most important, because if work isn't also pleasure, then it's hard to talk about being creative. The typewriter bought with your first author's honorarium is a clear indication that literary work today pays more than it did before. I received a letter from Tuśka, a very sad, not to say desperate, one. It inspired me to write you a letter that same day. You've probably already got it. Krystyn received your letter a few days ago. I'm very pleased that your strictly personal matters will probably work out well. Please remember that love, if it is true Love, will conquer over all.

I hope that, as you think, your feelings are real. If so, they are worth something and will triumph over everything, if, however, they just seem that way then there is nothing to regret, better to wait. Right? Janusz is now with his friends, I received a letter from him yesterday. He sees Ann often, and was accepted at the polytechnic and in three years will be a mechanical engineer with a London diploma. Workshop experience, together with his interests, will make a good professional out of him. He'll undoubtedly quickly fall in love, because there are a lot of females there, and, with his abilities in that direction, one needn't be a prophet to foresee this. Krystyn is studying architecture voraciously, I don't see him too often. I don't know what to write about myself. I think that I'm very tired emotionally, and I've become very bored with everything. "Auschwitz" is finished. I'm giving it a great deal of publicity, however, I'm meeting up with tremendous problems with transporting it. I don't even know how I'm going to solve them. Our affairs are like Pan Twardowski's[32] ladyship's: for the fourth month we're hanging "on the moon." It's a bit unpleasant. Krystyn has thrown out the idea of arranging the matter of publishing "Auschwitz" in Poland with Tadeusz L. I'm writing him a letter about this.

I think this wouldn't be bad, and would bring you some funds. It certainly wouldn't hurt you, and I think we could earn quite a lot. Maybe you could arrange something with him—if you wish to, naturally. I will have to see him. I think he'd get papers without difficulty and could come here. Do you know him, because he's actually an acquaintance of Janusz and Krystyn? I'd like you to also benefit from this. Juliusz translated one chapter into the English language.

Only to have some sense of it, naturally. It has aroused a lot of interest. Władek Stankiewicz's book has come out well. I forgot to write you that I have a copy of *Imiona nurtu* for you covered in leather. It's truly lovely. If I get some opportunity, I'll send it to you together with a copy of "Auschwitz."

So, what else to tell you? You know, I'd be most pleased if you'd write a short farewell poem for Mr. Anatol's funeral, I'm so sick of life. And meanwhile, dammit, I'm dragging on. What can one do? There's no remedy. I was recently driving from Frankfurt and the engine fell to pieces, but only after I'd arrived when they were taking the car to the garage. Had it only happened a little sooner, on the road . . . unbelievable luck, goddammit. Juliusz even suggested offering up a Mass in thanksgiving. Now I've got a new engine and a severe injunction: drive politely. I'm not allowed, either, to sit at the driving wheel on the autobahn. My love of sports has got it in the head. And even the drivers are scared. I await your promised letters,

Sincerely,

Tolek

23. OCTOBER 2, 1946 [WARSAW]

[to Wanda Leopold, Wrocław; the text is torn, unsigned, handed personally to the addressee]

My dear, beloved Wanda,

I'm turning red even though the paper is yellow. I should have replied, oh, such a long time ago! But, Wanda, you know! When there are conferences, two editorial offices that have to be run around, a sick brother, and a troubled mother, and my eternal absent-mindedness, then it is not so much hard to write a letter, as it is simply to mail it. The previous one got crushed in my pocket; yes, I'm reconstructing it afresh—like Borowy did Norwid's "Vade-Mecum"[33]—and this is the result: Listen, Wanda, I think that when I come to Wrocław (and this is supposed to be soon, on some literary Thursday), and read some little story there, I think that we'll be able to talk to our heart's content and then, dear God, I would like to thank you for the faith that you have in me. Because, you see, we all have our individual struggles and it often seems that it would be good to leave the field of battle before one compromises oneself in some way. But then it later turns out that one can do otherwise: not give in to compromise and—live. Sometimes, one looks at oneself in amazement, or, with distaste: So, this is how

it is? So this is what's called love, and this despair, and that—loneliness? And then the one passes, the other fades, and so one lives, from day to day. But you know, later, when one looks at one's life, one sees meaning, and continuity, and lasting value in it. I thought more than once that it was Satan's (that was when I was reading St. Augustine)[34] gift to man that man was able to assess the value of his actions only after he'd performed them. I might see this differently today. But basically fragments of life, people and events, fall from us like leaves off a tree, and new people, new events come along until we will pass, become a leaf, an event to others.

Our loneliness! Meditations over a book, on the street, under an evening lamp!

24. OCTOBER 16, 1946, ZAKOPANE
[*from S. Marczak-Oborski, express mail*]

Citizen Tadeusz Borowski, 23 Bednarska St., Apt. 30, Warsaw

Tadeusz,

I've just this minute received a short, overly terse, letter from you. To say that I went ballistic would be to put it far too mildly. So! What position have you left me in? What's going to happen with that unfortunate issue that has cost me so much effort, money, and God knows what all? We finally assembled about 20 coworkers, put the whole of *Kuźnica* on its feet. And now what? Think, buddy. Soberly. Write immediately what it is you're imagining, what did Żółkiewski write back to you? And in general. Ugh. My hand is shaking, and my goat's up to the point that it's stinking out the room. I'll probably have to air it.

Moreover, since you decided to write to me, you should have added a couple of sentences. What's new? What are you doing? How are our buddies?

And why did you not, you asshole, scumbag, cretin, creep, write all this? Are you no longer capable of a few sensible sentences? Do as you like, but you have to see to this somehow. In any event, communicate with me immediately. I'm sitting here in this Zakopane cut off from the world, and I don't even know what's actually stirring in the bushes.

And so, dear Tadeusz, write in order:
1) What's with *Kuźnica*?—possibilities, perspectives, horizons, point of entry and exit.

2) What's with "Płomienie"? Tell them to send me their prospectus and first issue, if it appears.

3) What's with the notorious "Klub Młodych Literatów" (Young Literati's Club)?

4) What's with *Pokolenie*? Have you decided whether or not to give them "Pamflet"? Tell them to send me Bratny's and Zalewski's books.

5) What's with you? Are you in the doldrums, are you overworked? What are you writing? How's your metaphysical state?

6) Give me our young chickies' address, which house on Górnośłąska, what room number? How's Ewa's health, what's with Silly Goose?

7) General gossip.

So Tadek: objectively, calmly, with dignity, as the Lord God commanded. And most important—immediately.

Hang in there, old man. I suspect you're suffering from some kind of mental diarrhea. Take comfort in the fact that it's damn miserable for me here as well.

Sincerely,

Your Staszek

25. OCTOBER 18, 1946, LUND

[*Maria Rundo to Mieczysław Grydzewski*]

Dear Mietek,

I leave for Poland on November 11. You are probably taken aback at my decision. Especially after what I wrote in my last letter. All talk of going to Ireland stopped. There were stipends to Spain, but only for devout Catholics, so I was turned down. I do not attend the local church on principle, so I don't enjoy a good reputation with the priest who has influence in these matters, on top of that I'm of Jewish descent, which absolutely compromises me. Conditions in the Polish community in Lund don't much concern me, that's not why I am leaving.

I'm leaving because I am fully aware that there's no chance of the situation changing. I'm terribly exhausted physically, and I know that I'll get sick if I carry on working like this for another few weeks. I dream of having a rest, just that. Tadeusz has promised me that I can rest for as long as I like. I'm not thinking further ahead. I'm convinced that, despite everything, I'll be able to get out of Poland more easily than Sweden. They've promised Tadeusz a stipend to Paris for next year, if he finishes his master's this winter. It looks as though he will. Of

course, if he gets a visa, I will as well. I plan to get a degree in Polish. Three years of wartime studies will count toward it. The same professors are still lecturing. If material conditions allow for further studies, I'll sign up for romance philology. A volume of Tadeusz's stories is coming out in winter, which will help with our studies.

I'll write to you from Poland through Sweden. A Swedish acquaintance of mine is working in a social organization in the Gdynia and Gdańsk area, and I'll easily be able to send letters through her. I plan to join that same organization in Warsaw as soon as I'm physically back in shape.

I've capitulated and feel very resigned, but, at the same time, I am inwardly calmer. I feel a certain fear at the thought of meeting Mother and Baśka. I've distanced myself from them a great deal, and I'm afraid that they'll notice. I'm totally ashamed that I'm coming back so horribly shattered and not bringing anything with me.

This return is very humiliating for me. I know this myself.

Sincerely,

Tuśka

26. OCTOBER 18, 1946, ŁÓDŹ
[*from S. Żółkiewski*]

Dear Sir,

What about the article for the young people's issue? Since it is not here as of today, I am delaying printing the issue by a week. But it absolutely must be here by 10/25, because otherwise there'll be another delay and since I have in view a piece of at least three installments that I've been putting off for a month because of you, your issue can go either on October 25, or not until the end of November.

I urgently request the manuscript.

Sincerely,

S. Żółkiewski

27. OCTOBER 23, 1946

[*to S. Marczak-Oborski*]

Dear Staszek,

As you probably suspect, I have not written the article for Żółkiewski. I'm sending a letter of apology to him. Otherwise everything's well with me.

Regards to your babes.

Sincerely,

Tadeusz

28. OCTOBER 24, 1946, ŁÓDŹ

[*from S. Żółkiewski*]

Dear Sir,

May you go rot! So what am I supposed to do? I'll bring out your issue, then, next week—without that article.

If you don't agree, let me know by 1st November.

I'll be in Warsaw 3–4/11. Get in touch with me. If you have time, come for the day to Łódź: we'll go for a vodka!

Send the promised reviews. I would very much like you to keep writing reviews for *Kuźnica*.

Sincerely,

Stefan Żółkiewski

29. OCTOBER 27, 1946, ZAKOPANE

[*telegram from S. Marczak-Oborski; sent 11:00 A.M., received 1:02 P.M.*]

Borowski Bednarska 23, Apt. 30, Warsaw

TO LOVE'S ARRIVAL, FAME, VODKA—STASZEK

30. NOVEMBER 1, 1946

[*from S. Żółkiewski*]

My Dears,

I was waiting for your article. Your refusal resulted in my having to decide to write the necessary introduction to the young people's issue myself. By chance, I suddenly have to go away for a few days. I learned about this precisely two days before starting to write. I wanted to have it ready for the 3rd–4th November. As a result, I have to put aside printing your issue until my return. Or, perhaps, longer. Having launched on Saturday Hertz's stories in three installments, I cannot interrupt them with the young people's issue. So your issue will not be able to run for another three weeks. It would be great if by then you were able to write that article. Your issue will definitely run in three weeks.

What's new? What about the reviews? You are a sluggard.

Sincerely,

Stefan Żółkiewski

31. NOVEMBER 20, 1946, WARSAW

[*telegram; sent 1:20 P.M., received 5:45 P.M.*]

Stanisław Marczak, Hrabina, Road to Biały, Zakopane

ESSENTIALIST GREETINGS STOP KEEP WELL STOP TUSKA TADEUSZ

32. NOVEMBER 23, 1946, MUNICH

[*from A. Girs*]

Dear Pan Tadeusz,

The promised letters aren't arriving. You were going to write often, in the meantime, apart from the one letter I received from you, nothing—a resounding silence. I, not knowing at all how to write letters, have written you three. This disturbs and worries me. I want to sell a few books to Poland in order to be able to send you bit of cash. Do not forget your old friends, and that is, perhaps, how you regarded us? Greetings from the author of the foreword to *Imiona nurtu*. He wrote that he knows nothing of you. I've had only one letter from Tuśka. I wrote

154

to her several more times, but received no answer. The mail here is erratic. I find my letters across the whole of Germany. Please at least write a few words.

Sincerely,

Anatol

33. NOVEMBER 23, 1946, ŁÓDŹ
[*from S. Żółkiewski*]

Dear Sir,

I returned today from three weeks in Moscow. Your review will run. If you want to submit an article for the youth issue, I must have it in Łódź by 12/3 at the latest. I would very much like it.

Please write a review of the books I mentioned. Perhaps you could write (but I would prefer positively) about Żukrowski (*Tiutiurlistan!*).

Sincerely,

Stefan Żółkiewski

34. DECEMBER 1, 1946, WARSAW
[*to S. Marczak-Oborski*]

Sender: T. Borowski, Polish Literary History Department, 36/38 Krakowskie Przedmiescie, Warsaw

Dear Staszek,

Forgive me, brother, for not lifting a finger for so long, but, see, it's been up and down: first, mental diarrhea (going on to this day!), second, Tuśka (she's finally arrived!), and third, I'm sick. Flu. On top of that I don't want to write anything, anywhere. The Commander-in-Chief after returning from Moscow (he's back, he was there for three weeks!) wants to write the article himself—May Terpsychora watch over him! I write a few reviews for them, I don't know when I'll do anything. I was 1) in Wrocław at a literary evening, read "Bitwa" [pod Grundwaldem] and drank for four days with T. Mikulski and others. Wanda Leopold is fine, but feels a bit despondent on the obvious subject. Something'll turn up, my seventh sense (the erotic one) tells me. 2) I was in Gdynia, Gdańsk,

Wrzeszcz, Olsztyn, and Łódź. This peregrination connected with Tuśka who kept thinking that NKVD agents were following her. She's calmed down a little, but not much.

3) I nearly beat the Bojarskis (seniors) up, because they're creating rows over Tuśka. She can't live here! (not married, dammit!) As a result, having thrown them out of the room, I'm moving myself. The rows were hellish. As a result of Mr. B.'s never having lived according to Christian–Bourgeois ethics.

4) I'm floating "Pamflet" ["Lampoon"] in *Pokolenie*.[35] May it go! There's such a Treuga Dei in polemics that it won't hurt to heat things up a little. To please Kuźnica, I promised the Commander-in-Chief to butcher "Ślad" and "Bohaterów" in my review—"balance of power"[36]—as the English say.

5. Has your hand stopped shaking in rage? If so, reply.

Regards to you, and your better half,

Tadeusz Bor.

35. DECEMBER 4, 1946, ŁÓDŹ
[*from S. Żółkiewski*]

I'm running your excellent review in the current youth issue[37] because I want to give it intellectual balls. But I would like to have your review for the normal issues immediately, if possible. So, please—send it to me. Perhaps you could come down, and hard, on Jan Wiktor's damned twaddle, *Skrzydlaty mnich* [*Winged Friar*]. I am also anxious to have a sensible evaluation of past literary works, e.g., *Wiatr od morza* [*Wind from the Sea*].[38] Or, perhaps, you'd try Comrade Suchodolski and his book on democracy: selection, who was chosen, what's written about whom?

On top of that, I'd very gladly see some of your new prose, especially about this independent, peoples', sovereign reality.

Sincerely,

Stefan Żółkiewski

Since your issue is running this week, talk to little Ewa and Marczak about new material. It's worth doing such things periodically.[39]

36. DECEMBER 6, 1946, ŁÓDŹ

[*from S. Żółkiewski*]

Dear Sir,

I'll be in Warsaw on the 11th of December and will stay a day or two. Send me word at the Sejm Hotel when we could see each other. The evening of the 11th at the Gruszczyńskis perhaps? Talk it over.

Sincerely,

S. Żółkiewski

37. UNDATED

[*from W. Żukrowski; probably hand-delivered, address on the reverse of the notepaper*]

To Comrade Tadeusz Borowski (former prisoner of Auschwitz, connoisseur of Plautus)[40]

Listen Borowski! Enraptured by the penetrating gaze and remarkable courage with which you dealt with the kindly, but defenseless, Dobraczyński (Bolcio hasn't yet got a fighting squad),[41] I suggest, and expect, an equally vehement review of Brandys's oily prose. If you are able to break out of that tight solidarity, to which even Żółkiewski succumbs (on the commander-in-chief model, he loses his head more often), I will have respect and a few observations, useful ones, for you; as payment in advance: glancing penetratingly through clothing, or, rather, a uniform buttoned all the way up, the Author of "Bitwa pod Grunwaldem" notices —a goat on the ensign's breast. A trifle, but amusing. I'm not getting at you. I impatiently await the next installment on the buxom quarter-Jewess. I truly do like the story. But I would still like you to pay close attention to the remains of the smug bourgeoisie gathered under the red flag in the area of the Łódź Olympus. Objectively, other than Rudnicki, the Left does not have a writer, apart from you, of course. Rudnicki is also a golden mean. I regret that we didn't meet, it's easier to talk than write, especially with a fever and after cupping-glasses.

A certain chaos, as a result, but I wish you a fine book, perhaps we'll still rub shoulders, because I promise a review no less vicious than yours of D., who really is weak, but not as much so as that whipper-snapper Brandys.

Sincerely,

Wojtek

38. DECEMBER 17, 1946, WROCŁAW

[*from T. Mikulski*]

Dear Tadeusz Borowski,

We reminisced at length, and very affectionately, about your scandalous stay in Wrocław.[42]

I'm taking the opportunity of Wanda Leopold's trip to Warsaw to send you a few words at the same time. Our *Zeszyty Wrocławskie*[43] are shortly (before Christmas) to appear in print. We are putting together the next issue less hastily than heretofore. Mrs. Kowalska remembers, and reminds us of, your promise to provide some fiction material for the second issue. In her, and my own, name I wish to remind you of this promise, and strongly request some manuscript for Wrocław as proof that you wanted to wind through our Thursdays and community. The deadline would, unfortunately, be soon, because the printers are unbelievably slow and we start issue 2 right after New Year. Please don't turn us down, but knuckle under, if the thing still requires it. As far as I know, you were cooking something up for us back in October. So, we anticipate no difficulties, just beautiful prose! Best wishes from my wife[44] and me. I kiss your wife's hand.

T. Mikulski

39. JANUARY 3, 1947, WARSAW

[*to T. Mikulski, the university, Wrocław*]

Dear Professor,

Please accept our* sincere, though somewhat belated, New Year's greetings, and I am taking the opportunity of enclosing my equally somewhat belated story for *Zeszyty Wrocławskie*. The story is written somewhat like Hemingway. Its shortcoming is its camp theme.[45]

I am very proud of the stay by the Oder, and am dreaming deep down about a spring voyage to Wrocław; at the moment, I'm preparing a volume of stories and getting ready for exams of which I have so very many!

My best wishes to you both and to the institute.

Tadeusz and Tuśka Borowski

* That is, Tuśka and me!

40. JANUARY 3, 1947, WARSAW

[to W. Leopold]

Dear Wandeczka,

Having moved to Apt. 37, 73 Filtrowa Street on New Year's Eve, I've been arranging our junk in the apartment for the whole of New Year; as of today, however, I'm sitting in college and writing letters. I'm sending a short story to Zeszyty, perhaps it will prove suitable, if it's no good I won't be offended if you return it. I'm also enclosing a letter for Pan Wojtek, hand it to him with a most beautiful smile.

I expect you had a good time during the holidays and got more than a little drunk, so written greetings aren't necessary. In any event, look after yourself and teach because the Golden Age—of conspiracy—is over.[46]

I enclose warm greetings to Wanda Leopold.

Kiss her for me,

Tadeusz Borowski

41. POSTMARKED JANUARY 8, 1947

Sender: Zbigniew Wojciech Żukrowski, 16 Harcerska Street, Oporów Wrocław
Tadeusz Borowski, Esq.
College of the History of Polish Literature, 26/28 Krakowskie Przedmiescie, Warsaw

Dear Colleague,

I share your view of Brandys and will play around with it a little. Also, I read your story "Chłopiec z Biblią" ["The Boy with a Bible"]. I think Wanda will edit it and make certain necessary revisions, which I loyally suggested to her: 1) on the first page, point out that the author is sitting in the cell and speaking like a ghost from the straw mattress; 2) get rid of the five-fold repetition of characterizations, which are supposed to bring the speakers into relief, you are not writing for idiots, a three-fold repetition should suffice, one remembers the last names. These are purely formal remarks whose soundness and need you perceive, yes? Another issue, why was this picture written? Is it, as I thought to myself, youthful coquetry in the face of death? A young Jew, captured for his Jewishness, goes off to be killed, in the eyes of the inmates the Bible saves the

Aryans, a "crime"—writing on the wall aggrandizes them, a mournful game, elevator shoes not removed even for a moment before death. Is that right?[47] I warn you that clearly this isn't in the text, it's I, rather than you, who is suggesting it. If the "idea" was different, then it didn't "come across." If there was none, it's a pity, because the above one plays with the surface of the picture. The dialogue is lively and good as always.

The burlesques I've written have the title "Piórkiem flaminga" ["With a Flamingo's Feather"], serving to make vomiting or contortions easier. If I manage to publish them, *Tygodnik Powszechny* turned them down in revulsion, I will lose the esteemed name of Catholic writer, which deep down, in fact, I am, even though I write in such a way as to lead my readers on, that is, I deliberately write ambiguously to guard against busybodies. Borowski, don't be overly humble, you know you have claws, and I'm not impressed by a master's degree, I could care less, because I've seen so many cretins with doctorates . . . We have one trait in common, other than our gender, of course, and that's laziness, which I value very highly, so we can go for a vodka.

Until we meet, sincerely,

Wojtek

42. JANUARY 15, 1946, WROCŁAW
[*from T. Mikulski*]

Mr. Tadeusz Borowski

Seminarium Polonistyczne, 26 Krakówskie Przedmiescie, Warsaw

Dear Tadeusz,

In chronological order I'm thanking you both, first for the nice holiday greeting, arriving by telegram from Olsztyn, then for the letter written "in normal prose," and the manuscript copy "Chłopiec z Biblią." We read the text here with satisfaction/pleasure, however, it doesn't rival "Grunwald." Your manuscript is currently in Mr. and Mrs. Kowalski's hands and a place is being reserved for it in the second *Zeszyty Wrocławskie.*

I unexpectedly dropped by Warsaw for a day, but didn't manage to track you down because it was still vacation time. But I heard that you had had some problems with accommodations, but apparently recently resolved. In any event, I'm availing myself of the old college address, regarding it as safer.

Prof. Krzyżanowski undoubtedly showed you the first issue of our quarterly. The second issue is supposed to be "better," a showpiece. We start printing in February.

On the threshold of the New Year of which two weeks have gone by, I send you both my warmest wishes for all things good and—the fastest possible meeting in Wrocław.

Sincerest greetings to you both,

T. Mikulski

43. JANUARY 18, 1947, ŁÓDŹ
[*from S. Żółkiewski*]

Dear Sir!

The royal creaming you got from all of the Catholic press for Dobraczyński is proof positive that it was on target, that your review was excellent, that it toppled that mainstay of "Catholic" scribbling. I believe that the only response to these attacks on you can be just one thing: further consistent obliteration of Catholic scribblers. I'm asking, therefore, for a review for *Kuźnica*. Something strong. Perhaps, for example, of Wiktor's *Skrzydlaty mnich*—it's fit to be eaten, and flushed down with water. You can also kill off Malewska, if you, as a newly married man, should wish to concern yourself with that broad. Please write me back what, and when, you will deliver. Quickly would be best. While they're still livid.

Żuławski will be approaching you on behalf of the General Committee of the ZZLP.[48] He'll offer you a stipend (100 thousand) to write a novel. You should agree, take it, write, and publish in a year. I strongly suggest it—strongly.

Sincerely,

Stefan Żółkiewski

44. JANUARY 22, 1947, WARSAW
[*to his brother*]

Dear Julek,

It's taken me rather a long time to reply to your letter and I'm afraid you are angry. But you know how it is at home: all day one goes here, there, and everywhere, and then is so tired that one doesn't want to do anything but sleep.

There was very tense pre-election action here, with rallies, resolutions, putting together letters, etc. In which connection I was supposed to hold rallies at the Electric Plant and the Ministry of Information and Propaganda, but politely got out of it on the basis of a sore throat, to the sorrow of Comrade Morawski.[49] It didn't however, spoil our relationship. The act of nation building itself passed peacefully and with dignity here, those who should get a mandate, got it. *Pokolenie,* which has been moving along like a fly through treacle for the past two months, and is planning to come into being any day (I gave them a review of Kossak's book about the camps),[50] has cost over a million to date, not counting the cash for storing the supplies at the printers (around two hundred thousand). I reckoned that for that money one could set up several nice libraries for students—and to greater effect. Since this journal, however, is a point of honor for several people, ergo, it has to come out, even if it cost another ten times as much. Let him have it! Comrade Żółkiewski is supposed, so it is rumored, to become Minister of Education—he or Skrzeszewski—or else Minister for Culture and the Arts. Oh, Christ! That'll be a shindig, since he's a good editor and journalist, but surely not an administrator, and with his attitude to universities we can expect wonders.

As you know from Mom, I've moved, for now, with my wife (!) and bedding to Apt. 37, 73 Filtrowa Street (to Col. Mankiewicz),[51] we've unpacked, tidied up the windows and floors (at night, obviously, since we're not home all day), put up a bookshelf (a very nice one), and made quite a pleasant, livable apartment. Tuśka is working at the Rada Szkół Wyższych [Secondary School Council], where Staszek Marczak's brother-in-law, Dr. Wieczorkiewicz, is—the work is neither absorbing nor hard, but is good for her frame of mind. I, as usual, am at the university, sitting over Orzeszkowa's[52] letters, which we will publish in time, but, for now, they have to be straightened out, I go to lectures and am reading for the Shakespeare exam, work for *Swiat Młodych* and *Pokolenie.* For the past few weeks, I've been writing a story, but it's not working out, maybe, however, something will come of it. And that's all. Write how things are in Olsztyn and what books you'd like to get from Warsaw. I don't want to buy blind, but I plan to send you something.

Love to you and the parents,
Tadeusz

45. JANUARY 29, 1947, MUNICH

A. Girs, UNRRA HQ US Zone, APO 757 US Army
Mr. T. Borowski, Apt. 3, 73 Filtrowa St., Warsaw

Dear Pan Tadeusz,

I received your letter of the 1st of January. I knew that lack of time, work, or other reasons prevented you from writing, and not for a second did such an ugly word "being angry" go through my mind. My affections do not depend on the number of letters. And you know how much I like you and Tuśka. Allow me to repeat the wishes for everything good, which I sent you mentally on learning about your marriage. I think she's going to be your good angel (angels are good thoughts, and not beings with wings), and help you on your life's, and literary, road. I sent you the Auschwitz books (a few packages). I don't know whether they arrived. I'd gladly send as many as you wish, but am not sure how. Because all kinds of mailings get lost. I will try to get some books for you. I'll also try to send books somehow. I'll probably shortly be leaving here. Far. I'll send you my new address when I do. I very much value your friendship, and thoughts, and always reciprocate them. Many good thoughts, and faith in your high, good ideals, and happiness in life,

from,
Anatol

46. FEBRUARY 20, 1947, MUNICH

[*from A. Girs; on decorative paper*]

To dear Tadeusz and Tuśka Borowski with all best wishes for their married life.
Anatol

47. MARCH 5, 1947, KRAKÓW

[*Kazimierz Wyka, on* Twórczość *letterhead*]

Apt. 8, 15 Basztowa Street
Mr. Tadeusz Borowski, Apt. 37, 73 Filtrowa St., Warsaw

Dear Sir,

I am approaching you to propose a more permanent than hitherto collaboration with *Twórczość*. The whole phrase "more permanent" is strongly euphemistic, since I have hosted you in our monthly only once, and as a prose writer. Nonetheless, I regard the fact that your post-Conspiracy debut was made in *Twórczość* as one of the successes of the journal. At present, I rather have in mind your critical works. Not because I don't follow your prose with pleasure and attention, but because the journal I edit devotes increasingly less space to original creative work. I am of the opinion that because normal publishers exist, books come out, it's their responsibility to provide original material, and mine—to pore over that material. When it comes to works of criticism, I should stress that my procedure is always to leave the choice of books to those doing the writing, to request I be informed about the choice, and then if I haven't already assigned the book to someone else, the matter is settled. I ask you to make a similar choice. The normal order of response differs only in the fact that I first await a reply from you as to whether this proposed collaboration interests you in principle, and depending on that decision, I await the remaining response. In order to avoid unnecessary resistance on your part, I should add that I am writing this letter after familiarizing myself with your conversation with Marczak-Oborski published in *Pokolenie*. I reserve my position on this matter for another occasion, but that is my business as critic, to you, on the other hand, I am writing as editor. The editor of *Twórczość* would also like to inquire whether you have a desire to take part in a questionnaire about the twenty years of independence? I haven't thus far sent you an official invitation, but this can stand in its place.

Awaiting your reply, sincerely,
Kazimierz Wyka

48. POSTMARKED MARCH 15, 1947, WROCŁAW

[*from W. Żukrowski, next to the sender's address a note:*] Better to write to Wanda's address, the institute. Gets there more quickly.

Dear Colleague,

It will come as a surprise to you that I'm writing again, but you are not giving me any peace. I am not "someone" from the "Oder" although in this case I thought likewise. But that's not the point, because even [the expression] "atavistic" prose, I regard as a compliment (just that arrangement with Bratny, but if it raises his spirits, so be it). I wrote about you to Jarosław [Iwaszkiewicz] telling him to give you some column to edit, so don't be surprised if he makes such a proposition (but maybe not). That was the first thing, because I think in your case independence is of greatest importance, and it's supposed to be that kind of journal. You worry me, as, for that matter, does the rest of *Pokolenie*. Those worries which make your blood run cold, I've plastered over, the resonance from your outbursts causes my ceilings to crack, amuses me a little, because it speaks of your youth, and angers me a little. The implication of your dialogue with Marczak is vague, chaotic, ruffling everyone. A lot of truth, and a lot of chaff—thrown in as a joke. One thing is correct, neither Iwaszkiewicz, nor Andrzejewski, nor Breza, Dygat, Miłosz, nor even Rudnicki, writing about the Uprising, as Brandys also did, lived through the occupation with "the nation." I think about you all with the same attention as I do about myself, in this case you have measure of my honesty, you all lived through the occupation to the end. That's why you cannot write about it without going apoplectic. About camp and prison, someone who has been there a week will not write better than someone who was crushed for years, the loss of freshness, the commonplaceness of the mortuary, the gaze of the professional, to a certain degree you are professionals of conspiracy and the whole patriotic butchery. That gets in your way. Dammit, man, I like you more and more, though you are treading a line heading straight to fascism. Do I need to prove it? I'm glad you've said you will come in spring, at Easter, perhaps? I would truly like to have an argument with you, perhaps I could be useful in some way? On my ground floor, a room with an unembarrassing bathroom at your disposal. I live on the first floor, so this would give me the opportunity to have the definitive upper hand in the projected discussions. If I'm in Warsaw before that, where could I find you? I may come to the retreat at *Dziś i Jutro*. Although you will assume a derisive pose in self-defense, I think the gears are grinding and the steering wheel is off. I continue to fill in the chinks,

and when they crack say: voila! the map of future conquests—if the whole thing doesn't come down on my head. I'm writing all this because certain surprises are in the offing, a foretaste of which you'll soon have. No, no, it's not about you, but me. I'm also going to find myself at odds with everyone who's pushing me around now, because . . . a lot to explain, above all, they bore me.

I'm pleased at the thought of our meeting, though I'm not promising myself a lot, we're different. But it would be good for you to know that in the place you expect to find enemies, there are also the well-disposed.

Sincerely,

Wojtek Żukrowski

P.S.   You were mean to Ożóg[53] by placing him next to a hack, he is, in fact, a poet, you hurt him more than you can know. He's a poor, beleaguered teacher in Radom, self-taught, in unusually hard circumstances, simplicity needs to be distinguished from coarseness and dissonance. In your column, there's more gibberish.

W.Z.

Trampling on insects is a sign of sadism even in literature!

49. MARCH 28, 1947, ŁÓDŹ

[*from S. Żółkiewski*]

Dear Sir,

I'm off to see alligators. The prose will come out—Brandys just wants to work some things out with you.

I'm not offended by any jokes. *Pokolenie* is getting increasingly better. The issue in which you write about Zalewski[54] is simply excellent. If *Nowiny* doesn't improve, you'll be the best journal in Warsaw.

Sincerely,

Stefan Żółkiewski

50. APRIL 1, 1947, WARSAW

[*piece of paper from S. Marczak-Oborski*]

Weird Citizen Tadeusz Borowski, hand-delivered

Tadek,

I'm getting over emphysema and am not in the office (which you can see in the picture). In keeping with our agreement, however, I'm sending you the type-script of your short story[55]—it gains a lot on second reading. I'm also enclosing the manuscript of the review. Tell the publishers to include a picture, it's well worth advertising this piece. If you've got money for me, leave it with charming citizen Nina Kinowska.

So, farewell, *Daragoi,*[56] kiss Tuśka for me, and happy holidays in the bosom of your family—when you get back, get in touch with me.

Yours,

Staszek

P.S.   My mother's here, on the Sunday after the holidays, Basia Bor[mann] and I are having a quiet wedding.

51. APRIL 2, 1947, KRAKÓW

[*from S. Wyka*]

Dear Sir,

I am very pleased at your agreeing to work with *Twórczość*. Naturally, as I expected from the beginning, most of your suggestions have already been taken, only Pytlakowski is available. Therefore, please start by writing about *Wielki cień*. [*The Great Shadow*][57] I am enclosing at the same time a review copy. I have already placed a review of *Medaliony* [*Medallions*] in the April issue, and have also submitted the poetry items.

I will also speak to Lichański, and maybe manage to extricate *Próg* for you. I do not see any interesting new items on the horizon. Please don't worry about my sticking you with Malewska, or Zawieyski, or even with the Boguszewski-Kornacki cycle. Please also remember about the twenty years of independence and also that *Twórczość* is always an outlet for your prose.

With sincere greetings,

Kazimierz Wyka

52. APRIL 28, 1947, ZAKOPANE

Sender Wilhelm Mach. "Lucylla." Parcele Urzędnicze
Mr. Tadeusz Borowski. Pokolenie. 8 Graźna St., Warsaw

Dear *Pokolenie* colleagues,

I am sending for your use my essay "woven against the background" of the
Kisielewski Case, which helped me formulate a certain critical concept in general.
In my piece, I discuss the unhealthy and harmful issue of critical factionalism
in evaluations of literature, in any case, you will notice this without additional
commentary, I began to write the piece at Easter and finished it today—in the
meantime, there were certain articles in the press about Kisielewski that, however, do not affect my basic arguments, and also clarify nothing when it comes
to the complaints I raise. For these reasons, despite the rather marked length of
the work, I request that you preserve it in its entirety without any cuts, or else
reject it and return it to me.

Sincere thanks for the issues of *Pokolenie* that you sent (most interesting and
pleasant) and also for other tokens of remembering me, I think in particular
of Comrade Bratny's letters, of good wishes conveyed to me—I remember all
this with gratitude. My poor health (still the same) and work on my own novel
prevent me from getting in touch with you as often and as I would like, but I
am powerless in the face of these obstacles. I assure you, however, of my "generational" solidarity, and I am happy you are there, writing, discussing, and editing.
The enclosed work connects me actively to your efforts.

Please send a couple of words in reply.

Sincere greetings to your honorable selves: colleagues Joanna, Bratny, Borowski,
Zalewski.

It is possible that at the end of May, I might drop by in Warsaw, I'd very much
like to meet (and get to know) you, so write whether I would find you in the
editorial offices, whether you are there every day, or where you meet.

If you see Mr. Staszek Marczak-Oborski give him my best regards.

Wilhelm Mach

53. JUNE 1, 1947, BREMEN
[*from A. Girs*]

Dear Tadeusz and Tuśka,

Your letter of 5/3 found me still in Europe. Actually at the gates of Europe. Every piece of news from you is a great joy to me. Thank you for your good wishes.

I am hopeful that your plans will work out. Difficulties, above our strength sometimes, are the fate of us all. Apparently they are necessary at this stage of our development. Mental *grajdolek* [depression] is always irritating, but is it always worth attacking? That I don't know. Perhaps it clears the air, but is it worth the price? I am very sorry that Tuśka is having problems with you, she does not deserve it after all the things she's been through. Fight off your depression. You are together and you probably don't well enough understand what great fortune that is. So where is there room for depression? How well you once wrote: "Perhaps I will meet you, and happiness, happiness is being sad together," and being sad together has nothing to do with depression.

I've sent the Auschwitz book to the States. Some got lost on the way, but some made it. I'm going to try make it known there. I think, however, that it would be worth bringing it out in Poland too. Do it together with Krystyn. I'll do everything possible to bring it about. The interest in it as a camp book is one thing, but it has other values, too, and these need to be brought out. It is a fight against fascist ideology. From this point of view, I maintain it is still relevant. If you would be willing to complete the projected trilogy by writing about the *auser kommandos* (I'm sure I've made a gaffe here),[58] I think it would be worth it. I'm thinking about the States. I've given *We Were in Auschwitz* to be translated, although everyone, including Janusz, thinks that book won't be a success. I hate it a lot when a plan doesn't work out for me. I cease to be interested in anything only when it succeeds. I also don't forget friends even if I don't hear from them for dozens of years. You know how much I like you. I'm hopeful that we will all work together again on some beautiful, good book that we like. I very much value my friendship with you and Tuśka, and am grateful for it. You can always count on me for whatever is within my power. Unfortunately, I don't anticipate having a moment's rest in the new world. On the contrary, just problems extremely difficult to surmount for someone in my situation. But we'll see.

Juliusz and Krystyna are staying in Munich for the time being. As is Pola. Our organization is being liquidated on the 15th of this month.[59] *Polonus* is

being finished. Unfortunately, it won't be totally done until after I've left. I'm reserving two hundred copies for myself. I'll send them to universities and acquaintances. Seven hundred copies I'm giving for the rebuilding of the National Library in Warsaw, and seven hundred for the rebuilding of the Gutenberg Society in Mainz. That's how I've planned it. I think it will sell well, and the cash used for the proper purpose. I think it should be able to sell for a thousand zloty. It's apparently the most beautiful book of its kind published after the war. I'm very curious what the critics will say about it. The German professionals are very favorable. Perhaps our native land will realize how good it is. You know, I don't require thanks, but about those books sent to Poland I've heard not a peep, not even a word that they received them. But never mind. It would, however, be nice to know that the books were finding themselves on the library shelves of a fine arts academy or architecture department. Wouldn't it be good for you to live somewhere outside Warsaw? A rest in the peace of the countryside would help you a lot. One can think quietly there, and words and thoughts acquire depth.

I would at some time like to create a quiet spot by a beautiful lake where my friends could rest or work by themselves or in company. Where there would always be a friendly smile and an understanding of others on everyone's face. Where art, music, literature, and philosophy would be at home. Utopia? Maybe it will work out. I've begun a series entitled "Nasi Współczesni" ["Our Contemporaries"]. It's an unusually difficult series and I don't know whether I'll be able to carry it out. I'm sending books for Professor Borów and also another man. I'm out of special editions now. I enclose many warm thoughts and lots of kisses for you and Tuśka,

your A.

54. JUNE 7, 1947, ŁÓDŹ

[*from S. Żółkiewski*]

Dear Sir,

I'm told that you have new prose (Pokój). I'd like it for *Kuźnica*. I'm also requesting a review of some kind—perhaps of one of the more important new books. Perhaps, in your own distinctive way, you could finish off that elephant Gołubiew.[60]

Sincerely,

Stefan Żółkiewski

55. JUNE 9, 1947, KRAKÓW

Sender: Wilhelm Mach, "Twórcość," Apt. 8, 15 Basztowa Street, Kraków

Respected Fellow Editor,

A month ago, I sent you, along with the issue, a critical article entitled "Na marginesie *Sprzysiężenia*"⁶¹ ["In the Margin of *Conspiracy*"], with the request for its speedy return in the event that you were not going to use it. The article was the only manuscript—I don't have a copy. I've had no word from you. I deduce from this that in a certain sense because of the long delay, the thing will, in part, not come to fruition; I ask, however, that you return it to me, I put too much work into it to lose the manuscript. Greetings to you and our colleagues,

Wilek Mach

56. JUNE 11, 1947, BREMEN

[*from A. Girs*]

Dear Pan Tadeusz and Tuśka,

Tomorrow, I leave Europe to which I am attached by no other feeling than grief. To all of you, on the other hand, my thoughts turn daily with warmth and friendship. I am hopeful that your wishes will be fulfilled. Perhaps, I, too, will still be able to do something good and interesting. Before leaving Munich, I wrote you a lengthy letter.

Now, certain thoughts have come to me about your plan to write a book about Dautmergen. I think it's a good project. But I would suggest that you still write something unconnected to the contemporary period. I even have a concrete proposal: something not too big—prose or poem—about Pan Twardowski. But not in the style of Mickiewicz. Something that would be very well suited for illustration. More or less 30–60 pages of typescript. Do you like this idea? If so, I'll give you others from the same series. I think on the whole that it would be worthwhile for you to write something completely different, from the world of fantasy and the olden days. Did you see Stępowski's *Legenda o masztowej sośnie* [*Legend of the Mast Pine*], which Barcz and I made? Do you know what happened to him? If you should see him, please give him my regards. Juliusz Panek will give 700 copies of *Polonus* on my behalf to the fund for the rebuilding of the National Library, I will also send you and Krystyn copies.

I'll close for the meantime, and once again many good thoughts and wishes to you and Tuśka.

Your A.

57. JUNE 20, 1947, WARSAW
[*to Wilhelm Mach*]

Dear Sir,

Only today (June 20) did I receive your letter of June 9 regarding the manuscript of your article about *Sprzysiężenie.* I did not receive this article. In this hellish pit on Grażyna St., where strange people operate, it can easily happen that articles disappear. I have run around half the day in order to find it because, quite apart from concern with common decency, it very much matters to me, and I was sincerely pleased that you sent it to the journal. I'm deluding myself that perhaps it wasn't addressed to me and got stuck en route, perhaps with Bratny. I will use all means to find it, and having copied it, print it. Anyway, over the next few days, I'll let you know of my attempts, and I assure you, again, that there's no fault of mine in this entire affair.

You have perhaps heard that *Pokolenie* is being turned into a monthly and changing its name to the neutral *Nurt.* I would like to reshape this journal in the form of a young *Skamander.* In the first issue, would run better and worse poems by Ziembicki, Gajc, Wirpsz, Różewicz, Gruszczyński, etc., fragments of Bratny's plays, translations of Sartre and Steinbeck, of criticism: your article if it turns up, S. Marczak's piece on formalism and, perhaps, I would write something about the temptations of naturalistic stories. I would be very pleased if you would wish to work with us.

I enclose sincere greetings. How is your health? I heard that you had been ill. I hope you are now feeling better.

Sincerely,

Tadeusz Borowski

58. JULY 6, 1947, WARSAW

[*to W. Mach, with postal order for 2000 zł. from the* Nurt *editorial board*]

Dear Colleague,

I enclose an advance for the article about Kisielewski. Since wonders happen in Poland, should the journal not come out, I will return the article immediately. Greetings from Bratny, Marczak, and me—

Borowski

59. JULY 8, 1947, KRAKÓW

[*from W. Mach*]

Dear Colleague,

Please believe me when I say that I am truly touched by your friendly willingness to see to the matter of my article. I wanted to write to you as soon as I got your previous letter, but was stopped both by a lack of time and by the promise of fresh news from you. The money also came at the best possible time in terms of my needs. But that's an issue for another time, since I'm always more caught up by "the question at hand."

That's a bit romantic, but it's how it is. And so. We know each other too little, too little to hit on the right word in a letter, and I will spare you "literary" praise because I get the impression that that isn't quite the thing for you either. Obviously, you write brilliantly, and you have a faithful and sincere ally in my modest self.[62] But I'd rather talk about this with others, not with the interested party—a bit romantic, too, but that's how it is. And so. I wish you success and joy in writing, a few more new enemies-Philistines, and *Nurt* a quick birth and healthy development. Other than that: any word from you will make me very happy, boost and refresh me—it's hard to live without such words, and even more so since I'm bashful.

Sincere respects, also for: Bratny, Marczak, and company. Thank them for their greetings.

Yours,

Wilek Mach

60. JULY 10, 1947, ŁÓDŹ
[from S. Żółkiewski]

Dear Sir,

At the end of July we are putting out the 100th issue of *Kuźnica*. I can't imagine this jubilee issue without you. So please send a manuscript by 20–21 July, preferably, perhaps, one of those little stories. I'm counting on it.

Respects,

S. Żółkiewski

61. JULY 17, 1947, NEW YORK
[from A. Girs]

Dear Tadeusz and Tuśka,

In five days, I'll have been a month in New York. I haven't achieved much in that time. But I've sweated like never before. Such heat that it's hard to bear. Both day and night, one is covered in sweat, your skin can't keep up with it, turns red. Your wet clothes rubbing against your skin makes it bleed. Apparently, it's an unusually mild and cool summer. I'm lucky. In air-conditioned places, on the other hand, it's wonderful. One's thirsty all the time. There are all kinds of marvels to drink which are unknown in Europe. The States is very like it is in movies. I'm writing this letter with very little on, it's night. Drops of sweat glisten on my skin.

The lack of language is getting in my way dreadfully. I absolutely must learn how to speak. I was in the library today. The city library's beautiful building resembles a palace with a garden. But a huge palace. It would be useful for our architects working on rebuilding to familiarize themselves with what has already been done, and to make use of acquired experience. And there are things to see. As you know, I'm not an architect, but the observations come to one themselves. You know, once seeing the constant repairs to our brick roads, I thought it would be better to use asphalt, which is more pliable as paving. I've already seen it here, it yields excellent results. America has already been discovered. It's not worth rediscovering over again. Just learn about things that have been done.

What interesting things are you writing now? I heard about some article attacking Kossak-Szczucka's book. I'm interested to know what you wrote there. Did you receive my letter with certain suggestions for some poem or prose on

the subject of Pan Twardowski? Not like in Mickiewicz, of course. He was an interesting figure from our Middle Ages. The Germans had Paracelsus[63] and several others; we were poorer, but there is little written in literature about what we did have.

When I was in the N.Y. public library, the Polish section interested me. Probably the smallest. As the director of that section told me, books weren't sent, and purchasing wasn't regular. The publishers in other countries, on the other hand, sent regularly. I think things have improved now. So far, I have not found a single book that I worked on before the war. It's strange. Naturally, I will give them the current ones as soon as Juliusz Panek sends them.

If you think it appropriate, tell them when you get the chance to send books to the libraries here, especially those in the larger towns, so that the Polish section looks more or less decent. Do you know whether the National Library has received the 700 copies of *Polonus* yet? Pani Pola[64] sent them through Major Wnuk of the consulate in Munich. A few days ago, I received a copy, doesn't look bad, although there are a lot of typos that they made after I left because they didn't pay attention to the specific instructions. But on the whole it's good. I think they'll be able to sell it well. Undoubtedly, as usual, they won't inform me about receiving this gift. Perhaps you'd be kind enough to check on it when you get a chance and write. My temporary address: A. G., c/o A. Bates, 180 Claremont Ave., New York City 21, N.Y., U.S.A. (the one is written like a stick here because otherwise they think it's a seven).

Sincerely,

A. Girs

62. AUGUST 8, 1947, WARSAW
[*to Wilhelm Mach*]

Dear Pan Wilhelm,

Having returned from vacation, I am immediately answering your letter, which has been lying on my desk for almost a month. Your article is now typeset and will come out together with *Nurt* some time in the first half of September, or, perhaps, earlier. Please forgive me for changing its top hat into a cycling cap, and giving it the title "Wstydliwa sprawa *Sprzysiężenie*" ["The Embarrassing Case of *Sprzysiężenia*"], it seemed more aggressive, and, as they say, in keeping with the tone of the article (quiet and yet caustic). In the first issue, of native stuff,

we are giving: poems (Gajc, Różewicz, Wirpsz, Ziembicki), an act of Bratny's play, Marczak's "programmatic" article and your piece about Kisielewski, then Bratny's remarks about innovative stories, and a bit of ballast, so-called "scientific." A lot of translations: a fragment of a Sartre novel, a Steinbeck story, Bush's article,[65] an Aragon poem; a few conversations; drawings and a colorful cover. In spite of everything, it's not as I would like it.

I would be truly grateful if you would be willing to send us something for the second issue. I would personally suggest putting Iwaszkiewicz on the carpet. R. Bratny told me that you have something in your file; perhaps, now, in connection with the prize, we should give him a touch of reality?

You see, Pan Wilhelm, you have to help us. Just don't excuse yourself with a lack of time or inspiration. Write about everything that lies heavy on your liver or heart. *Nurt*, if it floats, will have bitter and biting water for many; it seems to me worth trying.

And incidentally, it's time to think about some critical syntheses; e.g., a discussion of Polish camp literature, or the neo-classical poetry of Jastrun and *Kuźnica*, or Catholic literature, or the chaos among the leadership of so-called Marxist criticism (principles? criteria?). Or the question of realism (Socialist? Catholic? Realism and censorship? Can realism be reactionary?). Or a hundred other matters about which you know a hundred times more than I do. So, if you don't want Iwaszkiewicz, but have something ready in your briefcase, or on your spleen, please tip it into *Nurt*. I hope we'll be basting one of your books of criticism before too long?

In the meantime, best wishes, thanks for your kind words, wishes for great success with your work, and good health, happiness, regards,

Tadeusz Borowski

P.S.   Please write to this address: 17 Kaliska St., the rotters took our space.

63. AUGUST 13, 1947, WARSAW
[*to S. Marczak-Oborski*]

Dear Staszek,

I'm reminding you to write about Tuwim or about Gałczyński, because probably, you old ratbag, you're seeking solace between—as Montaigne says—"the

thighs of a woman." We need profiles for the second issue, and these you have to supply by the first of September.

Happy debauchery,

T. Borowski

P.S.   Give my regards to Alfred de Musset, I've heard you're sharing the same room.

64. AUGUST 21, 1947, WARSAW

[*to S. Marczak-Oborski*]

Oh my, Staszek, give me word by express on the progress of our groundbreaking work on Tuwim, because there's going to be trouble and misery in the second issue without it.

I'm very overworked and fed up with life, which I also wish you—as long as it is to the profit of the editors.

Yours,

T. Borowski

Editor-in-Chief, *Nurt*

Literature x) — education (!) — life

X) yes! look at the signature

65. AUGUST 16, 1947, NEW YORK

[*from A. Girs*]

Dear Pan Tadeusz and Tuśka,

Today I received your letter of July 8.

This is my second month of being in New York. My acclimation is going very slowly. I now know how to walk along the streets, buy in shops, travel by metro (it's called "subway" here). I observe people and am learning a lot. I don't have any work yet. There are very erroneous views about America in Europe, both on the plus and the minus side. Everybody works very hard here, but as a result have a high standard of living. What's difficult in Europe is easy here, and

vice versa. It sometimes creates a weird impression. Unbelievable opulence in the shops. Factory-made goods. However, what isn't machine-made is expensive. After arriving in New York, I felt semiconscious. I was simply asphyxiated by motor car fumes. On top of that horrendous heat, 96 degrees F. in the shade. The hot air was full of humidity, like at the baths. Several showers a day and iced drinks don't help much. Sweat streams down one's face, one's shirt is wet, one's suit as well; same thing at night. Unbelievably hot. Electric refrigerators nearly everywhere, they're of help to housewives. The lady of the house prepares dinner in literally half-an-hour (longer for parties, of course). The technology is wonderful.

I'm very pleased at the possibility of Czytelnik publishing *Auschwitz*. That's very good.[66] I wanted to tell you that when you criticize some work, by Kossak-Szczucka, for example, separate your criticism of her treatment of her subject from the woman herself. She's a very able writer and very nice. It's possible to criticize her work, and to praise her. The end product will be markedly better. Anyone can be wrong, but only the wise understand that. Respect is owed to the wise, compassion to the ignorant. It's better to have many friends and fewer enemies. An enemy is always a stupid person, and stupidity is the worst. Publishing a periodical is a splendid idea. After a while, you'll undoubtedly find people to write and to draw. Where are you having the journal printed? Send it to me when it comes out.

I may publish *Słowo o polku Igorewe*[67] here in translation. I'm starting to work on its graphics. I'll send it to you, of course, when I do it. I've met several professors of Slavic languages here, very nice people. I'm terribly pleased that you have your own apartment. Congratulations. I don't as yet. I'm renting a room in a beautiful area (academic). From the moment I got off the ship, I haven't had to report anywhere, nor are there address offices in the States. One simply melts into the human mass. It's very hard to find anyone. So I will always give you my changes of address. As to Mr. J. Z., naturally, I'd be very glad to speak with him about anything connected with cultural issues. You know my views on the subject. I have the rights to translate the book about Rembrandt (Pani Pola will send them to you). If it would be of interest to anyone, you may talk about it. The same with *Polonus*. Do you have any desire to write something historical, for example, about Pan Twardowski, about the Dragon of Wawel, about Wanda, etc.?[68] It might be interesting. Give my best wishes to Prof. Borow, I wrote to thank him for Norwid, which he sent me. The Munich publications arouse admiration in the States as well, I just don't know why. It's of little value

(moneywise). Unfortunately, there's almost no Polish readership here. I'd like to familiarize Anglo-Saxons a little with Slavic literature and art. Are they continuing to publish the monographs on Polish artists that I started?

My future plans (under totally new conditions) are not yet completely set. The dollar reigns here, it's expensive. Workmen are expensive. Print is expensive. Mass production cheap. Nothing can compete with it. Doing what I would like to do would be a marvel that will only be valued after my death. I don't know whether I'll be able to bring it about. I've seen many Polish prewar publications. About art, about graphics, about the book. A lot about X and Y who received awards of some kind at overseas exhibitions, but about me and about Barcz, that we received as many as five Grand Prix overseas—not a word. Apparently, they didn't consider us Polish artists. A bit strange. A lot about Półtawski's typeface, nothing about ours. Perhaps because they gave Półtawski subsidies, but not us, I don't know. I'm writing this so you know that words of recognition are of little worth, brief. You must write, and not just articles, but books. That's important. And publicize yourself. By yourself.

Because others will prefer to forget. Especially if you do something better than they. Collaboration with others is important as well. An exchange of thoughts and criticism is of inestimable value. But you don't need me to tell you this. I hope that you will make *Nurt* into something truly interesting. It can be done. If you'd care to write about *Polonus,* please do so. Same with *Goślicki.* I also wanted to write that the best printing blocks were made (and probably are being made) in Łódź, by Borkenhagen, 108 (?) Piotrkowska St. If Bork. is still there, tell him that I am requesting that they do things for you the way they did for me. That means very carefully. Cheaply, as well. Write to me about everything. If I'm able to advise or to help, I'm always glad to do so. I don't need to write, surely, that my feelings haven't changed. And you know how much I like you both.

The sea voyage was good. Fantastic food, unbelievable quantities. Then something completely new—New York. I lived practically on the corner of Broadway on the eleventh floor of a luxury hotel (two weeks), and then by my own resources. And now, sit down or you'll faint: Juliusz Panek married Krystyna (Miss Piggy);[69] I don't remember whether you knew her, she was kind of our new secretary. P. Cie returned to Toruń. That's all for now, even gossip. Fond kisses to you both, and all the best in everything.

Your A.

66. SEPTEMBER 5, 1947, NEW YORK

[from A. Girs]

Dear Pan Tadeusz and Tuśka,

A month has gone by since your last letter. How quickly time flies. My "acclimatization" is slowly moving forward. Were I younger, and not so tough, I would have crumpled and "acclimated" myself a long time ago. In the meantime, it's moving along somehow. Truth to tell, I've met up with a couple of disappointments, e.g., that the Poles here don't, on the whole, read books—but in the final analysis there are worse tragedies in life. It's so hot here that it's literally boiling. Other than that, for us Europeans, life without a suitcase of documents, without having to report, and without other nice things of this sort, is dreadful. Dreadful it is, but what can one do. Maybe I'll survive.

I'm very curious about your most recent work, I can't get it anywhere. Perhaps, when you have the opportunity, you could send me "a story of some kind"? I'm also waiting impatiently for an issue of *Nurt*. When are you going to do your doctorate? It's worth getting that out of the way, too. Even though my situation, like that of every emigrant, is uncertain financially, I am, however, starting to think a little about future work. I want to do a series "Masterpieces of Slavic Literature" in English, it's a difficult task. To start with, I'm preparing a translation of Gogol's "Nocz pod Rożdżestwo" [written in Russian]. A thought has occurred to me in connection with what you wrote about Mr. J. [?] Zawadzki. Would he not be interested in a simultaneous Polish edition? I think that, knowing Russian, you could, for example, translate it for him. I'm sure you'd do it excellently. The edition would be unusually opulent, with illustrations. The format like *Polonus*. I imagine it this way, that it would be a publication of the Oficyna made especially for Sp. Wyd. *Wiedza*. Talk it over with him, when you get a chance. They practically cursed me in Munich for choosing Gogol. Only Juliusz and Krystyna (now Panek) defended me bravely, but without greater success. I'm wondering what to choose from Polish, something not too long (for my humble means), which could be illustrated, and understandable, if exotic, to the West. I considered *Monachomachia*,[70] but they'd ultimately condemn me, even though such a worldly person wrote it. Going back to your new books, I'd also like to give them for review here. Our countrymen here should know about young Polish writers. I would also be very pleased if you would sometimes raise other subjects of interest to the whole world, historical—or whatever. Kossak's *Krzyżowców* [*The Crusaders*] or Sienkiewicz's *Quo Vadis* would be comprehensible to more

than just Poles. On the whole, however, our literature can only be understood by Poles. Please think about this. I once wrote you that our literature is, with a few exceptions, strictly for internal use. Practically nobody knows about our art, either. Or knows wrong. Because people who haven't a clue concern themselves with it. Unfortunately. We could boast about someone like Wyspiański, but we don't know how to do so. Do you remember the "Rembrandt" I started to make? Krystyn knows this well because he was for the "wrong" translator. I bought the English and Polish rights, not the German ones, however, because the author himself noted that not a single German would read a book written like that. As it happened, influenced by his friends' opinion, he published the book and it was very popular. Well, one can always be mistaken. I was also mistaken about Polish books in the States. I don't know how I'm going to get out of it. About "Rembrandt," I think I'll bring it out in English next year, and, if there is any interest, one could also think about a Polish edition. Perhaps you'd accept an order from me (unpaid at the moment)? There's a beautiful poem by Aleksey Tolstoy (the old one, not the present one, written in Russian) entitled "Grzesznica" ["The Sinner"]. I'd like to publish it in Polish, in a tiny edition perhaps, because I don't know if it would go, but very luxurious.

If you would want to, and if it wouldn't be too hard for you to translate, I'd also persuade Mr. Kuleszyn to illustrate it, and I'd publish it. I just ask you to be completely honest, without any "buts," because that would make me feel truly bad. Please give my regards to Krystyn and our acquaintances.

Very sincerely,
Your A.

New address on the envelope.

67. ŁÓDŹ, SEPTEMBER 22, 1947
[*from S. Żółkiewski*]

Dear Sir,

Comrade Z. Pióro of *Po prostu*[71] was here and said that *Nurt* had been finally throttled. Before it burst forth. Exactly as I predicted. He told me the reason was the contents of the issue: Sartre, Koestler,[72] Steinbeck. Evidently not such much young literature on the attack, as old Trotskyites. But that's a joke.

On the other hand, you have to get serious. The situation requires it. Don't

be childish. Your shutting yourselves up in a "youth" ghetto is an absurdity. How young are you? Hertz is 28 years old and a grown-up. Bratny—27 and a "youth." Brandys, an old writer, 30—and you, young lad, about 25. It's rubbish. We are the same generation.[73] We have to stick together. Because we hold the same artistic and social ideals. Give up those ideas for youthful ghetto journals and work with *Kuźnica* in a normal way. Or else those louts from *Po prostu* will cream you. Because the journal is lively and developing well. You also have to be in it, write in it, and give it tone.

Instead of historical-philosophical articles for *Nurt,* write reviews for *Kuźnica,* that will make better sense. And above all, once every two months publish a story in *Kuźnica.*

Left-wing literati aware of the needs of art are scattered. And the time requires cohesion and a conscious formulation of cultural politics. Bitterness about *Nurt* being throttled should teach you that the situation is difficult and requires common sense. That's also why I'm proposing coming to an understanding. All of you write for *Kuźnica.* We have to come to an agreement about details, who is to do what. That's why I suggest: come to Łódź in September—all you main ones from *Nurt:* you, Bratny, Oborski, Miss Fiszer, Gruszczyński—anyone who was important there. We'll feed you, put you up for the night, and organize a night of long conversation between fellow countrymen.

Send a telegram a few days before the date you decide on, when you'd be coming, so that, just in case, we can settle the date.

I await a reply,

Sincerely,

Stefan Żółkiewski

After all, the person who would write a weekly critical piece about poetry for *Kuźnica*—and I will take anyone who would write regularly—would control Polish taste.

68. OCTOBER 22, 1947, WROCŁAW
[*from T. Mikulski*]

Dear Tadeusz,

I write this letter for two reasons. First, I offer you very sincere best wishes on the occasion of our close and mutual name day. I wish your book, about which

news has been circulating for a long time, good speed, but we'd prefer to already have it in our hands. And now, not on account of the name day, we wish you a beautiful literary future and know that you will achieve it for yourself, and for us, as well.

And now the second matter. Wanda once mentioned that you would like to give a new manuscript to *Zeszyty Wrocławskie*. If I'm not mistaken, it is supposed to be not too long, about life during occupation schooling, but I'm not certain about this. In any case, if the piece is ready, and doesn't exceed the length governing our monthly, I ask you most sincerely to submit it to us.[74]

Issue 4 of the *Zeszyty* has just come out in print, and the next issue (5) is almost full. If you would accept our Wrocław request quickly, the piece could appear precisely in issue 5—issue 6, at the latest. I'll also make sure that the manuscript doesn't lie in the editorial offices, but we somewhat limit space in *Zeszyty* (the issue to ten pages) so as not to put our budget on a collision course.

I shall await your reply—perhaps a visit by you to Wrocław—with impatience. We both send you our most sincere best wishes. Greetings to your wife.

T. Mikulski

69. UNDATED
[*from W. Żukrowski*]

Dear Pan Tadeusz,

First, a kiss on both cheeks together with name day greetings—health, a quiet head, clear thoughts, and creative work still free from the demands of the feelings of the masses.

I'm pleased by your every letter, I'm pleased with every new article, the memoir in *Nurt* is good, but it's not the "great" Borowski.[75] It's good you are going, I am also supposed to be going to Russia for two weeks, I won't be at the conference, but I figure that even without me they'll manage to trade. The derisive book will be ready literally in days, I'll forward it without being reminded, because I'm counting on help and protection, since everybody from Dobraczyński to Żółkiewski will persecute me for it. I'll probably be in Warsaw shortly, perhaps I'll find you, then we could talk further.

For now, with respects and greetings to your wife,

Ever without a halo,

Wojtek

70. OCTOBER 22, 1947, WARSAW
[*to W. Leopold*]

Dearest Wanda,

To all intents and purposes, the Wrocław business isn't looking too rosy, because up until now I've had no time, nor will I be at the conference because—tomorrow I'm going to Yugoslavia.

Overworked, I wasn't able to squeeze a word out of myself, nor—I must confess—did I try very hard. So "Wielkie zmęczenieę" ["The Great Weariness"][76] remains unfinished and awaits my return. Anyway, I don't mind because the concept of that large story in twenty individual fragments is beginning to change a little, and I want to think the matter through properly. It's about, to put it briefly, the issue of a new war and our attitude toward it.

I'm promising myself, however, after returning from Broz Tito's fatherland (?) to make a whirlwind visit to Oporów and chat with you and Mikuła, because, you know Wanda, that one has terribly few people with whom one can speak completely openly, and not just mutter. And one ultimately longs for such people very much.

It turns out that Tuśka has a heart condition, and I have rather low blood pressure and am also on medication, getting strychnine injections from Tuśka in the evenings and huge doses of lecithin and some kind of powder of which I'm to consume ten bottles.

I'll gladly send you Saroyan as soon as Tuśka gets it back from Prof. Helsztyński who's supposed to write something on him.[77] Perhaps *Awir* would precede Ms. Stanisławska's translation with an essay on this author? Of course, Helsztyński sometimes writes like Boy, and, sometimes, like a hack, but perhaps this time he'd write—like Boy. I'll also send you (as a loan, because it's the only copy) John Lehman's *New Writing,* it would be good to familiarize Polish readers with English creative work. I, myself, would willingly take something for the obscure *Nurt,* if Ms. Stanisławska were willing to translate.

I was truly delighted that you are decidedly becoming a Slavophile, and are really engaging in scholarly work—something has to remain of our generation, and up to now there's so little![78] You know, I've become concerned about Wojtek: the guy's not exactly in the first blush of youth and he should have his crises behind him. It's a bit sad, ultimately, and a bit funny to be the contemporary Wokulski[79]—don't you think? Especially when one is burdened with Catholic complexes and life plays out according to dictates from above. I'm writing a

separate letter to him and am trying to buck him up—because I understand him all too well.

It's more or less the same thing with M., who is declining physically before our eyes; for days toward the end of the month he doesn't eat, and squanders his wages at the beginning of the month on girls. His eyes are like a hunted animal's. I help him as I can, but that help, it seems, costs him a lot.

Hold your head high, Wanda, because autosuggestion is an essential thing, and, on top of that, who the hell should be an optimist, if not people with experience?

Sincerely,

Will write as soon as I return,

Tadeusz

71. OCTOBER 23, 1947, WARSAW

[*to his parents*]

My dear Olsztynians,

So don't be angry with us for not writing to you, because Tuśka is still more or less dependable, but I'm a total sluggard and hate writing, and on top of that I'm going to Yugoslavia tomorrow, so you darling Moms, and you, dear bro, and you nice Daddy, cheer Tuśka up as best you can, and, in exchange, I'll bring you back a bottle of wine. The trip came up very unexpectedly, so that I barely got stuff together, bought (or rather Tuśka bought) extra socks and a bar of chocolate, and tomorrow I depart.

So: at dawn on Halloween, Tuśka wants to go to Łódź, and invites you to come with her, Moms. Write and tell her whether you'd like to.

I'm very curious how you liked my first issue of *Nurt*—the second issue will be made without me, but I've put it together and, when it comes out, Tuśka will send it to you.

May the radio play beautifully for you, my dears, and Julek, may books read beautifully and usefully.

Many kisses, and thanks for the marvelous package which we haven't yet managed to finish eating.

Your traveling son,

Tadeusz

72. OCTOBER 28, 1947, PARIS

[*sender: Piotr Słonimski, 172 Rue de l'Universite, Paris VIIe*]

To Tuśka and Tadeusz Borowski

My dears,

I got a big charge out of *Nurt*. Thank you very much for it, it's a success. Congratulations and sloppy kisses.

Since at this moment I've been transplanted into completely different soil, and, on top of that, since this is the first Polish journal that I've had in my hand for six months, you might be interested in a few remarks that occur to me in connection with *Nurt* (it's highly likely they're for the birds, but I don't have anyone much to talk to, so once in a while I need to empty my bladder!).

1) France, for Poland at the moment, is the existentialists (Nurt—3 positions). My information about them is as follows:

    a. in the laboratory where I work (the community is red on the whole), no one knew anything about them, and a few people (out of 20) reckoned it was a religious sect, or else a new hairdressing-tailoring genre.

    b. they wear knee-length jackets (an imitation of Warsaw fashion), beards (the drawing); pants rolled up to mid-calf. One sees this, and everyone knows it.

    c. I tried to get into their saloon, but because of the swarm of Americans (no Apaches and brothels were closed), Buicks, and so forth, I gave up. For a large sum of money, apparently, one can pinch Sartre himself in the course of writing a new play.

    d. in the papers [two words unreadable] about existentialism.

    e. "Les jeux sont fuites"—fantastic film.

Conclusion: The French are nitwits, and only Poles know how to appreciate French existentialists.

2) The Warsaw Uprising:

Obviously, "posthumous children," "complex," "fixation." I understand that it's an unresolved complex about the truth about the Warsaw Uprising, a necessity for debunking, but doesn't the possibility exist of creating an Uprising 2 psychosis precisely because one talks, writes, analyzes, chews over, fishes out "the naked truth of facts," and looks for social-domestic causes? The reaction of the masses and the leaders is sometimes completely irrational

and goes against the desired effect. I'm not saying this to you, but the Bratny and *Pokolenie* company.

Since I meet up with normal people who, of course, have neither on the whole heard, nor wish to hear, about the Uprising, I'm asking you whether the possibility exists of meeting such in Poland? I think not. That everybody is more or less abnormal. But if such did exist it might be worth breeding them, selecting them out, as an inoculation against heroic-romantic poison, and one would have the hope that in the next generation the entire population of Poland would be immune. Worth a candle!

3) The dedication is splendid.

4) Hemingway is a scribbler judging by the film "For Whom the Bell Tolls," which has very good technicolor and the marvelous Ingrid Bergman, and by the excerpt from the book published in *Paris-Presse* (the most readable "red press").

5) What else are you two doing? Kiss everyone for me: Basia, Maria, Ewa, Staszek, Mundek, Andrzej.

6) I might come to Warsaw for Christmas. I would ask you not to say anything about this, because it's not certain. Since I'll be completely without money, I would very much like to earn some. Write me, Tadek, what type of thing you'd like and how much. Make me a normal request (if, of course, it suits you), so that, when I arrive, I could have around ten pieces, since in Poland I've nothing but debts. I'll try to find good stuff. Do you still want illustrated stories? This is very important to me, write to me quickly if you'd be able to pull something like this off.

Lots of kisses, and hang in there, kids,

Piotr

Nothing new here, am working a lot unfortunately, rather strange stories are emerging that might prove interesting. I only have time on Sundays and then I mooch around pictures and theaters. Good night, 'cause it's late.

Because your name day is around this time, accept, oh Master, expressions of adoration and homage from a worshipper.

73. OCTOBER 28, 1947, BELGRADE
[to Maria Borowska]

Sender: T. Borowski, Polish Embassy, Belgrade, Yugoslavia

Dear Tuśka,

I've finally received pocket money from the Union of Serbian Writers—as Morton[80] says—which has enabled me to write and send this letter.

We had an interesting journey with athletes going to Bratislava for a match, and the Brandys's going to Silesia. There's a lot to say about Slovakia, about the river Sawa or, maybe, Danube along which we traveled, but the most interesting probably are our literary group (clearly taken from cavalry races), which is made up of totally fantastical people, and Budapest, the liveliest and noisiest city, along with Paris, of any I've seen, filled with neon, flags, colorful shops, hot chestnuts on the street, the Salvation Army singing church hymns, and poor, gray, harried people with aged faces.

Yugoslavia—at the moment presentations and internal wrangling among the group. More or less two receptions a day, more important and ceremonious by the day, I'm not kidding. Yesterday, we were at the Ambassador's, then at an official lunch, then dinner with a theater director, before that, the theater itself. My casual pants will finally spare me the most ceremonious ceremonies. I'll be able to walk out of European hotels and descend into the lower depths, because Belgrade lies on mountainsides and the proletariat resides on the lower streets. I have a ceremonial breakfast in a moment, in the evening of my name day I'll write you a second letter.

Your Tadeusz

P.S.   Go to the institute! And tell the Professor that I'm sorry, but it is, however, a month.

74. OCTOBER 30, 1947, BELGRADE
[*to W. Leopold*]

Dear Wanda,

Instead of being in Wrocław, I'm in Belgrade. I could say a lot about Yugoslavia from the window of a Chevrolet, but I'll tell you in person. I've become friendly

with Adolf Rudnicki, who reacted very cordially to your letter, and, as he told me, didn't manage to reply, because he would have had to put too much of himself into the reply. Give my warm regards to Professor Mikulski, and promise him, on my behalf, some Serbian books that the Union is preparing for us. Hang in there, you'll get the report from Serbia straight out of my own mouth.

Greetings,

Tadeusz, in other words, the foreigner

75. OCTOBER 30, 1947, BELGRADE

[*to M. Borowska; postcard*]

Dearest Tuśka,

It's a veritable cauldron here. A lot of work, long days of receptions, they last eighteen hours. We look very carefully for ourselves at what they show us, we are feted as Polish literature and are very tired. Tomorrow we are leaving for Macedonia, then we'll be in Slovenia, Herzogovina, and other Yugoslav republics. I've already learned a lot, although getting to know a country from out of the window of a Chevrolet doesn't appeal to me. I've made a few acquaintances among the residents and have learned many interesting things. At any rate, this is a very young country, very lively and enthusiastic, although the layer of culture, as with us in Poland, is relatively thin. Don't be angry, dear one, that I'm not writing much. I take daily notes, and, to your great joy, will read them out to you when I'm back. Keep well, and go to the institute.

Tadeusz

P.S.   Fondest kisses!

76. OCTOBER 31, 1947, BELGRADE

[*to M. Borowska; postcard*]

My dear, we're still in Belgrade being feted. To the outrage of the delegation and the embassy, I'm not going to the receptions, however I'm willingly visiting factories, pioneers' houses, and small, poor, town restaurants, which I wish you, too.

Your Tadeusz

77. NOVEMBER 3, 1947, OCHRIDA-BITOLA

[*to M. Borowska; postcard*]

My dear, we rode the whole night from Belgrade to Skopje (in a club car), and then by car through the mountains of Yugoslavia (Macedonia). The entire day to the minster on this picture (ninth century). Now dusk is falling, we are about 200 km. from Skopje where our luggage is, we're looking at the Macedonians and their gorgeous frescoes from the eleventh and twelfth centuries, as well as at beautiful mountains.

Kisses—Tadeusz

78. NOVEMBER 4, 1947, BELGRADE

[*to M. Borowska*]

My dear Tuśka,

We came back today from the Macedonian mountains where we rattled around by car in search of old monasteries. I'm the only one of the whole delegation who is more or less well, the rest are indisposed, and we'll probably come back to Poland earlier. Macedonia is a beautiful, but very poor, stony country that received its independence only after this war and has probably the youngest literature in the world—four years old!

Of course, the people there are very pleasant, enthusiastic, and rather cultured, although the farm laborer uses a wooden plow, and the literati read only Gorky. The capital of their people's republic, Skopje, is half Turkish, and some of the women wear wide trousers on their legs, and on their faces—veils. However, in the army building (former royal castle), the young Serbian guards dance the swing like everywhere else on earth.

In twenty minutes, we have some lunch reception. My head is still spinning from not having slept in the train (club car!), and they're already dragging us again into an elegant lifestyle. This elegance costs me a lot of nerves especially because Adolf and Morton are sick—one with dental problems, and the other in his notion that Yugoslavia is the "Majestic" hotel (the counterpart of the "Polonia"). As a result, our relations have rather deteriorated, and we've mutually had enough of one another.

I've learned a great deal here, and continue to learn. Literature isn't the chief occupation of young and old writers, and there are three, maybe four, professional

writers—making a living only off writing—the rest concern themselves with matters often far from literary, and that are primarily useful, and only after that beautiful. Perhaps this is better. In any event, Yugoslavia is a young country, and its young people are truly wonderful, working hard and with purpose, very social-minded, it seems. I made friends with a couple of people in Macedonia and when I return, I'm going to correspond with them.

I'll tell you the rest when I get back, because it isn't well suited to letters.

Love and kisses,

Your Tadeusz

P.S.   And how, dear one, goes the institute? And the injections? If you've omitted anything, your lot will be hard.

79. NOVEMBER 4, 1947, NEW YORK
[*from A. Girs*]

Dear Pani Maria and Tadeusz,

Thank you very sincerely, Maria, for your very nice, and completely undeserved, letter.[81] I know and love you as I do Tadeusz, Krystyn, and other people close to me. I know what you are to him and what you can still be. It's a great joy to me that you are happy and pleased with your work. I believe in Tadeusz's talent and his and your worth as people. These are normal friendly feelings that you merit 100%. What you perceive as unusual isn't me, but the philosophy[82] that I myself accept with rapture and wonder, that's all. I was able to give Tadeusz so little in Munich, that I can only be ashamed.

It's just your good eyes that see something different. I know that you are an inspiration and help to him. You are a very brave, dear, and loyal woman. Puppy has won the lottery.

I'm endeavoring to do something in my field. I don't know if I'll succeed. But I think so—after countless and fantastic difficulties, annoyances, etc. The difficulties in Munich were as nothing compared with the ones here. Especially for someone dumb, like me.

As for translating Gogol, I think that I may be able to correct it with the English edition. I am not counting on the Poles here, because they're not much interested in books. I think that such an edition would be interesting to Poland. With some of the money we'd get we could order something for a future publication, and

the remainder would be yours. But we'll see. I haven't yet received the monthly *Nurt*. I'm sending you *Polonus,* but by normal mail, so it will be slow. If you'd care to, give it appropriate publicity. They're already writing about it here. Leopold Wellisz wrote, and Professor Halecki is supposed to write. General admiration—platonic, unfortunately. Please give my regards to Professor Borowy and other bibliophile friends.

Fondly,

Your devoted A.

80. NOVEMBER 5, 1947, BELGRADE
[*to M. Borowska*]

My dear Tuśka,

Having made himself ill eating the natives, Adolf is going back to Poland and taking this letter with him. So you see: this is a completely different country, fixated on the east, and completely blindly imitating the Union. Between official and ordinary life there is a chasm unimaginable, despite everything, in Poland. It's tiring and funny that they show us the best sides of national life, while I, myself, visit the worst—and that's hard to reconcile "at heart." It's very hard to grasp what the truth is. In any event, that very observing with one's own eyes is an unbelievably primitive writing instrument. I've concluded that in order to get to know a country, one has to live, and be treated, like a citizen of that country. The journey to Macedonia gave me unbelievably much: both from the point of view of customs and literarily. I also came to know my famous travel companions better and there is a lot to tell about them.

As for me, I'm quite tired and am starting to feel nostalgic for Poland. I'm up to my ears in the local racket, and am repelled at thought of the formal receptions in Zagreb and Lubljana. I'd very much like to visit Czarnogóra, on the other hand, but probably won't manage to because my companions prefer not to go into the mountains.

All Yugoslavia is preparing for the great 30th anniversary of the October Revolution. The nation is going to really celebrate it. That at least is how it seems. Important Polish happenings, on the other hand—the flight of the president of the Polish Peasants' Party—seem like side notes; large national problems diminish at a distance.

I very much want to return to you and to literary work. Not writing (and living in general as in "Nowele włoskie" ["Italian novels"]) is very corrupting. It'll probably make you sad, but apart from books I won't be bringing anything back, I am spending money on various attainable goals and pleasures (including movies and cheap restaurants, where I eat as an experiment), but not on purchases.

Lots of love and kisses,

Tadeusz

81. POSTMARKED NOVEMBER 8, 1947, VRBA

[*to M. Borowska; postcard*]

My dearest, this is the family village of the greatest Slovenian poet, Dr. [France] Prešeren, the counterpart/equal of our Mickiewicz and Russia's Pushkin. The area is painfully beautiful, village gorgeous and clean, the roads asphalt and cobble. The Alps are marvelous, like in Słowacki's drawings, and the people very pleasant.

Tadeusz

82. NOVEMBER 8, 1947, BLED

[*to M. Borowska; postcard*]

My dear,

We are in Slovenia, right by the Alps and right by the Adriatic, in Bled, renowned Yugoslavian health resort. Gorgeous country, cultural level higher than in Poland, but picture postcards are so dreadful that I'm giving up and sending— sitting at a table in the hotel—this card. We wandered endlessly around mountain spirals and I'm a bit seasick. This evening, we're leaving Lubljana (Kraków in miniature) for Zagreb (a slightly larger Kraków) for Croatia.

Kisses, miss you a bit,

Tadeusz

Since we're going to be drinking cognac in a minute, I'll raise a glass to your health, dear.

83. NOVEMBER 8, 1947, WARSAW

[*M. Borowska to W. Leopold*]

Dear Wanda,

I'm sending books. As to Saroyan, I've not been able yet to pry him out of Helsztyński. I'll try to send it after Sunday.

Tadeusz doesn't come back from Yugoslavia until after the twentieth. Because he left rather unexpectedly (he was informed at the last minute), he didn't finish the promised stories for *Zeszyty*. He'll probably do so when he gets back. Tell Prof. Mikulski that the stories have nothing to do with the school of occupation times. Anyway, I think that you are aware of their nature.

I'm a bit down about being alone, but I'm very glad that Tadeusz will get some mental rest and gather a few impressions. He left me a mass of instructions, so I'm running around town and don't have time to feel sorry for myself. I'm very disappointed that we won't be at your conference. I'd come myself in order to chat with you, but I've got financial problems, which Tadeusz's return will resolve. I don't know how to deal with issues of this sort (as Mrs. Żukrowska does) and the sight of publishers makes me feel helpless. One way or another we'll get to Wrocław this year still. I've recently read a couple of good French books and feel spiritually uplifted. I really admire Camus's *La Peste,* I plan to go to a Swedish class being given by my Swedish friend. Apart from that, nothing interesting is going on around, or with, me. Scribble a few words,

Fondly,

Tuśka

Wanda, if you deem it appropriate, thank Prof. Mikulski on our behalf for his greetings to Tadeusz and give him the same in our name. I somehow couldn't get myself together to write back, and now it's too late.

84. ŁÓDŹ, DECEMBER 3, 1947

[*from Żółkiewski*]

Dear Sir,

Write something for *Kuźnica*—dammit.

Best regards,

Stefan Żółkiewski

85. DECEMBER 5, 1947, WARSAW
[*to W. Leopold*]

Dear Wanda,

Thank you from the bottom of my heart (truly) for your letter from Yugoslavia, I've brought back a few books, unfortunately not Polish historical documents, because the letter reached me on the last day (literally) of our stay in Belgrade where we went after Lubljana and Zagreb. If their literature interests you, I'll gladly send you something, I have Krleža, Andrić (their—the Serbs and Croatians) most outstanding prose writers, also a bit of literature from Slovenia (Voranc—a very talented novelist, apparently) as well as from Macedonia, a country whose literature is only four years old, because before the war nothing in their language, which is close to Bulgarian, came out, not even newspapers. I've returned with a slightly tired head, the journey itself was most unpleasant, the company quite simply fantastically ill-assorted, starting with Narcissus Rudnicki—a marvelous man but very aware of his own worth—who immediately went back to Poland out of boredom, and ending with Morton, a none-too-swift political provocateur. We made a very strange impression, something between surrealists, gluttons, hypochondriacs, and counts. The Serbs and the others—because there are six republics and the inhabitants of each baptize themselves differently—are very cordial, work extremely hard, and, probably sincerely, admit that there's poverty in their country and that, perhaps, things will get better. They're industrializing the country rapidly and at any price. The renowned "Żeleznik" factory near Belgrade, built on a volunteer basis by young people, resembles both a scout and a concentration camp. Apparently, something must have reached them and on high, because in the speech at the opening of the great railway to Sarajevo built by young people, Marshal Tito—incidentally, the most gorgeous man in Yugoslavia over whom all the women there go crazy—said that young people will not be asked to make great physical efforts, but will have to study in order to raise the future national standard of living. Meanwhile in Sarajevo, the Muslim women go around in niqabs and burkhas, that is veils over their faces, and appropriate sacks completely hiding their bodily charms, and in Macedonia they continue to work stony plots of ground with wooden plows.

We spent the whole month looking at enormous museums filled with art from the early middle ages, Byzantine period and earlier—Graeco-Roman (Thrace, Macedonia, and Illyria), at some spectacular minsters from the ninth century. The shift in art from the Middle Ages to the Renaissance occurred there, so they

claim, a hundred years earlier than in Italy, but I somehow didn't want to believe it. Ważyk claimed it was true. Since with the second issue *Nurt* wilted and died, I had to look for other work and for the moment I'm employed as program supervisor at the radio, that means they give me texts and I review them, in addition, I have stupid jobs like reading some scenario and the offer of an eventual collaboration and working on a literary translation of Gall for TUR [Workers' Universities Society]. These are truly disarming jobs and I'm writing you about them openly. When it comes to so-called serious writing, unfortunately I haven't written a word for a whole year, the little stories completely didn't work out (I read them all) and I'm absolutely not going to be able to show them off. I'm in a bit of the same situation as Mr. Wat about whom it is generally said that he's a good writer but no one has seen any of his work.[83]

Best regards,
Tadeusz

86. UNDATED POSTCARD

Sender: Adolf Rudnicki, Apt. 22, 8 Bandurskiego St., Łódź
Tadeusz Borowski, Apt. 39, 17 Kaliska St., Warsaw

I remembered the care you gave me and had a great desire to give you a kiss. Please accept this card as coming from my heart in which you have a place.
Rudnicki

87. DECEMBER 29, 1947, STANNINGLEY

Janusz Nel Siedlecki, 11, Frasley Old Road, Stanningley, Nr. Leeds, Yorkshire
Hiya Beautiful![84]

First, many, many best wishes to you both! (I apologize for the lateness.)

So very much time has passed (and I still have nothing from you) that I don't even know whether I can address the Great Man of Letters as "Puppy," it doesn't matter, anyway, because for me you will probably always remain a "Puppy" growling at Tolek, and barking at all the dignitaries beginning with Pół. Panek.

I know from the papers that you were (or are) in Yugoslavia—congratulations! Other than that, I know absolutely nothing—I haven't heard anything from Krystyn, either. If you get a moment, write.

It's boring here and nothing happening. I sit and plug away, think back to good (?) times. In October, I took first year London University exams, and right after that seasonal ones in college, and now I'm making up a whole lot of labs and so on. I'm generally a bit fed up with everything. Mother and I spent Christmas Eve in Leeds, and for Christmas we both went to Pontefract. I've had very little news from Loda.

I sometimes curse the fact that you are not here—you'd get a laugh out of the natives, and maybe we could enter into some kind of partnership again—I've had a few short story–novel ideas, and piles of scribbled paper lie in a drawer, and I have absolutely no time myself to do anything with it. Though I think that I've had (or rather thought up) several good ideas, I imagine that, like the devil and holy water, you're shuddering, and blessing the moment we parted. Well, anyway, they're just inconsequential trivia like Krystyn's poems. During summer vacation, I drew a little—the results: a perfectly passable "Ex Libris," which made one of my female friends happy at Christmas; a pile of "Christmas Cards," which are sent out with greetings here, and so on. But now I have absolutely no time for this.

That's it about me and my doings here. I await with impatience some sign of life from you. Again, I offer you and Tuśka my very best wishes for future happiness.

Farewell,

Nel

[*postscript by Nel's mother:*]

I send you both my very best wishes for the New Year. Tadeusz's stories about Tuśka were so colorful that I feel that I know you personally and think that we will certainly meet some time—but when?

Very best regards,

Siedlecka

88. DECEMBER 30, 1947, ŁÓDŹ
[*from Ryszard Matuszewski*]

Dear Sir,

Our mutual acquaintance, Miss Wanda Leopold, in a recent conversation with me, suggested that you might now have a little time as a result of the sad fact that *Nurt* has folded. Because you have not written for *Kuźnica* for a long time, and independent of the requests for collaboration in the area of prose, or else poetry (I don't even know whether you still write poetry), which Żółkiewski and other of my editor friends have made, or will be making, I wish to propose permanent or occasional (depending on your ability and desire) writings about books. We now pay particularly well for reviews. We have many unreviewed books, and while they may not always be masterpieces, nevertheless I think you'll probably agree with me that good criticism does not depend, or, if it does, then not to a great degree, on the value of the work under discussion. In any case, there are, for example, reissues like R. Rolland's *Colas Breugnon,* articles need to be written about reissues of Boy and Parandowski, it would be worth writing about Remarque's *Arc de Triomphe,* it would be worth discussing Gołubiew (you could do this superbly, comparing him to Iwaszkiewicz's *Czerwone Tarcze* [*Red Shields*]). There are reasons to write about Conrad (*Typhoon, The Pirate,* I think), Mauriac, L. Tolstoy—I'm suggesting various things, and awaiting your counter-proposals, and, in any event, counting on an answer. Friday–Saturday (2–3), I'll be in Warsaw. If you would let the editorial office of *Polska Zbrojna* [*Armed Poland*] (tel. 88 350) know where it might be possible to meet you during the day, I could spare you having to write a letter, and we could take the opportunity of getting to know each other.

Very truly yours,

Ryszard Matuszewski

89. JANUARY 9, 1948, WARSAW
[*to R. Matuszewski*]

Dear Sir,

I deeply regret that your letter did not find me in Warsaw, and that I did not have the opportunity to see you in order to discuss material for review. I currently have in my hand a lousy little work about the Medana Group (as

an expression of French naturalism) by a certain Zygmunt Markiewicz (PAU, Philosophy Dept., Kraków, 1947), which ought to be discussed. The book is similar to Teodor Jesk-Choiński's famous work on positivism; under the disguise of scholarship it expatiates in a fairly indiscriminate way on French naturalism, propagating a marginal cognitive relativism (as much reality as cognitive factors in a work). As for novels, I'd gladly write about Remarque's *L'Arc de Triomphe,* it seems to me, however, that reviews of Markiewicz or Ingarden (*Szkice z filozofii literatury* [*Sketches from the Philosophy of Literature*]) are more necessary. Metaphysicians with publishing houses and academic institutions at hand have gone on the offensive in the area of literary scholarship (Górski, Ingarden, Kleiner, and others). The review of Markiewicz, as possibly of Ingarden, I could send only after Nieborow (literary kindergarten) where we will be for a week.

About other works—reissues—only after I write about Markiewicz and Ingarden.

Will you be in Nieborów? We could verbally discuss a whole series of matters about which it is hard to write.

With best regards, and again apologies for not being able to be in Warsaw.

Tadeusz Borowski

90. JANUARY 10, 1948, WARSAW
[*to W. Leopold*]

Dear Wanda,

As you know I have periods of not writing and periods of writing, which normally occur before some trips. This afternoon, I'm going to literary kindergarten organized by the Ministry . . . and . . . (of Art and Culture, but since there is neither art nor culture there, I maintain that only "and" remains) at the cost of half a million zloty at the Radziwiłł Palace in Nieborów[85] where there is one of the three most famous heads of suffering NIOBE in the world, as well as a whole series of Brueghels, nymphs, thousand-year-old Slavic statues, incunabula, and whole cupboards of third-rate French literature, read by Janusz Radziwiłł and his wife, since the cupboards stand in the bedroom. Thank you very much for your letter, although it's not the same as a conversation, but since I'm leaving that lousy Korbutianum (please don't repeat this epithet to the Professor), perhaps there'll be a bit of time to come and chat. I spent the entire holidays either in Łódź or in Zakopane engaged in dirty work—dialogues for a film[86] cobbled together

by Kott and Żółkiewska about a printing house, People's Army, of course, and heroic, of course, not a word of truth, nor a single real human being, the only real thing the 600 thousand which they, together with the director, received for the scenario, and my hundred pieces that I got for fixing their scrawl, symbolic rather than radical in any case. There was a lot of work, but I got through it in two weeks, and promised myself never to get mired down in film filth again. You have no idea what tribulations I had with Kott and Stefan's wife! But these are funny stories and there's a lot to say about them. Let's talk about other things. Rudnicki. He appears to me to be an energetic man and admirable since he has the great ambition of writing something on the level of *Faust*. The greatness of a writer and his achievements consist in large measure of what he wants to attain. Also, he's cut himself off completely from the Łódź menagerie and is working diligently. As is known, he's the unofficial Jewish bard,[87] since they translate him into various languages and he rakes in cash—as a certain Kowalewski puts it, I don't know if you've heard of him. That he's in the Polish Workers' Party is a matter of total indifference. When I was last at his place, I said, "You know, Adolf, Dobraczyński is joining the Polish Workers' Party. You'll have a colleague." He took offense for three minutes, but it's true about that Dobraczyński. He went with his wife to Sokorski and said that he's looked things over, that he's going to factories, that he'll write a workers' novel, that when he's rendered services, he'll join. I don't know how embellished this depiction is, embellishments live hand in glove with Sokorski, but the fact is he's left *Dziś i Jutro*.

Other matters. *Nurt*. Closed down, because the political situation changed, and the attitude toward me of my young colleagues from the AZWM organization, *Życie*. I never did get along with them, but I told myself, when they asked me for an editor, that I did not need political rookies (along the lines of what we talked about with Gen. Spychalski in spring). It turned out, however, that the situation was changed and my friends wormed and squirmed until they brought in a certain high-ranking dignitary who seized on Molski's article about Schaff (a piece on Marxism),[88] an unbelievable row arose, side-splitting. I no longer regret a single experience, but a few innocent heads fell at that time. Bratny joined the AZWM, but he's sad, he wrote a play which no one wants to put on, even though it's supposed to be good. Staszek Marczak is still in a stew, heaven knows why.[89]

As for cash—as long as one has hands and a head, one can live, but not too easily. As you know, radio reviews for local stations are not of much interest (18

thousand a month), that dialogues for films (65 thousand in practice, paid in installments) are not of much interest, that translating Gall (a translation into archaic language of a certain lady) is not too interesting (supposed to be 80 thousand, don't know when, in any case in the distant future after the work is finished), etc. I've finished my short stories, of which I'll send you a couple. I think of them as exercises, I'd like to do something larger, some story in the style of Kleist or Defoe, but for that you need ten hours' time and to know that what you're doing is to the point.

Polish studies. I was in Zakopane, as was my professor with his morganatic wife; he gave us a performance of affection and concern, he drinks a lot, she moderates his drinking a little, hisses sometimes—to Pelc[90] or me, killingly sweet to Tuśka.

To hell with all of it. The professor encouraged me to finish my studies and to write my thesis on the language of Young Poland, that he would publish it in *TNW*, but he was slightly drunk, so can't be taken seriously. In effect, it's you, Wanda, who are right, Polish studies is shit hard to wade through, especially today. Under the pretext of scholarship, one just gives an outlook on life. And not just that.

A cult of hard facts, an amassing of details, a lack of classification methods, of any sense of order, of healthy judgment . . . imagine someone like Pelc being seriously involved with Ingarden! I'd chuck all this up, but pride won't let me. I want to finish, and then begin to clean up the dirt. Have you read Markiewicz on the Medanu group? The guy's gone nuts on the quiet, apparent objectivity, but he's utterly buried Zola.

Piórko flaminga? Yes, artistry there. Nice weather, opulent world. Other than that a slight feeling of boredom. A bit of tomfoolery. I thought that *Tiutiurlistan* was something marginal, but valuable, of Wojtek's.[91] But actually it was *Z kraju milczenia* [*From the Land of Silence*] that was marginal, that's not good. The reportage is weak, Kott's is better. Wojtek has neither written nor sent me books. The wrapper on it—"Not for everyone." Apparently not for me either. I'll do without. I'll read Homer finally translated into normal English—prose. In the foreword, the translator says that Homer is the best storyteller, and he's right. I'll send you the book, read it.

For the moment, I give you my sincere regards and await a long and exhaustive letter. Don't upset yourself about the Wrocław quagmire. Apropos of which, they are organizing a Literary Institute in Warsaw (Mikulski should know something

about it, he's on the committee), Kott said that they are looking for experts in Polish studies, good conditions apparently, perhaps you could write to Kott, he's not as stupid as he seems in what he writes.

Kisses,

Tadeusz

91. JANUARY 19, 1947, WARSAW

[to W. Leopold, the year corrected by the addressee: 1948]

Dear Wanda,

Write us how conditions at home have worked out for you and how your mother is feeling, because we are as worried as all get out. I met Hubert Drapella in Nieborȩw where I'd gone for literary studies and he told me a bit, though somewhat vaguely, about your problems, and just yesterday when I came back to Warsaw I found your card saying it was completely awful. Of course you cannot be so simply foolish as to get married for the sake of peace, because it won't give you peace at all and in the long run living with somebody one doesn't love must be somewhat tiring. Are there really no other possibilities for making money other than being up to your ears in idiotic work? A literary institute for the study of the history of literature is coming into being very shortly, with a million a month at its disposal—with departments in university towns. Jan Kott told me that Mikulski will also be in the institute and they need staff immediately, in Kraków, for example, it's to be Markiewicz (that would-be critic, but actually student of Polish)[92]—the conditions are apparently supposed to be quite good, and four or five hours of work in order to make it possible to study. This wouldn't be bad for you. Apart from that, if you'd like to write on the side some short reviews of books that I could send, I'd put them into Warsaw journals. For example, reviews of works in Polish studies are much in demand—Ingarden's *Studia z zakresu filozofii literatury* [*Studies in the Area of Literary Philosophy*], [Zygmunt] Markiewicz's on the Medan group (Zola), and so forth, new histories of literature, of course from, shall we say, a healthy point of view. For reviews like that, there's a very eager journal *Po prostu,* where the pay's not bad and they publish quite quickly. Apart from that the group that made *Nurt,* plus a few other members, is probably going to make a new journal—perhaps something along the lines of a literary express—and also publish separate pamphlets. The matter is being discussed with the KC PPR[93] representative by the name of

Stefan Żółkiewski, it'll probably come to fruition. Some possibilities will emerge in connection with this, more or less in a month.

Nothing new with us. I got the proofs of *Pożegnanie z Marią,* changed the title of some of my short stories to *Kamienny świat,* because the concept of the cycle changed. I gave it to *Kuźnica,* Stefan is to do battle with his personnel to have them print it, because it's full of allusions to literary figures: Hertz, Dygat, Rudnicki, Ważyk, just a little encounter with mendacity. I'm giving up the assistantship and going to study the domestic way.

Keep well, write immediately, lots of hugs, so chin up.

Tadeusz and company

92. POSTMARKED FEBRUARY 15, 1948, ZAKOPANE

[*from A. Rudnicki; postcard from "Wołodyjówka," Zakopane*]

My very dear Tadeusz,

Don't accuse me of being a "touring company," say, rather, that unless one is kept down by force it's difficult to sit in one single place in Poland. For the past two weeks I've set up my tent in "Wołodyjówka." I've only changed the backdrop, the company is coming with me. On the other side of the wall, Jakub Gold,[94] father Żółkiewski, brother Wat, the lover of young poets, Paweł Hertz, Szpalski—old Jews tired of life. They sit and write and write. You'll receive *Niekochana* [*Unloved*], naturally with a very tender dedication and tribute. What's happening with *Ucieczka z Jasnej Polany* only God knows. The rabbis have apparently said no. I think, at the moment, the collection is doing the rounds of Warsaw rabbis who have not yet issued their verdict. I had very interesting conversations about literature here with chief dir. of "Książka" Comrade Werfel who said: either Polish literature will render reality in an objective manner, or it will cease to exist. He apparently wrote to Warsaw about *Ucieczka* but so far—nix. Perhaps Wanda knows something? God, if only the rabbis would take their protective hands off my head! In the meantime, I'm riding on skates, on skis, living like God in France. I'm curious what's with your Berlin? Oh, Tadeusz old man, if I were only your age!

Sincerely, and regards to your "life's companion"—A.

93. UNDATED, WARSAW

[*to editor Karol Kuryluk*]

To the editor of *Odrodzenie,*

In Czesław Miłosz's review of Jarosław Iwaszkiewicz's *Wiersze Wybrane* [*Selected Poems*]—"Nad książką, czyli cudze chwalicie" ["On the Book, or Praise of Others"], *Odrodzenie* [no. 4, 1948], one reads the following two sentences:

"It is not easy in Polish poetry to find three excellent sonnets about activities at home and in the garden. It is probably only possible through a deliberate search for examples in the literature of the Golden Age." With all due respect, I would like to say that it is possible not only "through a deliberate search for examples in the literature of the Golden Age," but also by reaching into a volume of Leopold Staff's poetry, *Dzień duszy* [*Day of the Soul*]. One cluster of sonnets in this volume bears the title "Dzień pracy" ["Workday"] and is devoted to "activities at home and in the garden."

In *Wybór poezji* [*Selection of Poems*] (Lwów, Połoniecki, 1911), the author reprinted the first four sonnets of this cycle, together with two others, under the joint title, *Z cyklu "Dzień pracy"* [*From the cycle "Workday"*], which doubles the number Czesław Miłosz desires.

Respectfully,

Tadeusz Borowski

94. FEBRUARY 5, 1948, WARSAW

[*to W. Leopold; postcard, in pencil*]

Dear Wanda,

You once asked me for Saroyan for Mrs. Stanisławska. Prof. Helsztyński only returned it to me today, after many requests on my part. Nothing new with me other than I feel really dreadful, am not working at all, have let myself go a bit. Books I read quite a lot, wander round town even more looking to make money. It suddenly turns out that I owe a lot of money to various institutions and people, and the Film, which owes me 55 thou., won't think of paying. *Odrodzenie* has folded and is recreating itself for a new readership (Borejsza is editor), Bratny is creating a new journal[95] and has written a ninth play at his friends'—shush. I'm sorry I didn't meet Prof. Mikulski who was here in Warsaw. I was sitting at

home all that time then, I broke up with the university in part because I don't know what to do there, overall I'd gladly take a break from the dear people of Warsaw.

Kisses,
Tadeusz

95. FEBRUARY 28, 1948, PARIS
[*postcard*]

Sender: Wilhelm Mach, Epoq' Hotel, 40 rue St. Charles, Paris XVe, France
Monsieur Tadeusz Borowski, apt. 39, 17 Kaliska St., Warsaw, Poland

Dear Tadek,
    You who understand so many different things will surely understand and imagine where my silence as a correspondent is coming from.
    I'm learning about the world, and that defines an "in" rather than "ex" direction.—I think about you both often, always with warmth and friendship. Long and very necessary conversations await us after my return. Please, if you are able, write a few words. What are you doing, what are you writing, what are our mutual friends doing? Give everyone my regards: Staszek Marczak (I haven't got his address), Bratny, Tadek Konwicki—warm hugs to you, if you will allow it, to Tuśka as well. Bye, my dears,
    Wilek Mach

96. UNDATED
[*to W. Leopold*]

Dear Wanda,
    Enclosed a few little stories from *Kamienny świat*. The dedications are purposefully chosen. "The Man with a Parcel" for Rudnicki. When you've read them, send them back and write what you think of them. What are the possibilities for the Polish "short story"?[96]
    Kisses,
    Tadeusz

97. POSTMARKED MARCH 26, 1948, KRAKÓW 2

[*from S. Marczak-Oborski; postcard*]

Citizens (ho! ho!) Maria and Tadeusz Borowski,
I wish you:
First: that Your Four books come out this calendar year;
Second: that the Grace of God be with you;
Third: that you would finally write to me, at length and in confidence.
    Yours forever,
    Staszek

98. APRIL 2, 1948, ŁÓDŹ

[*from Kazimierz Brandys; on* Kuźnica *letterhead*]

Respected colleague,
    It is with sorrow that I am returning *Kamienny świat,* which was supposed to have gone into print in the next issue. I hope that you will not refuse us some new prose.
    Thank you (also in Hertz's name) for the unexpectedly pleasant reception on the part of you and your colleagues at our evening at the club.[97]
    Sincerely,
    Kazimierz Brandys

99. MAY 7, 1948, WARSAW

[*to Mieczysława Buczkówna*]

Dear Mietka,
    Forgive me for writing to you at the editorial offices, but I haven't remembered your address (I'd get there by instinct, but a letter wouldn't).
    You'll probably be seeing Hanka[98] (because why wouldn't you be seeing her?), tell her I am dreadfully sorry. I undoubtedly caused her a huge problem with my childish telegram; the only justification for it was the heat and tiredness; also the many deep feelings which I have for her.
    Nevertheless, however, a room awaits you both in Zaborów; it's available either immediately, or, whenever you, Hanka, or both of you together, would

like it. All you have to pay for is food—cheap in any event, around 100 or 150 zloty per stomach.

Hanka wanted to write her master's thesis in summer: she'll get the needed reading materials. You could get a solid rest and study, and eat strawberries and cherries—very necessary to poets.

If you decide on this "summer resort," write to this address: Edmund Kujawski, Legal Adviser "Lot," "Lot" Airlines, 39 Hoża Street, Warsaw. He's the owner of the joint in Zaborów, a great friend of mine. He'll explain everything to you in detail. If you choose to eat somewhere else, write as well, because otherwise the room will have been reserved in vain. If you can spare the time, write to me; the same address will suffice (to my attention). Don't flinch at this enigmatic style; the fine art of epistolography has fallen sharply; the fashion of placing one's hand on one's heart and pouring feelings out as from a faucet has been replaced by the art of silence and clenched teeth. That's why literature is as artificial and dead as a prosthesis and we're embarrassed to express feelings which are—let's say— painful. Hanka told me several times en route that I had been helpful to her in her tangled and dismal affairs, I believe that she spoke out of conviction not politeness. (This happened a bit at my expense, but who could have foreseen it?)

* * *

The terrible heat is drying the city out to the bone. We move around more slowly and think lazily, we go to sleep with a headache from the roar, smoke, dust, swelter. You detest Łódź, actually you should detest only Piotrkowska Street, you can always escape into side streets, quieter and cleaner. There are no streets like that in Warsaw; the dust floats around in clouds; the ruins offer no shade, just emit the stench of cellars worse than the smell of socks. Whole days I wander around town getting ready to leave. I'm looking for a place where I could write and read, maybe overcome the apathy that is plaguing me. But never mind that.

Hanka told me that you have very real problems and that she's worried about you. Actually, all three of us are as gloomy as burned-out light bulbs, more needed, however. I'll suggest a small antidote: have you read Miłosz's "Traktat moralny" ["Moral Tract"]?[99] It dropped like a stone into water, it would be worth fishing it out, and bashing the author with it. Write an antitract—as St. Thomas Aquinas wrote against the pagans, like Engels against Duhring, like Brzozowski . . . I'm not at all joking: Miłosz's tract is a great poetic happening, but how much perfidy is buried in it! Next to sensible, but banal, thoughts. The constellation of Polish poetry is not at all strange: the whole is "humanistic,"

but these humanisms are various! metaphysical humanism, the humanism of an individual person (Miłosz, Malraux, Blum, etc., actually like a third power, don't you think?) Finally, that which *Kuźnica* is doing. Think about it and you'll see it's so, and not otherwise; think—the cold of the intellect weighing the "flowers of feeling"—and this matters to you, too. No matter, it's a joke.

I've read this letter from the top: it's as heavy as Broszkiewicz's *Oczekiwania* [*Expectations*]. Have you ever waited three hours for anyone? So, I've been sitting in "Angola" for the past three hours; understand the state of my soul, and you'll forgive the style of the letter. Once again I ask you to defend me to Hanka a little; I hesitate to write to her; it couldn't have been very pleasant for her. (I'm talking about the telegram; I presume that why she didn't come; I'm a rationalist after all.) A final request: be more cheerful, both of you, but not wiser; wisdom dries out the heart. In the end, the most beautiful moment for me was late night when we came to you.

Sincerely yours, don't be lazy, write.

Tadeusz

100. MAY 14, 1948, KRAKÓW
[*from T. Różewicz*]

Dear Tadeusz,

You probably got my telegram? If the thing [100] is still on, and the end of May suits you, write to me—and give me the exact date. If it's not possible, we'll put it off until fall—I would ask you, of course, for the opening words—as we discussed in Łódź. Here in Kraków passing precipitation, the theaters are showing indigenous plays and Lope de Vegas "Owcze zrodlo," apart from that "Dziennik Literacki" comes out. So much for artistic and cultural life and the town's climate.

Sincerely,

Różewicz

P.S.   It would be better, of course, if the cost of travel were payable in advance. T.

101. MAY 20, 1948, OLSZTYN
[*from his father*]

Dear Tadek,

A swine you are not, because everyone sometimes forgets about their father, but I'm concerned about something else and, after that, I'll call you swine with a capital S.

Thank you very much for the book and although I'd read the stories, I'm reading them again, and always finding something new. We read *Kamienny świat;* Julek says it very good; Mom that she doesn't understand some things; and I find that some things are heavily stressed. In any event, Tadek, you possess the divine spark, but remember not to trivialize it. You, like a certain woman here, are easily influenced, like an animal that gives in to pressures, I don't know how to say it in one word, I'm not a student of Polish. See, Tadek, you are not following your own path, you are being pushed by others who want to bake their roast in your oven, or to pluck chestnuts out with your hands. Retain your individuality and your outlook on things, and don't listen to whispers from either the one or the other side.

You strut around with your "atheism" like a hen with her egg, and you know that you are a miserable worm and with a single nod, I won't say of God, because God doesn't concern himself with such shits, but his power, only a puff of smoke will be left of you. You see, Tadek, it is perhaps his will that we went through so much in life and are together. As you see, I'm not devout, but it amuses me that a mere squirt who gets a sniff of school immediately thinks he's conquered the world, and I'm telling you all that you are all stupid. What does it matter that you scribble a little? You are losing the ground beneath your feet, and remember that all those who are trying to lead you astray will be happy when you lose your "I." You are breaking off with your real friends, and becoming friendly with people who have nothing to do with friendship, but have their own interests in sight. I suggest you don't offend your mother or her feelings. She organized your apartment for you with such eagerness and sacrifice, and, I might say, devotion, and you blew her feelings and blessings away. Such things need to be honored and you may not trample on what Mother regards as holy, because life will take vengeance for it.

You are going to consider my remarks as stupid and not on the level, but one day you'll become convinced they were correct. We are all well. Julek is studying,

I'm over-working, and Mom, as usual, does nothing for herself but everything for You. Give Tuśka my sincere regards.

Kisses,

S.B.

102. MAY 31, 1948
[*from Paweł Jasienica*]

Dear Sir,

Thank you very much for *Pożegnanie z Marią*. This is now the second book that you have sent me. What my reading of *We Were in Auschwitz* resulted in, you already know—but only in part. When in January of this year I visited Auschwitz—doing so for the first time ever—I thought about it in terms of your book. Our newspaper "acquaintance" began with your review of Z. Kossak's book. I am not suggesting that I have completely changed my opinion about this review, but I've understood that the persistent didacticism made you see red. It is a pity that I did not read both these accounts about Auschwitz—hers and yours—in reverse order. Perhaps then my review might have been more intelligent.[101] I am reading *Kamienny świat* diligently. I had wanted of late to argue with you a little about those reviews of yours of that conspiratorial-partisan book (I've forgotten the title and author),[102] or rather about the conclusions, but it somehow got put off and fell by the board. But please do not think that I had reservations about the "debunking" of the underground. On that we agree.

Perhaps on the occasion of some trip to Warsaw, I will drop in on you, if you would allow it. I would like to get to know you in person. Should you be in Kraków, please stop by our nest of black reaction. We will be glad to see you.[103]

Please accept my sincere regards,

Paweł Jasienica

103. POSTMARKED JUNE 3, 1948

[*postcard*]

Send.: T. Różewicz, 22 Krupnicza St., Kraków
Mr. Tadeusz Borowski, Apt. 39, 17 Kaliska St., Warsaw

Tadeusz Borowski!

I'm waiting for your book—you've probably sent it off to all the literary luminaries, so, OK, I am reminding you of your promise. If it was you, instead of me,[104] who read those (short stories) coming out in *Nowiny*,[105] then I'm happy—because I liked the stories. I'll visit Warsaw again probably in June, so we'll see each other. No changes in Kraków's cultural life, only that my neighbor acquired a dog (anyway she's a highly educated old lady). Imagine this very funny story—I dreamed that I received from you a book with a violet cover signed in red pencil—where did such a dream come from? Write a large, epic (and good) novel.[106]

Write back, hugs,

Tadeusz

104. POSTMARKED JUNE 7, 1948

[*from A. Rudnicki; postcard*]

Dear Tadeusz, An hour ago, I returned from Zakopane after a five-week absence and found your books. Thank you with all my heart. I am always full of admiration, and full of concern, when it comes to you. I'm writing now, so that you won't think me heartless; I'll write more fully after I've read them. Fond kisses. Nose and olfactory system not good.

Your

Adolf

105. JUNE 7, 1948, KRAKÓW

[*from Stefan Kisielewski*]

Dear Sir,

I received the book with the dedication. Thank you very much. I follow your literary activities with interest; unfortunately, I find with sorrow that you

are decidedly sinking into a sensory-expository type of literature, limited to a bare relating of facts, for me personally somewhat unexpected in a person who survived a camp. It is impossible to draw any intellectual, ideological, or moral conclusions from the beautifully written, in any event, prose pictures in *Nowiny Literackie*. What does it matter that the dancer who looked like a woman turns out to be a man?! I truly don't understand you—there's some kind of basic weakness in it. Anyway, I write more fully about these matters in *Tygodnik Powszechny*, no. 24, in an article "Idea i wizja" ["Idea and Vision"] (if, of course, our beloved censors don't utterly castrate it). Meanwhile, yet another matter. In my time, I sent to *Odrodzenie* a correction to your article that was a review of Sowińska's book. The correction, of course, did not appear, but I'd like to know whether it came to your attention? In it, I corrected historical inaccuracies in your article, which you had repeated after Sowińska. They concerned the following matters: 1) Of all the Polish organizations (not excluding the Communists who supported only their own members) the most intensive help for the Jews during the Occupation from came from Catholic organizations, together with the Catholic Youth organization headed by Witold Bieńkowski who, at the time of uprising in the ghetto, was personally there. 2) The delegation of the [Polish] government in London gave outstanding material help to the Jews. 3) Military help to the defenders of the ghetto was directed on behalf of the Home Army by Colonel F. Niepokólczycki, later sentenced to death in the Kraków WiN[107] trial. I trust that a knowledge of these details would not be without influence on the general tenor of your article, nor on certain of its specific parts—I have absolute faith in your good will.

Sincere regards and best wishes,
Stefan Kisielewski

106. JUNE 8, 1948, SOBIESZÓW[108]

[*to T. Mikulski*]

Dear Professor,

I apologize for the delay in sending you the finally rewritten little story, "Ojczyzna"; the reason for the delay is the beautiful weather of which we are both gladly making the most.

I apologize for any possible spelling errors and typos, I think I corrected them all.

We enclose our sincere regards to you both.

Tadeusz Borowski

107. JUNE 10, 1948

[*on a torn sheet of paper, typed, to W. Leopold*]

Dear Wanda,

Sincere thanks for *Panorama,* it gave us much real pleasure.[109] I once cursed the foreword to the unfortunate *Imiona nurtu*—maintaining that it had damaged my poems (not my best ones at that); I am changing my mind. Already a second reviewer (the first, a Swiss editor of *Horyzonty* [*Horizons*]), uses it quite adroitly. Apropos—did you read what Kowalski wrote in *Zeszyty* about provincial Polish scholars? As you see, I am an ungrateful beast. I read Wyka's[110] review with mixed feelings: a lot of unmerited compliments in it (about that rare kind of prose) and, it seems to me, a bit of confusion. The first has to do with the story "Pożegnanie." Wyka doesn't like the annoying and diffuse language of the story (probably the opening section), but praises the same language in Baczyński. I wanted to write the story in the language of clandestine poetry and to reveal clandestine reality in its light. I wouldn't want to justify the mistakes in that story. I have some sentiment for it, because it gave me the greatest difficulty. You wrote in *Kuźnica* about the strong feelings that connected people to each other, don't you think that I tried to criticize the romanticism of clandestine love? The problem is that between "Pożegnanie" and the rest of the stories there's a lack of a kind of connection, this connection, in my opinion, is the sketch from the stripes—"Auschwitz, Our Home," that's why I want to reprint it in the book next to the story about Wacek. Ah well, according to old Goethe's wise advice it's always better to write than to talk about writing. And better yet, to argue

in person which, I think, we shall do. The article in *Kuźnica* was quite decent except that one could clearly see its limitations—a pity. But one always has to raise these matters so that things don't get too comfortable. A great pity that your university is extending [its session], but come over to see us. Sun as bright as all-get-out, grass is almost steaming it's so luxuriant. We were at [?], but nowhere else, I'm sitting and trying to write, not much, truth to tell, is coming of it. I've written about fifty typed pages, of which I was able to make a little story about a guy who wrote maxims (and was a corpse) on his chest, and about a woman who, having given birth to a child, marched on Berlin with him.[111]

This last—very little—is to close that section of the book where the middling stories will be ("Chłopiec z Biblią," "Ojczyzna," and others). I tried taking a leaf from Bojarski, but having covered a dozen or so pages with two or three sentences, as disheveled as a straw mattress after a dog's been at it, I'm no wiser than I was.[112]

Damn these floods! I have a great urge to go to the flooded areas, but it probably won't work out. I'm going to keep chewing on Bojarski for the next few days, and then will write to you.

And so: don't hesitate to drop by, the tram from Jelenia Góra leaves every half hour; from the stop, you follow the tourist signs right to the paved road, and that's Wiejska (to paraphrase *Wesele*).

The rest we'll talk about when you get here. Sincere regards to your mother,

Hugs,

Tadeusz et Co.

P.S.   I sent Prof. Mikulski "Ojczyzna," be so good as to ask him whether he got it and whether it'll be useful to him? Tad.

108. JUNE 1948, SOBIESZÓW

[*to T. Różewicz*]

Great, famous, and beloved Tadeusz, I have gone on vacation to Sobieszów in Karkonosz, and only today received a whole pile of mail from Warsaw, to which, as God ordained, I'm responding, and to you as well, although this is called going away for a rest. I'm sending my wife to Jelenia Góra, because our pot got broken, and has to be replaced for the boarding house, so perhaps she will get my book, and then I'll write you a dedication, but not in red pencil because I don't

have one. I didn't send you my publication because I never expected prose to interest a poet, since it doesn't interest even me, and I can absolutely no longer read what is being written in Poland. Have you already got Roman's *W karty z historią* [*Playing at Cards with History*]? It's a collection of verse, lyrical-political poetry, I read it all, and am going to argue with him, because at times the guy doesn't know how to write in Polish. But always better than Florczak and Flukowski.

It's a strange thing how in Roman the purest, and most daring, poetry mixes with dreary graphomania, pictures that have a lot of grace and freshness (you know what I'm speaking about, the so-called renewal of the poetic image) are expressed in such language that you want to scream. On the whole, however, he's the most Socialist-Realistic poet of People's Poland.

So much for Roman. He's going to be here toward the end of the month, so I will curse him out in person, I think you'll do it in letters, the boy needs to get used to criticism.

I read my short stories at the club. It took me six months (!) to cook up those thirty pages of typescript, in truth I was editing that stinking *Nurt* at the time, and going off on delegations, but still the end product is miserable. After writing that epic collection, I rested for another six months. I've now written a few small things, but when I read them, I get nauseous—I'm not exaggerating. I envy Broszkiewicz who, like a Tibetan mill, turns the handle once, and the text is ready. So this novel is just dross. I express nothing about People's Poland, I wanted to write a story "Russkij wopros,"[113] but they dissuaded me.

So, dear, famous, and great Tadeusz keep well and don't make fun of your poor colleagues who offer you their sincere good wishes.

Tadeusz

I'm sorry that we won't be seeing each other, but perhaps you could come to Sobieszów? It's not far from Kraków. Sun. Pool. Mountains. Sand, just like in one of Rudnicki's stories. You'll be fed at my expense. No floods here.

109. JUNE 11, 1948, WROCŁAW
[*from T. Mikulski, postcard*]

Mr. Tadeusz Borowski, ZAiKS, 1a Wiejska St., Sobieszów near Cieplic

Dear Pan Tadeusz,

Thank you for the copy, it did not arrive too late. I like "Ojczyzna" without reservation, Mrs. Kowalska hasn't seen the manuscript yet. One part on p. 9 is unclear ("they bring old clothes, ide, the women"—could you explain?).[114] We're finishing up, but still have to tackle a few jobs before vacation. When you are going through Wrocław, please remember us. Perhaps we could find some free afternoon. Our greetings to both of you, most sincerely,

T. Mikulski

110. JUNE 17, 1948, SOBIESZÓW
[*to his father*]

Dear Daddy,

Tuśka and I have been having a rest for the past two weeks in Lower Silesia, near Jelenia Góra, in a ZAiKS house situated in a small health resort. We're in Lower Silesia for the first time and have to admit that it's truly beautiful country. The little towns here are completely unruined by war and, it seems to me, much richer than the Mazovian ones.

Partly, this is a result of German politics, which developed strategic roads here; partly, industry, and partly the health resorts. The Karkonosze mountains are truly beautiful and accessible on foot, not like the Tatras where one apparently has to be very careful. We've also been in Wrocław, which is getting ready for the Exhibition of the Recovered Lands. The work of clearing has been intensified throughout the town, but it's hard to imagine that Wrocław, which is surely more ruined than Warsaw (it defended itself longer than Berlin, and before capitulation the Germans systematically burned down streets), will be cleared in time for the exhibition, in any event a lot is being done. The weather here, until today when it has clouded over, has been wonderful the entire time, and we only knew about the floods in Lower Carpathia from the news. We've taken many walks in the area, and today are going off to visit Jelenia Góra, where there are old churches and a famous town hall.

I've been writing quite a lot here. I have to speed up my work because in

the fall I want to give Czytelnik a completed collection of stories. One of the items in this collection will be "Kamienny świat." I'm taking two stories out of our "German" book (the one in concentration camp stripes), which enjoys great renown among "experts" in Poland, but is not more widely known. I still lack a lot for the new collection, but I have done some. One of the new stories will probably come out in *Zeszyty Wrocławskie* in an issue being published on the occasion of the exhibition. I'm now sitting over a long story, which, please God, let me get done during June, July, and a bit of August. When I finish this volume, I intend to sit down to a novel; Czytelnik, which would publish me in the "*Odrodzenie* Club" if I give them the manuscript in time, is very much urging me to do so. I'm hoping against hope that they will take my volume of stories for the club. So as you see, there's a lot of work on top of the professional, because a book brings income only after publication (I haven't received anything from *Pożegnania* yet). At the end of June, or in the first days of July, I'm returning to Warsaw because my vacation from the radio is coming to an end. I would still like to go to Wrocław for the Youth Meeting and I'd like to persuade Julek to go with me. The problem with this is that he would have to arrange his vacation for that week. I'll write to him separately, in any case, and we'll talk because I'd like to come to Olsztyn for a few days in the middle of July. Write and tell me, Daddy, when your vacation is and whether you're not planning to go somewhere in the summer; from my own experience, I can see that it does one's spirits good.

Fond kisses to you and Mom,

Tadeusz

P.S. I don't think your last letter, Daddy, was fair, you've known for a long time, after all, that I'm not a believer. I don't think that this should deny me the right to respect; after all, I'm neither a thief, nor a bandit, nor a cheat, nor an opportunist. "Believing" writers (or better yet, Catholics) get along quite well here and let's not create legends of martyrdom. When it comes to me, people on the whole consider me to be honest (they have other reservations instead, e.g., unreliability, laziness, light-mindedness, etc.); that it is so is evidenced by the fact that I have a few pen friends even in the editorial offices of *Tygodnik Powszechny*, in other words, among people officially charged with defending the faith.

Your T.

[*On a preserved envelope, his mother's remark:*] How delicately my most beloved son excused that bad advice from his father.

111. JUNE 21, 1948
[*from S. and I. Wygodzki*]

Dear Tadeusz,

I didn't write earlier since I was extremely busy, but have to today because Rudziński read the text[115] and declared the following: The text can serve as a point of departure, but the basic thing in the opera is conflict, which would add "timeless" character and meaning. I cringed inwardly, but swore, however, to create this conflict, thinking, of course, of you, because as a result of Michalski's[116] absence I am unable to think about anything, I am so overwhelmed with work. Love conflict of course—not stressed enough by us. I suggest changes at the point when the girl decides to stay by the sea. Situation: she comes back from France with "someone" and then has to break up with this "someone" because she fell in love with the one at the port. How do you like it? But it still has to be written! Will you do it? Apart from this, there are too many children, but we'll take care of that, Rudziński also wants some room for 3–4 ballets, they have to be packed in such a way as not to appear artificial, perhaps at the moment of the arrival: those returning (the trio) dance, the Kashubians, the displaced of Wilno, and also the Czechs' dance. Think about where to put this. On the pier after arriving might be best, don't you think? I'm counting on your finding a bit of time to mull over these things, and also to write. Remember that you assumed a certain kind of responsibility since you talked about it in the interview given to the press. The money has come back, but I haven't picked yours up at the radio yet, because I don't have the time to stop by to pick up my own. It won't disappear, and anyway I believe that you'll be back on July 1 with 5 kilos of written pages. . . . [*unclear*] Lewicka will create a lot of work and somehow it'll work out. O shudder!—I've become secretary of the writer's circle—Wanda, the good times are over.[117]

Write. Regards to you both,
Your Stanisław

[*Wygodzki's wife adds a postscript to Borowski's wife*]

Dear Tuśka,

As you already know, I feel v. well, and am glad that it's all behind me.

I'm now finishing a course, and would gladly go to the seaside, but don't know whether I'll manage to since I still have to copy almost the whole of Kisch.

Are you happy with your stay there? I think you will both return rested and with new reserves of strength and energy for work. How much longer are you staying? Write back! Kisses to you, and you kiss Tadek in my name (if you feel like it).

Irena

112. JUNE 23, 1948, SOBIESZÓW
[*to W. Leopold*]

Dear Wanda,

For a week, we've been penned up in here bored stiff, the weather's a bit lousy, cold and windy. For the first week of "vacation" I wrote, even quite diligently, then it started to seem to me that we should go back in order to write because here I couldn't. So we decided on this plan of action: we'll wait until this Saturday (26th) for Roman Bratny to arrive with the money and news, after which we'd like either on Monday morning or Sunday evening (it depends on the schedule) to escape from here to Wrocław, to you, in other words, and—if you would have a couple of days—take some excursions (or sit at home, it's up to you) or else—if you have a day—walk around and talk. It seems to us that this would be better than sitting in this hole (because Sobieszów really is a damned hole in this idiotic weather). We'd gladly take off today (never mind Saturday!), but Bratny prevents us. How does this seem to you? Would it not be a problem for you, especially since we'd like to stay until the first (Tuśka maintains that's the opening of the exhibition).

It is absolutely necessary to stick your nose in about IBL,[118] but it won't hurt to promise Fatty, he's understanding.

About Palestine, you're right, it's very comical. If in the future I manage to write several "small anecdotes," philosophical tales, clean of any aesthetic ornamentation, targeted at the taste of our Marxist burghers, one of them will be about the German doctor Brand who experimented on people and at the foot of the gallows recently said to the executioner and to American journalists that a nation that performs experiments on people should not hang people who have done the same.

As for your review, that promise that you'll write about my next book, I'm calling on it for *Pożegnanie;* write and don't spare dark colors, there's a bottle of wine waiting for you here. (What do you expect, my dear, I, too, have to take care of reviewers.)[119]

We have to talk further about Wyka and Żółkiewski. Wyka, as usual, carefully, Kraków-style, professorially, exhaustively, has just not noticed one thing: that today Rudnicki is the Jews' impassioned ideologue, he is helping them rebuild their faith in themselves as a nation and as a people; that's why, in him, the general character of adversity forms the background, the exception comes to the fore. According to the false, but effective, formula of the Christian Rusinek (! in the discussion about "Etap"): "One good man redeemed the hideousness of Auschwitz." Adolf thinks that the best cure for fascism is to show the beauty of those dying as a result of it (through this, he obscures the very mechanism of fascism—if people were like this, how could what happened have been possible?); but, perhaps, I'm being unfair. At any rate, for me, Rudnicki's problems lie completely somewhere else than where Wyka sees them. Well, this is for a further discussion.

Sincere greetings to you and your mother,

Tadeusz + Tuśka

113. POSTMARKED JULY 28, 1948

[*from Tadeusz Różewicz; postcard*]

Bierut St., Wolin—M.V.R.

Dear Tadeusz,

I was very pleased that *Odrodzenie*[120] singled you out, although you are probably unhappy? Dear one, do you always use Chinese titles in letters? I ought to address you: "O Brilliant Son of the Sun, White Elephant, Tower of Babel, Exalted Maiden, Vessel of Conceit, etc., etc." The fact that you cannot read what is being published in this country speaks rather well of you. As to other matters, e.g., "Ruskij wopros," I'll write you another letter about it. The Socialist-Realist and surrealistic poet, R. Bratny, is in the national horse stables—so I won't worry him with poetic matters, anyway Citizen Woroszyłski[121] already did so in the last poem published in the unfortunate *Dziennik Literacki.*[122]

Kisses,

Tadeusz

114. AUGUST 4, 1948, WARSAW
[to his family]

My dears,

I apologize for not having written for so long, but truth to tell we are both up to our ears in work. Tuśka is currently at the radio, which, together with monitoring, takes her the major part of the day, especially since a third reviewer has gone on vacation. I've been engaged by the press office of the Intellectuals Congress in Wrocław, which is to take place at the end of August. We have to gather materials about the guests—literati who are coming from all over the world to this congress—these materials go to the radio and the press. There's a more than hellish amount of running around and making so-called connections, but somebody has to do this work. I can't leave town. We'll go to Wrocław for the congress to organize a congress paper and bulletins there, as well as information for the Polish and foreign press. It would be good if Julek had a bit of time, he could spend a week in Wrocław and combine the beautiful with the useful, viewing the exhibition while looking at a few foreign guests such as Picasso or Huxley, an enticing thing if only from the point of view of snobbery.

We're very curious how the Mr. G. affair ended? You might, if only out of obligation, write a few words.

As you must know, I was mentioned in this year's *Odrodzenia* prize. It doesn't give much honor, but it's always nice to find oneself among the best writers, if only for a day. It will also bring a practical advantage—the book will sell more quickly.

The weather is truly summery—we make the most of it sometimes by going to the pool. We're hoping that after the congress we'll manage to find a couple of weeks for a prewinter break.

Hugs and kisses,

Tadeusz

When does Julek have vacation? Julek, I got your letter a moment ago. I'm in Warsaw all the time. Come, we'll decide on what to do next! T.

115. OCTOBER 4, 1948, STANNINGLEY

[*from J. Nel Siedlecki*]

POET Tadeusz Borowski, apt. 37, 13 Filtrowa St., Warsaw

Tadeusz—because I daren't make so bold as to address you in the old familiar way.

A great deal of time has gone by. I don't know whether you got a single one of my letters; as evidence of good will I'm enclosing one of the very old ones which was returned to me.

I again offer you both lots of good wishes—in all sincerity.

My situation in brief: I'm still studying ("mechanical engineering") in Bradford. I should finish college in a year (get a diploma—worth little). At the same time, I'm trying to take the university exams (the equivalent of our "engineer"). A great deal of work, and since I'm old and even lazier, it's going very hard. The country—so-so; climate and weather—lousy; people very friendly and very good; boring (and I don't feel like doing anything).

Tolek is in America, but it's also not going very well for him, or more simply—absolutely not going at all (don't mention this to him, should you write). He's enchanted with the country. I've had no news from Krystyn for about a year. I receive all the Polish journals here (rather: nearly all, and not regularly) and I've frequently come across your poems and articles. I remember to myself Pinzenauer and the rest, and I think it was a very good thing you went back. I, however, am also pleased with my decision—though I often feel lousy here.

Once again, best wishes to you both,

Nel

116. OCTOBER 19, 1948, WARSAW

[*to T. Mikulski*]

Dear Professor,

It's only today that I've been able to write a note about the congress newspaper; I apologize for the delay.[123] I justify the slightly ironic tone that can be detected in the article on the grounds of the disproportion between the amount of work we put into it, and the modesty of the result. Work on the paper was one great improvisation, and the people who allowed this to happen should be

beaten around the head. I cannot do so (how can one beat Borejsza[124] around the head?). So I passed over these matters in silence.

Sincere regards to you both,

Tadeusz Borowski

117. OCTOBER 20, 1948, EAST BERLIN
[*from Gerhart Pohl 246; original in German*][125]

Dear Tadeusz Borowski,

Please accept my most sincere thanks for your nice letter of October 5 and for the dedication in both your books, which I was very happy to receive.

I immediately gave the volume of stories to my Polish translator to read, because I myself cannot at the moment apply myself to reading that book. Please suggest which stories are the most representative and the most suited to a German collection of Polish stories. Then I will write what our opinion is.

Your observations on the subject of the journal *Aufbau* interested us very much, and I thank you for them in the name of my colleagues who work on it.

I can very well understand your aversion to Grotzinger's social psychology. If we decided to print this sketch, it was chiefly because it was an attempt to maintain contact with the at least semi-progressive circles in the western region. Grotzinger plays an important role in Munich.

We print such articles in *Aufbau* in order to explain situations and to create points for discussion, and to arouse criticism such as yours, dear Tadeusz Borowski. Only in this manner, will there gradually arise in Germany discussions on a wider spiritual plane. During the Nazi period, people became completely unaccustomed to it.

We will send you *Aufbau* regularly. I have paid the subscription for you, and later we'll be able to translate it into books or something similar.

I requested that you be sent my story "Between Yesterday and Tomorrow," from the complimentary copies. Unfortunately, I cannot send you Kasak's novels, my sister-in-law in Poland has one copy. If you were to ask her, I'm sure she will gladly lend it to you. Her address is: 138 Wilcza Poręba, Karpacz, Jelenia Góra, Lower Silesia. Write her a few words.

I would be most happy for us to stay in contact with each other in the future. I request speedy information, particularly about which stories you would suggest for the anthology.

You need not apologize for your German. You have mastered our language splendidly. Please don't forget to send in your next letter the address of Witold Wirpsza to whom I promised journals and a book.

Friendly greetings,

Your Gerhart Pohl

118. OCTOBER 26, 1948, WARSAW

[*to Helena Teigova*]

Dear Madam,

Thank you very much for thinking of me, and I wish to express my regret that we did not manage to meet in Wrocław. I was working in the congress press office then and did not have a free moment, while at the end of the job I fell sick and lay in bed unconscious.

I did not wish to impose with *Pożegnanie z Marią,* which was very poorly published. In a short time, however, my collection of short stories, *Kamienny świat,* will come out with Cztytelnik, and I will send it to you immediately.

To date I have had one, very negligible proposition for a translation of *Pożegnanie z Marią* into Czech, which I did not, in any event, take seriously (it was a Czech student from the university in Kraków). I don't know whether for a Czech reader all the archly Polish issues in the book would be comprehensible and engrossing (e.g., the Jewish issue in the first story, bourgeois youths—the matter of the Polish postwar camps in "Bitwa pod Grunwaldem," etc.). At present, after publishing *Kamienny świat,* I'm writing a third volume of stories of varying length and subject matter, encompassing, for the most part, the postwar period. The main subject—the difference between our understanding of humanism and Western "humanism." I'll finish the typescript by December, where and when I will publish it, I don't yet know, I think, however, the book should be off the presses by spring.

Out of these three volumes, it would be possible to make a collection for a Czech reader. I wouldn't wish to persuade you of anything; it would be best it you read these books and, if you consider them useful, choose something yourself.

I enclose my biography, beautifully written on a machine. There is not much of it, but I had too varied a life to write at length about it.

Sincerely,

Tadeusz Borowski

119. OCTOBER 1948, KRAKÓW
[*from W. Mach, postcard*]

Dear Tadek,
   Warm hugs. Wish you well. I think of you as a dear brother.
   Wilhelm

Give my very warm regards to your very nice wife! W.

120. OCTOBER 30, 1948, WROCŁAW
[*from T. Mikulski*]

Dear Tadzio,
   Thank you for the little article for *Zeszyty Wrocławskie,* which arrived in time. Very sincere thanks to both of you for the name day telegram, although I'm mortally embarrassed that I allowed you to beat me to it. Belatedly, but most sincerely, I wish you all the best. Will *Kamienny świat* be ready soon? We are putting together a belated *Zeszyty,* other than that—everything else goes along in the established Wrocław way. More students, less time. Do you have plans to come our way? You are always invited for a chat and a vodka.
   Sincere regards, greetings to Tuśka,
   T. Mikulski

121. NOVEMBER 1948, WARSAW
[*to Wilhelm Mach*]

Dear Wilek,
   Thank you in a brotherly way for your card, which I got sometime, somewhere, with a beautiful view of Kraków. On the other hand, author of *Rdza* [*Rust*], you could scratch out a few longer words and tell us what's going on in the wide world. And you could tuck some little book under your arm. But God be with you! Friends' legs are short.
   I have written, as you probably know, a certain *Kamienny świat,* which is to come out with Glucksmann[126] in Kraków, and they are predicting a thousand

unpleasantnesses for me for my nihilism and existentialism. Like a rabbit placed in a cage with a rattlesnake, I await the blows with resignation.

Where are you now? I'm promising myself to come to Kraków at some point, and will fish you out. I met with Wyka several times, but I was afraid to ask him, because he's become completely professorial and humanized himself, which could be seen at the Polish scholars meeting in Łódź.[127]

I kiss you on the cheek several times. Tuśka is asleep, so she's greeting you in her dreams.

Tadeusz

122. NOVEMBER 11, 1948, WARSAW
[*to T. Mikulski*]

With thanks for the copies of the Górski[128] review and for the good wishes, with sincerest regards,

Tadeusz Borowski

123. NOVEMBER 13, 1948
[*on the back:*] Citizen Marczak-Oborski, p. 242

Dear Staszek,

We didn't find you in, are leaving flowers, name day greetings, wishing you health, happiness, fame, going sadly home.

Tadeusz

Tuśka

[*a drawing of flowers in a pot, on the base written:*] 5 P.M.

124. NOVEMBER 28, 1948, WARSAW
[*to Wilhelm Mach*]

Dear Wilek,

I don't have to remind you what an epic swine you are not having written me a single word since your return—other than a lousy card! Truth to tell, I'm also a swine, but at least I didn't go anywhere.

You know, I've heard that Tadeusz Różewicz is tearing himself to bits now, we have to help him somehow. That fat scribbler S.R.D. wrote about him so idiotically.[129] Roman Bratny is going around in a rage. I think that we should organize an evening for Tadek at our club—and the case will be resolved. We'll ask Dobrowolski to explain himself.

Wilek, I'm in a bit of a fighting mood, but it passes quickly, and I wander around again free of care like a dog on a lawn.

Write what you are reading, doing, thinking. When will we see each other? I'm going to send you a new book soon.

Kisses,

Tadeusz

Is Prof. Wyka still putting on weight?

125. DECEMBER 2, 1948, SZCZECIN
[*from Witold Wirpsza*]

Dear Tadek,

As the editorial secretary of *Tygodnik Wybrzeża* [*Coastal Weekly*], I am writing to remind you of the promise you made during your stay in Szczecin[130] to write something for us: commentary, memoir, letter to the editor, or something of that kind. It can also be a story. We pay like *Odrodzenie*—15 a line.

And now another matter.

In talking with Bratny, we hit on the idea that—for the issue for the writers' conference—you write jointly with him an article that would be a kind of "manifesto" of writers of our generation. It's not a question of a contest with *Kuźnica,* or generally with the older generation. It's more about taking a position on literary matters in general, and, in particular, on the problem of the writer's connection with the working masses. The journal with this article would be

distributed at the time of the meeting and, in this way, even during the deliberations, certain people, at least, will be forced to think through certain matters.
The deadline for submitting this article is before the holidays. 6–8 pages typed.

I am furious with Sandauer, out of all my *Stocznia* [Shipyard] he chose two
most "formalistic" fragments which play a certain part within the whole, but on
their own, however, create an impression of ideological incompetence. I don't
think this has done me a good service; at the same time, it throws a certain light
on the section's new editor who is going to be enraptured with the same stuff
that Ziembiński was enraptured with, or even worse. That people—in literature,
at least—who are over thirty years should be afraid to call things by their true
names, always be needing either innuendos or a symbolic fog! The tyranny of
such editors is at base throwing sand under wheels.

My best to Tuśka. If she'd like a good rest, let her come down to us. You
said that you'd both like to hide out somewhere during the holidays. Come to
Szczecin—I won't tell anyone and no one will know about it.

Sincerely,

Witek

P.S.   I'm crawling out of the financial pits, I'll repay the debt very soon.

126. DECEMBER 6, 1948, WROCŁAW
[*from T. Mikulski, postcard*]

Dear Tadeusz Borowski,

Zeszyty came out a few days ago, and you have already received (or are receiving this moment) an author's copy. I remember your promise of a few months
ago to provide us with an article in the nature of a general review of literary
theory. If it is ready, we'd like it without delay. But I know well that long articles
are written slowly. Perhaps, however, you have something a little shorter at hand?
Issue 3 came out without reviews, because that was how it was decided. With
issue 4, on the other hand, we want to build this section up. So I am earnestly
requesting some material for the review section (prose, poetry—whatever is in
your heart) as well as a concrete suggestion so that the book you have reserved is
not given to someone else. Little time, unfortunately: up to two weeks. As you
know, I am ambitious about our publication, and that's the reason why I am

troubling you. Please write what you think about the issue. Our sincere greetings to both of you. Until we meet in Warsaw in January,

T. Mikulski

127. DECEMBER 6, 1948, KRAKÓW
[*from W. Mach, letter with torn top right corner*]

Dear Tadek,

You're right: you are [here, drawing of an angel], and I am [a torn sketch]. Hugs and kisses for remembering me, you perhaps don't realize how dear and valuable that is to me. I was in Warsaw 10th–11th, XI, for an editorial meeting at Czytelnik, and it wasn't because my legs were too short, but because my psychic (!) stomach was heavy after having eaten all the ideological and stipulative delicacies prepared for us, which resulted in the sad fact that I didn't see you. Ask Tadek Konwicki, at whose place I spent the night, how very much I wished to do so. It was impossible, I was actually in Warsaw one full day (completely bloated with meetings), and had to leave the following day. And I had such a moral hangover, that I preferred to get over it on my own Kraków garbage, rather than pollute your aesthetic innards. And as to writing, what happened was that, truth to tell, I wanted to every day, but my goddamn work wouldn't allow me to fulfill the desire. Wyka isn't here, he's gone to Czechoslovakia for a month—I had to cook up issue 11 of *Twórczość*, now I'm battling with 12—you can guess the rest. That's how it is.

Tadek, I'd very much like to talk with you, at length and about various things. But face to face.

Letters are beyond the ability of such a conversation. I'm tormented by various fears, loathings, contradictions, pleased, in turn, by various good signs—the world in some of its parts provokes rebellion, in others hope—I get lost in all of this, wander around, and cannot find my own place. And with all of this, I am a man of "lange Leitung," I'm slow on the uptake—and it's all completely entangled with more or less personal issues, with "good will," and with "impossibility," and so a pernicious "ideological alienation" torments me, and "integral humanism" troubles me, and a lack of education, and inappropriate reactions, and a feeling of inadequacy, small capacity—if I'm a little vessel, can I bear more than a couple of swigs of something, and, here, they shove the whole world into

me, and order me to acknowledge receipt—oh, Tadek, I'd rather chat with you because I miss your reaction—face, voice, your wisdom, and, finally, goodness.

Now I will tell you: you belong among that number of my friends that forms a very distinctive group. On a "personal," "everyday" level I don't know you as well as the others. I've seen you two or three times. Mainly what you write. And yet I turn to you in my thoughts, hopes, and fears, more often, and more willingly, than one normally turns to people one scarcely knows, even if they're actually highly worthy. In this, there's nothing of "literary friendship," of which by nature, laziness, and abnegation, I'm incapable. So why? Some kind of "ellipsis," some kind of crossing of an intermediary "acid test" [the text is broken here] long months or years of "acquaintance"—to immediately arrive at a stage of real understanding. Why it's so—I don't know, but it is, and you can be sure of it, if such a certainty is needed at all.

I read *Kamienny świat* while still in Paris, and I will simply say: I was enraptured. I wrote to Tadzio Konwicki about it then. Don't worry about being picked on—the dogs bark, the sun shines. I'm sorry I no longer write about books, because I would write about it with pleasure. But I easily persuaded myself that I have no right to write anything.[131]

I'm consoling Tadek Różewicz. The dogs won't do anything to him, either, never fear. An author's evening for him—a good idea, arrange it for him. He deserves the satisfaction.

You ask me about many things. But I'm not answering. I don't feel like writing. I'd rather send thoughts to you, and talk, if possible.

Sincere regards, Tadek. Best wishes to Tuśka.

Wilek

128. DECEMBER 7, 1948

[*from W. Wirpsza*]

Dear Tadek,

I'd like to ask you for a certain favor. After Słucki's article in *Odrodzenie,* I sent my "remarks" there. Because I explained certain things in it not too diplomatically, and certainly riskily, I'm afraid that *Odrodzenie* will be unwilling to print it. If, however, the possibility exists of printing it with certain changes, I'd prefer it if you, rather than anybody else, should take care of it. In connection with this, in sending the article to *Odrodzenie,* I wrote this to Konwicki.

In my opinion, if two fundamental points cannot be kept—my conception of the development of the youngest Polish poetry, and the stressing of the class character of the controversy on the subject— it's pointless to print the article. In this event, I will try to place it in *Tygodnik Wybrzeża* at the time of the literary conference.

I'm counting on you, just in case.

* * *

If you really do intend to come to us for the holidays, which both of us really truly would like, let us know!

* * *

Remember about the article for *Tygodnik Wybrzeża.*

* * *

Many warm regards to you both.
    Witold

129. DECEMBER 9, 1948, WARSAW
[*to T. Mikulski*]

Dear Professor,

Sincere thanks for the card and the invitation to *Zeszyty* of which I am a faithful admirer. I expect the third issue any day. If someone hasn't already taken Ingarden, I would gladly write something very critical about his *Szkice*. It would be a somewhat longer piece, but would, however, fit into the normal framework of a review. But I am afraid that its harsher tone would perhaps deviate from the calm of *Zeszyty.* If someone else is working on Ingarden, I propose a discussion of several publications not known to us (or nearly unknown) talking about man's fate during war. I am thinking here of Koestler's book, *Crusade Without a Cross,* Anna Seghers's *The Seventh Cross,* Graham Greene's *The Power and the Glory,* Hemingway's *For Whom the Bell Tolls,* Polewoj's *Story of a Real Man.* One might be able to give an overview of the various concepts of what our mutual friend calls "The Structure of the Human Fate."[132]

I am also taking the opportunity of sending you, sir, *Kamienny świat,* which has finally appeared in print and—as my friends predict—will create a great deal

of unpleasantness for me because of its supposed existentialism. Unfortunately, here in Poland they don't yet know how to read literature correctly (especially the so-called Marxists). They would have noticed long ago that *Kamienny świat* is a stinging, not only literary, but also political, lampoon.[133] It was written, finally, at a time when we didn't yet have beautiful critical and self-critical arrangements.

So I await, Professor, your decision as to the subject of the work, I promise that I will submit it on schedule (I have Ingarden underway, I'm now worrying *Spór o istnienie świata* [*Controversy About the Existence of the World*]. I will write about *Zeszyty* as soon as the post hands them to me and—I enclose best regards to you both.

Tadeusz Borowski

130. DECEMBER 10, 1948, WARSAW
[*to Maria and Witold Wirpsza*]

Dear Wirpszas,

Thank you very much for your letter, which, however, tells me nothing about Olga Kern. From this, I deduce that she left happily. I gave the letter to Jackowski and spoke to the necessary people, I don't know if it helped. I'm caught in the very midst of my own problems from which I don't quite know how to extricate myself. Probably, it'll come to having to waste some time (some two months), but truly—I'm going to have to go with Tuśka and my brother to the mountains or Lower Silesia, if conditions permit, of course. We will come to Głębokie, but probably in summer when you will already have two Punteks.[134] Witek will nurse the smaller one, and I will go for walks with the bigger one.

Don't upset yourselves about Sandauer—he's a psychopath. He's got an unbelievable mess in his head and obviously understands nothing about what's happening in Poland. It isn't surprising that he likes precisely what you don't, Witek. Anyway, the situation is like that in all the literary journals, as we've already bemoaned more than once. I think that after the Unification Congress a lot of things will improve. I am sending you, Puntek, *Kamienny świat*—published, bound, and with a dedication. It is, as is clear, a tiny lampoon of our friends on the Left and the Right—chosen at random (that means as they suited the general purpose). This for the moment is it: my next book in two years.

When will *Stocznia* [*Shipyard*] appear? How is the work with the Gdańskites coming along? Won't you be publishing some chapter somewhere? And how

232

is Maria feeling? Apropos the cash: don't send it, we'll consume it in summer, that'll be better.

I wrote a little report about our visit to Pomerania, which will appear in the Congress issue of *Odrodzenie*. For literary reasons, I've ripped the collar of your black coat a little, I hope you won't take offense.

Kisses to you both and to black Puntek and we're waiting to see what the new one will be: a guy or a girl.

Tadeusz

131. DECEMBER 14, 1948, GŁĘBOKIE
[*from Maria Kurecka-Wirpsza*]

Dear Tadeks,

Our letters are chasing each other in circles, and that's why certain things haven't been made clear yet. I'm writing on Witek's behalf today, because he is dreadfully overworked right now, and we wanted to thank you quickly, Tadek, for *Kamienny świat* and your letter. I, on the other hand, personally find it hard to forgive you for that ripped collar on Witek's coat, because, man, you have to understand that had you mentioned it once, you'd just be an ass, but 5 (five!!!) times on three pieces of paper . . . !!! In what kind of light are you showing me to posterity, bequeathing such a tattered silhouette of my hubby to our national literature?! I console myself only in that you probably treated the above unfortunate collar as a *per procura et figura* picture of the poetic pocket and if that is how things actually are, then I'm sorry that you didn't mention it five more times. And since we're talking of pockets, we would be grateful if before the holidays you could find out whether a few papers are due to us from the Union. I was in Warsaw in November, so Rymkiewicz made me write to the Head Office asking them to give me a bit of cash for the birth of little Wirpsza, but, as of yet not a peep, and that little creature won't ask about cash at first, but will appear on earth in a very short time.

But here I am bothering you, when you, yourself, write that you have a heap of worries. Why do you have to lose two whole months? The two of you aren't by any chance ill, are you? Those four thou. we could have given back to you with a clear conscience, because for the moment there's cash for grub, and it probably won't be too bad in January, either, because I've finally signed a contract with Czytelnik for that accursed Luidsey (except, again—goddammit—they're

not sending the money!). But if you get into some dire straits, write—maybe you and Witek could work something out. Oh, have you already received Witek's letter about that controversial article on poetry for *Odrodzenie*? It would be very good if you could read it and tone down the aggressivities in it a bit, because, in truth, you're aggressive enough for four yourself, but it's probably easier with someone else's text than one's own. And Witek very much wants that article to appear before the January Conference [in Szczecin], because it really is time to raise these matters.

It's a pity that you won't be showing up here for the holidays, however, even though it's a long time till summer, we're taking you at your word that you will come here for at least a month! Witek has also decided that he has no intention of nursing the smaller Puntek at that time, but of . . . flirting with Tuśka! What say you to that, Tadeusz? The work on the "Gdańskites" is practically at a standstill, because one has to eternally run around and wrangle over a whole load of daily matters and trivia. But perhaps Witek will be able to write a bit over the holidays.

Tuśka says nothing about being poisoned by our currant jelly, from which I'm prone to suspect that Tadek imbibed it along the road! But in summer there are whole swarms of currants, so you'll be able to rustle some jelly up for yourself. Bratny wrote that he'd spoken with you, Tadek, on the subject of an evening for Witek at the club, and you're apparently aiming for January. Would this take place before the conference? That would be wonderful!—If you get a moment after all the congress confusion and you decide on a definite date, write—okay? E. Kern left happily and without greater cataclysmic events, because the Ministry of Foreign Affairs sent her boat ticket (but not money, and she had to borrow from the Andrzejewskis!). She wrote to us again afterward, because she got stuck in Sopot, since, of course, the ship's departure was delayed, but now she's probably landed in her Brussels.[135]

So, keep well, sneeze loudly and through both nostrils at any problems, and have a good Christmas. Love and kisses,

Signed, Witek

Maryla

Puntek

and "something" little[136]

132. UNDATED, ŁÓDŹ

[*from R. Matuszewski*]

Dear Tadeusz,

Thank you very much for the book. As it happened, the day before I got it from you, I grabbed a review copy that came to *Kuźnica,* and I'm already familiar with it. It's excellent. I read it with real pleasure. I also want to write about it, and the review begs the title, "Sztuka niedomówień" ["The Art of Understatement"]. You are, of course, right that it isn't a form that you should stick with: the foreword is pertinent and—what can't always be said of forewords—necessary. But in thinking about the "art of understatement," I want to suggest to various lovers of dotting the i's the benefits of not doing so.[137] The profile of Zawadzki from *Wiedza* in "Zaliczka" is fantastic. Did you send him a copy with a dedication? The picture "Pod bohaterskim Partyzantem" should have been dedicated not to Jarosław, but to J. A. Król.[138] Morton against the background of Dubrovnik in "Dziennik podróży" is brilliant. In a word, you've finished the guy off forever. Of your last stories, I liked "Zabawa z wódką" better than "January Offensive," I am generally very curious whether you could manage to become a "positive realist" because derision drips from each of your pores and it'll be hard for you to avoid the taint of conversion. Perhaps you would visit the Matuszewskis on the third day of the holiday, apt. 104 (IV kolonia), 18 Krasiński Street, Żoliborz. My wife will be there, nothing threatens in the kitchen.

Deepest respects to your wife. Don't let her take offense: obviously every wife knows her own kitchen only, and apart from that, Wanda reckons that it is her; I, on the other hand, think the stove exploding, together with your unequaled eloquence, the most attractive act of the evening.

You apparently don't return books, in light of that bring "short stories" when you come. I warn you just in case, that in Żoliborz there isn't a single interesting book to "marvel at," the whole library is in Łódź.

Sincerely,
Ryszard

133. UNDATED, WROCŁAW

[*from W. Żukrowski*]

Dear Old Man,

Thank you for *Kamienny świat*, I'd bought it for myself earlier, now I am sending mine to Grudziński in London, asking for it to be discussed. Yours with the dedication—I'm keeping. Listen, you probably consider me the ultimate procrastinator because I promised you a review of *Pożegnanie z Marią*—so get this, I've finally written it, and it will appear in *Odra* together with a discussion of "świat"—in short, water's water, but we Poles prefer vodka. I tried to establish the spirit and humanitarianism of your position, so I will support you from an angle you didn't expect, but on the other hand I capture all the malice in the dedication, especially when it comes to the armchair Communists, and Jarosław to whom you devoted the story about the lesbians. See, Tadzio, the ceiling weighs down on you, too, I'd like to remind you of our summer agreement, and I still maintain that you can depend on me, if that's worth anything. "Ojczyzna" is very good, delightfully perverse, but the healthy climate of the proletariat will not be able to stand this type of truth, socialist realism is very conventional truth, the perceived rather than the one that surrounds us.

Apparently *Ręka Ojca* [*Father's Hand*] has already come out—you are now going to be witness to an amusing "dog fight" about my metaphysical position. The Catholics are afraid of meaty observations, the Marxists of faith-based ones, so I am swimming against the current, I think you'll soon be joining me. I'm not living in the new place yet, I'm settling a few accounts, reviews I owe, writing a very gloomy novel—that's about all. Wanda came out at least a week too soon with that congratulatory telegram for Mikulski, because the PPR still has its own candidate, Dygat. I think that M. will win out, but today, that is the 12th, there's still no decision. Don't tell her, because she'll feel bad, I don't know who put out that piece of gossip before time, Kott, probably. I'd like Tadeusz to get it because he's a straight guy, and Dygat—apart from the Congress declaration—has done nothing.[139] Sorry, I'm doing him a wrong—he lives in our hotel and forced the city to renovate my apartment, that's already a great deal.

Nothing remarkable here. If I might ask—send a copy to Giedroy, editor of *Kultura* (*Kamienny świat*)—they are incredibly isolated.

Very sincerely,

Wojtek

P.S.   I think I'll offer you my Christmas wishes! May those few days go by propitiously, don't stuff yourself too much and don't get plastered, because that would be beyond the bounds of Congress activity. T.W.

P.P.S.   I don't feel like repeating my assessment of *Kamienny świat* twice, you'll read it yourself—it's very complimentary, but without compliments! T.W.

134. DECEMBER 15, 1948, ŁÓDŹ
[send. Paweł Hertz] 96 Kosciuski St., Łódź

Dear Sir,

I sincerely thank you for sending *Kamienny świat*. I know this book in part from reading the press. I would like to tell you how very much I like this genre and the way in which you develop it with your prose. And your suspiciousness, and lack of naive enthusiasm, and seeing evil and good things in human matters—all of this wins me over to that which you write.

Please don't take it as nastiness when I say that of all of them *Kamienny świat* appeals to me the most, and that's why I thank you for dedicating it to me, although these thanks were probably not part of the intent of your opening dedication.

Warm regards, sincerely

Paweł Hertz

135. DECEMBER 18, 1948, WROCŁAW
[*from T. Mikulski*]

Dear Pan Tadeusz,

Thank you most sincerely for thinking of me and for the copy of *Kamienny świat,* which arrived over a week ago. We read it immediately and discussed it intently in our little Wrocław community (Wojtek Żukrowski, Miss Kowalska). We also savored the literary dedications at length and some of them seemed to us very well aimed. Perhaps the best among them—the pages for Żółkiewski and our little Wojtek.[140] One would very much like to talk to the author about other (and these also) fragments of the book—and perhaps we will manage this before too long (10th January I will be in Warsaw).

Thank you very much for complying with my editorial request. You must now have received issue 3 of *Zeszyty*, since the editor's secretary has finally passed his oral exams in reading (it turned out that it was precisely this that was putting the brakes on some of the administrative functions). You promise—as I read from your last letter—to write about *Zeszyty* somewhere. That announcement made me very happy and I shall be eagerly watching for it to be realized.

I'm also awaiting with great impatience your new scripts for us. I am reserving space in the review section, which we want to expand in this issue, for your articles: the report on Wygodzki's little volume[141] and perhaps precisely for the review of war novels (but please remember that not all of them, as it seems to me, have freedom of distribution in Poland).

I would ask for Ingarden, too, provided you put it together courteously (I will tell you honestly that I would prefer not to get entangled in polemics with my former *gimnazjium* teacher with whom I maintain relations to this day). It is precisely for these personal reasons, that I ask you rather for other things previously mentioned.

I can render you nothing sensational from our Wrocław backyard—out of lack of sensation. About ordinary things, we'll talk in Warsaw. I'd be very sorry, were I not to find you home.

For the approaching holiday and the New Year, I send you both my best wishes, and you, my dear Sir, a warm embrace.

T. Mikulski

136. DECEMBER 19, 1948, KRAKÓW
[*from Paweł Jasienica*]

Dear Sir,

Thank you very much for forwarding *Kamienny świat* to me. It seems that Kisiel is thinking of writing a review of this book. I had hoped that I would be in Warsaw before Christmas and that we would see each other. I had planned to come for the purpose of arranging the matter of my book (reportage) with the censors. It took place without my presence in Warsaw, because I received a short note prohibiting printing, and also the manuscript returned. So, as you see, not everybody is allowed to participate in the building of the culture, for which you so unambiguously called in the issue of *Dziennik Polski* of the 15th day of the current month. Kisiel and I perused that article of yours with enormous interest.[142]

I don't know when I will be in Warsaw; perhaps in January or February. If I may—I will visit you.

Sincere regards to you both and holiday greetings,

Paweł Jasienica

137. JANUARY 2, 1949, OPORÓW
[*from W. Żukrowski*]

Dear Tadek,

Damn you, you ought to get a literary prize for that joke—it's brilliant, I howled with delight reading that carol, tell me, out of what archive did you shake that postcard? You really did pull it off! But now on a more serious note, conversations between us, you know, are strangely feverish, a screaming of two monologues at our faces, and I would like to talk with you. I very much do not like what you wrote in *Dziennik Literacki*, I understand that the idea is 1) dynamic, 2) in a period of rearmament uses totalitarian methods, destructive and brutal tricks, but why the hell praise this, dignify it as art? Maybe I'm wrong, perhaps stripping things down has its own sense—but I read it with sadness. I am sending you the book with the request that you not write about it, except directly to me. You see, I'm not at all pleased with it, I can see all its errors clearly, how every attempt at objectifying this turning point in time is subject to discussion and to an appropriate choice of citations, that it may have a murderous meaning, and, anyway—I'm shrugging my shoulders here—it has ceased to amuse me. I'm quoting from a letter from Grudziński to whom I sent *Kamienny świat*—"Borowski is too young and too green in relation to his writing ambitions and the talent at his disposal. Aggressiveness and provocation take the place of wisdom and literary reflection in him. He would like to 'philosophize' everything he's lived through as fast as possible, and he has no sense of the decadence in which we are living. In literature, there's no art in repeating there is no God, I don't believe in God, it is not enough to have oneself taken for an atheist, one has to be able to show why one doesn't believe, and the permanence of art depends on this ability." I'm not writing the praises because you have enough of those. He stresses the maturity of the prose and talent many times, of course. If you think about it calmly, you'll admit he's a bit right. I think he's one of the few emigrants with whom one can talk, and even, perhaps, come to an agreement with, since, growing numb in sterile torment, they thirst for a human word. You've spared

me so far, you know the story in *Kamienny świat* dedicated to me is like a friendly jab, for that reason, don't get angry for what I said above. Literati are so sensitive, it's worse than treading on eggs. I came by your place at the time of the PZPR Congress[143] but no one was in. A pity, because you know, in the end, even the impression that someone is listening is a relief. Neverending monologue is tiring. What are you writing? If you are alive, jot down a few words, and say what offends you about *Ręce* [*Hands*]? Will you not be somewhere in Szklarska or Wrocław? Warm regards. I wish you a new book and a prize in the New Year, unless the Stoczkowcy[144] stifle our voices—with symphonic gunfire.

Your Wojtek

138. UNDATED
[*from S. Wygodzki*]

My Dear Tadeusz,

I've learned that you are fooling around and do not want to take on the secretaryship.[145] Well, you are not allowed to handle the matter this way, because it thwarts us, and the guy currently secretary-ing can on no account do this, if only for the reason that he's not entitled to do so. You must take up the secretaryship(!), at least for a short time until we find some other way out of this situation, otherwise we'll never crawl out of this quagmire.

Regards,
Stanisław Wyg

139. JANUARY 17, 1949, EAST BERLIN
[*in German; from G. Pohl*]

Dear Tadeusz Borowski,

I'm thanking you at last for your nice letter of 1 December (which took rather a long time to get here) and for the truly wonderful gift (*Satyra w konspiracji* [*Satire in the Conspiracy*]).[146] I am enraptured by this wonderfully conceived work, will most definitely write about it here.

At the moment I am working a lot on Mickiewicz. For his jubilee, I have to prepare a few sketches, a radio program, and a speech for the official festivities of the Mickiewicz Society named after Hellmuth von Gerlach.

The anthology of Polish stories is slowly moving forward. The translations of 10 stories are ready. Of yours, we've already translated the story "Pożegnanie z Marią." Horst Holzschuher has put together a very good translation. All our friends here at the publishing house and in the Cultural Union who have already read your stories think them very good. The debates that have arisen about them in Poland are different in Germany. A foreign country's poetry is judged abroad in terms of literary merit above all. When you, for example, translate a collection of German stories, the internal criticisms and debates that evolved around them are not so important after all. Anyway, Jan Koprowski wrote me that he is preparing such an anthology. Andrzejewski's *Przed sądem* [*Before the Court*] made a great impression on the readers of *Aufbau*, provoking lively discussions as well. Andrzejewski ought to speak on the issue of readers' opinion. It could be most interesting.

I was most grateful to have received your book, *Kamienny świat*, but I have not yet read it. Witold Wirpsza, meanwhile, approached me himself. I have already sent him the books and periodicals he requested, and am going to write a German chronicle for his paper. I've just heard that *Nowiny Literackie* [*Literary News*] is to cease publication.[147] Is this true? And why? Sincere thanks for your kind wishes for 1949. I am hopeful that during this year many things that are troubling the nations of the world will be resolved in a positive way.

In warmest friendship,

Gerhart Pohl

I've just heard from the gentlemen of the Polska Misja Wojskowa [Polish Military Mission] that you are coming. A warm welcome!

140. JANUARY 24, 1949
[*from A. Rudnicki; postcard*]

Adolf Rudnicki, "Wolodyjowka," Sienkiewicz St., Zakopane

Dear Tadeusz,

Why didn't you come to "Kopciuszek"? I waited half an hour. I was unable, unfortunately, to go to you.—Jackowski of the MSZ[148] told me about your Berlin. He inquired. I responded as best I could. From this I deduce that your Berlin will pop up in a few days. What a shame that I can't go as your toilet bag.

I know from the papers that you were in Szczecin. So how did it go? The KC telephoned me to come as a guest. Was it a bit sparse in terms of stars?[149] Write a few words, old man.

Sincerely—A.

141. JANUARY 3, 1949, WIETZE/CELLE

[*from Kurt Knuth-Siebenlist; in German*]

My dear Tad,

I don't know how to tell you how happy your letter of January 6 made me. I was amazed to realize that I still have friends from those times. I now have contacts with the whole world, since I receive mail from all parts of our earthly globe. I almost have the impression that I am being flattered, was I really such a good guy? I was simply fulfilling my obligations as a colleague, and will always behave like that under similar circumstances.

So, as you see, not all Germans are bad people. I could not prove it in any other way than through my being open to total collegiality, which, after all, was not always so safe for me either. And yet I behaved in this way willingly because we all had to pull the same rope, and that was devilishly hard sometimes. And yet we managed. I must tell you, unfortunately, that when I finally got out of the camp I had imagined everything differently. Life mixed people up in all manner of ways. And things didn't always work out for me as I had imagined.

Toward the end of the first period after I left the camp, I was nominated head of the political police in Ebensee in Austria. I tried to be always fair and to behave in good conscience. As you might imagine, one also made enemies. I have to keep stressing that former Nazis are still being sheltered in some way, unfortunately. Even though I ignored it, it wasn't a matter of indifference to me either. So in 1947, I left Austria and moved to Germany. I am with my adoptive parents whom I got to know in 1945 in Austria. My dad is director of the German Crude Oil collaborative. I have two attractive little sisters, big actually—one is 14, the other 18 years old—but to me they are a symbol of blood sisters. So this is how I've built a life for myself. I wished it otherwise, but had to adapt to circumstances.

I've published a small book, and have now finished my book, *The Helots*. It's written in the form of a novel and covers the years 1943–45. It's three sections in one volume, the second section covers Birkenau. I wrote it as I saw it, and wherever I have presented it, it aroused general interest. I want to publish it in

other languages; since your letter got to me, I thought about you. So now I am asking you: do you have the means to translate and publish it? If so, let me know quickly, and write whether I can send you the manuscript. I completely depend on your working on my behalf in every eventuality.

For many other reasons, also, the book will be of interest to you and to Poles in general, because I saw everything with my own eyes. I've given all the individuals their real names, and the initiated, that means those who were there, will have to conclude that, unfortunately, this is no novel but the bitter truth. It's actually a mixture of novel and fact and I hope that you will read it with great interest.

And now I'd like to ask you something in particular. Does the possibility of visiting you and other of my friends exist? Here in Germany I am a member of the Association of Those Persecuted by the Nazi Regime (VVN),[150] whose secretariat-general, FIAPP, is in Warsaw. I'd be enormously pleased to be able to talk a whole week away with you. I was delighted to learn that you had married, and I hope that you are happy, you deserve to be. Please convey my best wishes and respects to your lady wife.

Should such a possibility arise, let me know quickly. Since I have you within my line of vision again, I wouldn't want to lose you. One has so few real friends. And those whom one gets to know later didn't go through the crucible that we had to go through.

Perhaps you remember Rapportschrieber Kasek Gosk from the men's camp, we are corresponding with each other. He emigrated to the USA in December and writes diligently. I had to help him one more time here in Germany when he was imprisoned in Frankfurt after being falsely denounced. The Polish bishop to whom he turned in his helplessness sent me a telegram and I immediately went there. I managed to get him out on the following day and to squelch the investigation. The witness testimony which I presented was considered reliable, and I am pleased that I managed once again to help a colleague.

As you see, Kurt remains the way he was. It doesn't matter to me whether or not I get to hear thanks. It's enough for me to receive a postcard on which is written: Still thinking of you. As you see life takes strange twists, but you can't make an ogre out of an idealist.

I await mail from you and steps in the direction of my offer.

I enclose my best wishes to all those acquaintances who can still be found there, and, with words of the highest esteem for your wife, remain your old and faithful friend,

Your old colleague from Birkenau, Kurt

142. UNDATED

[*from T. Różewicz*]

Dear Tadeusz,

Is that business of that radio-reportage course you mentioned to me during our conversation still active? If so, during what period—be so kind as to write about it—you'll recall I said that I'd like to be there for it. The letter (this letter) was supposed to have been very long and exhaustive—various observations on the subject "From the time peace came I am afraid of everything" (I think that's how you captured that "feeling" on p. 146 (?) of one of the stories from *Pożegnanie z Marią*). Enormously interesting subject. Why is it that when someone knocks at his door my colleague first peers at great length through the peephole, and only then opens the locks and bolts? A very interesting story that would be, very interesting. Write also about how the conference in Szczecin worked out for you.

Contrary to our practice hitherto, I think it wouldn't hurt to exchange letters (thoughts?) sometimes. I'm writing a poem that begins this way: "Do you think that one can live without faith and eat broth and macaroni for forty years?"— rhetorical question, yes? My dear!

Write—warm regards,

Tadeusz

143. FEBRUARY 1, 1949, WARSAW

[*to T. Różewicz*]

Dear Tadeusz,

I'm writing on the machine because it's easier for me (my pen is leaking). Of the radio course—nothing, Wygodzki who proposed it to me is keeping mum. If anything should transpire, I'll let you know at once by express mail. But I don't know whether I'll have time for a letter because now—during carnival—Warsaw writers have turned into MSZ clerks and three times a day go to receptions on the occasion of the visit to Warsaw of Soviet writers. A little of our time was also taken up by the good old man, Leopold Staff, to whom were given, in front of witnesses, decorations, flowers, recitations, and money. He was placed on the stage at the Polish Theater in a woven little granny's armchair, and representatives of ZAiKS and of publishers approached him one after the other handing him "Modest Souvenirs" in envelopes. The souvenir handed by ZAiKS

(S. R. Dobrowolski) was indeed modest: a hundred thousand. For postage stamps to the end of the honoree's life. With trembling hand Staff placed the envelopes into his pocket. Tuwim who was watching all this from the presidential table reckoned that Staff would make around a million zloty at his Jubilee [seventy years]. When we started to laugh, Tuwim raised his eyebrows in amazement. "Why are you laughing?" he said. "That's a serious matter." At this matinee in the theater, actors recited hideously chosen Staff poems. They didn't want to get up from the table until with raised voice Zarembina convinced them that one should not make light of even an outdated poet. They recited badly—it wasn't worth their while—as they said—to learn a part for just once. Then there was a reception at the Sejm, lots of wine, vodka, and flowers given out by Marshal Kowalski, a few of which—a tulip and something yellow—I brought to my wife (oh, belated winter love!).

It was more or less the same in Szczecin. The most tragic figure—I am telling you this in confidence—was Jerzy Andrzejewski who couldn't understand what was going on. Behold Sokorski at the podium engaged in polemics with Zawieyski, but just give them a shot of Starowin brand vodka and watch: they're kissing one another! "One should play them the polonaise!" muttered Jerzy, referring to the scene in *Popioly* [*Ashes*] (remember at the Monopol). Stefan Żółkiewski graded our work. As to me, he withdrew from his previous, long-standing praise. He declared my creative work youthful, pointed out and condemned its immoralism, left the door open for the future with the words that "it is hard to assess him as yet." It'll be easier when they hit me on the head. Anyway, you can read Żółkiewski's article in *Kuźnica*. Because he spoke in a quiet, gentle voice, his judgments seemed at first glance gentle, but when read—God have mercy! Contrary to my hero, I'm not afraid of anything at the moment, though this sounds like the reassurance of a child in a dark room. In the end, no one will do for me what I must do, and I've time enough, I am not dying at the moment. My wife, on the other hand, has complexes and when somebody knocks after eleven gets palpitations and can't sleep for a long time after.

When you see Wilek Mach, tell him that I am living very weirdly and squeezing a letter out is hard for me, especially since he's not exactly guilty of diligence either. You can also tell him that his predictions about Polewka were correct! But I'll survive somehow and defend myself! Let me know when you've written the poem. I irritated Jastrun a bit. I told Matuszewski to inform him that Staff learned a lot from you. I'll be speaking about that this Thursday at the club on the occasion of Bratny's poetry.

On top of that, I still maintain that, as compared to the great literatures of the world, Polish literature (I'm speaking about prose, my poet!) is decidedly third rate.

Warm regards,

Tadeusz

144. FEBRUARY 8, 1949, STANNINGLEY

[*from J. Nel Siedlecki*][151]

Dear Tadeusz,

Thank you very much for your letter. I've come across your name (even a photograph once) and a few fragments of your creative work in the Polish daily press, which I still get from the Embassy. I am very pleased that you are managing and writing. I remember our time together fondly and sometimes regret that you are not here.

To tell the truth, though, I think you'd be rather lost here—you know, like a fish out of water. I am eagerly awaiting the promised book, perhaps I will see a little, as through a keyhole, of what's happening with you, or, at least, what you are currently thinking.

I've had nothing from Krystyn for a very long time.

I still correspond with Tolek—he's managing somehow and is generally happy, though I think things are rather hard for him.

My mother is well and speaks of you very often, she asks that I send both of you her very best thoughts and wishes.

I am still studying (and am up to my ears in it), though it's very hard for me (of which I'm also up to my ears). I like the country, the people on the whole are much more honest and pleasant than on the continent—however, all of us here are (and will always be) "dirty foreigners."[152]

Apart from my engineering, I've tried to write a bit (many ideas, but it's not "coming out" too well and there's no time because there's a lot of work). My latest effort is a "short story"[153] in English!!!

Regards to Tuśka.

Congratulations on the bathroom.

Best wishes to both of you

Janusz

P.S.   I didn't know about the children of sea horses,[154] now "am worrying to death"[155]—because what if . . . and how and why?

145. FEBRUARY 15, 1949, WARSAW

[*to H. Teigova*]

Dear Helena Teigova,

Yesterday, I sent you *Kamienny świat* together with two stories recently printed in *Odrodzenie.* Unfortunately, the conditions under which I am currently living force me to write slowly so that I have nothing new (apart from two other stories printed in *Zeszyty Wrocławskie* and one short journalistic piece in *Nowiny Literackie*) at hand. I have two stories started, but God only knows when I will finish them. So that the announced volume of semijournalistic stories will probably only come out at the end of the year. I don't have a decent photograph, but will make one and send it to you. At present some disgusting photo of me in which I look like a bandit is circulating in the papers.

As for translating something of mine into Czech, the situation stands as follows: ZAiKS approached me with a proposal to translate *Pożegnanie z Marią* into Czech (Mrs. Pluharowa); a "serious" publisher wishes to bring it out. I have not responded to them yet (as you know, I let letters just lie there); I will await your decision.

I'd be extremely pleased, of course, if you would want to translate *Pożegnanie z Marią,* but I don't think that specific book would arouse particular interest among the Czechs. It would be better to put together some selection of stories from three of my books. The third, *We Were in Auschwitz,* I will send when I get a chance. We could also do it this way: not touching *Pożegnanie z Marią,* publish other stories of which quite a handful has already amassed.

If need arose, I would be willing, after writing the screenplay I'm sitting at now, to quickly round out the volume with two or three short stories.

I leave the matter for you to decide. In any case, I would like to know how to respond to ZAiKS. I have gone on extensively about my own matters, but only out of official duty. Please write a word or two about how Gałczyński's Czech visit worked out. Pilarz was at the writers' conference in Szczecin, he knows how to drink wine. And they said that Czechs only drink beer!

Sincere regards and apologies for all the delays.

Tadeusz Borowski

146. FEBRUARY 19, 1949, DETROIT

A. Girs, 4855 Proctor, Detroit 10, Mich., USA

Dear Tadeusz and Tuśka,

I got a letter today from Sea Horse enclosing a letter with a note saying more or less this: "letter from Puppy." I haven't written recently because I got no reply to several letters.

I decided, therefore, that something must be causing this and stopped writing.

I am very pleased to have news of you, Tuśka, and Krystyn. It's good he's happy with his work.

I occasionally read your articles (unfortunately not all), which they sometimes send me from Poland. The last was "Zabawa z wódką"—good.

After being in New York for a year, I have gone to Detroit. Smaller city, land of Ford, General Motors, and other Cadillacs, a big village. Nice houses.

And also countless cars. I have discovered, in America, the inconvenience of cars, as long as you are driving—fine. But when you have to park, it's a disaster. Hard to find a place.

So far, I have not published anything, I've somehow been unable to assimilate. Europe has not a clue about America. It's a little better now, because I can find my way around a bit.

I'm shortly also going to print books, but differently than in Europe. I will print them myself, because I can't afford to pay a worker. It'll work out to the advantage of the publisher anyway. I'm making a small poem cycle by J. Pietrkiewicz. He also provided me with illustrations (plates) according to the dimensions I gave him. I think it's going to be a little gem. I want to finish it in fall. I am shortly going to get a press on which I will print. Naturally, I will send you a copy.

I also have Gogol ready, but that I will publish later.

Pani Pola has sent "Auschwitz" several times to your address. They returned it to her a few times. She's now trying again, because she's shortly leaving Europe.

I am closing for now, because I don't know whether this letter "*dojdiet.*"[156] I enclose sincere greetings for Tuśka and you, and wishes for success and in general.

A.

I enclose a newspaper cutting for Tuśka.

[*translation from the English:*] Joke for the day. Mother: "You're not afraid to go to the hospital—what a good little boy you are." Little boy: "But I won't let them foist an infant off on me, like they did you. I want a puppy."

147. FEBRUARY 27, 1949

[*to T. Różewicz*]

Dear Tadek,

Do you already know that Roman Bratny jointly with Jan Aleksander Król is to edit *Wieś*, which will be called something else? He dropped by with this news and right afterward went to Zakopane to ski. He's promising himself a lot of work at Król's on poetry—God have mercy—what'll it be? You are completely right, nothing is happening in poetry here, even Ważyk repeats his ideas and from time to time pilfers (compare Chinese poem).

Because the grotesque battle between Jastrun and Roman (the bone of contention, as is well known, is a woman) is gathering national momentum, the minister of arts and culture wants to organize, through our club, a meeting of young poets from the whole of Poland and a discussion something like a Warsaw Niebor. What do you think, is it worth dabbling in this? Since the time that Sofronow, that Soviet writer of comedies, on returning from a trip to Poland,[157] wrote in some Russian paper that I am a nihilist and a Céline-ist (something my obliging friends must have informed him, because he read nothing himself), not an hour goes by that I'm not offered condolences on it and an immediate corroboration of the words of the master. Best of all was old and deaf grandpa Lucjan Rudnicki[158] who drew me aside at the author's evening at our club and said, "I read it, I read it, but don't worry, Comrade; when I, myself, read your book, I thought to myself: how could they have printed such a thing!" So it's also not surprising that I'm not on any list of authors to be translated; I'm tolerated more out of sentiment for my person than for my work.

I've already written the script of the film *30 kwietnia* [*April 30th*] with Jan Rojewski,[159] actually, he wrote it and I transcribed it onto the machine. It consists of four stories; one, as Jan says, will be published in *Trybuna Wolnosci* [*Tribune of Freedom*]. Glance through a few of the current issues, maybe you'll stumble on it. Title: "Dwa worki mąki" ["Two Sacks of Flour"], a sensational little story with fire and shooting.

Drop by when you're in Warsaw. I liked your poem in *Twórczość*, but people won't understand its perverse meaning.[160]

148. FEBRUARY 28, 1949
[*to T. Mikulski*]

Dear Professor,

Please forgive my indecently long silence and for letting the editor of *Zeszyty* down by not sending the promised review. My only justification is that since the beginning of December I have rather difficult work conditions. My brother who has been living with us over the past months had a nervous breakdown. More serious work got swept into the corner and I grabbed at less pure literary jobs: I'm writing weekly columns and, together with Jan Rojewski, churned out the story for a film.

All of this looks very paltry and is no excuse, but please believe that I was unable to do any work. I couldn't even lay a finger on my little volume, started long ago and which should have been finished by February. I promise to work in spring—but don't myself know whether anything will come of it.

I'm very sorry I missed you at the Institute Conference, Professor, where I dropped by a couple of times. Wanda, however, told me that your duties left you no free time.

Warm regards,

Tadeusz Borowski

149. FEBRUARY 29, 1949, GLIWITZ
[*from T. Różewicz*]

Dear Tadeusz,

I didn't reply immediately (as I have the habit of doing), because I thought I'd be in Warsaw on the 15th and so would see you. But before that I'm going to Szczecin, and will be in Warsaw at the end of the month and will drop by—I want to talk over various things. You know that Kraków is a strange city, it's hard even to talk here. Your opinion about prose (third rate) is correct, but out of politeness (?) you were kind about poetry—and in this country the little verses are mostly totally devoid of meaning or poetry! Rubbish is what they mostly write—I truly prefer Biernat of Lublin[161] or Andrzej Morsztyn;[162] from that "representative of the Baroque movement" (as Łos writes) our young poets could learn economy of language, clarity, logic, etc. (see the lousy poems in the latest *Kuźnica*). Tadek dear, when one reads all this (prose and poetry), one starts to

think that the innovator and discoverer in literature here is the guy who writes with sense and correctly. But enough of this whining.

How's your work on the waterworks? About which *Lidove Noviny*[163] also wrote. Why are you not on the list of authors recommended for translation into other languages (an oversight)? I glanced at it in one of our journals.

Warm regards, and until we meet,

Tadeusz

150. MARCH 4, 1949, WROCŁAW
[*from T. Mikulski*]

Dear Tadeusz Borowski,

Thank you for your letter of the 28th February, which I received yesterday. I very much appreciate your thinking of me and the friendliness that I've experienced more than once. We missed you in the current *Zeszyty,* but, after all, it's not the last issue, and I will again turn to you more than once for material. I am sorry we did not see each other in Warsaw. But I dropped in for two days and really did have quite a lot of matters, institutional and personal, and on top of that stayed farther away from you than last time, and, as a result, was unable to drop by for even a minute. But everything points to my being again in Warsaw in April, and I will make sure that we don't miss each other.

I was truly concerned by what you wrote about your working conditions, but I think you will be able to deal with them. In a few weeks, we will talk extensively about the "Borowski affair," there's reason to do so even in the current *Zeszyty*—and about all the others. Your columns get into our Wrocław *Słowo Polskie* [*Polish Word*].[164] And the author? We will always be pleased to see him here. Best wishes to you, dear Tadeusz Borowski, sincere regards to Tuśka.

T. Mikulski

151. MARCH 12, 1949, KRAKÓW
[*from T. Różewicz*]

Dear Tadek,

I am feeling miserable and writing only a few words. A long letter to you was written and not sent (you smile—yes, it's almost a sentimental story). You ask

about the "poets' meeting." I think that they have nothing interesting to say at the moment—I have something in Warsaw, so that "meeting" is to my interest—but it's probably a waste of money. After all, those people crazy about Jastrun would again speak only about him. With the Wirpszas, it's a serious symptom. Slap Roman on the head, maybe he'll get over it, the poor thing! It is so funny, after all, that sometimes tears just well up spontaneously in my eyes. I heard, Tadek, that you are going as a diplomat—is this just a rumor? I haven't come across the story about the flour, a pity. You've set all this up very well. "Controversy about poetry in Poland"—the beautiful Helen, of course (God have her in your keeping). Achilles—Agamemnon, and a crowd of Atreides and Ajaxes [*a note in the margin:* perhaps it's different in this *Iliad*] and us among them. The story about the guys who offer you their condolences on account of Sofronow—is fantastic, I'll tell you something along the same lines from my own experience when we meet.

Sincere regards, very sincere,

Tadek

152. MARCH 7, 1949, DETROIT
[*from A. Girs*]

Dear Tadeusz and Tuśka,

Thank you for the letter of February 27. I received it today. Is it worth writing registered mail? Letters rarely get lost here. I've gone through a lot of changes as well. I've swapped New York for Detroit and am very happy about it.

I can't boast about any new publishing successes. I've produced nothing new since Munich. Even worse, I've sold none of the previously published books.

I want now to acquire a hand press and start to print beautiful things *antiquo modo.* I'm working on Pietrkiewicz's poems.

It's very bad that Tuśka is ill. What do the doctors say? She needs to get better as fast as possible. She should also not tire herself out working. Would a vitamin cure not do her good? Please look after her.

How did Krystyn become such a workaholic? Is it worth it? I, for example, am starting to regret that I worked so much. As the saying goes—wise after the fact.

I have asked Pani Pola to send you all the remaining "stripes."[165] For some reason, the post office returned a lot of them after a few months. If I could afford it, I would send you more.

I am pleased to have seen a chunk of the world and how people live in other places. Please believe me that this is exceedingly interesting. I also like the atmosphere here. I am not working hard. I've now taken up painting. I'm painting quite a lot. But more for my own pleasure than for buyers. It's very pleasant to do something just for one's self without depending on buyers.

I forgive the long silence, and if I don't receive an answer quickly to this letter, will send the next registered.

Naturally, I'd be most grateful for books. What kind of a question was that?!

Best wishes to you and Tuśka, and to the lazy monster of architecture from

A. Girs

153. MARCH 15, 1949, ŁÓDŹ

[*from Kazimierz Brandys; on* Kuźnica *letterhead*]

Dear Colleague,

On behalf of the editors of *Kuźnica,* I am turning to you with the request that you send some excerpt or story that might strengthen our prose section.

As you have probably noticed yourself, things are not going too well lately in this section. Lack of valuable materials and good names. That's why I am anxious for you not to let us down this time, and to put the terrible misunderstanding about *Kamienny świat* out of your mind. We are counting on your sending one of your new pieces, which, as I heard, you currently have at hand. If you don't have them in publishable shape yet, we will willingly accept something from your so-called files, some old trifle or sketch. You, yourself, will decide this best.

I repeat again that we are counting on this greatly. Personally, I would like—after the break—for your permanent collaboration with *Kuźnica* to be renewed. There's nothing, surely, that divides us, and a great deal that unites.

For now, regards,

Kazimierz Brandys

154. MARCH 24, 1949, SZCZECIN
[from W. Wirpsza]

Dear Tadek,

On her return, Maryla told me that you plan to arrange an author's evening at the club for me and that you'd like me to set a date. For me, next Thursday would suit best, i.e., *prima aprilis*.

Namely because I have a number of things, apart from reading poems at the club, to discuss in Warsaw, which need to be discussed as soon as possible. It concerns publishing matters, or, else to link up with some editorial office as a reporter—because this is the only way, really, that I can ensure sufficient income to support my numerous family.

I can, of course, also foresee the possibility that it won't be possible to organize that evening next Thursday. In that case, I accept any close date. Just in case—in particular, if the first of April date doesn't suit the club—I would ask to reply by telegram because, as you know, even radio programs take three weeks to reach Szczecin.

The rest of the letter will be completed by Maryla, for whom I and the neighbors arranged a noisy welcome, and who will definitely be able to convey most rationally all the good wishes which, in terms of you both, I share in equally.

Witold

They've called me a pessimist here, and refuse to believe the proverb that even "among good friends, the dogs ate the hare."[166] In light of that, I am sending you, Tadek, an application to the Union for a loan and I am hoping that we'll somehow squeak by in April. But Witek is already stressing that from the moment of my return black prospects for the future are looming. Ah, well—tough. I'm closing, there's no sense in troubling you any further. Please accept once more my most sincere thanks for all your "support" both moral as well as "nutritional" which I received from you, and be in good health,

Maryla

And Lindsay I will send through Jerzy Andrzejewski who is going to Warsaw Monday. Just arrange that evening for Witek reasonably soon, Tadek, okay? Would you prefer a reading from Stocznia, or a revised in the meantime with Miłosz "Traktat polemiczny" ["Polemical Tract"]?[167] We await a wired reply!

155. APRIL 14, 1949, WARSAW

[*to H. Teigova*]

Dear Helena Teigova,

Sincere thanks for the letter, I apologize for the long silence, caused in truth by Slavic carelessness and Germanic overwork, and I hope that you have completely returned to health, in which case I wish you *bon appetit* for the Easter holidays, which, in Poland at least, are traditionally holidays of great, epic gluttony. Why should it be any different in Czechoslovakia? I am truly grateful to you for the pains that you took translating *Kamienny świat*,[168] but I am fully aware that these little stories neither chill nor warm the Czech reader. I have to admit to you that it's the same with the Polish reader, and even my friends of the pen couldn't quite grasp that it isn't a collection of short stories, but simply a political-literary lampoon of which there are many in literature.

Today, I see that had I provided a different foreword and added a couple more items to the volume, its satiric tendencies would have come out more clearly. But I don't know whether in that case *Kamienny świat* could have come out at all. I was concerned about the criticism of "bourgeois" literature (that's how we call it, but we have in mind pseudo-realistic pieces, which from time to time *Kuźnica* announces in prophetic tones) and pointing out exit strategies. But the form was unusual and the concept hidden out of faint-heartedness. One has to learn! I'm now writing articles/columns and essays, a collection of which I will publish with the Państwowy Instytut Wydawniczy, where the clever Karol Kuryluk is director. I'll finish this book up in May, and only then turn to the stories that I again want to finish in summer. I'm not in a rush, because I don't know how to work hard, and a lot of time is taken up with reading and organizational work, which I don't do well, but even careless work takes time.

When I finish the book of stories, I'll send you the manuscript—perhaps you'll like it, especially since I'm going to make the meaning clear in the foreword. It's not the best system, but it's hard to learn to write otherwise; I try, but it doesn't work. Mrs. Pluharowa is translating *Pożegnanie z Marią* (so ZAiKS informs me). I'd prefer, truth to tell, to make a collection of stories out of my three books, but don't know if anyone would agree to this.

Dear Mrs. Teigova, I have gone on at such length about myself, but what is a so-called writer to write about? I admire your diligence about which legends circulate in Poland, and I too would like to profit from it a little: specifically, I am very interested in Czech publications of criticism: I've already picked up

Mukarzowski, Fuczik, Neumann. I don't, however, know to what extent they give a full picture of Czech criticism and Czech aesthetic ideas. If you would be willing to enlarge my debt by sending me a few newer critical works, I would be sincerely grateful and ready always to perform the same service, with that, once again, wishes for a happy, gluttonous, holiday, and I remain as always very truly yours,

Tadeusz Borowski

156. APRIL 14, 1949, WARSAW
[*to his parents*]

My Dears,

Sincere apologies for not having written for such a long time, but I truly am overworked as I never before have been, there are so many conferences, deliberations, meetings, and conventions. The end result is that a person who isn't working anywhere and considers himself a freelance writer, leaving the house at nine, appears at two for lunch, and again vanishes only to return in the evening, and then has to apply himself to various kinds of literary work—columns and articles—to say nothing of reading. I've undertaken a number of commitments, by April 22 I have to take care of a lot of film and other matters. Since my trip keeps getting delayed and the Ministry with a scrupulosity peculiar to itself is silent on the matter, I've linked up with Film where I've assumed the literary directorship of one of the literary groups for a few months. The work is arduous, but interesting. On top of that, I've negotiated a contract with PIW for a new book of articles, which I also have to finish soon. All in all, I'm a bit tired, but cannot move until 22 April, so that I really cannot come to you for Easter Sunday and Monday, but will try to come for a few days between the 22nd and 30th of April so that I can finish up some things I've started in Warsaw. Tuśka is doing the rounds of doctors who are always discovering new postcamp things in her. The girl gets up at six each day and runs to rinse out her stomach. She has tremendous hyperacidity, which could result in ulcers if she doesn't embark on an energetic cure.

I think, however, that she'll pull out of this with a bit of care. We're sending razors, we couldn't get them here, either, for a couple of days, what a strange country where everything goes off the market, meat and razors, but people go around well fed and, what's weirder, shave as normal.

It worries me a lot that Julek doesn't feel completely well, but perhaps he's started to go around town and study. It seems to me that all his energy should go into finishing his studies—a degree is increasingly starting to count for a lot in Poland. The worst, however, is to drop out of a normal way of life, or to vacillate for too long over what to do, because then time is wasted. The most important thing is to do something, and then it always turns out that one was right.

Dear Mom write how you are doing financially, we, thank God, have crawled out of the pits and can always help considerably. We've bought a small bookshelf, and Tuśka has bought me a beautiful suit, jacket out of homespun and the dark trousers out of flannel or God knows what. In her opinion, I look in it like Rudolf Valentino, except that Valentino never had such a beautiful suit.

We both send you our warmest wishes for Easter and heartfelt kisses,

Your Tadeusz

157. APRIL 15, 1949, SZCZECIN

[*postcard*]

Sender: Wiktor Woroszylski, 29 Pogodna St., Szczecin-Głębokie
Citizen Tadeusz Borowski, 17 Kaliska St., Apt. 39, Warsaw

My dear,

I'm holed up in Szczecin, far from the civilized world, kill mosquitoes, write, and engage in other, equally insignificant, community matters. And imagine— I'm happy. I'm not convinced that one could put up with provincial languor for long, but at the moment it provides a pleasant respite from the Warsaw hell of hurt pride, mutual jealousies, backbiting, and "great politics" or very small people.

I don't know about you, but it lately really got to me. If you are not going abroad, and would also decide on the provinces even short-term, with your wife or by yourself (or just your wife instead of you)—I offer you the hospitality of my palace.

And now to the purpose—since, of course, I'm writing this card out of self-interest. I am editing the literary section of the local Party organ here. I'd like to ask you to send me something to reprint: a) the last story from "Pewny żołnierz, b) "Zabawa z wódką, c) all the historical-literary articles written for the general reader, e.g., about Mickiewicz, reviews, and so on, d) whatever you consider

appropriate. Speed is of the essence in relation to point b ("Zabawa z wódką"), because I want to put it into the First of May issue, which I'm already working on.

Write how things are with you.

Warm regards to you and your wife,

Witek

158. APRIL 19, 1949, ZAKOPANE
[*from Adolf Rudnicki; postcard*]

Dear Tadeusz,

Ewa wrote me that you are going to enter into a discussion about "Ucieczka."[169] I'm very pleased. I'm pleased that I will see, hear, and be able to hug you. I hear that Berlin is becoming a reality—heh, beloved pal, happy pal! Give your wife my regards.

A.

159. APRIL 21, 1949, WARSAW
[*to Wiktor Woroszylski*]

My dear Witek,

Many thanks for your card, and, as you see, I am carrying out points a and b right away, they're mindful of publicity; on the other hand, point c regarding articles I cannot arrange since I have neither cuttings nor copies of the articles scattered in *Pokolenie* (the new one), *Światło,* and *Niedziela na wsi.* It would be more appropriate to speak of planting rather than scattering—there were only two of these articles—one about Mickiewicz, the other on Balzac. I envy you sitting there in the quiet. As usual, I spend half the day in town going after money, taking articles around, making plans that will never come to fruition in any case. We are now in the grips of total madness organizing the First of May: parades, slogans, artistic productions, and so on. Some committees are gathering, somebody's arranging something, but so far nothing is known. The single positive result of my meanderings—a loss of weight and a signed contract with PIW for a collection of articles that I will put together for them in May. My Berlin will probably become a reality only after the fifth or sixth war.

Wouldn't you like to do something for a film? I've taken on something along the lines of literary directorship in the "Warsaw" collective (Starski and co.), which insists very much on collaboration of any degree and kind and will gladly cover all costs and offer assistance. I suggested something about the port to Wirpsza; I don't know, of course, whether he'll agree and whether the subject will suit him. If you'd like to think about something (subject, kind of treatment—whatever) let either me or Zespół "Warszawa," 69 Narutowicz St, Łódź, know directly, they will provide you with all the information (including payment).

I am going to take up your invitation to the villa sooner than you think—I am setting out in the first days of May for a several-day trek around villages, why not go to the Szczecin ones? As a native, of course, you could accompany me around the area if you'd like. But most certainly instead of going off into the countryside, we'll talk some long evening away. What are you writing? You write me nothing about what you are writing, write.

To go back to the daily again: if you need some not too exhaustive pieces— I'm always willing. I don't know whether I could write regularly, but from time to time I could whip something out, just think something up.

Warm regards to you, your wife and villa.

Tadeusz

Forgive the typewriter, but my pen broke.

160. APRIL 19, 1949, DETROIT
[*from A. Girs*]

Dear Tadeusz and Tuśka,

Thank you for the letter of April 14, I received it yesterday. I am truly not at all annoyed about not receiving immediate answers to my letters. I fully understand that when one talks a lot, one does little, even though talking can be useful too.

Thank you for the books you sent, but why the bibliophile ones? I have neither a library nor my own house. In this regard, not mentioning the others, I am poorer than the average worker who usually has his own house, a car for himself, and often one for his wife, and the homes are furnished like little jewels. I was most amazed by this state of affairs at the beginning of my stay here. Naturally, if someone is addicted to alcohol or other things, he lives in poverty. But

not in hunger. It creates a strange impression by comparison with our prewar conditions.

I could send you something out of the literature here, books galore, in every bookstore one can get everything from extreme leftist to practically fascist authors. Only to the deceased Hitler does this freedom of speech not apply. The books are not very cheap. However, the library network is phenomenally well organized. They're free. Everybody can take out three books a day and keep them for a month. If a library doesn't have something a reader's interested in, they can get it on the average within two to three weeks (bureaucracy takes time). In addition, every library has luxurious reading rooms where one can read from morning till night in beautiful rooms in comfortable chairs. There's no limit to the number of books you can access in the reading rooms, nor on the number for scholars, writers, etc., to take home. Where there aren't libraries, reading is interestingly organized. You order it by mail.

It's always good to see the world. I can now see why our prewar "powers-that-be" made traveling abroad so difficult for people. And I first understood how useful it is when I went to the Leipzig Fair. I am very pleased to have seen a bit of the world and got to know many things in literature with my own eyes and often on my own skin. As a certain kind of experiment, my departure was interesting, although many would doubtless describe it as crazy. I landed on the ground of the New World with three dollars in my pocket. Not having an affidavit from an organization, they denied me after a week the aid that they normally give emigrants for the first few months. I didn't want to appeal for help to any private persons or organizations.

Wanting to try to manage "on my own," I hadn't supplied myself, as experienced acquaintances suggested, with something for "a rainy day." So I had rather a lot of these rainy days. Sometimes just like in Jack London. But it was interesting. I gathered an entire suitcase of good advice during this time. I'm keeping it "for posterity." It's possible that some acquaintances counted on my having certain material means. They probably couldn't imagine that in making "handsome," in their estimation, gifts to the National Library in Warsaw or the academy there (the last didn't get there, unfortunately, scoundrels stole them), to the Gutenberg Society, etc., one could possess nothing. I remember a literary moment, when I spoke for close to five hours with somebody in his gorgeous institute and it was my second day of "dieting" on account of a lack of cents. I was also invited one evening for dinner by a poor guy I knew. I was offered, instead, expensive cognac, which I don't drink. With what gusto would I have

eaten something more. This year, not the easiest in my life, was, however, very interesting . . . from the artistic and literary point of view.

Thinking of Krystyn, I often watched construction workers. A few dozen workers are building a huge skyscraper. Dressed in overalls, colorful caps, gloves, moving slowly, they operate machines. Enormous iron constructions fly precisely and exactly, elevated to a height of five stories by a crane mounted on a huge truck. Up above, gloved workers screw these chunks of steel with lazy movements, but it goes so quickly, you're filled with amazement. Only at the finish do a lot of workers work. I seriously regretted then that I don't have work experience. Such a one gets from 2 to 4.50 dollars an hour. In two hours he's made enough for a pair of shoes, and when he's out of work, he receives such unemployment benefits from the government, that a lot go to California or Florida instead of looking for work. There was even a scandal about this, because the benefits offices sent them money there. Isn't it funny for people not to know what unemployment is? Unfortunately, DPs (displaced people) don't have such privileges.

The *antiquo modo* typography is slowly moving forward. But American tempo is machine, not human, tempo. Tempo of the dollar. And I have neither machines nor people. To say nothing of dollars. That's why for me it goes slowly, I don't over-tire myself too much. Some workers I know in their sixties or older could not work anymore, but they'd get bored. I wouldn't think they were over fifty. They're very nice and intelligent, though different than in Europe.

I am closing and send warm regards to you and Tuśka.

A.

[*postscript by hand:*] Tuśka's ill state of health has concerned me greatly. One has to deal with it seriously and not neglect it. I understand that you, Tadeusz, want to have more time to work. Writing articles can be interesting, but doesn't have too much value. In the same way, one cannot always live in camp memories. It was written about and one needs to let it go. Otherwise one will never be an artist of the pen. Naturally not everyone is Shakespeare. Just as nowadays there were poetasters, and sometimes true poets, writing "panegyrics" in praise of various great men, but those simply remained as something amusing. Only works of art have endured. When you get a chance, please confirm receipt of this letter. Bye!

161. UNDATED, WARSAW

[*to W. Woroszylski*]

Dear Witek,

The evening will be toward the end of June, title—I think "Poezja polityczna" ["Political Poetry"] is better. If you think it expedient, I could open for you, as they say, but I don't know whether you wouldn't prefer a poet. I sit and write, it's hard going as I promised myself and Karol Kuryluk. I'm already a couple of days late, please God may I finish the immortal work three weeks after the deadline! Thanks for the cash. Although it didn't help me. I wasn't home and Tuśka appropriated it.

When you get a moment, write when you're coming: the second or the third? Hug Janka from us, and buy her a crock of pickles. She's earned it!

Best wishes,

Tuśka and Tadeusz

162. MAY 3, 1949, KRAKÓW

[*from T. Różewicz*]

Dear to my heart Borowski,

Your letter (just as you said) was waiting at the door, thank you very much (once again) for the thought (this in connection with that FP). Laughing at W. Burk's weight was the reason why I didn't eat the eggs (soft-boiled) that your good wife prepared for me for the Last Supper (do you know that word?). And, of course, we didn't chat with one another as I had wanted to setting out to your place. We'll certainly see each other again before you depart. I read Miłosz's "Toast" a bit carelessly—I have no opinion about him. You mentioned Roman during our conversation; judging by what he's been recently printing, e.g., in *Odrodzenie,* he ought to edit a lot out of the poem (there were only a few little lines of poetry in it (?) and a lot of chatter)—but that's his business.

As for me (as I mentioned to you): I published two poems in *Wieś,* where in the first they made an error and wrote "taken away" (should have been: "taken off," and that's something else) hm, hm! Do you have Mickiewicz's "Nad wodą wielką i czystą" ["By the Great and Pure Water"] at hand? I'd like to talk with

you about that poem sometime. Are you going to be in Warsaw until you leave? Get in touch sometimes. NB why do you call me "Oh, my hope"?

Regards,

Tadeusz

P.S.   Greetings to your wife—T.

P.S. 2   As to FP, I will apply at the appropriate time.

163. MAY 4, 1949, ŁÓDŹ

[*from K. Brandys, on* Kuźnica *letterhead*]

Dear Pan Tadeusz,

On returning from Zakopane, I found your letter at the office. *Kuźnica* counts greatly on the mentioned prose and asks, through me, when you will send it? For the next few weeks still, probably until June 1, the journal will be coming out of Łódź, so please send the above-mentioned by post, or give it to R. Matuszewski in Warsaw.

How does the business of your departure stand? In Zakopane, Krzysztof Gruszczyński and I talked about the necessity of assembling the best people at the Warsaw editorial offices of *Kuźnica;* I fear that Berlin would stand in the way when it comes to you. And that would not be good.

I read your review of "Antygona" ["Antigone"][170] from cover to cover, and agree, for the most part, with your objections. I simply cannot concur with the business about the bag. Also the three imprecisions in the details that you raised in "Samson" (Tomb of the Unknown Soldier, the dove, and the placing of Jakub on the bed by the girl from Solc) merit discussion. But of that when we meet in person. In any event—I am pleased that such an interesting essay was written about my book, and that it came from a pen I value. I remind you once again about the promised sexual-legal story.[171]

Sincerely yours,

Kazimierz Brandys

164. MAY 17, 1949, LENINGRAD
[*postcard*]

Send.: Wiktor Woroszylski, Hotel Astoria, Leningrad
Cit. Tad. Borowski, Apt. 39, 17 Kaliska St., Warsaw

Dear Tadeusz,

I will probably come to Warsaw next Saturday, 5/21. I will be there for a few hours, on Sunday I drop into Łódź, Monday back to Warsaw, and in the evening drive to Szczecin. If you are not yet in Berlin, or are not at my place in Szczecin, I would very much like you to come with me to Szczecin on Monday evening. Think about it, if so, get ready for the trip. I don't know if I will manage to get in touch with you on Saturday, but Monday I'll definitely drop by.

Sincere regards to Tuśka and you,
Witek

165. MAY 24, 1949, SZCZECIN
[*postcard from W. Woroszylski*]

My dear,

Yesterday evening I forgot to pay back the debt, even though I got a load of cash during the day. So I am now sending you 1100 zł. (that's how much I believe I took yesterday morning?). In regards to my evening at the club either on June 2 or toward the end of June, I propose the title "Poezja polityczna" ["Political Poetry"] or the title of my collection, "Smierci nie ma" ["Death Doesn't Exist"]. Decide which would look better on the posters. Also be so kind as to think about who could open. I'd prefer it not to be Bratny.

We await your arrival. Maybe Tuśka will also decide to come?

Best wishes,
Janka and Witek

P.S.   Your "Zabawa z wódką" went into *Głos*. I'll be at the editorial office tomorrow and will make sure they send the cash if they haven't yet done so.

166. JUNE 3, 1949, DETROIT

[*from A. Girs*]

Dear Tadeusz and Tuśka,

The day before yesterday, I received *Pożegnanie z Marią* and *Kamienny świat*. I read them with interest. Thank you for the dedication, but I had no hand in the making of *Pożegnanie*. The books that I would have projected would certainly have been written differently. That doesn't, however, mean that I think these two books are of little value. By no means.

When it comes to my point of view, I think that in the given case one could have given fewer personal matters—very well captured, in any case, with clear Freudian influence—in favor of a general landscape of relationships, connections, etc. The book would then have greater historical value. The artistic form would only have increased its worth. You use the titles "Actor," "Singer," etc. Even though it is not a clear giving of surnames, some of this gossip was not worth writing about, unless one were 100% certain that it was not just gossip. Because otherwise, one does people unnecessary harm. Just as I am an advocate of writing the most brutal truth, so I am a believer that every one of these "truths" should be checked, so that there is not even the shadow of a doubt about its truthfulness (authenticity).

After reading the first chapter of *Pożegnanie*, I was enormously pleased to ascertain that it didn't end as "artistically and tragically" as in the book, but with the most "banal" happy ending, as in dozens of films. Dear Mrs. Tuśka, heartfelt congratulations, and I am happy for you both that the farewell was only temporary and crowned with a "banal" ending in marriage. I wish you both many, many years of happiness.

If I may offer advice, it seems to me that it is worth putting an end for now to the camp theme. Perhaps a historical thing would be good as an antidote. There are, after all, enough subjects, as you well know. I once thought about a certain true history artistically rendered about Jan Hus.[172] I think there is a lot of material unearthed out of archives. This isn't a suggestion, just a general observation.

So much about books. I might also add that the paper is poor. It will turn to dust in five or ten years.

I looked at the Polish section in the New York Library. How very incomplete. Those who should have taken care of it, didn't take care. The results are

miserable, masses of books turning to dust. But it's not worth talking about, it's the same now.

I wrote you that Pola sent a lot of books, among them more than seven hundred *Imiona nurtu*. I wonder whether you will get them in their entirety.

With best wishes to you and Tuśka and warmest regards,

A. Girs

IV.

JUNE 1949–JULY 3, 1951

BERLIN AND WARSAW

Good times

1. JUNE 23, 1949, BERLIN

[*to his wife*]

T. Borowski—address through the Ministry: Press Information Office, Polish Military Mission in Berlin, Post Office 7, Warsaw; by normal post: T.B., Polnisches Informationsbiuro, 3 Neustadtische Kirchstr., Berlin NW 7

Dearest Tuśka,

Having arrived by comfortable sleeping car, I've fallen into a maelstrom of matters and concerns that I don't quite know how to handle and I am somewhat depressed. The office is located in the center of the city, which is completely destroyed; the workers' apartments are in the residential suburbs several dozen kilometers from the so-called "Stadtmitte" (look at the dictionary). For the locals, the communication system is simple; for the new arrivals—dreadful. So, for the moment, I've taken up residence in a hotel near the office; one pays a lot, truth to tell, but it's convenient. I was offered a beautiful room on the outskirts of Pankow near our consulate, but I wanted at least two or three rooms right away. We'll see what happens. In any case, it doesn't make the job any easier, especially since one needs, practically speaking, to see to everything for one's self. For the first few days, I was furious and hungry (one also had to pick up rations for one's self; one had to find out where, etc.); now I'm just furious. But that will probably pass.

I can't quite get used to the part of "office worker" and having to sit behind a desk for several hours; but that'll pass, too. Berlin itself—a vast city! The town center ruined, other districts lying beyond the surrounding highway—practically untouched. A funny impression is created by the division of the city, which uses two monetary systems: boarding a tram—you pay in one, but if you want to return in the same tram—you have to pay in the other. (Westmarks and Ostmarks.) You'll see for yourself, anyway. The director has already written to Warsaw to hurry the passport along; I've been promised all kinds of privileges, but we'll have to put the pressure on, as everywhere. Haven't been either to the cinema or to the theater. I've bought several books, I read for several hours a day. I am sometimes so tired that I sleep half the day.

Together we'll set ourselves up a bit better and more comfortably. The conditions, objectively speaking, are magnificent, I just don't know how to make the most of them.

I await you like salvation. At the moment, I can't write anything. I simply know nothing. A lot of time will have to pass before I learn something.

Regards to Staszek Wygodzki and tell him that he'll get *Sinn und Form* soon. I'll send a few journals, perhaps I'll manage to subscribe. Truth to tell, I haven't looked around yet.

Kisses. Go to Jackowski and remind him about the passport.

Your Tadeusz

2. JUNE 31, 1949, BERLIN

[*telegram; sent 5:15 P.M., received 7:12 P.M.*]

Maria Borowska, Apt. 39, 17 Kaliska St., Warsaw 22, Poland

ENORMOUS CITY STOP MUCH WORK STOP SETTLING IN STOP BRINGING YOU OVER STOP KISSES MISS YOU STOP TADEUSZ

3. JULY 4, 1949, BERLIN

[*telegram to his wife; received 2:35 P.M.*]

CHINUP STOP SETTLED IN WONDERFULLY STOP WILL NUDGE THE NECESSARY PERSON STOP MONEY ODRODZENIE STOP KISSES TADEUSZ

4. JULY 6, 1949, BERLIN

[*to his wife*]

Dear Tuśka,

If you only knew how your silence worries me. I don't know how you are feeling, nor whether you still have some money, nor what you are doing. I have sent two letters to you via the Ministry and a telegram by post; I got a book from you but there wasn't a word in it. Every day I expect a letter from you.

The first several days were very hard for me; I was homesick and nostalgic and instantly developed a loathing for Berlin, which I have to this day.

If only you knew what I ate in the first days! Now I am more or less managing: I am to receive a three-room apartment with furniture; canteen and apartment

are to be in the same area, so I won't have to return home in the evening. People here know how to get by so well it almost makes you sick.

Director Halpern has already called Warsaw several times in the matter of your and other wives' passports; the matter—as they say—is being resolved. You need to go to Jackowski (Department of Press and Information, 4th Floor, MSZ).[1] We will go to theaters and cinemas together, I don't feel like it right now. You will be able to learn German with student tutors. Take our transcripts, perhaps we'll be able to audit some courses.

I'm sparing you descriptions of my work and the town because I want you to form your own opinion. In any event, the pay is good: 4,000 Western marks (or over 600 Eastern). In the Eastern sector a book = 6 to 90 marks; in the Western, five times higher. However, on the average = 6 marks. Handbags, dresses, watches—gorgeous. A lot of pornographic photos in the Western sector.

Gorgeous parks. Very ugly German women. Ice cream out of egg whites! Ghastly food. You need to take some crackers, then we'll both look around, because, as you know, I don't have much initiative myself.

On the whole, I'm living a makeshift life and waiting for you. You are like health, your worth can be known only by someone who, like me, is your husband, and has gone to Berlin.

Write, Dear.

Tadeusz

5. JULY 7, 1949, BERLIN

[*to his wife*]

Dear Tuśka,

The lack of news from you concerns me a great deal. As of yesterday, I have arranged an apartment, three beautiful rooms, unfortunately with old furniture and an even older landlady. Beautiful neighborhood, we'll be comfortable. I think that the matter of the passport will be settled by the end of the month. Probably—I don't know yet—I'll be able to get away for a few days in order to come and fetch you. I'm starting to get used to things and settling in.

I'm transferring money (20.000) to you through the MSZ on Monday, I think you will have it by April 15. You have no idea how much I am missing you and feeling the weight of the "single" life. But we'll arrange it beautifully and

I will find time to write. I'm sending this letter through someone. Write how you're managing with your health and with money, what's with the passport (have you been to Jackowski already?), what's with Julek, etc. You know, when one has no news for so many days, one doesn't want to go on living.

But I've had a breather and am relaxing a bit, the rest I'll tell you, there's enough for long evenings (that's it!). I've bought myself a pair of glasses and around 30 books, I haven't yet gone off to delve through the French bookstores, but I'll do so and send you something.

Write, Dear.

Your Tadeusz

6. UNDATED, BERLIN
[*to his wife*]

My dearest Tuśka,

Don't worry about anything, I've set myself up nicely. I now have a three-room apartment with some old ladies in a pretty neighborhood, am eating well. I'm gradually buying books, reading nothing, and missing you very much. In connection with this, I am sending you my photo from my officemate's new camera. When you come, we'll buy a load of various things. I am waiting for you so we can look around Berlin together, I don't feel like doing so by myself.

I will be writing something, but Osmańczyk[2] advises me to wait a bit and get to know the terrain better. He's a walking encyclopedia, unbelievable guy. The only one who has honestly helped me.

Darling, don't upset yourself about the difficulties with the passport because they have promised to arrange it on time. If they make faces about it now, you know that I won't stay here without you. The main thing is that you don't over-work too much, and that you don't tire yourself out. We're often going to take trips here. If not, then we'll manage to make the most of summer in Poland.

Kisses,

Tadeusz

Eat well, as I'm doing, go to the beach (look at the photo), read a bit, and think about me, as I very often do. Really! I never even expected it! Old love.

7. JULY 14, 1949, BERLIN

[*telegram to his wife; received 5:15 P.M.*]

EXCELLENT WEATHER STOP GOOD MOOD STOP SEND LITERARY JOURNALS STOP
YOU'LL RECEIVE FRENCH BOOKS STOP KISSES TADEUSZ

8. UNDATED, BERLIN

[*to his brother*]

Sanatorium, Wonieść, Bojanowa Stare, Kościan near Poznań

Dear Julek,

Thank you very much for your very optimistic letter. You have no idea how happy I am that you are boring yourself stiff in a positive way and swimming in the water. Apparently, actually, the weather where you are was not too good either, here it rained all the time and was as stuffy as a bedroom. I'm performing the first part of your program: boring myself stiff with idiotic work, but am not making use of either the sun, nor of water, nor of air, because I get very tired.

I can't even write. Fortunately, I was able to send a little volume of articles to the publisher before I left. I worked on them day and night the last days and managed exactly on time. I read a little. I'm sending you Kisch's book about America. Kisch recently died in Prague, he was a great reporter, a middle-class liberal. Writes well. Wygodzki translated his *Jarmark sensacji* [*Market of Sensations*]. *Chiny bez maski* [*China Without a Mask*] also came out in Poland. Read, it's worth it.

Give my regards to Krzyżanowski's Polish student. She's probably changed her surname, because I can't recall it, but don't tell her because she'll feel bad. Ask about her maiden name.

Stay as long as you need to, of course, then leave immediately. I think it might be good to arrange a short vacation in the mountains or by the sea for yourself, and then go to work. When Tuśka comes, I'll try to help you a bit.

Write a lot and extensively,

Kisses, Brother,

Tadeusz

9. JULY 20, 1949, BERLIN

[*to his wife*]

Dear Tuśka,

I don't at all know what the situation with your passport looks like, since everybody here promises, but no one does anything about it. After July 22, Halpern, who promised to intervene himself, is to go to Warsaw. I have semi-officially announced that if by the end of July you do not have a passport enabling you to come before August 25, then I am going back to Poland, particularly since I don't amount to much here. I detest office work, as you know, rummaging through letters, etc. Conversations with Germans exhaust me immensely. They imagined for themselves here that when the "literati" arrived he would write brilliant articles and essays every day and serve the entire German press. They don't much understand that writing an essay means a week of absolute quiet. "But you can write after three P.M."

I've become very friendly with Edmund Osmańczyk, who has shown me much kindness. He's a very wise guy. I go out of town with him on Saturday and Sunday, practically to the Baltic, and have rested up well. I get a lot of pleasure from books, which I go crazy over in antiquariats, I've collected a few and am reading a lot. I'll start to write something and send it to Poland, but it is coming with difficulty because I have to orient myself about German issues and start from scratch. Nobody wants to offer me either help or advice. I'm used to it by now, but I was surprised.

I've set myself up splendidly, in other words by comparison with others I've landed on my feet. I've got three rooms with old furniture, very comfortable, with a balcony. Two little old ladies creep around the apartment, but you can't see them. One cooks for me and supports me.

I needn't tell you that I'm not in great humor and am furious at my stupidity in coming here without you. It turns out that it's best not to trust anyone, not even the great directors of MSZ.

Write how you're managing with money and whether you got the transmittal from MSZ. Julek wrote me a letter, he's in a wonderful mood.

Write, chin up, don't upset yourself. One way or another we'll see each other in three weeks.

Love and kisses,

T.

10. JULY 27, 1949, BERLIN

[*to his wife*]

Tuśka, Dear,

Director Halpern left for Warsaw the day before yesterday and promised to stop by during the week to let you know what he was told by the MSZ. I made huge and unpleasant scenes here, and am sabotaging work out of fury. In general, huge disillusionment with conditions: I knew more about Berlin in Warsaw, than in Berlin itself. Paperwork tires me and I cannot write anything. That's why Starski's suggestion to write Prus's *Faraon* [*Pharoah*] has pleased me immeasurably. It will be a great relief to me at work and will finally establish me in a rightful place.

Darling, you must write to Hager that he make every effort on behalf of my arrival. They don't much understand here that a so-called writer came, and not a shit from Dung Street; in Berlin, the world ends with the Ambassador-General, from behind whom Poland cannot be seen. I'm also writing to Hager, but there's not much time. I'd be very glad if I could manage to tear myself away from work and sit down to write. On top of that, I'd be coming to you! At the thought of that I'd not only write a story from *Faraon* but *Faraon* itself and three other films.

Another summer isn't working out for us! I'd thought that we would go away for weekends together and roam around antiquariats and Berlin theaters. I don't do so myself and I miss it terribly. It would have been better to sit in Poland and write decent reportage about villages and factories, I'd very much like to. Berlin is also an interesting hub, but have you ever known a so-called clerk of the 8th category to have time to read and see everything? He doesn't need it anyway. So I buy with my own money the German papers—of which there is an unusual amount, I get practically no Polish papers and am supposed, you see, to create "culture." I don't know how to argue about things, it immediately makes me sick, and I wave it aside. I dream about our being together: we'll shut ourselves up and study without anyone's help. A little longer and I'll take up writing, but I don't know whether it will be pleasing to people.

I'm very concerned about your health, I regret that I left in summer, I could have kept an eye on you in some health spa and, as it is, you're breathing dust and choking from the heat. But I'll get to writing stories and will never move out of Poland without you! Just let them try to do anything.

I think I wrote to Mother once. I truly have no time. I leave the office at three, then two hours for lunch, and I return home around six so tired that I usually fall into bed and sleep till the following day, or else read rather stupid

novels and sweat from exhaustion. Perhaps it's the summer, or perhaps nerves. I lost self-control a few times, and made enemies for myself, who are now outraged. But, you know, right is usually on my side in arguments. I don't know how to get used to things.

So, Darling: even if walls crumble, I'm definitely coming to sign the contract for the story and will not leave without you, I will not make such an idiot of myself a second time.

Fond kisses, Tuśka, hang in there bravely, wife,

Tadeusz

11. JULY 26, 1949, 40 BERLIN
[*telegram to his wife; received 5:45 P.M.*]

CHIN UP STOP WANT TO COME TO MAKE FILM STOP WE'LL ARRANGE EVERYTHING STOP KISS ON THE CHEEK TADEUSZ

12. AUGUST 18, 1949, BERLIN
[*telegram to his wife; received 3:20 P.M.*]

UP TO MY EARS IN WORK STOP MISS YOU VERY MUCH THOUGH EATING WELL STOP PICK UP PASSPORT THURSDAY FROM DIRECTOR ZBOROWSKA MSZ STOP PRESS DEPARTMENT STOP DIVISION FOREIGN SERVICE ESTABLISHMENT STOP TELEGRAM WHEN YOU ARE COMING STOP KISSES AND AM WAITING TADEUSZ

13. AUGUST 23, 1949, GŁĘBOKIE
[*M. Kurecka-Wirpsza to M. Borowska*]

Dear Tuśka,

If you haven't already left, then definitely give some sign of life as soon as you receive this letter. You have no idea how much has been spoken of late about you (and you in particular) in Głębokie . . . First of all: a week ago, Witek was in Warsaw for a few days, and banged at your door a few times to no avail; second of all, my school friend, Iza Belke, was here recently, who, as it turns out, knows you from childhood days. So we chatted about you more than once, and even

though we should no longer harbor any thoughts of your coming here, I decided to write in order to learn what's with you. Have you finally got all those papers? Are you going to that Berlin for long? We thought that perhaps Tadek would write to us, but not a whisper, not a word from him, Woroszyłski got some books from him, but also "without words." How's your health? Write, woman. A card at least! If you haven't left by September, perhaps I'll try to find you on your home turf, because I'm setting off on a great fishing expedition to Warsaw, in other words, I quite simply want to get some translation work. I've been poring over Goethe and Mann a lot lately, from such translations I can certainly learn a lot, but earn little, and winter's at the door, and one has to think about potatoes, coal, and boots, rather than making "art for art's sake."

Tuśka, dear woman, I'm writing this letter in stages, because my little one is a bit sick—a few cooler days and she came down with flu—and in the next room Puntek is playing "trains," which is not conducive to collecting my thoughts. Every other moment, somebody or other arrives as though in spite: chimney sweep, mailman, etc. I've come to the general conclusion that I'm going a bit mad, because I've lost the ability to write even a decent letter, and I simply wanted to write to you to show a sign of life and concern about your person on the part of people who hold your memory dear to their heart.

Have you laid hands yet on the first issue of the "philosophical series" from *Nowe Drogi* [*New Roads*]? It's a very interesting selection of translations of various Marxist philosophical works: cognitive theory, genetics, etc. I'm rummaging through it right now, and have a great desire to talk on the subject with someone, however, Witek is terribly worn out, working and writing a lot at the moment, and when he's not writing or else not sleeping or not eating, he's at the radio station, or at various meetings and conferences. So I have a feeling that over time I'll become famous for being a female of extremely few words, because by dint of the fact that I have no one to talk to, I simply won't talk! I keep on regretting that there's no way you can come here. The weather's wonderful, the long, sunny Pomeranian fall is starting, and that truly has to be the most beautiful time of year here. But I cheer myself up with the thought that when you are settled in that Berlin, perhaps you'll both come here for a vacation. In any event, if this letter still reaches you, write a couple of words at least about yourselves, yourself, when you are leaving, how you are feeling, and whether I have any prospects of seeing you in September in Warsaw. Sincere regards from me and from Witek, and I really am waiting for some news from you.

Maryla

14. SEPTEMBER 22, 1949, WARSAW

[*from S. Żółkiewski*]

Dear Tadeusz Borowski,

I received the books. Thank you very, very much. I was terribly pleased. They're extremely necessary to us here. A lot of work—and no sources.

You're a decent guy for remembering. How is it in Germany? What does literary and scholarly life look like there? It would be good if you'd write—for *Kuźnica—Twórczość* some at least very informative article.

No important changes here. Rather, a certain torpor in literary life. Only that Bratny is going to govern *Odrodzenie* instead of Sandauer. Is Kruczkowski going to be shown in Berlin? Best regards to your wife. Kisses from mine,

Sincere regards,

Stefan Żółkiewski

15. SEPTEMBER 15, 1949, BERLIN

[*to Jerzy Andrzejewski*]

Tadeusz Borowski, Polskie Biuro Informacji Prasowej, 3 Neudstadtische Kirch-strasse, Berlin NW 7

Dear Jerzy,

I am taking the liberty of sending you a fragment of the German *Popiół i Diament;* the German editors bear the blame for the errors in surnames. *Zeit im Bild* is the most serious, together with *Tägliche Rundschau* (Soviet paper), of illustrated journals, edition of 200,000.

Best wishes to you both,

T. Borowski

16. SEPTEMBER 29, 1949, WARSAW

[*from Leon Kruczkowski*]

Dear Pan Tadeusz,

Despite a lack of news from Berlin, I am assuming that there have been no changes in the matter of performing *Niemcy* [*The Germans*] at the Deutsches

Theater and that the play is being prepared. In connection with this, I am sending you a somewhat "edited" text of the epilogue. This arose at the time the play was being worked on at the Teatr Współczesny in Warsaw, during discussions with Axer and the company. As you will easily see, the new "edition" does not contain any major changes in the plot and only insignificant changes in dialogue—it simply rests on changing the sequence of scenes. Previously, the epilogue was constructed of three successive "duets" of Sonnenbruch: 1) with Bennecke, 2) with Hoppe, 3) with Willi. Currently, it begins with the conversation with Hoppe (almost unchanged), followed by the conversation with Bennecke (also almost unchanged), the significant change is the bringing of Willi into Bennecke's presence, as a result of which I gained a certain "thickening" of the mood in the final scene—the epilogue's finale: Sonnenbruch's decision happens immediately against the antagonist and not, as previously, with Hoppe's intervention. I think that in the new formulation I achieved a richer cadence in the dramatic line, a stronger point, and the figure of Bennecke also acquired several additional features. I would be most grateful to you if you would convey the new text of the epilogue to the translator and the theater for whom the introduction of such insignificant but productive changes should not create too big a problem at the present stage of the work.

On the card attached to the text, I also suggest to the translator and the theater the addition of a few words in Act III, along the lines which Langhoff suggested in conversation with me.

I also wish to inform you what the dates of the premieres of *Niemcy* look like here. The first will be performed by Dąbrowski (Kraków): 10/22; the real, however, and "official" world premiere will be performed in Warsaw at Axer: 10/29. That same day is earmarked for the Wrocław premiere.

In accordance with what we decided in Berlin, that premiere should not take place sooner than a few days after the Warsaw one—I'd be most grateful if you would inform me how it looks "calendarwise."

I am sending you my photograph for eventual press use. Incidentally, I recall that you graciously promised to send me our photographs from Weimar[3] and Berlin, they would be useful for the long report that I am preparing for *Odrodzenie*.

I await news from you, and enclose sincere regards also to your wife, Mr. and Mrs. Osmańczyk and the Podkowińskis, as well as to all my Berlin acquaintances.

Sincerely,

Leon Kruczkowski

P.S.   In a few days, we will send through the Mission invitations to German writers for the Goethe celebration in Warsaw (around 10/20). In connection with this, please send to my address biographical materials on those writers who will make up the delegation—for press purposes. Perhaps you would come to Warsaw with them?

17. OCTOBER 3, 1949, BERLIN
[*to his parents*]

My Dears,

I've been traveling for several days and wasn't able to write back to Dad or Julek's letters, which arrived just then. Hot days in Germany now, the peacetime battle is in full swing, a mass of demonstrations and conferences, which one has to attend. Until three months ago, it was quite sleepy here and only dissenting railroad workers in Berlin were on strike, and the inhabitants had to go by foot, or cram themselves into the subway. With distances of up to 60 km. from one suburb to another—not much of a pleasure. After the reactionary railroad workers' strike a great peacetime action was announced: concerts, cinemas, processions, etc., throughout fall. Only here does one see how serious these actions are. And that's why I roam around here and there a little: from Weimar to Frankfurt, from Forst by the Nysa to Quedlinburg on the border of the English sector. Unbelievably interesting meetings, but nerve-wracking.

Tuśka is having dental work, diathermia, and working in the Women's League. It takes her the whole day. On top of that, she's trying to speak German with the landladies, which creates an amusing impression since the landladies speak with a Berlin accent, and Tuśka thinks that she knows how to speak German. But they communicate splendidly with the aid of gestures. We got the medicines for Julek, we are waiting for the occasion to have them taken or sent. We'll arrange it in the next few days (we can't through the post). I sent you a bit of cash in September, I wonder whether you got it, because the bureaucracy here is disgusting and will probably last until the Day of Judgment. There's no cure for it.

I don't have much time or energy for writing. My book is coming out any day with Kuryluk in Warsaw (PIW). They wrote that they have started printing it. Ah, well, we'll see what happens, I wrote it in a hurry.

Write what's with you before winter. How is it going with Julek's university?

280

How's Mom's health? Moms, perhaps you'd write us a word? Tuśka sent a letter, and there's been neither sight nor sound.

Kisses, and keep well,

Your Tadeusz

18. OCTOBER 15, 1949, BERLIN
[*M. Borowska to W. Leopold*]

Dear Wanda,

I haven't written for a long, long time, but it was because I had to get acclimatized here, which I have been completely unable to do, and neither has Tadeusz.

Tadek plows fallow ground, gathers so-called experiences of various kinds, and operates no worse than an insurance clerk. The worst is that he can't write. He rarely has free afternoons or evenings, and so we just as rarely go to the theater or the concert. I think that our authorities here don't much believe that he's a writer because he announced that he couldn't "create" in the office in the company of a secretary pounding on a machine and many, many clients.

Anyway, I'll tell you everything in detail in the future, because it's not convenient for me to write about it. In any event, conditions here are not the best climate for people lacking street smarts and possessing an ugly flaw—honesty.

It's only here that both I and Tadeusz have come to value our friends and acquaintances and we think with tears in our eyes about the integrity of their characters and miss them dreadfully. The moral of this is: as soon as Tadeusz gets free of his responsibilities, we return to Warsaw immediately. I'm also not going to describe my impressions of theaters and concerts. I'll just tell you that the most magnificent performance I've ever seen, and the most harmonious in every respect (songs such that tears flowed freely)—was Brecht's *Mutter Courage*! Such theater, of course, can only be seen in the Eastern sector. And the concerts—I tell you, even the deaf would hear them.

And in the West—luxury behind window displays, prostitution on the streets, and despair in the heart. There's even an Existentialists' Club here, to which we're always planning to go, but somehow never have enough time.

We repeat every day that Berlin is a magnificent, radical cure for cosmopolitanism, that Berlin is a corpse, and Warsaw a newborn—but it somehow doesn't

comfort us, and we would very much like to return. The one plus of our stay here is a comfortable and large apartment and attentive staff.

I'm making fairly good strides in German, but don't tire myself out studying. The whole of September, I felt quite well, and now I'm again plagued by various organs. The worst's with the teeth, which they alternately either put in or remove.

Tadek's physical appearance is assuming the shape of a boxer. He bought himself some strange, string gadget, and twice a day wrestles with it enthusiastically. It looks very funny.

So far, we've taken three compulsory expeditions through the terrain, but we profited from them a lot in terms of getting to know both people and monuments.

There's generally going to be a lot to tell, enough for several sessions. Tadek has scraped together quite a few books. German, of course. It's quite hard to get French literature here.

I'm closing for now and sending kisses to your mother and you from Tadeusz and me,

Tuśka

Write a few words about what you're doing and what you're into. Perhaps we'll drop into Warsaw in November.

If by chance you learn anything about courses in building be so kind as to let my sister know. Her address: Barbara Rundo, Apt. 26, 11 Kilinski's Street, Łódź.

19. OCTOBER 16, 1949, SZCZECIN
[*from W. Woroszylski*]

Dear Tadeusz,

I'm taking the opportunity of Mrs. Osmańczyk's trip to Berlin to send you a few words. First of all, I'm tremendously grateful to you for Lukács and Brecht. They're wonderful—each in its own way—books! I've recently been envying you that Berlin. For how many days did the radio speakers emit: "What's happening in Berlin?" You probably saw all those things at close hand. I'm not convinced, actually, that history seen at close hand is always very engaging. But I believe it was this time. Write me something about it, will you?

Not much has changed for me since we last saw each other. In September

I was at the SFMD conference in Budapest, other than that I'm sitting in my Szczecin backwater and, on the whole, lauding it. My first three "works" have finally come out: a volume of poems, volume of satires, and a poem-cycle about Jarosław Dąbrowski. I'd like to send them to you, so give me your address. My collection of reportage from the USSR is in print and the translation of Kirsanow's poems[4] that I once had in *Odrodzenie*. Other than that I've written several poems during this time. Prose still doesn't work out well.

And you—what are you writing? I've heard that things didn't go too well for you in Berlin with apartments, work, etc. That's not too conducive to writing. But I judge that the arrival of Tuśka, who took up the task with her usual energy and industriousness, changed the situation—and you're no longer going around hungry, unwashed, homeless, and exploited by the cruel Zygmunt Radka. So, perhaps, you are also writing? Let me know whether you are getting journals and books from Poland. If not, I might be able to organize something for you.

I'll leave Warsaw and Szczecin gossip for our further correspondence. For now, I'm closing, regards to Tuśka and you, too—from Janka and me,

Witek

20. OCTOBER 16, 1949

Sender: Witold Wirpsza, 24 Pogodna St., Szczecin 11

Dear Tadek,

The following circumstance has caused me to get over my hatred of letter writing: on behalf of Polish Radio in Szczecin, I am to establish official contact with progressive German literati, Szczecin's new radio station is to work up these matters—beginning sometime in December—for an all-Poland program. In connection with this, I have written two letters so far to BIP and have received no reply. It's simply a question of BIP sending to Szczecin radio the addresses of those writers with whom one should establish contact. Since this matter is pressing at the moment, and BIP does not respond to any requests, I would be most grateful to you if you would be willing to personally take the matter up. Regardless of this, it would be very good, if you'd be willing to send us bimonthly a German cultural chronicle (four typewritten pages double-spaced). We would pay 10,000 apiece, and independent of that, I would give it to *Głos Szczeciński* [*Voice of Szczecin*].

As to my personal matters, there are no great changes. My two books have come out—I'm not sending them to you at the moment because I haven't got the author's copies. As soon as I get them, I'll send them. Maryla is in Warsaw and has been working in the Konkurs Szopenowski [Chopin Competition]—I get the impression that she's got a bit of water on the brain. It'll pass—probably.

My health isn't wonderful, I'm gradually falling apart, I recently lay in bed for two weeks and am still in a feverish state. I don't go to the doctor.

I'd be most grateful for a speedy reply and for your private address.

Warm regards. Hugs for Tuśka,

Witek

21. OCTOBER 18, 1949, BERLIN

[*to W. Woroszylski*]

Sender: T. Borowski, Polskie Biuro Informacji Prasowej, Sammel NR: 425166, 3 Neustadtische Kirchstr., Berlin, NW 7

Dear Witek,

I envy you as well, that you are able to sit quietly finishing books for publication, may there be many of them. Our literature hasn't been erring on the side of taking firm stands lately, one waits longingly for every honest book. I learned from *Przewodnik Bibliograficzny* [*Bibliographical Guide*] that your books had come out and immediately wrote asking that a copy be sent to me, but don't yet have them in hand. If you can, send them to the above address.

My collection of reviews and articles will come out with Kuryluk sometime this year. I was promised the middle of September, but one has to wait patiently. I finished it in June, and since that time wrote only a filmscript "Faraon" at the suggestion of Film Polski and—as with everything one does for film—it was turned down. A month and a half of work in Berlin went down the drain.

The stay in Berlin teaches one thing, as do all stays abroad, anyway: that the important things are happening at home. The great happenings in Berlin are simply echoes of the decisions that are taken up in the Soviet Union and Poland, and a demonstration of that power that is being created in our country. German democracy is going through that honeymoon period that we went through four years ago. It's amusing when one discovers the same trains of thought in young writers and composers here, which we, ourselves—thank God!—have already

gone beyond. The young workers, however, are different, very mature and decided. Cultural life? I have little occasion to take part in it. Periodicals you know, books—other than the huge flood of dime novels, not many outstanding items. Lukács, Brecht, H. Mann, young Kuba's poems, Abusch's essays, some of Anna Seghers's pages—that's about all that is really worth remembering.

The rest is typical literature for internal use. On the other hand, they have interesting periodicals, edited in a lively way. *Ost und West, Aufbau, Bildende kunst,* the West's *Wandlung, Monat,* and others—give a close-up view of the class struggle in the area of culture. Sometimes it takes on an amusing shape, e.g., when Plivier, the author of "Stalingrad," escapes to the West and becomes an "integral" humanist, or when German reaction slings mud at the not very progressive Thomas Mann.

For me, personally, life is tolerable, although there's never a shortage of stupid and nasty people. I'm supposed to be a good office worker, and only thanks to my stubborn nature, I've persuaded people I'm not going to be one. Tuśka is very sick, lying at home, and is getting nothing out of her stay. She goes around to doctors who exert themselves even less than the ones in Warsaw.

Best wishes, and am awaiting a letter. I get a few books from Poland the official route, but strangely not a lot. One could tell volumes about how valued journals from Poland are in our office. I feel as though I were in Patagonia.

Greetings from Tuśka to Janka and from me to you both,

T. Borowski

22. OCTOBER 19, 1949, BERLIN

[*to Aleksander Wat; on* Polskie Biuro Informacji Prasowej *letterhead*][5]

Dear Aleksander,

I'm sending beautiful photos from the West's *Die Zeit.* Did that visit to Tops[6] take place in Venice, or is the information imprecise? The photos are with Kruczkowski. Unfortunately, I didn't manage to get the prints. Infant cries in Berlin: a new people's democracy is being born.[7] May we have ever more of such infants! Sincere regards to Ola and Andrzej.

Tadeusz

23. NOVEMBER 12, 1949, BERLIN

[*to W. Woroszylski, on Polskie Biuro Informacji Prasowej letterhead*]

Dear Wiktor,

Sincere congratulations on your recent successes. In eighteen months, you have become one of our best poets. That's a lot, since Polish poetry (as opposed to prose and drama) can without shame measure itself against the best.

But why did you omit to send me your pile of volumes? Is that how a friend behaves? Hugs to Janka, and to you a poke in the ribs.

Tadeusz

24. NOVEMBER 18, 1949, GŁĘBOKIE

[*from M. Wirpsza*]

Dearest Tadeuszes,

Witek is now in Wisła in Lower Silesia, because Film Polski brought him there for a conference, then he'll probably go for a day or two to Warsaw, and when he gets back he'll send you his books, because I don't want to send them without him and a dedication.

I see that you have no taste for Berlin life—but you'll probably snatch up some books. Tadek, could you not find me something decent to translate, because actually I am making one book for PIW, but a dreadful one, and another for Czytelnik—but that again—Lindsay!!! In a word, enough to make one crazy. Wyka recently upbraided me that what I'm doing is "prostituting translation," easy for him to say, when cash is needed and "serious" publishers give one such "dross" to do! I stayed in Warsaw for six solid weeks, because on the occasion of the Chopin Competition, I was helping various foreigners on the jury communicate with the Poles and vice versa. I got dog tired, but on the whole the event was quite a success and interesting—and a bit of money came my way, so that we've somewhat provided for the house, kids, and ourselves for the winter.

Puntek is going to preschool and is growing up a storm, Pucka already has seven teeth, is beginning to walk and talk—funny little tots, and very much loved.

Three weeks ago, the Woroszyłskis' son was born—he's to be Felek—as fat as a watermelon (4 kg 300!!!) and unbelievably good. The young papa is as proud as a peacock about it! Witek is working a lot and feeling quite well lately, at the

beginning of December we're opening a new radio station here, so there's a mass of work.—And how's Tuśka's health? What is life like "in general" for you there? Write something decent, and not just those little notes! In Szczecin, recently, there's been a bit of action—a few concerts, quite decent, and on top of that the literary director of our theater is . . . no other than—Roman Bratny, who has to look in here sometimes on that score, since he usually travels with a "retinue"— S. Marczak-Oborski and A. Braun accompanied him recently (the latter even stayed for a few more days in our abode, because a sudden frenzy of work came down upon him!). Tadek Różewicz has at last gone to Prague with—Kornel Filipowicz, he's supposed to return the end of November.

Some German women at the competition told me that there apparently exists some new, excellent book of Brecht's. Do you know it? and what's it called? I would still like (maniacally) to find out about the possibility of getting Mann's "Lotte in Weimar" and "Roman eines Romans"—but I think it's a lost cause! Write again, dear people; here in removed from "the world" Głębokie every sign of life from you gives us pleasure. Surely, Tuśka should take the opportunity of this Berlin escapade to get solid treatment, because apparently, as the Osmańczyks say, there's no shortage of doctors in Berlin, and good ones at that. Who on the whole do you see—the Osmańczyks, Podkowińskis? Is Słucki still at BIP? Teleg's woolliness shouldn't be a cause for getting upset, Tadek—he's a truck missing all its wheels! He's still wandering around the streets of our city with a haughty and sullen expression, but that's all there is to the wandering. Better if you send Wyka something decent yourself,[8] because he was complaining to me recently in Warsaw that he had no material. Could you not drop by Szczecin instead of Warsaw sometime? What are you doing about the holidays? Always remember that our madhouse welcomingly opens its doors to your disposal.

Warm hugs to you both from us four, and Witek will write and send books when he returns.

Maryla

25. NOVEMBER 21, 1949, SZCZECIN
[*from W. Woroszylski*]

Dear Tadeusz,

It really was not nice on my part to put a letter and the books off for so long. My justification lies in the fact that for the past three weeks I've been lying in

bed with flu, which was not conducive to writing letters. Today, I've got up a bit for the first time.

Let's start with the matters raised in your first letter. I was very pleased by what you wrote about young German workers. It's quite natural, anyway, that we can rely most of all on young people—and not those of our age, I think, but a few years younger. In certain old Communist-intellectuals one can observe a strange attitude, not always clearly expressed, that only they are the bearers of Marxist-Leninist ideology and all young people are reactionary, hah, fascist! A rather typical expression could be found in both of Kruczkowski's plays. This attitude is not only nonsensical, but also politically incorrect, harmful, backward. As it seems to me, there are many correct observations in Osmańczyk's review of the Berlin performance of *Niemcy*.[9] Write and tell me what you think about this.

You say that in German literature there aren't many outstanding figures and you mention Brecht, Lukács, H. Mann, Seghers, Abusch, Kuba. In our postwar literature, however, I couldn't list as many names worthy of regard. Apropos, who is Kuba? I've been hearing about him lately from all sides, but his work hasn't yet reached Poland.

Tuśka's illness worried us a lot. Janka and I wish her a speedy return to health.

I'm curious whether you finally became a decent office worker, or whether your "authorities" let themselves be persuaded that you would not become one. If it's the last eventuality, you are doubtless making better use of your stay in Berlin.

In your second letter, which I received a few days ago, you congratulate my successes and maintain that "within eighteen months I have become one of the best of our poets." You gave me great pleasure, and I don't doubt that you really think so. I, however, don't feel this way. Not only because my poetry is no social fact, because no one buys or reads my books, any more than they buy and read those of my colleagues. But also because I see all the primitiveness, superficiality, meagerness of everything I have written so far. The writing of every poem is several days' toil. I don't know whether I'll ever learn to write better. Perhaps I'll soon stop writing completely.

News from Poland. First—that last KC[10] plenary assembly, about which they are probably talking a lot where you are. Some details of the discussion are shattering. How deeply agents can reach! Perhaps at the Lechowicz and S-ki these facts will be brought to public attention.[11] Second communiqué from Poland:

10/29 of the current year, a son was born to me. Huge fellow, he's called Felek. Janka, in her role as mother, feels as though she's done nothing but this for years. I, in the role of father—not so good. Perhaps in time I will get used to it.

That's probably it for now. I enclose the books. I'd like you to write what you think of them.

Sincere hugs and regards for Tuśka. To you—Janka returns hugs, and I—a poke in the ribs.

Witek

26. NOVEMBER 25, 1949, GŁĘBOKIE
[*from W. Wirpsza*]

Dear Tadeusz and Darling Tuśka,

I received the letter with its well-deserved curses. As to the books, I only recently received author's copies, literally three days before my departure to Wisła, so that there were so-called objective obstacles. I trust you will consider me exonerated.

No list of German writers has so far reached Szczecin. At the moment, I'm not much concerned about these things, on the 22nd of this month, I broke a leg at Bacewiczówna's (I had wanted to flirt a little for once and it didn't work out; Maryla is laughing at me and says that in light of this she is giving me a completely free hand) and I have a six-week, somewhat compulsory vacation, so I'll finally be able to quietly get to work. As a matter of fact, for the past few years, I've been dreaming of breaking a leg. It turns out that such dreams are very easily fulfilled. We'll just have to see what the benefits are going to be.

I'm writing a bit now, although, like nearly everybody else, I'm experiencing a so-called block. I try not to succumb, however. I sometimes arrive at the conclusion that things are going too fast for the pen to be able to keep up—I don't know how to run, have heart palpitations, don't want to use mechanical means of locomotion, so sometimes one is reduced to the somewhat out-of-date device of his own conscience. In other words, it's a question of philosophical matters being turned from intellectual constructions into honest poetry. However, despite all difficulties, I don't want to give in. Honest poetry is, at the base of things, a question of honest effort.

One has to bring one's self—*und wenn es Steine regnet*—to make this effort. But it's only—in a word.

Don't upset yourself about Telega! He's a decided idiot—of great caliber. Anyway, he hurt only himself with his statement, probably Zarząd Swietlicy, of which Andrzejwski is president, will send the appropriate corrections to Wyka. Telega has finished himself off in this area with that whole story.

I was in Wisła for four days, where PP[12] "Film Polski" threw another four million in the mud. The conference produced no results; apart from the repetition by the significant and the insignificant of already known platitudes, nobody said anything concrete. Organizational matters remain as they were, writers are going to write stories, Ford is going to write screenplays, the few gentlemen's little shop is going to keep prospering, until someone gets seriously interested in these matters. I fear, however, that there will then be weeping and grinding of teeth.

Personally, I'm prospering quite well, the children are healthy, Maryla is fortunately not getting pregnant. I bought myself a carpet for my study, as well as a set of the works of Jules Verne. It's wonderful reading! Perhaps, you could come to Szczecin for a weekend sometime? Only four hours by train!

Witek

Sincere regards—write to the plaster-of-Paris invalid and to me as well!

Maryla

P.S.   Large request: I cannot get decent ink either in Szczecin or in Warsaw. All of it clogs up my pen. Perhaps Tuśka could suggest something?

27. DECEMBER 4, 1949, WARSAW
[*from Wanda Leopold*]

My Dears,

Actually, I don't know where to start this letter, nor how to justify my silence. I'll begin with thanks that Tuśka dropped by for a minute, and I got a bit of firsthand information, and I am completely abashed by the gift, because it is total indulgence and I don't see the reason, etc. Which didn't stop me from flashing them at Barbara today, I fear, unfortunately, that they'll reach her already after Sunday. I asked her to confirm their receipt either to you or me. Of course, that dumb Ryszard who apparently spent an entire Sunday with you (were you bored to death?) managed to tell me nothing other than that you were very nice. I said that wasn't news. What I'd most like to know is whether you will manage to get

back to health in Berlin, whether there won't again be a shortage of medications and whether conditions won't get worse? When I wasn't getting any news from you, I'd ask Staszek Wygodzki about this or that. Things are apparently not well with him. I was once so despondent about you that I warned Wygodzki that I'd visit him, but Tuśka's letter came so I didn't go.

Now I must outline a bit of gossip about myself, which isn't interesting, but if you were in Warsaw, I would have been to see you at least ten times under all manner of circumstances, so you're at a clear advantage. First—had the III Plenary Session been a bit later,[13] I would probably already be in the Party—now I have scruples again (my Home Army past!), in addition, there's no group at the institute, *Kuźnica* is in the "creative" circle, it's hard for me to decide on an area. In any event, I'm going to clear up these matters in the shortest time.

At the institute it's rather gloomy—first part of the handbook finished—not worth a hoot. Every lecture—not Marxist (Wyka, Wyka!). There's now going to be a journal—we'll see (a quarterly, *Zeszyty Wrocławski* taken over). Stefan Z.[14] is going crazy and reveling in the university. A born teacher. Things are going quite well for him here, only he's practically not working himself, says that he now sees that his scholarly work is junk, and that in a while he'll land up as some honorary vice president of an Academy of Learning. Apart from that, in the higher seminar there are two very intelligent neo-Positivists who are lording it over him, and Stefan is wallowing in it because it's his past, after all, and we regard this with horror and wanted to write an article "When Does a Professor Stop Being a Marxist?" As to my "scholarly" work it's a bit unclear—other than occasional work for the institute, I've done nothing, I always get involved in organizational matters, and, apart from that, who the hell knows whether I'm suited to it. I can always manage to criticize everything beautifully, but do nothing myself. If this drags on, I will resign from my position at the institute and will only do things for them occasionally, because I am embarrassed. Stefan wanted me to run classes at the university this year, but the college wouldn't agree because I am a "traitor," and Stefan was not willing this year to push it through the Ministry. Our old man (i.e., J.K.) sucks up to Stefan unbelievably, invited them to his house for some big university reception, and introduced Barbara to everyone: "Pani Professor Żółkiewska." Barbara says she nearly hit him out of rage. Apart from that, Barbara has a very pleasant friend Eva Dorota, about whom, I think, it's known also in Berlin.

In my other "area of work," on the other hand, I have "advanced," that means that I have lately decided to join the *Kuźnica* group and act as deputy to the

editorial secretary, that means working closely with Paweł and beginning to slowly change the journal. What happened was simply that old Paweł (that is, Hoffman)[15] and I got to like each other very much and somehow agreed on many issues contrary to the rest of the group. At the moment we are slowly planning many changes, but these have to be connected, of course—to a certain extent at least—with a change of people. You know, Tadek, that there'll certainly be a push on you in this regard when you return. I don't think there's anything to fear. The Old Man is very good to work with, it's just they who sometimes can't, and also there is no chaos or bawdy house in the editorial office as there was in Łódź. The Old Man has a phenomenal nose for politics, but has to be helped with organizing literary, critical, and such like material. And it isn't true that he's not knowledgeable about it, as Brandys claims. It's simply that he's less interested in it, and one has to suggest it to him. It's just that they either don't have their own judgment, or they're afraid, or, at bottom, admit that they're ideologically incorrect, but don't want to acknowledge it. And the Old Man likes people who are quick, and with decided opinions (again, despite what they say). I don't think it would overburden you, we'd be a trio with the Old Man, Ryszard usually agrees to everything and works, we're also talking about Bartelski, so that there's no question of any "backbiting" and who knows if we won't manage to do a decent job over time.

The fact is that one way or another *Kuźnica* will not stop coming out—so perhaps let's try it? Anyway, I'll get better acquainted with it this month and will write to you again. It seems to me, at the moment, that it won't be so bad.[16]

Now about mutual contacts and acquaintances—I continue to run to Silber[17] when I suddenly need cash, he continues to be charming. I was supposed to translate *Clochemerle*, which Tuśka once reviewed, the sample translation apparently came out well, but the French wanted too much cash for the rights and it wasn't bought in the end. Anyway, at the moment I don't have time for translation because at this institute there's constant minor mess.

Other than that, and this is the last bit of news and the most personal—I've fallen in love and am getting married. That sounds incredibly funny! Especially the "getting married"! But I feel unbelievably good about this, after so many years, when I came to doubt that I'd be able to "dredge up" any feeling out of myself. As it turns out, I didn't need to "dredge," it came and exists. Completely different, but certain. At first I was very afraid that it might only be attachment, loneliness, friendship, regard for him, and the like—because then it surely wouldn't be right to get tied—however, I'm certainly not "talking" myself into anything,

I've reassured myself of this and feel very well, particularly since it is intensifying. We'll probably manage to arrange the formalities at the BGK in February (he has a wife with whom he hasn't lived for a long time already, but a divorce has to be gone through; a law is now to be enacted that five years' separation nullifies a marriage, so that will make it easier for us; but an official divorce and "wedding" is necessary for reasons of accommodations). Of course, the apartment peripatetics will go on for a while. But, of course, we'll make it through all of this. I am also very happy that he and Mother literally love each other, and the family idyll is in bloom. He's an incredible maniac and painter, practically self-taught, a yokel, and with the face of a bandit. Incredibly talented, hot-headed, a scoffer, mischievous, without a trace of so-called "refinement," neurotic, fantasist, etc. I was somewhat taken aback at first and didn't know what to make of it. But apart from these traits, he's emotional to the point of supersensitivity, with incredible intuition and powers of observation, so-called "upright character" to the highest degree. And he doesn't react the same way others do to the so-called "windmill of matters," from the most private to the most general, and still other things about which every woman could talk without end, but it's not worth it. I simply want you to like him and not be turned off at first meeting. He had an unusually entangled and difficult life, and even though he is a Communist, he's been left with a number of prejudices about "educated" people, and "proletarian" complexes. I think, anyway, that he and Tadek should get along well. Both of them are excellent and wicked raconteurs, like to "observe" people, have quick reactions and vehement attitudes to things. On top of that, Kajetan writes really truly well, better, I fear, than he draws, but he's certainly not going to write. So much about him for now. Oh, one more detail, I know that he loves me very much and that we'll be well together. Those in on the secret make the spiteful claim that we've both changed for the better even externally. As to formalities, he's called Kajetan Sosnowski[18] and is the technical editor of *Kuźnica*—so, therefore, if sometime in the nearest future our mutual acquaintances come to Berlin, please keep this information to yourselves, because working at this journal, I wouldn't want the place to be buzzing like a beehive for long. In a few months, anyway, Kajetan will move out of *Kuźnica*. At the moment, the *Kuźnica* gossip on the subject of me vacillates between him and Jastrun, and poor Rynio is completely disoriented and tries to draw me out from time to time, which amuses me greatly. Enough about this.

To finish with the gossip, Adolf has given his new novel to be published, doesn't know what he himself thinks of it, is a bit scared, solicits the opinions of

publishers and people familiar with fragments, is safeguarding himself with the subject matter of the next one—in a word, being Adolf. I don't know the book as a whole. K. and I are going to him next week for a further part of the fragments, which, he claims, are to be "close" to me. Meanwhile, I don't see this "closeness" and don't know what it consists of. But we'll see.[19] We could, of course, multiply these tiny pieces of information from our little world into infinity, but it's of little importance and I'm fortunately increasingly distanced from it.

And as to the larger world—I hope that you know more interesting things than I, and will tell me sometime. It's interesting that it's all hellish. And what's with literature? I've gone on a lot and unnecessarily. I'm very much awaiting your return, and if it gets delayed, send a card sometime. Tuśka get better as fast as possible—to hell with those Warsaw diagnoses; are those doctors really so dumb? Also write anytime you need something arranged, or prepared, in Warsaw. It's not a burden, and I'll at least have news of you. Warm hugs from my mother, and me, too, of course, and thank you very much for writing to me. Keep on doing it and come back, and be well (literally, and as "*Vale*").

Wanda

28. JANUARY 1, 1950, PANKOW, BERLIN
[*telegram*]

Borowscy, 5 Pocztowa St., Olsztyn
HAPPY NEW YEAR—THE TADEUSZES

29. JANUARY 5, 1950, BERLIN

Ed. Lesław M. Bartelski
Polish Radio, Literary Dept., Myśliwiecka St., Warsaw

Dear Lesław,
I've just read your "O zachodzie słońca" ["On the Setting of the Sun"],[20] a very beautiful and pleasant story; it would be worth arguing over a few details, but also worth being jealous.

I enclose my very best wishes for the New Year. Warm greetings to the lady.
Tadeusz

30. JANUARY 10, 1950, WARSAW

[*I. and S. Wygodzki to M. Borowska*]

Dear Tuśka,

Thank you very much for the greetings, and I hasten to ask how your hubby's respected appendix is? Did it get removed? If so, how does Tadeusz feel? And what about the glands? I'm terribly pleased that you are coming to our beloved Warsaw and are longingly awaiting you.

I've arranged a subscription for you with KDK and KO[21] for 1950, and also for Basia who was with me last week. Everything is fine with her.

Today I received a letter from Mrs. Prawinowa concerning the payments from the deposit. Tell her that the matter has been settled.

Everything's fine here. In February, we're going on "vacation." Stasiek is going to the factory to write, and I want to go to Zakopane for two weeks. But we'll meet before then.

Tuśka, I have a request, if it won't cause you too much trouble to buy two nylon tablecloths, do so, but truly only on condition that you won't go to too much trouble.

Until we meet.

Sincerely,

Irena

[*postscript from S. Wygodzki:*] Best wishes for the New Year and warmest regards,

Stanisław

31. JANUARY 14, 1950, SZCZECIN

[*from W. Woroszylski*]

Dear Ones,

First of all thank you very much for the Christmas Brecht. His poems gave us all (Felek, too) great satisfaction.

We' re enclosing the post-Christmas Kirsanow. Tough. Nothing interesting to be seen in the bookshops, and Kirsanow has at least the virtue of being "mine." Apropos—for several weeks, Tadek, I've been reading advertisements in journals for your volume, but getting it in Szczecin is out of the question. The distributor

is unprofessional! What's with you? Nothing sensational here. We're mummying and daddying. God's Will!

Bye, keep well—Janka and Witek

P.S.   Tadeusz could you get me numbers 4, 5, and 6 of *Aufbau* from 1949?

32. JANUARY 26, 1950, BERLIN

[*to W. Woroszylski*]

My Dears,

Thanks for Kirsanow. We know the poem from *Odrodzenia* and I, personally, like his defiant romanticism.

(Damn this machine, I made the spaces too small, and on top of that there are no Polish keys.)

You are not allowed to complain about 1949. Apart from the poem entitled "Felek," you published a small library, worked harder, surely, than anyone else. A writer—finally—is a small factory of ideology and is obliged to produce something. Only after achieving a certain level of output can one make demands about quality. Naturally, some will answer that works of art are different, that machinery . . . etc. But these jokes are not at all funny. I blame myself a lot for laziness. We need huge amounts of literature immediately; quality somehow arises during the course of work.

This is me thinking out loud; it doesn't concern you. In reading the volumes for the second time (I read lots in the press, as you know) I found many fine things; Tuśka read the piece on Roza Lee to some old biddies in the Polish community here; they wept.

I sent you Kuba's poems; he's the one the German younger generation likes to read the most. He wrote a cantata for Stalin's birthday: poetic sensation. Unfortunately, it hasn't yet come out in print. Here, too, publishers work for the day after tomorrow.

My little book is a collection of articles from *Rzeczpospolita*,[22] which cannot be read a second time without distaste. Journalism has to be good in order not to stink.

We're returning to Warsaw shortly (within weeks). I didn't learn much in this here Berlin, lots of office work that deadened my mental faculties for a few months.

I've collected some materials, mainly newspaper journalism, which we'll be able to go through in Warsaw.

Regards to the numerous Woroszyłski family. I'll send *Aufbau*. Kisses (but only for Janka).

Tadeusz

33. JANUARY 28, 1950, BERLIN
[*to L. M. Bartelski*]

Dear Leszek,

By return post, I'm sending you the requested issues of *Blick nach Polen* [*A Glance at Poland*]. You will also receive books as honorarium.

Thank you very much for the words about the last little volume. I had intended to gather materials in Berlin for a further volume on those subjects. Unfortunately, my work (apropos: send me other of your stories, if you have some, because we, unfortunately, send them out) did not always allow me to.

Maybe I'll manage to write something sensible in Warsaw.

Regards to the family,

Tadeusz

Enclosure: Bill for L. Bartelski's honorarium from *Blick nach Polen* for the sum of 120 marks.

34. UNDATED, BERLIN
[*to L. M. Bartelski*]

Dear Leszek,

Am sending you books; don't be angry if they're not to your taste.

Regards—Borowski

35. FEBRUARY 5, 1950, WARSAW
[*from Julian Tuwim*]

14 Wiejska St.

Dear and Respected Sir,

Thank you very much for *Deutsche Literatur Zeitung* (nos. 10 and 11) and I courteously request a permanent subscription. How and to whom should the dues be sent? Would it be possible to obtain a bibliography of books devoted to parodies? (*sehr wichtig!*)[23] One further request—almost a plea: that German antiquariats (Leipzig, Berlin, Dresden, Munich, et al.) keep sending me their catalogs. The areas that especially interest me are: ethnography, folklore, comparative linguistics, culture history, "Kulturgeschichtliche Curiosa,"[24] literary history.

I will be most obliged to you for arranging these matters.

Sincerely yours and warm regards,

Julian Tuwim

36. FEBRUARY 22, 1950, BERLIN
[*to Julian Tuwim*]

Respected Sir,

Only now on receiving a list of periodicals from "Deutsche Bücherei" in Leipzig am I able to offer you some information. No bibliophilic journal comes out either in East, or in West, Germany. The last issue of *Zwiebelfisch* came out in October 1948; *Zeitschrift fur Bucherfreunde* and *Philobiblion* have also ceased appearing. I have sent a few of Gerd Rosen's catalogs. Eastern antiquariats do not put out catalogs for reasons of price instability. Generally, since the so-called financial reforms German periodicals are under threat of catastrophe. *Ost und West* has ceased operations, *Frankfurter Hefte* has dropped from an edition of 60,000 to 5,000. I have been promised a few publications in the area of parody. I will endeavor to send them.

With sincere regards and apologies for the delay,

T. Borowski

P.S.   The enclosed list comes from "Deutsche Bucherei" in Leipzig, thus from the German National Library. But how incomplete it is!

37. FEBRUARY 13, 1950, SZCZECIN
[*from W. Woroszylski*]

Dear Tadeuszes,

First of all, we thank you very much for Kuba and for that women's brochure with my poem. Unfortunately, I already have that Kuba from Osmańczyk. I'm not especially impressed by him, anyway—I think that he's very much a chatterbox, ideologically ambiguous in places (perhaps this impression comes from my not having the best knowledge of the language), and that he examines specifically German problems. I only liked some fragments. You won't hold it against me (or maybe you will?) that I have behaved most indecently: I tore out the page with the dedication, and gave the rest to Wirpsza.

Has *Odrodzenie* reached you yet, and *Kuźnica*, with our discussion of poetry?[25] What swine, what swine—makes your hair stand on end! One thing's good, that there's some kind of discussion, and that we have finally achieved the possibility of saying what we think of colleagues who somewhat prematurely act like monuments to themselves. I'm very much counting, Tadek, on your taking part in the discussion. Primarily because, despite your Berlin "posting," you are not a diplomat, and will say what's bothering you.

It's good you are returning to Warsaw. I think you'll finally apply yourself to creating our good prose. You complain about your laziness. How well I understand you! Every time I sit down at my desk, it takes all my energy not to sit on the couch and read a book that someone industrious has already written. And that beginning—brrrr.

Janka and Felek thank you for your greetings,

Witek

38. UNDATED
[*to W. Woroszylski; postcard, City Hall in Leipzig on the reverse side*]

In Warsaw on March 1. Wrote to *Odrodzenie*.[26] Hang this city hall above your desk. Luther argued there with the Catholics.

Yours,

Tadeusz

39. FEBRUARY 21, 1950, WARSAW

[*from J. Tuwim*]

Dear and Respected Sir,

I am exceedingly grateful to you for so many favors. I received the "Zwiebelfisch" catalog, the bibliography of parodies, the list of periodicals, in a word—everything for which I asked. I am aware that you are soon returning to Warsaw, at that time I will thank you again, and request the so-called "bill," because someone had to pay for all this. You made me very happy by sending me the issue of *Weltbuhne* with the translation of my letter to Aragon. I was once a faithful and diligent reader of that journal, when such wonderful Germans as Tucholski and Osiecki (Ossietzky!) still worked for it. I want to believe with all my political will and hope that people of similar stature will be reborn in tragic Germany.

I congratulate you on your article in *Odrodzenie*. The observations about those "antifascists" who, in next to no time, are caught up in the clear waters of fascism are excellent, although not new to me. I saw many such idiots in America.

When you are back in Warsaw, please come and visit me.

Sincerely,

Julian Tuwim

40. EASTER 1950, OLSZTYN

[*to his brother*]

Dear Julek,

And so, I've been back from Berlin for some time. Toward the end I had a lot of work in Berlin in connection with the Leipzig Fair, and then with our departure. On my return, I had to look around for work, a lot of which piled up.

They dragged me here and there, finally, however, I've landed up at *Nowa Kultura*. My recent article in *Odrodzenie* and, before that, the article by my friend Witek Woroszyłski, resulted in the two journals being deemed redundant, correctly so.

My friends expected me to meet up with "unpleasantness" and were very happy. In the end, however, I have taken on the journalism section at *Nowa Kultura,* where each week I cook up a weekly chronicle. On top of that, masses of other work, paid and volunteer. My Tuśka has become very independent and

has gone to work for *Przyjaciółka* [*Friend*], where, from time to time, you can admire the fruits of my spirit.

I had expected to get an apartment in Warsaw by spring. Unfortunately, the matter will drag on probably until fall. I have been promised two rooms. In my room, I've laid out books from Germany. I was going to write a second volume of my *Opowiadania z książek i z gazet*. It ought to be ready by fall. I'm thinking of traveling a lot around Poland in summer; I'd like to opt for the Mazurs with their production cooperatives.

So much about me, Bro. Forgive me for not writing to you for so long. There wasn't always time; one wasn't always sitting at home.

Write and tell me how you are feeling and when you're returning home.

Hugs and kisses,

Your Tadeusz

41. APRIL 23, 1950, KRAKÓW

Sender: S. Kisielewski, 22 Krupnicza St., [Kraków]

Dear Sir,

I've got you hellishly stuck in my throat, and, unfortunately, I can't give vent to it because—the censors won't allow it. Your article about the exhibition[27] got me so riled up that I couldn't settle down anywhere. I consider you a journalist of great talent and equally great ignorance. You formed your ideas about the world in occupied Warsaw, in the hell of Auschwitz, and in debauched occupied Germany. That's hellishly little. You remind me of the Malayan girl in Conrad's story: a girl who, reading only the local paper consisting of reprints from European papers of news about accidents, comes to the conclusion that Europe is one great slaughterhouse . . .

But let's get away from general matters—perhaps we'll still talk about them in person sometime, if the ever-increasing totalitarianism of your psyche, which, with ever-increasing anxiety, I observe in you, will allow it. At the moment, I'm concerned about art, about which you write, and about which you know absolutely nothing. One can do so, but it would be worth your while to at least interest yourself in someone else's opinion, an opinion that won't be an easy to put down with demagoguery of the "Let's all go to Bagdad" type. Have you ever seen in the original any painting of Cezanne's? Must the building of socialism go

hand in hand with the destruction of artistic values which we see at the Exhibition? If I were in your place, I wouldn't think so badly of Socialism! I enclose a section of my article about Warsaw, comprised of my impressions of the Exhibition. I wrote it in conciliatory terms, circumspectly, "under censorship"—despite everything it got irrevocably confiscated. Perhaps this might make you inclined to revise your a la Malaysian girl thought processes. I'd be grateful if you could send it back to me after you've read it. I am sending it because, despite all appearances, I consider you a man of good will. I ask only for discretion: this is, after all, "illegal publication."

And one more thing. You accuse a painter of your acquaintance of not coming to the discussion at the Museum out of cowardice. Are you aware that there was an individual who once took an invitation to a discussion seriously, and in the Festival of Artistic Work in Poznań took up a dissenting voice? It was in any event, rather gentle dissent, based on the claim that among the classical Marxists (have you ever read them?) there is no conception about music, that the case is an open one, and suitable for discussion not only by politicians but also by professionals. Do you know that within a week that individual was fired from his position as conservatory professor? That individual was me. After this experience of mine, no one is taken in by a discussion; it's the type of discussion that Irzykowski wrote about Słonimski: "I suggest a game of chess to him, and he gathers up the pieces and throws them at me." And there aren't too many suicides.

I doubt, anyway, that I can stop you on the intellectual slope down which you are heading. But I want my conscience to be clear: that I warned you. Anyway, I am, as is known, a formalist, so I read you not for content but for form: this time, however, I got angry.

Appropriate greetings,
Stefan Kisielewski

42. APRIL 24, 1950, POZNAŃ
[*from W. Żukrowski*]

Dear Tadek,

Your telegram chased me around a long time. I'm finally replying from Poznań. Here's the column, but it's hard not to write something banal. Either rah-rah politically, or exactly like this one, which, apart from a certain grace—doesn't mean much. If you can use it, keep it, if not, return it to me at home,

i.e., Wrocław. Would like to talk to you, haven't seen you for years. What's with Osmańczyk? You've sold yourself to *Kuźnica,* but in six months they'll sell you as well. For now they are feeding you out of the sweetness of their hearts and setting dogs on whoever's convenient. I'll be in Warsaw May 7th. Write where to find you. Regards to Tadek Konwicki.

Sincerely,

Wojtek

43. MAY 6, 1950, WARSAW

[*to Bożenna Lewandowska, Polskie Biuro Informacji Prasowej, Berlin*]

Sender: M. and T. Borowski, Apt. 39, 17 Kaliska St., Warsaw

Dearest Bozenka,

The fact that we haven't written for so long is not at all the result of our laziness, nor of shortness of memory, and not, above all, ungratefulness. I (that means Tadeusz) thank you most sincerely for the piles of periodicals. They're a great help at work, but must be a lot of labor for you. We both have work up to our ears. When I (that means Tadeusz) make up the balance sheet for the weeks I've spent in Warsaw, I barely have room to put all the articles, chronicles, stories written and verbal, not to mention the sessions, conferences, consultations, meetings . . . This affects a little the book, which I haven't yet delivered to the publisher; the matter will be delayed by a few days. Tuśka hasn't got better, in truth, but she's started to work at *Przyjaciółka,* as a so-called "Literary Director." The apple doesn't fall far from the tree! She, also, can't complain about a lack of things to do. When you come, you'll see: there is stuff to do in Poland.—I heard that your Tadeusz is having certain difficulties; I shared his rage. We chat about this and that sometimes, either over a wine, or over black coffee. Dear One! If you're passing through, stop by Kaliska: lots of books, working mood, in a word—high time to talk. Drop a few words on a card sometime, perhaps you need some books, magazines, whatever? We'll send them right away. Hugs and kisses from both of us,

Tuśka and Tadeusz

P.S. Are the people in town still so irritable? If not, give them my kind regards—T. (that means Tadeusz).

44. MAY 22, 1950, BERLIN-PANKOW
[*from Alfred Kantorowicz*]

Very Dear and Respected Mr. Borowski,

Many thanks for the information. I, too, hope that during the summer I will finally receive an invitation to Warsaw, and will take the opportunity of visiting my old friends and colleagues from Spain, but also of seeing new friends, like you. I asked our ambassador, Prof. Dr. Friedrich Wolf,[28] during his short stay here, to arrange such an invitation for me. I am hopeful that he will not forget.

Sincere regards,

Your Alfred Kantorowicz

45. AUGUST 1, 1950, KRAKÓW
[*from Jan Paweł Gawlik*]

Dear Sir,

I am enclosing a note written in the margin of "Kłopoty pani Doroty" which (the note, not Dorothy) the Kraków censors, apparently overprotective of your reputation with readers of *Tygodnik Powszecnny*, decided to erase. I think it happened without cause. The censors' ugly action (not the first when it comes to you) deprived me of, apart from a good supper, the opportunity of showing you another point of view ("from the trenches of the Holy Trinity") of the truly literarily excellent *Kłopoty* [*Problems*]. In order to straighten this, and because the remarks made in the margin may be of some use to you, although coming from a different world view, I'm sending "proofs."

I enclose sincere regards and wishes for future achievements and personal success.

J. P. Gawlik

P.S. I've just learned of your being awarded a National Literary Prize. Hearty congratulations. I must admit that the third class was a surprise to me—I expected to see your name in the second or even the first group. The names Wilczek, Hamerlak, and Woroszyłski were also a certain surprise to me, when one considers Wygodzki, Kubiak, Różewicz.

There are so many other splendid writers (Parandowski, Szaniawski, Iwasz-kiewicz). Could it be that their creative work holds no value for Socialism? After

all, even the most ideologically correct writing is never going to be literature without correctness of "form," without that which is the basis of good prose or true poetry. Are you doing the right thing, Gentlemen, preventing Szaniawski from being shown, passing Parandowski over in silence? Compared to other countries we already have an inferior literary tradition—the "formal" values it represents are trivialized. Do you think, Sir, that a great literature can arise without being based on the literary output of older generations, even though their representatives didn't shout "Let Live," and concerned themselves with "bourgeois" problems?

J.P.G.

46. AUGUST 9, 1950, HOHEN NEUENDORF

[from Kurt Barthel; in German]

Dear Tadek,

First, congratulations on the National Prize. I know that youthful honors weigh one down. We were all enormously pleased. Give Comrade Jastrun my regards, as well, and congratulate him from me.

Yes, yes, Tadek, I very reluctantly allowed you to leave. But when one gets a National Prize! What will we do now? You won't have foreign currency problems, because you are invited. The publishers of *Neues Leben* and the Central Counsel of FDJ (Free German Youth) have prepared everything for our journey. For now, I've written a report for the young people's paper, *Junge Welt*. You often appear in it, Witek [Woroszyłski] too.

But what about our reportage? I know that being so honored you are going to have a lot to do. Wisdom brings suffering, honors—as well. Despite this, it would be very good if we could bring the matter to completion.[29] Can you give me an answer? I'm presently working on a new program for the People's Police. New songs, new choruses. I enclose a few of them. What are you up to? Are you still celebrating? Warm regards to Witek. I'm sending each of you "Cantata for Stalin" and am with you in Warsaw in my thoughts. Ruth is completely in the Brandenburg steel works where she's spending her vacation. The woman's barely been emancipated and she's already spending her vacation in a steel works. Give my regards to your beautiful wife (perhaps she, too, is away from home?). Warm regards to you as well,

Your Kuba

47. UNDATED, WARSAW

To the Polish Press Information Office in Berlin

I wish to inform you that so-called graphomania is not so-called pornography, and that is why I respectfully request that you not make difficulties over sending books and periodicals to Poland. I buy them with my own money, but not in my own self-interest. Please present a bill for the cost of sending them.

T. Borowski

48. UNDATED (BUT AFTER JUNE 10, 1951), WARSAW
[to his brother]

Dear Julek,

It so happened that I haven't written to you for a good few months. In the midst of work, constant travels, one somehow couldn't get himself to sit down at the typewriter. Spring of this year was industrious, but not very fruitful. Constant trips. In May, I was in Berlin twice. Once with the president's visit in the guise of journalist.[30] You know from the papers that the visit took place in an unusually good atmosphere. There was much to look at. Especially in Leune Werke near Halle, where they employ twenty-eight thousand workers, and stretch across an area of a hundred square kilometers at least. It's the largest chemical combine in Germany, now producing artificial fertilizers and medicines. The second time, I was at a congress of young artists in Berlin.[31] Also an interesting event. Especially that story with Helgoland. That island is bombed by the English air force, used as a firing ground. Young Germans decided to land on it, in order to not allow it to be destroyed. Courts, demonstrations, uproar. In West Germany in general, a fierce battle is going on. It's not as easy as it seems with that militarization. I have a great deal of literary work. I gave two books consisting of chronicles and articles to the publisher;[32] I've written a story for an anthology of Polish stories;[33] I published a small brochure for young people about the battle for peace;[34] now I'm putting together a volume of stories. Having lately been at the Zarząd Główny Związku Literatów, I am to take care of young writers, which requires going around our provincial centers. I've just been to Bygdosz, Poznań, Katowice, Wrocław; in the space of a week we examined around a hundred literature students; one's head aches from the constant reading, conferring, lecturing.[35] We are seeking out able people, capable of offering

something to literature. At the moment—half are weak. Polish scholars at the universities don't know the world, though they have a certain refinement; the workers who have literary aspirations, on the other hand, haven't got refinement. One will have to write essays, lectures, etc., for them. And above all—send them to a good, systematic school.

So much for me. Tuśka is having a baby, wants a son, I maintain it'll be a girl, but we don't argue about it especially. She was a bit sick in the middle of the pregnancy, now she's like a young goddess. Evidently, women bear the last months the best. As you see, one continues to learn and acquire experience. It concerns me very much that I can't come by medicine for you as quickly as I would like to. Unfortunately, my friend, on whom I was greatly depending, has shamefully let me down, he took the prescription and to this day hasn't appeared, even though he promised to take care of it at once. The Warsaw pharmacies didn't have it; one has to work through, so to say, connections. I'll wait a while, and then write to Berlin asking them to try to get it there.

Write and tell me how you feel, and whether you are going out to bask in the sun. I'd so much like to lie on the beach, but it's totally impossible at present, so much work.

Hugs and kisses,
Your Tadeusz

49. JUNE 27, 1951, WARSAW
[*telegram to Teofila Borowska, 2 Post Office St., Olsztyn; received 6:21 A.M.*]

TODAY YOU HAVE A GRANDDAUGHTER STOP JULEK A NIECE STOP TUŚKA FEELS WONDERFUL STOP TADEUSZ

50. JULY 3, 1951, WARSAW
[*unsigned telegram to Borowskis, 2 Post Office St., Olsztyn; received 11:50 P.M.*]

COME IMMEDIATELY STOP TADEUSZ SERIOUSLY ILL

APPENDIX A
Letters from the Private Collection of the Family of Anatol Girs

1. MAY 31, 1946, MUNICH
[*to Anatol Girs*]

Dear Pan Anatol,

In connection with my return to Poland, which will make it difficult, if not simply impossible, for us to stay in contact with each other, I very much request that any money from the sale of *We Were in Auschwitz* be sent to *Maria Rundo,* presently residing c/o Brown, 5 Siriusgalan, Lund, Sweden. Mr. Mieczysław Grydzewski, 10 Sussex Mansions, London, W.7, who is her uncle, will know her permanent address.

Tadeusz Borowski

2. MAY 13, ROZBRAT; WARSAW, JULY 14, 1946
[*to Anatol Girs*]

Dear Pan Anatol,

Forgive me for not writing for such an indecently long time, but various family and university matters, as well as the establishment of literary relations, didn't allow me time for reflection and placed restrictions on my way of life. I arrived in perfectly good order right to my burned-down house, and, for the time being, am sharing a room. I found my family whole and well, my friends unchanged and honest, they willingly help me. I am going to continue my studies in the fall as an assistant to one of the professors in the Polish Literature Department in Warsaw. I probably still have a year left to complete my master's—I've tended to most of my affairs, and shipments. Since the last few days, I am in Warsaw permanently.

As to literary work, at the moment, my situation is very good. I've become quite well known since the publication of two of my stories in *Twórczość*— "A Day at Harmenz" and "Transport." These works provoked some discussion about the problem of Auschwitz morality. The courage with which we set about addressing the camp complex was stressed both in the press and in spoken opinion. For both these stories, I received nine thousand zloty, from five hundred to a thousand for the poems. This machine, a small Continental, was bought with the honorarium. So much for material things. I saw Mrs. Barcz, she's managing very well, and, anyway, she's going to write to you personally. I also gave her the packages for Szustra, as I was leaving the same day. I saw Pani Loda[1] personally, and told her a lot about Janusz. She feels fine, she's just a bit subdued— not surprising, she misses him. I know that feeling well. I lost my great—and ambitious—match for the love of a certain lady overseas. I received a letter from her, saying that under no circumstances does she wish to see me. This, we did not anticipate, Pan Anatol. I'm a little bitter. Please forgive the reportorial tone of my letter, and deficiency of details that might have interested you, but, truth to tell, I don't see any point to my life. I wonder, is love really eternal?

Sincere regards to you, Mr. Juliusz, Miss Anna and the boys,

Tadeusz Borowski

3. JANUARY 1, 1947, WARSAW

[*to Anatol Girs*]

Dear Pan Anatol,

I ask you most sincerely to forgive me for not having written for so long. Over the past six months, I've been settling myself down in Warsaw, and I wanted to write when I knew what was happening with me. In summer, I tried to go to Sweden, but it didn't work out. In light of that, I brought Tuśka to me, and in mid-December 1946, we got married in the capital. I've begun to study. It goes rather slowly because of a lack of time. Working as an assistant is rather dull and consists of cataloguing books. But who else, after all, should be doing this? Apart from that, I contribute to a few journals, but I write rather little. In all, I've published two new stories and a few reviews, as well as several poems. There's a large demand for such things, but I'm not in a hurry. The bottom line is that these "things" be good and that I not be ashamed of them. I've had quite a few successes in life! I've obtained an apartment for Tuśka and myself, Tuśka is

not working, just studying a little, and bossing around the maid who serves us and the family of a certain colonel who lives with us. My plans for the immediate future are very simple: thoroughly clean the apartment, publish a volume of stories, which I have almost ready, and go, this summer, perhaps, to France to study. I was offered a stipend for the fall, but didn't want to without Tuśka and with unfinished studies in Warsaw.

Dear Pan Anatol! Please neither send cash, nor sell books with me in mind. Think about yourself, above all. Truly, dear Pan Anatol, I am managing very well for myself and would feel guilty robbing you. I would, however, like to ask you for one thing, or, rather, several things. If you were able to send me a few of the Auschwitz books (the stripes), and a few of the Bruckmann books, I would be most grateful and would like to repay you with something. However, should it cause difficulties, or the cost be great, then, of course, it's not worth it.

Dear Pan Anatol, for the New Year, I send you warm and sincere wishes for that happiness and cheerfulness of spirit that you, yourself, manifested during difficult times. I do not know how to thank you, sir, for the care that you showed for me and Tuśka. I wish that, wherever you find yourself, you will find devoted and good friends, friends such as we didn't know how to be, but which we would like to remain for you forever.

Tadeusz and Tuśka Borowski

4. MARCH 25, 1947, WARSAW

[*to Anatol Girs*]

Dear Pan Anatol,

I haven't written to you for quite some time, but my day life is rather tiring, a lot of work and there isn't always the possibility or the mood for writing. Both Tuśka and I thank you sincerely, very sincerely, for your good thoughts. They were among the very few received from friends. We've somehow settled ourselves down and are trying to maintain a quiet life. It doesn't always work out, but what can one do? I would like to learn, study Polish history and foreign literary criticism, however, apart from occasional critical work, I cannot engage in solid studies. There's a lack of books and, above all, of time. I'm slowly reading English, and learning Russian, reading journals and Russian prose. After mastering the languages and publishing further books, I am planning a trip abroad, most probably to Paris or to London, to the British Museum. There are even stipends,

though it's difficult to get them at the moment, especially since I don't have my master's.

If you go further afield, please write to me quickly. Sincere regards to you and our friends,

Tuśka and Tadeusz Borowski

5. MAY 3, 1947, WARSAW
[*to Anatol Girs*]

Dear Pan Anatol,

We were sincerely pleased to get news from you. I hope that this letter will still find you in Munich, and I send best wishes for a happy journey from this uneasy continent, which brought you, and us, so much worry and unhappiness, together with the sincerest hope that that country will greet you in a hospitable and humane fashion.

My plans are coming to fruition with great difficulty. Truth to tell, with a couple of short stories I gained the name of the leading prose writer of the younger generation (that means, those writers who emerged after the war), but this doesn't go hand-in-hand with what I might do were there greater intellectual contact with world currents. This parochial Polish mindset irritates me a bit, and, every once in a while, rows break out on my account (I'm also writing literary criticism), anyway, they clear the air. This year, we both will finish attending lectures at the university, sometime in fall we will take exams, before then, barring any obstacles, I will write my master's thesis. Tuśka is having some problems with me—as you did a year ago—because I sometimes fall into psychic depressions, perhaps as a result of our not having had any rest for a long time. I've recently submitted a volume of stories for publication to one of the publishing companies ("Wiedza"); when it comes out (end of November this year), I'll immediately send it to you. I think it might be a good idea to reprint "Auschwitz" in the Polish press in the USA, at least some excerpts. I think that such stories as "A Day at Harmenz" or "This Way for the Gas" might cause a sensation there. In Poland, they're considered among the best of the camp ones; they've been translated into French and Czech. The rest are nothing to be ashamed of either. As to issuing "Auschwitz" in Poland, I'll look into it, although interest has rather died down of late. Janusz should write a few words to me. It's true that I sometimes

don't write back for a few days, but, dear God, that's no reason to take offense! I'm maintaining very cordial relations with Krystyn.

At present, after taking care of the most pressing scholarly matters, I'm going to apply myself to good literary work, probably a novel. Perhaps it'll be a tragic-comic tale about Dautmergen, perhaps something else, I don't know yet.

Dear Pan Anatol, please don't trouble yourself overly much about books. If it is hard to send them, simply don't send them. And if you have them ready and it would be a pity to waste them, please try to send them to the attention of Edmund Osmańczyk (Polish Military Mission, Berlin, I don't know the street), a Polish journalist, who knows my name, of course (he wrote about *Imiona nurtu* in *Przekrój* [*The Review*]), and he would be able to send these things to Warsaw to me (Dept. of the History of Polish Literature, the University, 26/28 Krakowskie Przedmieście). Dear Pan Anatol, I know that you are one of those people who doesn't forget their friends. When you leave for overseas, please write us a few words. We will await the letter anxiously and impatiently, best to also address it to the university (sometime in summer we are moving into a new apartment). On our part—as you will know—we always remember you and would willingly help you in any way, if only with our thoughts. I think that knowing that somewhere far away we have sincere and devoted friends helps us live. You have such friends in us. Once again, our most sincere wishes for a happy journey, for rest after the experiences of this continent, and we await a few words from you from this and the other side of the sea.

Warmest kisses,

Tadeusz and Tuśka Borowski

6. AUGUST 8, 1947
[*to Anatol Girs*]

Apt. 39, 17 Kaliska St., Warsaw

Dear Pan Anatol,

Having received your address the day before yesterday from Krystyn, I was truly pleased that you are already abroad, and—as Krystyn told me—acclimatizing yourself quite well. I would wish you to get some rest in better and quieter conditions, but I know that you are not by nature one who likes rest. You will undoubtedly find a load of work and take on a mass of responsibilities. Viewed

from the perspective of that land, our concerns must seem paltry and insignificant, however, with joy—and even a certain pride—I wish to brag that at last we have our own apartment, truth to tell, a one-room and very expensive (I've got into debt over it, but will manage), but finally our own. One can work and live comparatively peacefully. One just doesn't know for how long, because sometimes one feels like a fly on the lid of a boiling pot.

This year, I am planning to finish university and get my master's. I am still working as an assistant (I had a six-month vacation that ends in a month) and will probably slowly tread down the scholarly road, albeit, as one says, it doesn't pay one's keep. The habits acquired putting together *Ziemia i Ludzie* are giving me hell. I am now putting together a literary-scholarly monthly *Nurt*, the first issue of which was supposed to come out in September. It's a monthly that brings together young artists, writers, and scholars; one of the numerous publishing cooperatives is providing the money for it. In its conception, the journal was supposed to be richly illustrated, on good paper, with many translations of the West and a keen artistic bent. Unfortunately, they don't much know how to draw here, these young people, and they are also lazy about writing. As a result, the journal will actually come out in the first half of September, but not as I would have wanted it. Apropos translations, do you know that my translation of Hemingway's "The Killers," which was in *Ziemia i Ludzie,* was the only translation of this writer in Poland, that the translation of Saroyan (also for you) is still the only translation into Polish of the author of *The Human Comedy*? I am very sorry that you are not here to advise me, nor am I the only one who is sorry. I was recently approached by Mr. Józef Zawadzki, director of the Wiedza/ Warsaw Publishing Cooperative (18 Daszynski St., Warsaw), who, on learning that I know you, would like to establish contact with you and, perhaps—if you would find it possible—some kind of collaboration. E.g., they collaborate with Wittlin and pay him in dollars. Wittlin is, of course, a translator, so the matter is easier. I'll send the manuscript and the finished journal.

Since we are on the subject of publications, perhaps even this year (or this winter season) my collection of stories *Pożegnanie z Marią* will come out, a small collection of sketches about the activities of clandestine education entitled *Pewien żołnierz* (you will be pleased, because although these sketches are not particularly weighty artistically, yet they do express—as I might put it—your philosophy), as well as a collection of poems entitled *Rozmowa z przyjacielem,* it will be partly a repetition of the Munich poems.

The Munich publications arouse wonder and envy here. Not one publishing company is able to produce any publication so magnificently. Miłośnicy Książki [Booklovers] published a few nice publications (among them, Rabska's sonnets), I'll try to send them to you. Krystyn and I have also decided to send you the prewar Oficyna publications. If they can be found. The Czytelnik publishing cooperative has expressed a desire to publish *We Were in Auschwitz* in spring or in fall of next year with the proviso that—in their opinion—the language of the book should be polished a little, and some of the numbers checked for errors in dates, etc. I would like to have your opinion in this matter.

This is an overly lengthy account of my plans and achievements, but please forgive me, Pan Anatol. I hope that you will write us an equally detailed account of your aspirations and problems, as well as your impressions of that continent. How was the sea journey? And your first impressions of New York? And, above all, what do you plan to do in the future? Will you work as a graphic artist? It would be bad if you were to take up other work!

Tuśka and I both wish you all the best, and await a letter from you.

Sincere kisses,

Stay strong

Tadeusz

7. SEPTEMBER 29, 1947

[to Anatol Girs, unsigned]

Apt. 39, 17 Kaliska St., Warsaw

Dear Pan Anatol,

A few long days have gone by before I was able to reply to your letter of summer, which reached me in August, let my justification be the drudgery and exhaustion from a whole series of work and problems that descended on me in fall. Editing, seminars, and my own work (I finally plan to get my master's this calendar year) took up a lot of my time, and the rest . . .

And so, we are working on *Nurt*, which will come out in the first days of October and I will send it to you immediately then. I'd be very pleased if you'd send me some little drawing or beautiful vignettes for the issue, however, I don't know about the transmission of money to N.Y. In any case, I very much want a critique of the issue—all right?

Here, summer was cold and rainy at the time that Tuśka and I went to the Mazuria lakes, and hot when we sat in dusty Warsaw. One cannot stay out long in town, because one's head starts to ache horribly, and one has to lie down and rest, there's so much dust.

Wincenty Mackiewicz has returned to Kraków, he's getting settled, but apparently not too well. The National Library claims it received the announcement about Polonus, but has not yet received the books themselves. As to Twardowski about whom you've been bugging me from the moment we met, please, Pan Anatol, I swear, I have bought the most serious Polish studies and, making use of acquiring knowledge of the period and its language, I will gladly write you something, prose rather than verse, but let's decide on a time? I'd prefer to write it sometime after Christmas on account of various started works (a volume of short tales modeled after the American "short story").

Apropos, the Institute of National Memory approached me today in the matter of writing a short monograph on the small camp, about which there are not many works in our rich Lager literature. Do you remember and would you be willing to write very briefly—and without devoting too much of your time, which I wouldn't want to take up—about conditions in the hospital in Dautmergen, giving facts and names of doctors and nurses? Perhaps the condition of the sick, etc.? I think I should also turn to Mr. Rudziński in this matter.

Tuśka is a bit sick, doesn't feel well, she didn't manage to rest up in summer, which really was busy and hot. The doctor maintains that it's a weakening of the heart muscle and prescribed a lot of injections for her, which she's finally taking faithfully.

Krystyn's father has returned from Scotland, Krystyn will write you better what he's going to do, where he'll work. In any event, it's better the family is together.

I have no news from Nel, has the boy taken offense or what? But I see no reason for it. Perhaps he's become completely anglicized?

I sense from your letter that you, Pan Anatol, are very impressed by the spontaneity of life in America and her wonderful discoveries. Correctly so, since technical might and the ability to make peoples' lives easier should be the leading principle of the life of nations. It's harder here in this regard, even in the area of printing, we've greatly regressed, and cannot even dream, not only about bibliophilic books, but we still haven't achieved prewar standards. Periodicals are very badly published and horribly edited. To a certain extent it's the result of the editors' lack of professionalism. One such editor, anyway, is me.

Well, never mind, it's getting better. I even hope that my book, which has been lying for six months at the publishers, will at some point—that means in a year—finally see the light of day.

Please write to us a lot and often, Pan Anatol, and give your address each time because I wouldn't want the letters to wander around when you move, and you'd then be apt to think that we weren't writing.

Kisses to you—mine on your right, and Tuśka's on your left cheek, which, as usual, is probably unshaven.

And sincere regards,

8. OCTOBER 24, 1947
[to Anatol Girs]

Apt. 39, 17 Kaliska St., Warsaw

Dear, beloved Pan Anatol,

A moment ago I received your letter of 9/30/47 and am replying immediately, because in a few minutes I'm leaving for a visit to Yugoslavia and on my return will think about the translation from Russian for you, I've partly organized the materials.

I will write you a long, long, long, long letter from Belgrade, and in the meantime, kisses and hugs from your sincerely faithfully devoted,

Tadeusz—Puppy

[Postscript from Maria Borowska:]

Dear Sir,

I am taking the liberty of adding my most sincere regards to Tadeusz's letter.

I know you, in truth, only from Tadeusz and Krystyn's stories, but I know you so well, that I am proud that Tadeusz has such a worthy and extraordinary friend. I am very happy with Tadeusz, and do not regret my return to Poland. I help him as I can in his work and I think that I look after him well. He's not only my husband and friend, but also my beloved son who totally fills my life.

I am fully aware how much Tadeusz owes to you, and how much he developed both morally and intellectually under your care in Munich—and for that, I am enormously grateful to you.

Maria Borowska

9. FEBRUARY 1, 1949

[to Janusz Nel Siedlecki]

Apt. 39, 17 Kaliska St., Warsaw

My dear and beloved Sea Horse,

It's true we haven't written to one another for a long time. But a certain lady came back from England and brought an exquisitely sealed letter from you. That's great! And what'll happen when you finish that engineering? Probably you'll come here and what will you build me—some bridge or ship or tunnel? For the time being—you're fine as you are: swallow fog, brother, and twist your tongue around English, I'm not in the least bit sorry for you. Krystyn—that lazy swine—is in architecture, the kind that builds towns—he travels across the whole of Poland planning the rebuilding of Bolesławow, Bolesławki, Skierniew, and other dumps, and he's thrilled with it. He sometimes brings back with him some fragments of holy figures and hangs them on the wall. Collects illustrated books. Dances. Talks about things he's discovered in his travels. Isn't marrying. Sometimes, he drops by my place in the middle of the night, and then we have long talks over black coffee. Goes back to his place—Mokotow[2]—on foot.

I, as you may know, was an assistant at the university at first, then I gave up this more than boring work and devoted myself to a craftsmanly literary career. I was an editor, journalist, reviewer, speaker, and God knows what all else. I published two books in Poland: *Pożegnanie z Marią* (stories, two taken from the stripes), and *Kamienny świat* (20 very short stories, extremely amusing, I'll mail it to you). I also published something for young people, wrote some scripts for one or two films, married a long time ago, got my own room with a bathroom (address above), was in Yugoslavia, was supposed to go to Bulgaria, also in a delegation, but talked my way out of it, because it's boring and I have an awful lot of work with a third book, the writing of which is decidedly not going well. I make quite good money from various occasional sheets of typescript, but the cash, like ice cream, quickly melts away. Just a few licks.

Tuśka is also working, she's doing all kinds of translations and editings, has a lot of chores at home.

Tolek and I don't exactly deluge each other with letters. Could you give me his address, because he forgot to, and I think he changed it?

How is your mother? Thank you for your good wishes, which are always current, regardless of the date!

Do you know that among sea horses, it's the males that give birth to children? Horrible!

Regards and hugs and also:

Hiya Beautiful![3]

Tadeusz

10. FEBRUARY 1, 1949

[*to Pola Kossobudzka*]

Apt. 39, 17 Kaliska St., Warsaw

Dear Pani Pola,

Thank you very much for thinking of me and for the books, which are of twofold value to me. They aroused a bit of recognition in Poland, but, because of the lack of copies, they were known only to a group of a few of my closest friends. Both packages arrived in wonderful condition—many, many thanks! I would most gladly recompense you in some way: would you allow me to send you a few Polish books? I don't think much Polish literature gets through. Unfortunately, I have not been in touch with Anatol for more than a year. Somehow, it seems, he changed his address and omitted to tell me about it. But I'll have to keep trying. Perhaps you could forward his present address to me? After two years of rather concentrated literary and journalistic work, I've become a fairly well-known person in Poland. I managed to buy myself a modest apartment in Warsaw (one room and a bathroom), however, I feel the painful lack of a second room "for writing" and books from abroad, which would familiarize me with foreign literature. But somehow one manages. Krystyn Olszewski is learning architecture, living with his parents (his father returned to Poland a long time ago), and planning to complete his studies soon. He's a wonderful boy! I also lost contact with Janusz, but a certain lady who returned from a delegation to England brought me his letter and I'll pick up the threads again.

I sincerely request that you write telling me how you are living and getting along, because, from the moment of Krystyn's arrival, I have heard nothing about my friends in Munich.

With very best wishes,

Tadeusz Borowski

11. FEBRUARY 8, 1949
[*to Pola Kossobudzka*]

Apt. 39, 17 Kaliska St., Warsaw

Dear Pani Pola,

On Saturday, the day before yesterday, I received a third package of books from you, for which I thank you most sincerely. They're of tremendous help to me, since there's a big demand for the "stripes" in bookstores. I have not, however, received any letter from you. My first letter has probably not yet made it to Munich. I have heard from Nel Siedlecki who is studying in England, shortly completing so-called "college."[4] His mother—as I learned from a chance acquaintance who had returned from London—works part-time in a hospital. Here, in Poland, she was guaranteed a university professorship in Wrocław.

Nothing new with me, other than work, of which there's always too much for a lazy man like me.

Best regards and thanks for your efforts and the mailing expenses, and, also, for remembering—

Tadeusz Borowski

12. APRIL 14, 1949, WARSAW
[*to Pola Kossobudzka*]

Dear Pani Pola,

Thank you very much for the nice letter and books, I'm writing back somewhat belatedly, but I hope that you are still in Europe and have not left the continent. Thank you very much also for the parcels of books, which, like everything which is beautifully published, create a big sensation here. I gave them to the Oficyna Księgarska, which likes artistic books, and they have already dispersed, Stankiewicz's piece about Goślicki[5] also has its readers, even though it is not as much of a revelation as we had assumed in Munich. The level of Polish scholarship on the Aryans and Polish democratic thought is high, and more is known about Goślicki here than Stankiewicz writes. But the beautiful publication of the book makes up for the errors in its substance.

As to German books, dear Pani Pola, I don't want to burden you with the cost, because, as Edmund Osmańczyk, our correspondent in Berlin, informs me,

these are expensive things. I occasionally get some items from friends in Germany who were at the peace congress in Wrocław, and since I ran the congress newspaper there, and worked in the press office, I made a few contacts.

My wife and I are working a lot, but I must admit that for a writer the living conditions are wonderful and everything that one writes is immediately printed and well recompensed. The country is making big concessions to artists, gives sizable stipends toward completing work, sends the most deserving people abroad. This last, however, not to the degree which we would like, but what to do—we're still a bit too poor! I have been living in Warsaw for nearly two years and the housing conditions have markedly improved. Where two years ago there was no question of artists (I am again using this milieu as my example, although it's practically the same with the others) having a room to work in, today, two and three room apartments are slowly being given, which really is a great success. By our calculation, by the end of this year, the most needy people in our profession will receive workshops.

I've gone on at length about our affairs, but that's not unusual: one boasts about what one sees.

I am sending best Easter wishes in the hope that the holidays will be more than good for you, they'll be joyful.

Tadeusz Borowski

P.S.   Thank you for the photo, why wasn't it signed? After all, we don't have all that many friends in the world!

APPENDIX B
Biographical Sketch of Tadeusz Borowski

Tadeusz Borowski, prose writer, poet, and journalist, was born November 12, 1922, in Zhitomir, Ukraine, and died in Warsaw, July 3, 1951. Borowski spent his childhood in Ukraine. Both parents in turn were sent to camps, so that he lived with an aunt in Marchlewsk, and there he started his education in a Soviet school. When six years later his father was released and exiled to Poland, the Red Cross repatriated his two sons. Until their mother's return, they lived at the Franciscan boarding school on Nowe Miasto Avenue. Borowski received his graduation certificate from the underground T. Czacki Lyceum during the German Occupation (1940), after which he studied Polish literature at the clandestine Warsaw University. At the same time, he worked as a guard and storeroom keeper at a building supplies company in Praga.[1] A group of artist friends, the Essentialists, associated with the left-wing movement, gathered around him (and began publishing *Droga* in 1943). On February 24, 1943, as he was searching for his missing fiancée, he fell into a trap, was arrested, and after a short stay in Pawiak was transported to Auschwitz (#119,198). He worked on various Kommandos; after getting over typhus he became a nurse in the camp hospital. From August 1944, he was in the Natzweiler-Dautmergen camp, and then Dachau-Allach.[2] After being liberated by the Seventh American Army (May 1, 1945), he was in the displaced persons' camp in Freimann, from which he was extricated by his camp companion the publisher Anatol Girs, who was setting up a family tracing service in nearby Munich. Not able to wait to be reunited with his fiancée, Maria Rundo, who had been taken from the concentration camps to Sweden, he returned to Poland in 1946; after some dramatic attempts to reunite with his love, he married her at the end of that year. Borowski continued his studies, worked as a junior lecturer in Korbutian and for the illustrated monthly, *Swiat Mlodych* [*World of the Young*], but in particular for the young writers' press: the biweekly *Pokolenie* and the monthly *Nurt,* which he headed. From 1947, he was active in the Club of Young Artists and Scholars (its president 1948–49).

In 1948, he joined the Polish Workers' Party. He was deputy to the head of the press office of the World Congress of Intellectuals in Wrocław and the editor of the congress newspaper, *W Obronie pokoju* [*In Defense of Peace*]. At the Szczecin meeting of the Polish Writers' Association promoting socialist realism in January 1949, his writings became the main object of attack in official lectures. Borowski attempted to go to the United States, but was not allowed. From among the realistic possibilities, he chose to work as cultural editor at the Polish Press Information Office in East Berlin. His stay in Berlin (June 1949–March 1950) coincided with the period of the partition of Germany and the intensifying confrontations between the superpowers; political considerations caused a radical change in his own position. On his return from Germany, he joined the staff of *Nowa Kultura,* and as journalist and columnist led a socialist realism campaign. Shortly thereafter—following a few previous attempts—he committed suicide.

He made his poetic debut with a cycle of catastrophic poems that he printed himself—*Gdziekolwiek ziemia* [*Wherever the Earth*] (1942), encompassing the manifested and bitter beliefs of the war generation ("There will remain after us scrap-iron and the hollow, jeering laughter of generations"). He wrote much, and variously (poems of friendship and epigrams for the Essentialists; "Księdze z dnia wigilii" ["Book from Christmas Eve"] and songs in Auschwitz; a vast explosion of poetry in Munich), but published little. In 1944, when Borowski was in Auschwitz, *Droga* put out a folio of his love poetry. In Munich in 1945, Girs published his bibliophilic volume *Imiona nurtu* [*The Names of the Current*], especially intended for Polish soldiers in the West, as well as a pamphlet of poems by Borowski and K. Olszewski, "Poszukiwania: Tracing" [*sic*] used as a Family Tracing Service receipt. Finally after Borowski's return to Poland in 1947, the poet put together a small volume, *Rozmowa z przyjacielem* [*Conversation with a Friend*], including an author's retrospective and a few new poems, which for unknown reasons never came out (the volume was discovered fifty-two years later and published in 1999). For reasons of circumstance, this poetic output largely vanished, and the few poems that survived were scattered around by the poet and distorted by publishers (see *Utwory zebrane* 1, 1954), blurring the poetic paths to the origins of the writer's conception of "periods of contempt" and human fate which find fuller expression in his prose.

The beginnings of this conception are in a collective work, written at the insistence of Girs by three young Haeftlings, Borowski, Olszewski, and Nel Siedlecki, and entitled *Byliśmy w Oświęcimiu* (*We Were in Auschwitz*), 1946; Borowski not only included four of his own well-known stories in this collection,[3] but also planned,

edited, and annotated it. The subsequent collection of stories, *Pożegnanie z Marią* (*Farewell to Maria*), published in Poland in 1947, was in sharp contrast to the emerging martyrological-heroic literature. For Borowski, the concentration camp was a model for a future society devoted to exploitation, force, and genocide, and automatic mechanism, since its victims were forced into criminal dealings (hence the creation of the vorarbeiter-hero Tadek to whose doubtful behavior he assigned his own name). The following collection of short stories, *Kamienny świat* [*World of Stone*] (1948), depicted the laws of the camp even more drastically and carried them over into postwar reality (in addition, the author dedicated them provocatively to various writers). These two behavioristic, unusually dramatic volumes led him to attempt to create a broader cycle of stories about "times of contempt," treated as harbingers in totalitarianism terms. The introduction of socialist realism put an end to this endeavor. Instead, he turned to writing a column in *Rzeczpospolita* [*The Republic*] entitled *Nasz wiek XX* (*Our Twentieth Century*), journalism—published as *Opowiadania z książek i gazet* [*Stories from Books and Newspapers*] in 1949, and awarded a national prize (third class). With the shocking article, sent from Germany, entitled "Rozmowy" (1950), he dismissed as worthless his entire literary output. On his return, he issued a weekly *Mała kronika* [*Small Chronicles*] in *Nowa Kultura,* became a journalist, and wrote contemporary prose, most of it obsessively political, which was published after his death in the editions *Mała kronika wielkich spraw* [*A Small Chronicle about Large Matters*] (1951); *Na przedpolu* [*In the Foreground*] (1952); and *Czerwony Maj* [*Red May*] (1953). On the periphery of the mainstream, there remains a little-known volume about Polish clandestine education under German occupation entitled, *Pewien żołnierz. Opowieści szkolne* [*A Certain Soldier: School Stories*] (1947), written immediately after his return, which was modeled on students' essays and, above all, on his own memories as a secondary-school pupil and student.

Reaction to Borowski's writings continues to be various. In addition to the primitive Catholic-patriotic criticism, the main cycle of stories met also with moralistic criticism ("contamination by death," "satire on the dead"). His former critics (Kisielewski, Jasienica) supported his defenders and fans. Borowski's sudden about-face to socialist realism lent a certain credence to his critics (the cult of the strong). But after his suicide, Miłosz corrected the portrait of Beta [Borowski] in *The Captive Mind*—"Na smierc Tadeusza Borowskiego" ["On Tadeusz Borowski's Death"]. World reaction (predicted by Iwaszkiewicz: "Borowski's stories cannot be compared to any of the world's literature") helped to stabilize his position in

Poland (included on school reading lists and in the National Library series), but the state of Borowski scholarship and of his personal papers is not improving (unverified texts, many papers dispersed). Only now is a deeper interest emerging on the part of the young generation of scholars.

MAJOR CRITICAL WORKS

C. Miłosz, "Beta, the Disappointed Lover," in *The Captive Mind,* 1953.

T. Mikulski, "Z marginesów twórczości Tadeusz Borowskiego" ["On the Edges of Tadeusz Borowski's Creative Work"], 1954, in *Miniatury krytyczne* [*Critical Miniatures*].

A. Werner, *Zwyczajna Apokalipsa* [*An Ordinary Apocalypse*], 1971.

T. Drewnowski, *Ucieczka z kamiennego świata* [*Escape from the World of Stone*], 1972, 3rd ed., 1992.

J. Ziomek, "Beta w oczach Mi" ["Beta in Mi's Eyes"], 1988, in *Praca ostatnie* [*Last Work*].

T. Borowski, *Utwory wybrane* [*Selected Works*], ed. A. Werner, National Library, 1991.

S. Buryła, "Na antypodach tradycji literackiej. Wokół 'Sprawy Borowskiego'" ["In the Antipodes of Literary Tradition. In the 'Matter of Borowski'"], *Pamiętnik Literacki* 4 (1998).

J. Szczęsna, *Tadeusz Borowski—poeta* [*Tadeusz Borowski—Poet*], 2000.

APPENDIX C
Biographical Information on Correspondents and Those
Mentioned in Correspondence

JERZY ANDRZEJEWSKI (1909–83) was the author of the novels *Lad serca* [*Mode of the Heart*], 1938; *Święta Winkelrieda* [*Winkelreid's Holidays*] (with Zagórski); *Popioł i diament* [*Ashes and Diamonds*], 1948; and *Miazga* [*The Mummies*], 1969. In 1947 he moved from Kraków to the Szczecin Writers' Colony. At the time, he was one of the Polish propagators of socialist realism, but he was also the first writer to react against it; in 1964 he allied himself with the democratic opposition, as a founder of KOR [Committee for the Defense of Workers] and the journal *Zapis*. Accordingly, he disassociated himself from the popular and officially promoted novel *Ashes and Diamonds,* but he did not prevent it from being reprinted and, together with Wajda, he wrote the screenplay for the film version (1958). Enthusiastic about Borowski's prose from the beginning, Andrzejewski endorsed the publishing of *Utwory zebrane* [*Collected Works*], 1959. As he put it in the foreword, this posthumous collection of Borowski's stories contains "several stories that have a chance of surviving as long as there exists a Polish literature and a cemetery of shattered dreams and illusions."

LESŁAW M. BARTELSKI was born in 1920 and made his debut as a poet during the occupation; he was a member of the group Sztuka i Naród [Art and the Nation]. After the war, he worked in the editorial offices of *Nowiny Literackie, Nowa Kultura,* and *Kultura* and for many years was the president of the Warsaw department of the ZLP [Polish Writers Association]. He published, among other things, books of essays about cultural life under the occupation—*Genealogia ocalonych* [*Genealogy of the Saved*], *Pieśń niepodlegla* [*Song of Independence*]—as well as collections of documentary biographical stories such as *Krwawe skrzydła* [*Bloody Wings*] (about Kaden-Bandrowski)[1] and *Rajski ogród* [*Paradisial Garden*] (about Dąbrowska). He and Borowski knew one another from the time of the occupation.

HALSZKA BODALSKA was a student in the first study group at the clandestine University of Warsaw where she and Borowski first met. She helped with sending packages to him in Auschwitz and was involved in the underground movement. Wanda Leopold, in her memoir, *Z dziejów podziemnego Uniwersytetu Warszawskiego* [*From the History of Warsaw's Clandestine University*], suggests that she did not survive the war; the postwar exchange of letters with Borowski contradicts this. Immediately after the war, Bodalska worked in the Polish Press Agency in Łódź.

JULIUSZ BOROWSKI (1919–87), Tadeusz's older brother, completed *gimnazjium* [which at that time corresponded to U.S. grades seven through ten], but after the occupation he suffered from psychiatric problems that prevented him from working more than sporadically. His last attempt to establish a career was to go in 1945 with a government procurator to Masuria, where he worked as a People's Council inspector. Thanks to his efforts, the family moved to Olsztyn, capital of the Mazury region of Poland.

TEOFILA, née Karpińska (1897–1993), and STANISŁAW (1890–1966) BOROWSKI came from Ukraine, of peasant families; they married in Zhitomir in 1917. They had two sons: Juliusz and Tadeusz. Stanisław, a bookkeeper in a beekeeping and gardening cooperative, was arrested in 1926 for participating in the POW [Polska Organizacja Wojenna, or Polish Army Organization] before the First World War and sent to Karelia to build the White Sea Canal. In 1930, Teofila, a seamstress, was sent to Siberia, to the town of Igarek near Jeniseje. In 1932, the Polish authorities exchanged Stanisław for Communists imprisoned in Poland, and the Red Cross arranged the repatriation of the sons. In Poland, Stanisław became a site worker and subsequently a storeroom keeper in the Lilpop factory in the Wola district of Warsaw. The boys spent the first years in a Franciscan boarding school on Nowe Miasto. After the return of their mother—who "tailored for the poorest"—they lived in the factory's apartment building at 2 Smolna Street (Smolna came right down to Ksiazeca Street then). When the apartment building went up in flames in September 1939, they moved into a nearby, half-destroyed warehouse. Despite the dreadfully difficult conditions after Tadeusz's arrest, they hid a Jewish boy, Jerzy Szulc, right to the end of the war. After the war and after moving to Olsztyn, Stanisław returned to his old profession and became bookkeeper of the Union of Agricultural and Forestry Workers. As can be seen from their letters, there was a special bond between Teofila and her poet son.

KAZIMIERZ BRANDYS (1916–2000), a writer, was published in literary journals before the war. After the war, he published the novel *Miasto niepokonane* [*The Invincible City*]. From 1945 to 1950, he was on the staff of *Kuźnica,* and for the next decade he worked at *Nowa Kultura.* In 1970, after joining the opposition, Brandys was on the staff of *Zapis.* After 1978, he lived abroad, taking up residence in Paris in 1983 and publishing *Obywatele* [*Citizens*], *Matka królow* [*Sons and Comrades*], *Wariacje pocztowe* [*Postal Variations*], *Nierzeczywistość* [*Fictions*], *Miesiące* [*The Months*], and *Przygody Robinsona* [*The Adventures of Robinson*]. Borowski fought against the "construction of the human fate" and the concept and style of "*Kuźnica* realism" that Brandys was developing at the time. Despite the conflict between them, Borowski's piece on Brandys's *Antigone* [2] (*Odrodzenie* 16–17, 1949) was not a spoof, but a principled polemic on the beginnings of the *Między wojnami* [*Between the Wars*] cycle.

MIECZYSŁAWA BUCZKÓWNA, a friend of Borowski's from student days, was born in 1924. A lyric poet and children's writer, she was married to Mieczysław Jastrun. Her poetic works include *Swiatła ziemie* [*Lights of the Earth*] and *Planeta miłości* [*Planet of Love*].

EWA FISZER (1926–2000), the daughter of Kazimierz Fiszer, a Warsaw publisher and bookseller, was a poet and translator, especially from French. From 1951 to 1969 she was married to Joris Ivens, a well-known film director. During the occupation, Fiszer was active in the underground and uprising and began Polish studies, which she continued after the war. Through S. Marczak, she met Borowski the day he returned from Germany and joined the Essentialist friends. She took part in the struggles of the postwar generation to establish their own journal, and she headed the literary department in the Klub Młodych Artystów i Pisarzy [Young Artists and Writers Club].

JAN PAWEŁ GAWLIK, a theater student and essayist, was born in 1924. He made his debut as a journalist at *Tygodnik Powszechny* in 1948; later, he served on the editorial staff of *Życie Literackie* [*Literary Life*]. Since 1970, he has been a theater director, especially of the Old Theater at the time of its development.

ANATOL GIRS (1904–90) was a graphic artist, publisher, and painter who was born in Simferopol, Crimea, into Polish-Swedish-Russian nobility. He studied in his hometown at the Izo-Iskusstw School and at the Szkoła Sztuk Zdobyczn ych

in Warsaw. From 1931 to 1939, he ran a graphics studio with Bolesław Barcz and subsequently published periodicals, books, and bibliophilic materials with Oficyna Warszawska, from 1938 to 1944. During the Warsaw Uprising, he was taken to Dachau,[3] where he met Borowski. Probably thanks to his connections with Christian Science, he set up the Family Tracing Service in Munich under the auspices of the Polish Red Cross. The production of camp stamps allowed him also to acquire funds to establish Oficyna Warszawska na Obczyźnie, whose first three publications were provided by Borowski and his companions. Borowski presents him as a figure out of Chesterton, a mixture of idealist and business-man. In 1947, Girs went to the United States, where he founded the Girs-Press, but he did not meet with success.

MIECZYSŁAW GRYDZEWSKI (1894–1970, original surname Grutzhandler, then Grycendler) attended schools in Warsaw. During the First World War, he began to study law in Moscow; after 1916, he studied in the history depart-ment at Warsaw University under Professor Marcel Handelsmann, with whom he eventually did his doctoral work. In the student setting, he belonged to the nationalistically oriented Kollataj Circle; he took part in the Polish-Bolshevik war. He felt himself to be, as he said, a Pole of the faith of Moses. His sister, Aniela, was a Polish Socialist Party activist and then a Communist. Grydzewski started his editorial work early: from 1917, as secretary of the academic "Pro arte et studio" (at the same time being night editor of *Kurier Polski* [*Polish Courier*]); from 1921, he published and edited the poetry monthly *Skamander;* from 1924, with Antoni Borman, he published the most widely read weekly, *Wiadomości Literackie,* as well as *La Pologne Litteraire* [*Literary Poland*] and *Przyjaciela Psa* [Dog's Friend]. In September 1939, together with his *Skamander* friends, he emigrated to Paris, where he and Zygmunt Nowakowski began to publish *Wiadomości Polskich Literackich i Politicznych* [*Polish Literary and Political News*], a publication that, after the fall of France, Grydzewski brought to London. They were closed down by English authorities in 1944 as being politically intransigent and uncomfortable. Grydzewski bridged the gap for two years with the vol-umes *Biblioteki* [*Libraries*] and *Wczoraj i dziś* [*Yesterday and Today*]; in 1946, he reissued what he called *Wiadomości* (without the adjectives) and ran it until he became ill in 1966. All varieties of the émigré *Wiadomości* differed profoundly from prewar *Wiadomości Literackie*—as Karol Zbyszewski wrote, their editor would not recognize Gombrowicz, was most willing to publish Z. Nowakowski,

and regarded Hemar as a sage—on the other hand, they gained prestige among émigrés, an expression of which is the *Książka o Grzydewskim* [*Book About Grzydewski*] (1971), published after his death. During the entire period of his working life, Grzydewski was regarded as "an editor who doesn't write." After his death, however, it was discovered that in all the journals he published he placed many valuable snippets, ran quite a few of his own columns, printed historical sketches (see, for example, *Silva rerum,* selected by J. B. Wójcika, 1994, and *Szkice* [*Sketches*], ed. P. Kądziela, 1994), and also published a couple of anthologies, several of which are left among his papers.

Before the war, Grzydewski took an interest in Tuśka, his fatherless niece, especially in her reading. Her letters to him in this volume reveal Grzydewski's close ties to his lost family in Poland and his continuing protective feelings toward her, which he acted upon.

PAWEŁ HERTZ was born in 1918. He made his poetic debut in *Wiadomości Literackie* at the age of sixteen. He studied in France and traveled widely. In 1940, Hertz was arrested in Lwów and sent to a camp in Iwdiel in Siberia. After receiving an amnesty, he worked in Samarkand. He then returned in military uniform and joined the staff of *Kuźnica,* where he ran the press review section. After October, he was one of the founders of the monthly *Europa;* when the authorities banned its publication, he and others left the Party. He published extensively in the field of nineteenth-century Polish poetry as well as authoring translations of Russian classics. Collections of his sketches and columns for the papers (chiefly for *Tygodnik Powszechny*) have been published. In connection with his work of the *Kuźnica* period—the story "Sedan" and pseudo-classical poems—Borowski dedicated the title story of *Kamienny świat* to him.

PAWEŁ JASIENICA (1909–70, born Leon Lech Beynar) is best known as the author of essays on Polish history. He studied history at the Stefan Batory University in Wilno. A Home Army officer during the war, at its end he remained a partisan in WiN [Freedom and Independence], for which he was arrested and jailed in 1946 (but, as a result of B. Piasecki's intervention, quickly freed). Jasienica was a popular journalist for *Tygodnik Powszechny.* When he openly joined the opposition in 1968, Gomułka publicly blackmailed him with spurious allegations about the time of his arrest. Jasienica was one of the people attacking Borowski for his review of Kossak-Szczucka's *Z otchłani* [*From the Abyss*],

1946. Jasienica's revision of his position after reading Borowski's books played an important role in the dispute about Borowski.

ALFRED KANTOROWICZ (1899–1979) was an antifascist activist and journalist who came from a conservative Jewish family in Germany. A volunteer in the First World War, shortly afterward he joined the German Communist Party. He studied law and literature in Berlin, where he met the leading figures of progressive German literature (Lion Feuchtwanger [pseud. J. L. Wetcheek], Bertolt Brecht, Klabund [pseud. Alfred Henschke], and Bruno Frank). He was Paris correspondent for *Vossische Zeitung,* first with Kurt Tucholski, then as his replacement. While abroad, he began preparing *Brunatna Księga o pożarze Reichstagu i terrorze hitlerowskim [Brown Book about the Reichstag Fire and Hitler's Terrorism].* He fought on the Republican side in Spain. Then, at the beginning of the Second World War, he went to the United States, where he became secretary general of the Association of German Emigrant Writers. He returned to Germany in 1947 and published a journal, *Ost und West,* in East Berlin; it never appeared in West Germany. Kantorowicz became director of the German Institute and head of the H. Mann Archives at the Academy of Arts before escaping to Munich in 1957, then settling in Hamburg. His most important books are *Spanisches Tagebuch [Spanish Journal],* 1948; *H. and T. Mann,* 1956; *Deutsche Schicksale, Intellektuelle unter Hitler und Stalin [German Destiny: Intellectuals Under Hitler and Stalin],* 1964; and *Politik und Literatur in Exil [Politics and Literature in Exile],* 1978.

STEFAN KISIELEWSKI (1911–91, also known under the pseudonyms Kisiel, Teodor Klon, and Tomasz Staliński) was the son of novelist Zygmunt Jan Kisielewski and nephew of playwright Jan August Kisielewski. He held degrees in Polish studies and philosophy from the University of Warsaw and in composition theory and piano from the Warsaw Conservatory. He wrote for *Bunt Młodych [Rebellion of the Young]* and for Giedroyc's[4] *Polityka* and *Pion,* and he took part in the September 1939 campaign and in the Uprising. From 1945 until the end of his life (with two interruptions, one in 1947 when he had to do penance for his supposed lewdness in *Sprzysiezenie [Blood Brothers]* and the other from 1953 to 1956 when the journal was suspended), Kisielewski served on the staff of *Tygodnik Powszechny,* for which he wrote his famous columns. He was also a member of the Sejm [Parliament] and the author of six novels with publishing houses abroad. Ever in the opposition, he was persecuted and attacked.

Kisielewski looked after Borowski when *Dziś i Jutro* attacked him. Valuing his talent, he warned him against "mental totalitarianism."

KURT KNUTH-SIEBENLIST was a German journalist who found himself a "black triangle" (designating apolitical status; apparently he was captured smuggling on the borders) in Auschwitz. Borowski got to know him in the hospital where he was *Pfleger* [a nurse]. The Polish staff were unfriendly to German patients, and Borowski apparently protected him from an attack of some kind. After leaving the hospital, Knuth-Siebenlist worked in Birkenau, where he was the most elegant functionary in the camp, becoming the first permanent letter carrier between Borowski and Tuśka.

LEON KRUCZKOWSKI (1900–62) was a chemist, teacher, and writer known before the war for his acclaimed novel *Kordian i cham* [*Kordian and the Boor*], 1932. A left-wing writer, he came out against the Moscow Trials. After the September 1939 campaign, he spent the entire war in a prisoner-of-war camp for officers in Germany, where he ran the Teatr Symboli. After the war, he served as underminister for Culture and the Arts and as president of the Polish Writers' Association. He switched to writing plays—*Niemcy* [*The Germans*], *Pierwszy dzień wolności* [*First Day of Freedom*], and *Śmierń gubernatora* [*Death of the Governor*]. *The Germans,* or rather, *Sonnenbruch,* was performed in Berlin for the inauguration of the German Democratic Republic. Exclusively for the German production Kruczkowski added an epilogue. As can be seen from his letters, he entrusted Borowski with arranging the festive premiere.

KUBA (1914–67, real name Kurt Barthel) was a German poet, playwright, and novelist who came from a workers' family and had been a Party activist since youth. From 1933, he led the "Communist work" in Czechoslovakia; he fled from the Brown Shirts to England. In 1946 he returned to East Germany, where he became a member of the Central Committee of the United Socialist Party of Germany and was exceptionally active as a writer and activist. His writings included *Gedicht vom Menschen* [*Poems about Man*], 1948; reportage from Socialist countries, *Gedanken im Fluge* [*Thoughts in Flight*], 1950; *Kantate uber Stalin* [*Cantata on Stalin*], 1950; and a dramatic poem, *Terra Incognita,* 1964. Kuba was friendly with young Polish writers and a number of Polish translations of his writing appeared in the anthology *Dopowiedzenie świtu* [*Addition to Dawn*], 1969.

MARIA KURECKA-WIRPSZA (1920–89) was a translator, prose writer, and poet who spent her childhood and youth in the Free City of Gdańsk. She studied Polish during the war at the clandestine University of Warsaw and was a nurse during the Warsaw Uprising. She had two children, Aleksander and Lidia. She left Poland in 1970 to join her husband and worked with *Kultura, Archipelag,* and RWE [Radio Free Europe]. She made her writing debut with a translation of part of Camus's *The Plague;* later, she concentrated on translating German literary works such as Hesse's *Damian* and *The Glass Bead Game,* and, with her husband, Thomas Mann's *Doctor Faustus.* She also wrote biographies of Andersen and Mann, among others. Her collection *Trzydzieści wierszy* [*Thirty Poems*] came out in 1987.

HALINA LASKOWSKA-SZWYKOWSKA was born in 1922 in Lwów and moved to Warsaw in 1936. She graduated from secondary school during the occupation, and began Polish studies in the clandestine study group conducted by Prof. Stanisław Adamczewski in 1942. At his house, she met Andrzej Trzebiński, and at literary gatherings and concerts she came into contact with Bojarski, Gajc, Mencel, Stroiński, and also Borowski. From 1943, she worked with the Sztuka i Naród group; at the time Ruch Kulturowy was founded, she directed the Upowszechnienie Kultury [Dissemination of Culture] division (under the pseudonym Marta). During the Uprising, together with Mencel, Sołtan, and Schwakopf, she worked at BiP [Biuro Informacji i Propagandy, or Bureau of Information and Propaganda]. After the capitulation, she was in POW camps; from the last one, in Oberlangen, together with T. Engelhardt and others at the end of April 1945, she went to France. A PWSK [Polska Wojskowa Słuzba Kobiet, or Polish Women's Military Service] volunteer, she was taken to England and drafted to study in London. When Borowski received Halina Laskowska's address from T. Engelhardt, a correspondence arose between them, and, through her, contact with Sweden; the poet addressed the poem "Do Pani H. w Londynie" ["To Miss H. in London"] to her. She returned to Poland in May 1947. She worked first at "Dziś i Jutro" and later with the film press and as a translator.

WANDA LEOPOLD (1920–87, Kazimiera née Ziemiecka), the daughter of Jerzy Iwanowski, was a literary critic, editor, and African scholar, as well as an engineer and a minister in Moraczewski's and Paderewski's governments. She emigrated in 1939. She studied law before the war and was active in the Związek Polskiej Młodziezy Demokrtycznej (ZPMD) [Union of Polish Democratic Youth] where

she met her first husband (Stanisław Leopold, a "Parasola" soldier and leader of the attack on Kopp who perished in the Warsaw Uprising). From 1940, she embraced Polish studies at the clandestine University of Warsaw, where she became friends with Borowski. Leopold was active in sabotage; after the birth of her daughter Joanna, she ran the distribution of clandestine papers for the whole country. She fought in the Uprising, and her daughter died a year later. In fall 1945, Leopold completed her studies and began to work as an assistant lecturer at the University of Wrocław. Her articles about Rudnicki and Borowski were well known. On returning to Warsaw, she worked at the Instytut Badań Literackich and for *Kuźnica* and *Nowa Kultura*. She married artist Kajetan Sosnowski, and they raised three children together. From 1960 to 1964, she ran the editorial offices of PIW [Państwowy Instytut Wydawniczy, or National Publishing Institute].

From 1964, she worked in Prof. J. Chałasiński's Contemporary Africa department on African literature (in European languages) and anthropological principles, for which she received a doctorate.

Beginning in 1968, Leopold became active in the opposition as a coworker of KOR. She died in a car accident. Borowski portrays her in the sketch "Profesorowie i studenci," where he cites a letter, now lost, which she wrote immediately after the war: "I am starting life afresh, as after reawakening. Ah, the doctoral thesis! Of course, I shall write it! Lectures? I will give them. But you know . . ."

BOŻENNA LEWANDOWSKA (1927–2000) was a secretary of the Polish Press Information Office in East Berlin who simultaneously studied at the Humboldt University there. She became friends with Maria and Tadeusz Borowski. Later, she ran the editorial office of the West German monthly *Polska*. After *Ucieczka z kamiennego świata* [*Escape from the World of Stone*][5] appeared, she offered me [Drewnowski] her memoirs of the writer's work in Berlin (annuals, *Blick nach Polen*, excerpts taken from Brecht, and so on).

WILHELM MACH (1917–65) came from the village of Kamionka near Dębica (in the Rzeszów district). A graduate of the Państwowy Pedagogium [National Normal School], he took part in the September Campaign. During the war, he worked as a clerk at the Ubezpieczalnia and in clandestine studies. He made his literary debut in *Odrodzenie* with the story "Rdza" ["Rust"], which he developed into a novel. From 1949 to 1950 (with a break for research in France), he was secretary and critic for *Twórczość;* he subsequently ran the prose department of *Nowa Kultura,* and young prose writers were highly indebted to him. He sided

with *Pokolenie* and Borowski generationally, in his correspondence with them. His own writings cover various genres: popular prose; social—*Jaworowy dom* [*Sycamore House*], *Życie duże i małe* [*Life Great and Small*]; experimental—*Góry nad czarnym morzem* [*Hills Above the Black Sea*]; and refined intellectualism—*Szkice literackie* [*Literary Sketches*].

STANISŁAW MARCZAK-OBORSKI (1921–87) was a poet, historian, critic, and theater director who used the pseudonyms Juliusz Oborski and, with Borowski and Bratny—Wiktor K. Ostrowski. He was one of Borowski's closest friends from the clandestine Polish studies days. Under the occupation, he also studied theater under Leon Schiller and directed the Students' Experimental Theater. By agreement with the Delegatura Rzadu RP [State Council] he organized cultural activities in occupied Warsaw such as concerts, authors' meetings, and theater performances. As Borowski writes in the epigram "Na Staszka Marczaka" ["For Staszek Marczak"], "He's got contacts here and contacts there, stage an act for him here, two acts elsewhere." His activities brought the ideologically divided groups of the younger generation together and widened the "Essentialist" circle. At the end of the occupation, he edited the left-wing journal *Droga,* which published the poetry of K. K. Baczyński and Borowski, as well as his own. He fought in the Uprising and was deported to a Stalag,[6] after which he underwent treatment for tuberculosis in Zakopane. Exceptional industriousness was typical of him also after the war; among other things, he and Borowski tried to revive *Droga* and published *Pokolenie* and *Nurt,* which also contain Marczak-Oborski's most interesting literary critical statements. He later focused on the theater: in the best periods he was literary director of the Teatr Dramatyczny and headed Teatr TV. After 1956, he worked in the Instytut Sztuki PAN.[7] He published a cycle of accounts of Polish theatrical works and theater life during the years 1918 to 1965, as well as popular theater guides.

RYSZARD MATUSZEWSKI is a literary critic and historian, a lawyer by training, who was born in 1914. He made his literary debut in 1931 in *Kuźna Młodych* and in the poetry club S. After the war, he was a critic for *Kuźnica, Nowa Kultura* (where he collaborated with Borowski), and *Literatura.* From 1960 to 1977, he was head of the literature department of Czytelnik publishers. In addition to many works of criticism and school textbooks, he published *Literatura polska 1939–1991* [*Polish Literature 1939–1991*] and two volumes of memoirs.

TADEUSZ MIKULSKI (1909–58) was a historian of Polish literature, a writer, and a professor at Wrocław University. Originally from Chobotow (Tombowska district), Mikulski studied Polish in Warsaw with Professor Ujejski and in Kraków with Professor Chrzanowski. He got his doctorate with Professor Pigoń. Mikulski specialized in medieval, Renaissance, and Baroque literature before the war (his works were collected after his death in the volume *Rczeczy staropolskie* [*Old Polish Things*]) and became a lecturer at Warsaw University. In 1937, he went on a research grant to Paris, where the focus of his studies became the Enlightenment. Throughout the occupation he lectured at the clandestine University of Warsaw, where Borowski was his student, and also at the University of Western Territories. He served in the Home Army (under the pseudonym Krasicki) and was taken prisoner of war after the Uprising.

Immediately upon his return, he signed up to work at the university being reorganized in Wrocław,[8] where as professor he generated a mass of activity. He initiated methodical, communal research and editorial and documentary work on the Enlightenment period (the larger part of the work was his); cofounded the Instytut Badan Literackich; and created what was later called "the Mikulski School," whose protégées to this day work on more than just Wrocław Polish studies. On top of that, he brought together Wrocław's cultural and literary circle (which made him friends with Anna and Jerzy Kowalski, and also Maria Dąbrowska). Under the auspices of Koło Miłośników Literatury i Jezyka Polskiego [Lovers of Polish Literature and Language Circle], he and Anna Kowalska edited the quarterly *Zeszyty Wrocławskie,* a journal important to postwar culture. At the "Spotkania wrocławskie" ["Wrocław Meetings"], he also raised a new literary subject: Polish traditions in Lower Silesia.

Professor Mikulski wrote an excellent piece about Borowski et al.'s *We Were in Auschwitz* (see *Miniatury krytyczne* [*Critical Miniatures*]). Borowski, for his part, excellently portrayed Mikulski in the memoir "Profesorowie i studenci" ["Professors and Students"] (in the volume *Pewien żołnierz* [*A Certain Soldier*]), as a fervent scholar and an unusually gentle and shy man who "blushed like a girl."

JANUSZ NEL SIEDLECKI (1916–2000) was a graduate of the Batory Gimnazjium and a member of Boy Scout troop 23WDH who served as a courier on a special mission to France in 1940 and became Auschwitz prisoner #6,643. After liberation, he came to be a friend of Borowski and Olszewski, with whom he wrote *We Were in Auschwitz.* Later he worked as an engineer in England and published a memoir in English, *Beyond Lost Dreams,* 1994.

KRYSTYN OLSZEWSKI is an architect and urban planner who was born in 1921. He graduated from the Warsaw Polytechnic. From 1964 to 1981, he was the general designer, in turn, of the overall plans for Warsaw, Baghdad, and Singapore, as well as the Lubelskie Zagłebia Weglowe [Lublin Coal Fields] and the cofounder of the Sląski Park Wypoczynkowy [Silesian Recuperation Area]. He is a UN expert and a lecturer at the Warsaw Polytechnic. During the war, Olszewski was a prisoner of Pawiak, Auschwitz, Gross Rosen, Buchenwald,[9] and Dachau. After liberation, he wrote the poetry pamphlet *Poszukiwania: Tracing* (1945) with Borowski, and *We Were in Auschwitz* (1946) with Borowski and Nel Siedlecki. He admits that, to this day, poetry remains his hobby.

TADEUSZ PEREŚWIET-SOŁTAN (1921–96, pseudonym Karcz) graduated in 1939 from Prince Józef Poniatowski Secondary School in Warsaw. During the occupation, he studied philosophy and sociology at the clandestine Warsaw University and at the University of Western Territories. From 1940 to 1941, he was a prisoner in Auschwitz. In 1942, he joined the "Sztuka i Naród" circle. He was a member of the Ruch Kulturowy[10] management, organized and ran the journal *Sprawy Kultury,*[11] and was an active journalist and critic in the underground press. A soldier in the Home Army, he worked for the Home Army's Office of Information and Propaganda. During the Uprising, he led tape-recorder patrol no. 1 (to sabotage the Wehrmacht divisions). After getting out of the Stalag in Sandbostel, he remained in the West (where, among other things, he was editorial secretary of *Defilada,* published by Gen. Maczek's Panzer division). In 1946, he returned to his native Rzeszów and served as secretary of the Provincial Headquarters of the PPS,[12] later the PZPR,[13] and director of the Siemaszkowa Memorial Theater. From 1950, he was a coworker at the PAX association in Warsaw and became a Pietrzak Prize laureate in 1984.[14] He published two collections of sketches, *Motywy i fascynacje* [*Motifs and Enchantments*], 1978, and *Z rachunków mojego pokolenia* [*From the Debts of My Generation*], 1988, as well as many disparate memoirs about the occupation. *Dzienniki krytyczne* [*Critical Diaries*] and a novel, *Złom żelazny* [*Iron Block*], remain in manuscript form.

GERHART POHL (1902–66) was a writer, journalist, and publisher. He came from Lower Silesia and studied German, art history, and psychology in Wrocław, Munich, and Berlin. His prewar books—*Symbol Oberammergau* [*Symbol of Oberammergau*], *Deutscher Justizmord* [*German Judicial Murder*]—had an influence on leftist youth. He was a friend of G. Hauptmann and found himself in

Berlin in 1946 in connection with Hauptmann's funeral. From 1946 to 1950, he was a proofreader at Aufbau publishers. In 1950 he "chose freedom"[15] in West Berlin. Pohl became a public figure in West German literary life, serving as president of the Union of Professional German Writers and president of the West German PEN club, among other things.

TADEUSZ RÓŻEWICZ (born in 1921, pseudonym Satyr) comes from a white-collar family in Radom. He made his debut in *Czerwone Tarcze* [*Red Shields*] with pastiches on the poets of the Twenty Years of Independence and then published pastiches in a section of a partisan brochure, *Echo lesne* [*Echo of the Woods*]. He studied art history at Jagiellonian University. His *Niepokój* [*Anxiety*], 1947, and *Czerwona rękawiczka* [*The Red Glove*], 1948, revealed a new type of verse stripped of metaphor and reinstating simplicity of language. Later, he fearlessly took it upon himself to reform drama, creating a naturalistic-poetic theater with works such as *Kartoteka* [*Personal File*]; *Stara kobieta wysiada* [*An Old Woman Gets Off*]; and *Pułapka* [*The Trap*]. Although he created great and original work that gained worldwide fame, in Poland Różewicz was long criticized and accused of nihilism (as was Borowski). He has finally received due recognition in his creative old age. Of their contemporaries, Borowski and Różewicz were closest to each other in their independent aspirations, but their personal acquaintance arose rather late and only for a brief time. In addition to a posthumous poem, Różewicz devoted many reflections on "pages torn from a diary" to his tragic colleague, as well as a foreword to a Swedish edition of Borowski's stories.

ADOLF RUDNICKI (1912–90) was already a recognized writer before the war for *Niekochana* [*Unloved*] (1937) and *Lato* [*Summer*] (1938). After the September 1939 campaign, in which he had taken part, he found himself in Lwów as a contributor to *Nowe Widnokręgi* [*New Horizons*].[16] Rudnicki returned to Warsaw in 1942, went into hiding, and took part in the resistance and in the Warsaw Uprising. From 1945 to 1950 he belonged to the *Kuźnica* group in Łódź. In Warsaw, he worked with the weekly *Swiat* [*The World*]. Until 1968, his writings were devoted totally to the Holocaust; he collected them in the volume *Żywe i martwe morze* [*The Living and Dead Sea*] (1952). Marrying a French woman, he lived both in Paris and in Warsaw. His later fiction has an existentialist dimension.

Borowski's writings fascinated Rudnicki. Borowski reciprocated his friendship; one of the hidden dedications in *Kamienny świat* was the dedication to him in "Człowiek z packą" ["The Man with the Parcel"]: "To Sebastian, dear

to us all." When in "Rozmowy" ["Conversations"], published in *Odrodzenie,* Borowski treated him, together with himself and others, brutally, Rudnicki tore the issue up and threw it out the window at Rada Państwa, where a conference about socialist realism was underway.

MARIA BERTA RUNDO (Tuśka), later Borowska, was born in 1920. She came from a Polonized Jewish family of rich cultural traditions. Her father, Jerzy, a grandson of Samuel Orgelbrand,[17] and Mieczysław Grzydewski's cousin, studied chemistry and architecture in Zurich. Her mother, Eugenia, the daughter of Stanisław Swierczyński and Mathilde Franzmann, finished ballet school, then performed in Warsaw cabarets including "Sphinx" and "The Black Cat." After her husband's early death, the mother and her two daughters moved from Milanówka to Warsaw to the grandfather's (a wealthy merchant) house at 8 Złota Street where her uncle lived and ran the editorial offices of *Wiadomości Literackie.* After finishing secondary school and the Konopnicki Lyceum, in 1940 Rundo attended the first clandestine Polish studies group directed by Professor Julian Krzyżanowski. There she met Tadeusz Borowski, to whom she became emotionally attached, and took part in the Polish studies and arts group known as the "Essentialists," which was forming around him. On February 23, 1943, wanting to help a school friend who had escaped from the Ghetto to get false papers, she went to the Mankiewicz family, whom she knew (they lived at the corner of Puławska and Szustra Streets), where the Gestapo had set up a trap in connection with a mishap at the *Trybuna Wolności* [*Tribune of Freedom*] printing house on Grzybowska Street (according to accounts at the time, it was to have been a self-denunciation of the Communist underground). The next day, her fiancé, who was looking for her, was also arrested there. Both were transported from Pawiak to Auschwitz on April 29. During her more than eighteen-month stay in Birkenau (#43,558), she suffered from all the possible camp illnesses (from which Tadeusz saved her to the extent that he was able). Shortly before the liquidation of the camp, her condition borderline, she was taken to Ravensbrück, where she registered for the Count Bernadotte transport to Sweden. After undergoing treatment in a sanatorium, she found paid work and studied. For a year after the war, she and Tadeusz were unable first to find one another and then to reunite. Only after Tadeusz's desperate return to Poland and his pleading letters did she return to Poland, and on December 18, 1946, they were married. In 1951, their daughter Małgorzata was born (currently Małgorzata is a professor of classical philology at the University of Warsaw). Despite the undoubtedly psychological causes

for her husband's suicide, Rundo also took responsibility. In 1954, she married Dr. Jan Bayer (1909–76). She worked as a journalist for *Trybuna Wolności,* for *Swiat i Polska* [*The World and Poland*], and was the chief editor of CAF[18] and then the monthly *Ty i ja* [*You and Me*]. She published her prison and camp memoirs in *Gazeta Wyborcza* (January 28 and January 29, 1995) under the title, "Pożegnanie z Tuśką" ["Farewell to Tuśka"], written in the style of Borowski.

PIOTR SŁONIMSKI is the son of Piotr W. Słonimski—a doctor, histologist, and embryologist—and Janina née Sobecka, who taught Polish at the Szachtmajerów Gymnasium (both his parents perished during the Uprising). He is also a nephew of Antoni Słonimski.[19] Born in 1922, he graduated from the clandestine Batory Lyceum in 1940, studied medicine in Warsaw, and after the Uprising, in Kraków. Słonimski belonged to the "Szare Szeregi"[20] during the occupation, was a cadet officer in the Home Army, and during the Uprising fought on the barricades. He was a founder of the "Essentialist" club. After 1947, he lived in Paris and married Hanna Kulągowska; they had a daughter, Agnieszka. Słonimski received a doctorate from the Sorbonne, and taught as a professor there from 1965 to 1992. He is the director of the French Center for Molecular Genetics; codiscoverer of mitochondrial genetics, mosaic genes, research on genomes, the structure and workings of genes and enzymes; and a member of many international academies.

ZOFIA MARIA ŚWIDWIŃSKA-KRZYŻANOWSKA (1920–68) studied at the first clandestine Polish studies group, organized in 1940 by Professor Julian Krzyżanowski, and there met Borowski. Immediately after the war, she completed her studies and became an assistant of "Korbutiana" at the Towarzystwo Naukowe Warszawskie. She organized the Orzeszkowa archives. In 1948, she married Krzyżanowski (they had a son—Julian Tadeusz). She took part in her husband's editorial work (among other things, she worked on Słowacki's letters to his mother) and organized his enormous scholarly bibliography. She also worked with ITI (International Theater Institute). She died in a car accident on Aleja Niepodleglosci in Warsaw.

HELENA TEIGOVA (1920–86, née Peszkova) was a Czech translator of Polish literature. She spent her childhood in Lwów and Bielsk and studied Romance languages at the Karol University in Prague. Over time, she devoted herself entirely to making Polish literature better known (she translated over a hundred works, among them Borowski's).

JULIAN TUWIM[21] (1894–1953) was a leading poet of the Skamander group, adored by Borowski, who in his Munich period modeled himself on Tuwim's satires, especially on *Bal w operze* [*Ball at the Opera*] (1936). His passions as a bibliophile and collector (a curiosity of the epoch!), in connection with which he approached Borowski, were also not alien to the author of *Opowiadania z książek i gazet*. From his return from emigration right up to his early death, Tuwim was unable to get to the bottom of the realities of the Polish People's Republic. And despite his natural leanings toward young talent, he was probably the only one who supported Borowski's marginally leftist *Rozmowy* [*Conversations*].

ALEKSANDER WAT (nom de plume of Aleksander Chwat, 1900–67). A futurist in his youth ("Ja z jednej, ja z drugiej strony mopsozelaznego piecyka" ["I on one side, I on the other side of a pig-iron stove"], 1920) and a Communist, he served as the editor of *Miesięcznik Literacki* [*Literary Monthly*] from 1929 to 1931. He was arrested in Lwów, imprisoned from 1940 to 1941, then sent to Khazakstan; this period determined his turning away from communism. After the war, he was editor-in-chief of the State Publishing Institute and a member of the Leading Committee of the Polish Writers' Association and the PEN club. Wat chose to emigrate in 1959 and committed virtual suicide by leaving.

During his lifetime he published *Wiersze środziemnomorskie* [*Mediterranean Poems*], 1959 and *Ciemne świecidło* [*Dark Trinket*], 1968. After his death were published *Pamiętnik mówiony* [*Spoken Diary*], with a foreword by Miłosz, as well as three volumes of *Pism wybranych* [*Selected Writings*]: *Swiat na haku i z kluczem* [*World on a Hook and with a Key*], *Dziennik bez samogłosek* [*Diary Without Vowels*], and a volume of prose, *Ucieczka Lotha* [*Loth's Escape*] (1988).

During his visits to Germany in 1949, Wat grew close to Borowski, whom he valued very highly as a writer (particularly for his *Kamienny świat*). One of his last remarks was about the final period of Borowski's life: "After his famous attack on non-Communist writers [*Rozmowy*] he justified himself to me saying that the arguments and even the sentences in the article were dictated to him over the telephone to Berlin. He had become completely disillusioned with communism in East Berlin. It was painful to watch Communist scribblers using this excellent writer as an errand boy. During the period when he was writing the most aggressive columns for *Nowa Kultura,* he'd come to me from time to time for a 'soulful confession.' When I warned him that he was in danger of becoming clinically schizophrenic, he maintained that, in fact, after Auschwitz, he couldn't go on living; he immersed himself in communism which, for him, was a kind

of 'ersatz suicide.' " ("I stand among you like a specter and ask about the source of evil," *Na Antenie* [*On the Antenna*], 43, 1966, RWE addendum to the London *Wiadomosci Literackie*).

WITOLD WIRPSZA (1918–85) was a writer and translator. Born in Odessa, between the wars he studied at the conservatory and at the University of Warsaw, in law. He made his debut in *Kuźna Młodych* with the poem "Sredniowiecze" ["The Middle Ages"]. He spent the Second World War in a prisoner-of-war camp. In 1947, he went to live in an artists' colony in Szczecin, then moved to Warsaw in 1956. At first, he was involved with socialist realism. After October 1956, he became one of the creators of "linguistic poetry" and the author of a dozen or so books of poetry and a couple of books of prose, as well as a collection of essays, *Gra znaczeń* [*Game of Meanings*]. He translated primarily from German (works by Johannes Bobrowski, Gottfried Benn, Thomas Mann, Hermann Broch), but also from Russian (Joseph Brodsky) and Portuguese. In 1960, he emigrated, first to Switzerland, then to West Berlin. Abroad, he published, among other things, historical essays such as *Polaku, kim jestes?* [*Pole, Who Are You?*] and a cycle of poems, *Liturgia* [*Liturgy*] (1985); he worked with the Paris *Kultura,* the London *Wiadomości,* and the Berlin *Archipelag.* Later, two volumes of his poetry came out in Poland: a long poem *Faeton* [*Phaeton*] (1988); a collection, *Apoteoza tańca* [*Apotheosis of the Dance*]; and, after his death in West Berlin, *Nowy podręcznik wydajnego zażywania narkotyków* [*New Handbook of the Efficient Use of Narcotics*] (1995).

WIKTOR WOROSZYŁSKI (1927–96) was a prose writer, poet, and translator from a doctor's family in Grodno. In March 1945, the family was repatriated in Łódź. From student days—first medicine, then Polish studies in Łódź and Warsaw—he was active in the Party and worked as a journalist and reporter for *Głos Ludu* [*Voice of the People*], *Po Prostu* [*Simply*], and *Nowa Kultura.* He made his debut as a poet with the volume *Smierci nie ma* [*Death Doesn't Exist*], 1949. In the spring of that year, he and his wife moved to the artists' colony in Szczecin (his correspondence with Borowski is from this period). From 1952 to 1956, he studied at the Gorky Institute in Moscow (at the same time, his wife, a biologist, had a stipend to Moscow University), and the confirmed young Communist underwent an abrupt political change. After October 1956, the *Nowa Kultura* group elected him editor in chief; two years later he was removed from the position. In 1964, he was thrown out of the Polish United Workers Party as

a revisionist. He was one of the founders of KOR and a known activist for the democratic opposition. From 1976 to 1980, he coedited *Zapis,* a quarterly that came out behind the back of the censors. He was the author of, among other things, *Dziennik węgierski* [*Hungarian Diary*] (1956, from Budapest) and collections of poetry, such as *Śmierć gatunku* [*Death of Quality*] and *Ostatni raz* [*The Last Time*] as well as documentary stories about Pushkin and Mayakovsky and many translations. Woroszyłski played an important part in the political changes in the literary circle, both in its being reconciled to the Polish People's Republic and its rebellion against it, and also in the changes in Borowski's political stance, which is strange since Borowski usually did not succumb to influences.[22]

IRENA WYGODZKA (born in 1922, née Beitner) was married to Stanisław Wygodzki. After being made homeless by war, she was arrested and sent to a camp in the Sudetenland where she became an Aussenkommando of Gross-Rosen. She managed by some miracle to get her mother and two sisters brought there, and thanks to the camp they all survived.

STANISŁAW WYGODZKI (1907–92), a writer and political activist from Będzin, was from early youth involved with the revolutionary movement. He was expelled from the *gimnazjium* before graduation. He made his literary debut in 1928 in *Wiadomości Literackie* [*Literary News*], taking part in a discussion on proletarian literature. He worked with left-wing and Communist journals, as well as the Moscow *Kultura Mas* [*Culture of the Masses*] and *Literatura mirowoj riewolucji* [*Literature of the World Revolution*], as a result of which his first volume of poetry, *Apel* [*Appeal*], was published in Moscow in 1933.

During the occupation, he was in the Będzin ghetto. He experienced an unspeakable tragedy: in a mutually undertaken suicide attempt, his wife and four-year-old daughter died, but he survived. After being liberated from the camps, he underwent medical treatment in Germany; there he married again to Irena, a girl from Sosnowiec, who had been more fortunate. [See her biography above.]

The Wygodzkis returned to Poland in 1947. Stanisław worked in the book department of the Ministry of Culture and Art, was literary director of Polish Radio, and was active in the Party. Two threads run through his postwar writings: works in the revolutionary tradition such as *Widzenie* [*Vision*] (1950) and *Pusty Plac* [*Empty Square*] (1955); and the Jewish-themed *Pamiętnik miłości* [*Diary of Love*] (1948) and *Koncert życzeń* [*Concert of Wishes*] (1961). The Wygodzkis and their two children emigrated to Israel in 1968. The writer had a bad accident

there. His new works were literary reexaminations of the past: *Zatrzymany do wyjasnienia* [*Stopped for Clarification*] (1968), *Pieskin został pisarzem* [*Pieskin Became a Writer*] (1973), and political poems.

Borowski came to know Wygodzki in Germany, most probably through the Family Tracing Service where he worked. Apart from the poem "To XXX," Wygodzki's misfortunes to some extent were the inspiration for the story "This Way for the Gas," whose original title was "Transport Sosnowiec-Będzin" ["The Sosnowiec–Będzin Transport"]. Their later relationship was not devoid of sharp political clashes.

KAZIMIERZ WYKA (1910–75), a historian, a literary critic, and an essayist, was a professor at Jagiellonian University and director of Instytut Badań Literackich. Immediately after the war, he ran the monthly *Twórczość*, and his literary judgment carried great weight. *Twórczość*'s distancing of itself from the Borowski stories it had published did not deter Wyka from soliciting material—criticism and burlesques—from Borowski.[23]

JERZY ZAGÓRSKI (1907–64), was a poet, essayist, and translator. He earned a law degree from USB [Stefan Batory University] in Vilno. A catastrophist, fantasist, and stylistic poet, he was coeditor of *Zagary* and *Piony*. During the war, he participated in the clandestine cultural life, edited the monthly *Kultura jutra* [*Culture of Tomorrow*], and, with J. Andrzejewski, wrote a burlesque historical play, *Święto Winkelrieda* [*Winkelried's Holiday*]. He served as a cultural attaché in Paris after the war, and then as literary director of the Kraków theater, before moving to Warsaw where he became a popular theater critic. Zagórski found himself in Germany in connection with the Nuremberg Trials, and Borowski was indebted to him for quickly reintroducing his work in Poland at the end of 1945. Out of those travels in Germany, Zagórski wrote a long reportage, *Indie w środku Europy* [*India in the Center of Europe*].

STEFAN ŻÓŁKIEWSKI (1911–91) was a historian, literary critic, journalist, and political activist who endeavored to conduct an open political culture and was especially sensitive to the needs of young people. He was remarkable for his broad horizons and exceptional inspirational and pedagogic talent. He held a degree in Polish philology from Warsaw University and was president of the Warsaw Polish Studies Circle. Before the war, he worked as a schoolteacher. In 1942, he joined the PPR and served as coeditor of underground cultural journals,

including *Literatura Walcząca* [*Fighting Literature*] and *Przełom* [*Turning Point*]. From 1945 to 1949, he was editor in chief of *Kuźnica* in Łódź, then served as editor in chief of *Polityka* (1957–58) and *Nowa Kultura* (1958–61). In 1948, he created the Instytut Badań Literackich [Institute of Literary Studies], which he directed until 1953, when he received the title of "Professor." He fulfilled many responsible national and Party functions, among others, minister of higher education, director of the cultural division of the Central Committee, and scholarly secretary of PAN. As a result of supporting the student strike in 1968, he was thrown out of the Central Committee and stripped of all positions. He devoted himself entirely to scholarly work at the IBL [Institute of Literary Studies]. He published, among other things, *Perspektywy literatury XX w* [*Twentieth Century Literary Perspectives*] (1960); *Przepowiednie i wspomnienia* [*Prophecies and Recollections*] (1964); *Kultura literacka 1918–32* [*Literary Culture 1918–32*] (1973); *Kultura, socjologia, semiotyka literacka* [*Culture, Sociology, Literary Semiotics*] (1983); and *Społeczne konteksty kultury literarckiej na ziemiach polskich* [*Social Contexts of Literary Culture on Polish Soil*] (1995).

WOJCIECH ŻUKROWSKI (1916–2000) was a prose writer, reporter, and author of works for children and young people who made his debut in *Kuźna Młodych*. He began Polish studies at Jagiellonian University and graduated from Wrocław after the war. He took part as an artilleryman in the 1939 campaign, then served as an officer of the Home Army ZWZ [Union for Armed Struggle] during the occupation, as well as working as a quarry worker and on the staff of Kraków's *Miesięcznik Literacki* [*Literary Monthly*]. He lived in Katowice and Wrocław after the war, connected with *Odra* and later with the PAX press. Shortly after moving to Warsaw, he went as a war correspondent to North Vietnam, then became an adviser at the embassy in India. After the Związek Literatów [Writers' Union] was closed down, he became president of the ZLP [Polish Writers' Association]. His works include *Z Kraju Milczenia* [*From the Land of Silence*] (1946); *Porwania w Tiutiurlistanie* [*Capture in Tiutiurlistan*] (1946); *Dni klęski* [*Days of Defeat*] (1952); *Dom bez ścian* [*House Without Walls*] (1954); *Kamienne tablice* [*Tablets of Stone*] (1966); and *Plaża nad Styksem* [*Beach on the Styx*] (1976).

Żukrowski was the most highly regarded young prose writer of that time. His letters to Borowski suggest an ambivalence toward him or, perhaps, competitiveness. It's a pity that the return correspondence was not found among the writer's papers.

NOTES

INTRODUCTION

1. 1873–1944. Novelist and literary critic.—TRANS.
2. The name of a poetry magazine and of an elite club of poets including J. Tuwim, A. Słonimski, and K. Wierszyński.—TRANS.

I. FEBRUARY 25, 1943–AUGUST 12, 1944

1. From Pawiak and Auschwitz, it was permissible to write only on prison cards and special camp forms in the German language. Tadeusz Borowski's letters were translated in writing for his family by his brother's friend, Andrzej Wakar. Not all the original letters in German survived; I am including mostly the later ones, written by the sender himself. When some of these letters, in abbreviated form, were published in *Twórczość* 8 (1961), the translations made under the occupation were somewhat edited, apparently by Iwaszkiewicz himself. I contributed minimally to this.
2. From the beginning, friends and acquaintances (even estranged ones, like Trzebiński) contributed to the family packages, or sent some themselves. They later, apparently, received some modest means for this from the State representative.
3. During the first period in Auschwitz, Borowski did not have direct contact with his fiancée, who was not far away across the wires in the women's camp in Birkenau. In a camouflaged way, he was asking for information about her via Warsaw.
4. Not only as a result of the time of year. After having typhoid fever, Borowski was retained in the camp hospital; at this writing he was performing the functions of a Nachtwach, a night guard. Shortly after being trained, he became a regular nurse and then chose night shifts, which isolated him somewhat.

5. Borowski managed to make initial contact with Tuśka through Kurt Knuth-Siebenlist, a German prisoner working in the women's camp; in other words, as the saying went, he "found himself a pair of feet."

6. Eugenia Rundo, Tuśka's mother.

7. Probably a reference to his own illness.

8. A reference to his parents' camp experiences.

9. His former girlfriend; surname unknown.

10. Reference to the artistic life in the camp: prisoners' creative work and readings.

11. The farm was functioning at the time. Before his arrest, Tadeusz gave food from it to Prof. Adamczewski.

12. From the start, apparently, Tuśka's mother made efforts to buy her out (or otherwise get her out)—first from Pawiak, then from Auschwitz. Borowski is referring to these efforts skeptically here.

13. Borowski swapped the hospital for the Dachdecker Kommando in order to be able to contact his fiancée.

14. Respectively, Żurawski, Kujawski, Słonimski.

II. MAY 1945–MAY 31, 1946

Munich

1. Most probably the chapbook *Poszukiwania: Tracing* [*sic*] containing Borowski's poem "Korespondencja" ("Correspondence"). [The epigraph on page 33 is from this poem.—TRANS.]

2. Causticity and pneumatosis.

3. Borowski was transported from Dautmergen on April 7, 1945, arriving in Dachau-Allach on April 12, 1945.—TRANS.

4. Janusz Stępowski, *The Legend of the Mast Pine*, 1934.

5. At that time, J. Zagórski was present at the Nuremberg Trials as a correspondent for *Przekrój* (*The Review*). When he was returning from there to Poland for the first time, Borowski saddled him with poems and stories for publication. Thanks to Zagórski, the news that Borowski was alive and the first review of *Imiona nurtu* appeared in Poland before the writer himself had returned. *Tygodnik Powszechny* [*Universal Weekly*] published Borowski's poems, and *Twórczość*, his stories. The stories that appeared in *Twórczość* were "The

Sosnowiec–Będzin Transport" (original title of "This Way for the Gas") and "A Day at Harmenz." Zagórski appears as "the poet" in Borowski's story "The January Offensive."—TRANS.

6. Borowski was twenty-three, not twenty-four years old, at the time.

7. It soon became clear that Wygodzki was confused and that the letter wasn't asking about Borowski.

8. Professional Writers Union.—TRANS.

9. Maria Rundo and Borowski were arrested at the Mankiewiczs' house by the Gestapo.

10. Halina (Natalia) née Marczak (1920–84), Stanisław Marczak's sister, had the married names Bojarska (she married the poet *in articulo mortis*) and Wieczorkiewiczowa. She was a nurse as well as an actress in clandestine performances. After the war, she was on the staff of the Theater Department of MKiS [Ministry of Culture and Art].

11. Zofia Trzebińska, presently Nagabczyńska, a painter; younger sister of Andrew, a friend, and then antagonist, of Borowski's.

12. Edmund Kujawski (b.1921) was a student of Polish studies and law at the underground university in Warsaw, cofounder of the Essentialists Club, and one of Borowski's closest friends. After the Warsaw Uprising, he was in Auschwitz and Lengenfeld. After the war, he was a lawyer for the Lot Polish Airlines. From 1925 to 1981, he served as director of the Center for Planning and Coordinating Research at the Polish Academy of Science and as advisor to the Scientific Secretary for PAN. He was one of the founders of the Alumni Association of the Batory School and coauthor of its monograph.

13. Arkadiusz Żurawski (1922–44), a painter. A friend of Borowski's from *gimnazjium* and the Czacki Lyceum, he designed the cover for *Gdziekolwiek ziemia* [*Wherever the Earth*]. He perished in unknown circumstances during the Warsaw Uprising.

14. The Essentialists was a social and arts club of students, active beginning in 1941 during the occupation. Its base was the underground Warsaw University Department of Polish Literature, but it was an interdisciplinary group. Its founders included literature students Tadeusz Borowski, Stanisław Marczak-Oborski, Zofia Świdwińska, Barbara Bormann, and Maria Rundo; musicians Norbert Karaśkiewicz and Jerzy Kreutz; artists Arkadiusz Żurawski and Olga Peczenko; lawyers Edmund Kujawski and Andrzej Gwiżdż; and also biological scientist Piotr Słonimski and philosopher Tadeusz Sołtan. Although it was a

politically diverse group, and politics were avoided during their gatherings, it had (particularly in contrast with Sztuka i Naród [Art and the Nation]) a leftist, or left-leaning, reputation. The meetings took place in various houses (the favorite places were Edmund Kujawski's manor, "Kujawianka," in Zaborów near Leszno, and the barracks on Skaryszewska Street where Borowski lived and worked), usually at night after curfew. Piotr Słonimski thought up the Essentialist Hymn, but it was collectively edited and revised:

> We are the essentialists
> ecclesiastic-futurists
> ooooo! ooo!

> We do whatever must be done
> but never where it should be done
> ooooo! ooo!

> In our studies and cabarets
> on top of women we do lay
> ooooo! ooo!

> We'll make it through eternity
> lauded by posterity
> ooooo! ooo!

> Away with poet medievalists!
> Vivat only essentialists
> ooooo! ooo!

Borowski was the Essentialists' "Mage," as Sołtan calls him, even though the club continued to exist after his arrest. His poetry set the club's tone: in the dark years it aroused faith in "the times of Saturn"—in learning and love, poetry and fun. The fundamentalists regarded this as blasphemous antipatriotism, even though most of the young people were active in the resistance movement; the Sztuka i Naród opposition simply regarded Borowski as a deserter (in Bojarski and Gajcy's polemic on his first work, *Gdziekolwiek ziemia*).

15. Andrzej Maurycy Gwiżdż (1923–98) studied in the clandestine law department. The Essentialists also met at his place on Sadyba. He was a professor at the University of Warsaw, chaired the Legislative Council, and participated in the work on the constitution of the Polish Republic.

16. Olga Peczenko (b. 1918, died in the 1960s), later Srzednicka, was a painter and a professor at the Kraków Academy of Fine Arts. Born in Siberia, she spent her childhood in Neuchatel, then lived in Poland after she turned twenty. Friends with the Essentialists, she introduced a repertoire of French and Russian songs.

17. Jerzy Kreutz, a musicologist, died in the 1950s. Zofia Kreutz, née Neugebauer, was a classmate of Tuśka's from the Konopicki Lyceum. The Essentialists organized a festive wedding for them.

18. Ewa Pohoska (1918–44), pseud. Halina Sosnowska. A journalist, playwright, and poet, she was daughter of the vice president of Warsaw during the Starzyński presidency. She studied ethnography at the University of Warsaw and together with J. Garztecki founded the social-cultural journal *Droga* in 1943 (hers was the leading article). Her *Schyłek amonitow* [*Decline of Fossils*], a satirically grotesque play about the underground, was published posthumously. She was shot to death near Pawiak.

19. Tadeusz Wiwatowski, an outstanding student and a Ph.D. candidate during the war, served as an assistant to Prof. Krzyżanowski. He ran tutorial sessions. Twice (in September 1939 and during the Uprising) he was awarded the Virtute Militari cross. Under the code name "Olszyn" he was deputy leader of the "Miotla" battalion, and was killed August 11, 1944 on Stawka.

20. In August 1943 on a transport to Auschwitz, Anka née Dab and Stanisław Wygodzki tried to poison themselves, together with their four-year-old daughter, Inka. Only the husband survived.

21. Wygodzki is referring to Władysław Broniewski, secretary of *Wiadomości Literackie;* to Stanisław Ryszard Standeg, who, after escaping to Russia, collaborated on *Kultura Mas* [*Culture of the Masses*] in Moscow; and to Aleksander Wat, editor of *Miesięcznik Literacki* [*Literary Monthly*], as poets and editors connected with the beginning of his poetic career.

22. Bruno Jasieński, as editor of *Kultura Mas,* an organ of the Central Department of the Polish Union of Proletarian Writers, helped with Wygodzki's Moscow debut, entitled *Apel* [*Appeal*] (1933), and Kruczkowski in the publishing of the next two volumes in Kraków: *Chleb powszedni* [*Daily Bread*] (1934) and *Żywioł liścia* [*A Leaf's Element*] (1936).

23. Andreas Gryphius was a preeminent German Baroque lyricist and dramatist whose creative work was connected to the Thirty Years' War; he used the Lower Silesian dialect and translated Sarbiewski's Latin poetry.

24. In Słowacki's "Ojcu zadżumionych" ["Father of the Plague-Stricken"]: "My wife fed a tiny child."

25. Stanisław Baliński, Skamander poet, an émigré since the war.

26. He's quoting from his poem, "Czytanie ruin" ["The Reading of Ruins"], in *Pamiętnik miłości* [*Journal of Love*], 1946.—TRANS.

27. Tuberculosis.—TRANS.

28. A revolutionary character in the novel *Nie-Boska Komedia* [*The Undivine Comedy*] by Zygmunt Krasiński (1812–59).—TRANS.

29. Pen name of Tadeusz Żeleński (1874–1941), an eminent satirist, theater critic, essayist, journalist, and translator. Killed in Lwów by the Nazis.—TRANS.

30. Juliusz Słowacki (1809–49), Romantic poet and dramatist.—TRANS.

31. Słowacki's long prose poem, 1838.—TRANS.

32. Słowacki poem of 1841 written in ottava rima.—TRANS.

33. Jan Chryzostom Pasek (1636–1701), prose writer.—TRANS.

34. The opening of *Sonety krymskie* [*Crimean Sonnets*].

35. If only from Z. Kossak-Szczucka's "Nieznany kraj" ["Unknown Country"] or "Na Śląsku" ["In Silesia"].

36. Bolesław Prus (1845–1912), a novelist.—TRANS.

37. Maria Konopnicka (1842–1910), a poet, and Adolf Dygasiński (1839–1902), a teacher and writer.

38. He's talking about the poem "Korespondencja," published in the chapbook *Poszukiwania: Tracing*.

39. People who claimed they were ethnic Germans.—TRANS.

40. Borowski included his January 6, 1941, speech about the four freedoms in the periodical *Ziemia i Ludzie* [*The Earth and People*], which he started publishing in Munich. He published a cycle of poems entitled "Cztery Wolności" ["The Four Freedoms"] in the collection *Rozmowa z przyjacielem*.

41. Designed and issued by Anatol Girs.—TRANS.

42. This discussion is simply invaluable. Since Borowski did not have the wherewithal to collect and systematically publish his poems and then later began to deprecate them, many of his works perished, many he gave away. Wygodzki's letter is one of the more reliable and fuller accounts of this poetry at the beginning of 1946.

43. Titled in English.—TRANS.

44. He's speaking, of course, about the poem "To xxx" (to S. Wygodzki).

45. Mistaken title: the ensuing discussion is not about "Koniec wojny" ["End of the War"] but "Spacer po Monachium" ["A Walk Through Munich"].

46. Borowski often said about his own stories that they were written in the manner of Céline, which later (starting with G. Herling-Grudziński's review of *Pożegnanie z Marią*) was used against him.

47. Quite a long time passed before it was established that K. K. Baczyński perished in the Blank Palace on Plac Teatralny.

48. Polish Academy of Theater Arts.—TRANS.

49. "Empty-Talksville." He's calling on images from Gałczyński's works.—TRANS.

50. Literally, Muslims, here means walking dead. See Drewnoski's explanation, note 7 in the Maria Rundo letters.—TRANS.

51. Reference to Zbigniew Namokel. The following words were inscribed on his grave in the Augsburg-Evangelical cemetery in Warsaw: "He lived 18 years. Died 5 September 1943 in concentration camp Auschwitz." (See L. B. Grzeniewski, "Chłopiec z Biblią," *Kultura* 40, 1970.)

52. Stefania Engelhardt-Frank, born 1922. After her university studies, the resistance, and Uprising, she and H. Laskowska made it to France and England. In 1946, she went to Munich in search of information about her father, with which Borowski assisted her. Currently, having met her fiancé again after many years, she is working at a university in America and translating from Polish.

53. Inaccurate information; even without counting K. K. Baczyński's hectographs, Borowski's *Wiersze wybrane* [*Selected Poems*] appeared simultaneously in 1942.

54. *Wiersze polskie wybrane. Antologia poezji od "Bogu rodzicy" do chwili obecnej* [*Selected Polish Poems: Anthology of Poetry from Bogurodzica to the Present*], London, 1946. Not so much an anthology as a large reader for Polish émigrés.

55. In reference to the poem "Korespondencja."—TRANS.

56. Reminiscence of the Romantic-landscape section of [Żeromski's] *Ashes,* vol. 2.

57. S. Wygodzki's second, newly wedded wife. "We received from him [Borowski] at that time," Irena Wygodzka wrote me, "a beautiful poem, which, unfortunately, got lost." It turned out to have been preserved at the home of Wanda Leopold's daughter, Honorata Sosnowska, among her mother's papers:

> To xxx
>
> You'll return to your country, poet,
> to Sosnowiec or to Będzin.
> you'll go to the Jewish market,
> the Umschlagplatz, the ghetto.

You'll return alone, unneeded,
like a strip of peeled-off bark—
from where your daughter floated
                    skyward in ashes
from the crematorium.

You'll return needed by no one,
enter a yard you know well,
a few windows, a lilac by the door—
and then you'll burst out crying,
                    "Daughter, oh, Daughter"

And I'll return, find my near ones
in Warsaw or in Milanówek,
we'll sit at the table together
slowly cooling our soup.

Someone will reply, "that was
                    interesting,"
Somebody sigh, "my poor boy."
And I will look on as at a waking
                    dream
so distant from these people
                    so other.

Tadeusz Borowski

58. Authorized by the United Nations Relief and Rehabilitation Administration, the 92-page *Ziemia i Ludzie* [*The Earth and its People*], no. 1, was printed at F. Bruckmann K.G. in Munich, May 15, 1946.

59. In Polish, the name of this English light bulb means, "I'll shit on it."—TRANS.

60. Zuzanna Ginczanka (1917–44), a talented poet. She was shot to death by the Nazis in a prison in Krakow.

Maria Rundo Letters

1. Anna Zboromirska, Tuśka's friend from Auschwitz, went on the same transport to Sweden from Ravensbrück. The wife of an officer in Anders's army, she soon went on to England.

2. Mendel and Drexler . . . Molow and Endress—Kapos in Birkenau and Auschwitz.

3. Mieczysław Grydzewski, editor of *Wiadomości* in London.

4. Monday, August 9, 1943.

5. Dautmergen, subcamp of Natzweiler.

6. Death reports.

7. According to "Auschwitz Terms" from *We Were in Auschwitz*, a *muzulman* was "physically and mentally a totally depleted human being who no longer had the strength or the will to fight for life . . . more than ripe for the chimney."

8. *** "Jabłonie stały przy drodze" . . . (in *Rozmowa z przyjacielem* it is entitled "Fragment," revised text).

9. Mikolaj Peim (b. 1916 in Ukraine, d. London, 1989), a teacher, was Borowski's bunkmate and friend in Dautmergen. He is the "Kola" of "Deszcz zacina po błocie" ["Rain Lashes the Mud"], *Imiona nurtu;* "Kolka" in "Bitwa pod Grunwaldem" ["Battle of Grunwald"]; and the person to whom "Do *** we Włoszech" ["To *** in Italy"] is addressed.—TRANS.

10. "Canada"—here, "symbol of the camp's prosperity" ("Auschwitz Terms").

11. Dachau-Allach was liberated April 30–May 1 by the 7th American Army; see the poem "Koniec wojny" ["End of the War"].

12. Barbara Leszczyńska, Maria Rundo's younger sister, worked in a cigarette factory.

13. Polish Tobacco Monopoly.—TRANS.

14. Foreword by Wincenty (Wintyma) Mackiewicz.

15. The idea for *We Were in Auschwitz* came from Girs, who noticed that Nel Siedlecki was writing camp memoirs. Borowski became its chief executor, not only the author of the few stories for which he is known, but also the author of texts based on the other people's accounts, coauthor of most of the other stories, and also of the editing work (preface, dictionary, forewords to the stories, etc.). Prof. T. Mikulski analyzed the issue of authorship of *We Were in Auschwitz* on the basis of Borowski's testimony in "Z marginesów twórczości Borowskiego" in *Miniatury krytyczne* ["*From the Margins of Borowski's Creative Work*" in *Miniatures of Criticism*].

16. The first appeared in *Tygodnik Powszechny* 49 and 57 (1945–46).

17. From *Bal w operze* [*Ball at the Opera*].

18. This text (formerly "Słońce Oświęcimia") was printed with small changes in *Rozmowa z przyjacielem* and signed: Dachau, 1945.

19. From the cycle of love poems, "Światło i cień."

20. A poem about his love for Maria with an untranslatable play on the word *droga,* meaning both "dear" and "road."—TRANS.

21. Mankiewicz.

22. One idea that was to facilitate their reuniting.

23. He added to them later.

24. Instead of becoming a "vade mecum," this subject became the basis of a *Reader's Digest*-type periodical, *Ziemia i Ludzie,* only the first issue of which was published—the American one (Munich, May 1946).

25. As can be seen, this term was thrown around recklessly.

26. Stanisław Wygodzki.

27. The periodical consisted of politicians' remarks, essays by philosophers and journalists, short stories, and anecdotes from American life—all in Borowski's translation.

28. Jerzy Pietrkiewicz (b. 1916) was connected with *Prosto z mostu* [*Straight from the Bridge*] before the war. He was an émigré professor of Polish and East European studies and a writer of prose and essays, usually in English (under the simplified spelling: Peterkiewicz).

29. In the United States.

30. The only postage stamps from the camps went into circulation and became a philatelic sensation, bringing enormous profit to the Polish Red Cross. Girs managed to free three of his young coworkers from Freimann in order to produce them.

31. C. T. H. de Coster's novel, *The Legend of Ulenspiegel,* based on a sixteenth-century legend, became the symbol of the Flemish resistance movement against Spanish domination.

32. Written in English.—TRANS.

33. See the poem "Kąpiel w Izarze" ["A Bath in the Isar"], whose last stanza reads, "Stormy, overgrown / like the Danube River / I gaze into the water. Remember: / water, German water."

34. See the story "Opera/Opera" in *Kamienny świat.*—TRANS.

35. *Poszukiwania: Tracing.*—TRANS.

36. Stanisław Lam (1891–1965), a literary historian and critic. Between the wars he was an editor not at Gebethner but at Trzask, Evert, and Michalski; he developed the department of encyclopedias and compendia. After the war, he remained in Paris, where at the Ksiegarnia Polska [Polish Bookshop], not at the library, he continued his émigré work.

37. Cil Loebel, a Romanian Jew, settled in France from where she was transported

to Auschwitz. In the camp, she became friendly with a group of Jews and Poles. She returned to Paris after the war.

38. An error; not Saint, but Sacre-Coeur.

39. Out of this comfort and idleness in Munich came three books and a tremendous flow of poetry.

40. Owners of Warsaw bookstores, open during the occupation, which clandestinely sold illegal publications.

41. Jadwiga Łobzowksa, Grydzewski's niece.

42. Wiśka's brother.

43. Ludwik Łobzowski, husband of Grydzewski's sister, Aniela, and legal guardian of Rundo's daughters (he managed their grandfather's graphics firm until it was requisitioned by the Germans).

44. Janina Sawiczewska, partner in the grandfather's printing shop, headed the bookkeeping department.

45. Paweł Rundo, Tuśka's father's cousin, director of the Rada Miejska [City Council] in Łódź.

46. Stanisław Rundo, another cousin, member of the Rada Adwokacka [Law Council] in Warsaw.

47. Wanda Rundo, the father's cousin.

48. Bolesława Rundo, Rundo's grandfather's cousin.

49. Tuśka worked as a nurse's aid in the hospital in the town of Jönköping.

50. Private tutoring.

51. M. Rundo studied philosophy, Slavonic, and Latin.

52. A foreigner who lacked a certificate of graduation from a *gimnazjium* needed permission from Gustav V to study. (The permit was issued by the royal chancery on the basis of recommendations from three professors. M. Rundo received it as the relative of Przybyszewski.) [Stanisław Przybyszewski (1868–1927), a Bohemian, writer, and editor, revered in "Young Germany" and "Young Scandinavia."—TRANS.]

53. A reference to Grydzewski's forthcoming anthology, *Poezja polska od "Bogu rodzicy" do chwili obecnej* [*Polish Poetry from "Bogurodzica" to the Present*].

54. Arthur Koestler, then a not much known anti-Communist writer.

55. Maria Lasocka (Landau), daughter of M. Grydzewski's cousin, came to Sweden from Ravensbrück.

56. At the beginning of the occupation, she belonged to one of the pre-PPR [Polish Workers' Party] Communist cells; she left when she was asked to prepare a talk about Stalin—as a scholar.

57. Związek Walki Zbrojnej [Union for Armed Struggle].—TRANS.

58. From Tadeusz's father they received radio programs and conspiracy materials first for the ZWZ, later the AK [Home Army], which they printed on the copy machine on Skaryszewska Street.

59. Russian was required for Slavic studies.

60. Tuśka applied for a visa to Belgium, where they had deluded themselves into thinking it would prove easiest to meet.

III. JUNE 1946–JUNE 1949

1. Throughout his correspondence with Borowski, Żółkiewski uses the Communist second-person plural form of address.—TRANS.

2. A group of Catholic poets (founders: J. Braun, J. Kierst, B. Ostromęcki) publishing in *Odnowa* [*Renewal*] and *Tygodnik Warszawski* [*Warsaw Weekly*].

3. This was not the first show of interest in the young by *Kuźnica*'s editor. Żółkiewski had earlier come out with a strong attack, "O młodszym bracie pamflet" ["Pamphlet about a Younger Brother"] (vol. 9, 1946). Now he was making a positive proposal.

4. A word play on the Polish word "*droga.*"—TRANS.

5. *Pokolenie,* issued by the ZWM publisher Płomień [or Flame; not to be confused with the socialist journal by that name in wartime], began appearing on September 25, 1946.

6. Jerzy Piórkowski (1924–90), pseud. Chram during the occupation, was shot and severely injured during the Uprising. In 1958, he was the main editor, after Woroszylski, of *Nowa Kultura* and from 1959 to 1976 of the monthly *Polska,* whose success was rewarded with dismantlement by the Party. He was the author of a collection of stories, *Niepodleglii* [*The Unconquered*], and a collection of historical sketches, *Warszawska lekcja europejskiej kultury* [*The Warsaw Lesson in European Culture*] (the title sketch deals with Baczynski's and Borowski's creative work).

7. Barbara Bormann, a student of Polish and a theater director, was the second wife of Marczak-Oborski; later she married Prof. Stefan Żółkiewski.

8. Untranslatable play on "*droga*" again.

9. See "Bitwa pod Grunwaldem."—TRANS.

10. "Death of an Insurgent" appeared in *Kuźnica* 33 and was reprinted in *Pożegnanie z Marią.*

11. "A Day at Harmenz" and "This Way for the Gas, Ladies and Gentlemen."
—TRANS.

12. In thinking about their own journal, Marczak and Borowski are calling on the wartime *Droga* (1943–44), of which only four issues—but very thoughtful and significant ones—actually came out (and in addition three "poetry leaflets"). Together with the publishing house Płomień, it brought together leftist, lay, and antinationalist youth (Krzysztof and Barbara Baczyński, Ewa Pohoska, Karol Lipiński, Jan Jósef Szczepański, and others). As a manifesto for the new journal, Marczak even proposed reprinting E. Pohoska's leading article of occupation-era *Droga* (a mature creative program, distancing itself from ideologically and politically controlled literature) as well as two poetic texts: Borowski's tract "O poezji i poecie" ("To be a poet—means to say no to the world") and his poem "O rozumienie" ("Dusk will be less black, if you look into it with a flame"). The new reality did not favor these plans.

13. Andrzej Jakimowicz (1919–92), an artist and critic at the time, later a professor of the history of art at Warsaw University.

14. Kapist was the name by which students of the artist J. Pankiewicz were known.

15. The Kraków group Inaczej [Otherwise], founded by T. Jęczalik and A. Włodek, consisting of people from the literary supplement of *Dziennik Polski* [*Polish Daily*], and, later, the periodical *Inaczej* (including W. Machejek, T. Sokół, W. Szymborska).

16. Examining the problem of political émigrés, Osmańczyk drew on two poems constituting a poetic dialogue, T. Borowski's "Jeżeli sie nie zrozumiemy, kolego, chlopcze z emigracji" ["If we do not understand each other, colleague, boy of emigration"] and J. Rostworowski's "Most" ["The Bridge"], *Przekrój* 67 (1946).

17. See letter 2 in appendix A.—TRANS.

18. Janusz Nel Siedlecki's friend in Auschwitz; she appears in "Fire Freezes" *(We Were in Auschwitz)*.—TRANS.

19. Zbigniew Folejewski, a poet, literary historian, and linguist from Wilno. From 1937 in Stockholm, then in Uppsala; since the 1950s, Polish literature specialist on the Nobel Prize committee.

20. Ministry of Foreign Affairs (National Armed Forces?).

21. He's referring to Jarosław Iwaszkiewicz (1894–1980), poet and novelist.—TRANS.

22. "Puppy" was the nickname given to Borowski by Girs.

23. The letter was unfortunately lost.

24. Anatol Girs.

25. Juliusz Panek, a prewar Polish judge, was in Dautmergen with Girs and became director of the Polish Red Cross Committee in Munich.—TRANS.

26. Girs's editorial works of art, devoted to two fifteenth-century figures: Stanisław Polak, a printer in Seville, and Wawrzyniec Goślicki, a liberal bishop and diplomat.

27. Anatol Girs was a Christian Scientist.—TRANS.

28. "Fire Freezes."—TRANS.

29. *Listy spod morwy* (1945) is a book by Gustaw Morcinek (1891–1963) about his experiences in Sachsenhausen and Dachau.—TRANS.

30. Graphic work by Anatol Girs.

31. A friend of Borowski's from wartime classes, Wanda Leopold became an assistant in the Polish department at Wrocław University.

32. Legendary Polish nobleman and alchemist.—TRANS.

33. The philological event of the day was the reconstruction by Prof. Wacław Borowy of the facsimile of the manuscript of "Vade-Mecum" (1947).

34. During the occupation, of course, probably at the recommendation of Prof. Witold Suchodolski and an older colleague in the course, Dionez Janiszewski (a Dominican).

35. T. Borowski, S. Marczak-Oborski, "Pamflet na starszych braci" ["Lampoon on Older Brothers"], *Pokolenie* 3 (1947, 9). A repartee on Żółkiewski's lampoon on the young, it was narrower and limited to literature ("The Apocalypse came and went, and in literature there's peace").

36. In English in the original.—TRANS.

37. A piece on J. Dobraczyński's novel, *W rozwalonym domu* [*In a Ruined House*], entitled "W oczach i uszach Courths-Mahlerowej" ["In the Eyes and Ears of Mrs. Courths-Mahler"], *Kuźnica* 49 (1946).

38. Novel by S. Żeromski.—TRANS.

39. In the end, the young people's issue [*Kuźnica* 49 (1946)] appeared with a long introduction by S. Żółkiewski. It consisted of the work of fifteen young poets (from Anna Kamieńska to Wiktor Woroszylski), prose (Czeszko, Piórkowski), journalism (Hanna Kulągowska), and criticism (Lech Budrecki). The central points of the issue were two things by Borowski: "Bitwa pod Grunwaldem" (section 1) and the piece on Dobraczyński. The youth issue was undoubtedly a major event, it united the youth with *Kuźnica;* however, despite Żółkiewski's efforts, it did not lead to periodic collaboration, nor to a deeper understanding with the younger generation.

40. Throughout the letter, he uses the Communist second-person plural form of address.—TRANS.

41. Bolesław Piasecki (1915–79), a politician and journalist. Leader of the ONR [National Radical Camp]; during the war, commander of the Konfederacja Narodu [National Federation]. In 1944, arrested by the NKVD. Freed, he published and edited, by agreement with the PPR, *Dziś i jutro* [*Today and Tomorrow*], and from 1954 directed the PAX Society. From 1965, a member of the Sejm, and from 1971 also a member of the Rada Państwa [National Council]. He wrote *Zagadnienia istotne* [*Relevant Issues*] and *Instynkt państwowy* [*National Instinct*].

42. On a literary Thursday in Wrocław, Borowski read the complete text of "Bitwa pod Grunwaldem," which had been published in excerpts in *Kuźnica*, and which, as Mikulski said of it, "took place again in the Polish camp in Germany." The work created a huge row, as did everything he was writing at the time.

43. A literary-critical quarterly from Wrocław from 1947 to 1952, by, in addition to Mikulski, Anna Kowalska, a Lwów writer (the first issues were mainly prepared by Jerzy Kowalski, her husband and coauthor and a professor of classical philology); the editorial secretaries were current students: T. Lutogniewski, J. Pierzchała, C. Hernas, and J. Gawałkiewicz.

44. Zofia Mikulska née Skrzędziewska (1907–77), married 1933; she looked after the publications and also published the work of her husband, who died young.

45. "Chłopiec z Biblia" (printed in *Zeszyty Wrocławskie* 2 [1974]), a short tale from Pawiak, combining autobiographical elements with the story of an eighteen-year-old cell companion, Zbigniew Namokel, whose bunk in the Auschwitz hospital Borowski occupied the day after Namokel's death.

46. The Golden Age—the days of Saturn—is a frequent motif in Borowski's occupation poetry. To oppose the nightmares of the time, the Essentialists tried to cultivate poetry, learning, friendship, and love.

47. A free interpretation, without foundation in the character of the hero.

48. Związek Zawodowy Literatów Polskich, or Union of Professional Polish Writers.—TRANS.

49. Jerzy Morawski, PPR activist since 1942, was editor of the *Trybuna Wolności* [*Tribune of Freedom*] during the occupation. Then in the directorship of ZWM [Fighting Youth Union], to which the publishers of *Płomień* belonged. Next, he held many responsible functions in the PZPR [Polish United Workers'

Party] and was counted as one of the so-called young Turks, in other words, a revisionist of the younger generation.

50.   The reaction to the piece against Z. Kossak-Szczucka's *Z otchłanie* [*From the Abyss*], entitled "Alicja krainie czarów" ["Alice in Wonderland"] (*Pokolenie* 1, 1947) was the culminating point of the attack on Borowski. *Dziś i Jutro* demanded his being tried as a war criminal, or, at the very least, being thrown out of the Union of Polish Writers for slander.

51.   In the Communist underground during the war, Tuśka and Tadeusz were arrested in the apartment of Maria and Czesław Mankiewicz. After the war, Maria was a journalist for *Kobieta i życie* [*Woman and Life*]. Czesław was in the army. When he was arrested in connection with rightist-nationalist leanings, Borowski (after a row with Hoffman) intervened with Berman on his behalf. He was later the head of Obrona Powietrzna Państwa [National Air Defense], with the rank of general.

52.   Eliza Orzeszkowa (1841–1910), a leading writer of the Polish Positivist period. —TRANS.

53.   Jan Bolesław Ożóg, b. 1913.

54.   T. Borowski, "Droga do kresu—czego?" ["Road to the End—of What?"], *Pokolenie* 4, 1947 (11). Żółkiewski's raptures were inopportune; *Pokolenie* was closed down with this issue.

55.   Probably "Portret przyjaciela" ["Portrait of a Friend"], printed in the first issue of *Nurt*.

56.   Russian for "dear one."—TRANS.

57.   Unfinished sketch found among his papers after his death. Borowski's views on the literature of war and occupation found their broadest expression here; printed in *Utwory zebrane* [*Collected Works* 3] (1944).

58.   Aussen-Kommando—Girs has in mind here not so much the groups of prisoners working outside the camp (as in "A Day at Harmenz"), but rather the small subcamps (e.g., Dautmergen) about which Borowski wanted to write separately.

59.   Oficyna Warszawska na Obczyznie, Girs's publishing company in Munich.

60.   Antoni Gołubiew (1907–79), Catholic writer.—TRANS.

61.   Stefan Kisielewski's controversial first novel, published in 1947.—TRANS.

62.   Literally true. The delivery of Borowski's first stories from Munich to *Twórczość* came into the hands of Mach, editorial secretary. As is known, the college was divided on the issue of the stories, and their publication was in doubt. (In the end they were published with a note, in which the editors distanced

themselves from them morally—see K. Wyka's information in *Ucieczka z kamiennego swiata* [1992, 145]. Throughout the controversy, Mach was the author's warmest supporter.

63. Paracelsus, actually Theophrastus Bombastus von Hohenheim, a fifteenth-century German doctor, naturalist, and philosopher, alchemist and chemist, was one of the precursors of contemporary medicine. He was the model for the Faust legend.

64. Pola Kossobudzka, a mathematician, worked in Munich at the Polish Red Cross Committee with Girs.—TRANS.

65. It did not appear in the two published issues.

66. The first, and only, edition of *We Were in Auschwitz* in Poland (without Girs's foreword and "Auschwitz Terms") was published by MON publishers in 1958.

67. Russian epic, "The Lay of Igor's Campaign."—TRANS.

68. Figures from Polish folklore.—TRANS.

69. Krystyna Zamoyska, author of *Have You Forgotten* (New York: 1989). Worked at the Polish Red Cross in Munich. Girs nicknamed her Miss Piggy because, as a result of wartime hunger, she ate immoderately in Munich.—TRANS.

70. *War of the Monks,* by Ignacy Krasicki, 1778.—TRANS.

71. AZWM students' paper *Zycie* (transformed into *Po prostu* [*Simply*] in the period of the October Revolution).

72. *Nurt* did not publish Koestler.

73. Statistics somewhat manipulated to make the point, and restricted to the youngest on *Kuźnica.* Anyway, as one knows, it's not just birthdates that contribute to generational awareness.

74. In question was the little book *Pewien żołnierz: Opowieści szkolne* [*A Certain Soldier: School Stories*], Płomien, 1947, which the professor didn't yet know.

75. T. Borowski—"Portret przyjaciela" ["Portrait of a Friend"] (about Trzebiński) *Nurt* 1 (October 1947).

76. Original title of *Kamienny świat.*

77. Stanisław Helsztyński was a professor of English and American literature at the University of Warsaw; he shortly published two collections of essays: *Od Fieldinga do Steinbecka* (*From Fielding to Steinbeck*) and *Ave Roosevelt. Panorama amerykanska* (*Ave Roosevelt: American Panorama*).

78. This Horatian question—"What will remain of us?"—pursued Borowski relentlessly. He connects many books and poems to his definitive response in the wartime "Pieśń."

79. The main character in Bolesław Prus's *Lalka* [*Doll*], 1890.—TRANS.

80. Józef Morton (1911–94), one of the main writers of the "peasant theme," was the author of *Spowiedź* [*Confession*] and *Apasionata* [*Apassionata*].

81. See Letter 8 in appendix A.—TRANS.

82. Christian Science.—TRANS.

83. Indeed, from after the war until October 1956, apart from translations, Wat published practically nothing. On the whole, however, especially as it emerged after his death, his literary output (both in Poland and in emigration) was considerable.

84. Written in English.—TRANS.

85. This was the first event of this kind, organized by MKiS [Ministry of Culture and Art] for thirty young writers. Its double intent shone through, it seems: quelling discontent by pointing out sources of income (radio, film, translations, etc.) and political machination (fueling generational animosity), which contributed to the breakthrough of socialist realism.

86. *Za wam pójdą inni* [*Others Will Follow You*], dir. A. Bohdziewicz, screenplay J. Kott, W. Żółkiewska, 1949.

87. At the time, Rudnicki was the most vocal writer on the Holocaust, the author of *Szekspir* [*Shakespeare*] and *Ucieczka z Jasnej Polany* [*Escape from Jasna Polana*] as well as the collected works *Żywe i martwe morze* [*Living and Dead Sea*].

88. *Nurt* lasted for an even shorter time than *Pokolenie,* scarcely two issues, but it left its mark. The reason for its demise was ostensibly Rafael Molski's review (under the pseudonym Henryk Zarowski) of Adam Schaff's *Wstęp do teorii marksizmu* [*Introduction to Marxist Theory*], accusing him of conservatism and lack of scholarship. A different version has it that the closing of *Nurt* was caused by the inclusion in issue 2 of a late photograph of Lenin as a laughing paralytic in a rocking chair.

89. A friend's unknown "offenses."

90. Jerzy Pelc, a student of Polish studies and logic and a professor of logical semantics at the University of Warsaw.

91. *Porwanie w Tiutiurlistanie* and *Piorkiem flaminga* by W. Żukrowski— grotesque fantasy for children and adults.

92. Henryk Markiewicz, a literary theorist and specialist in Polish Positivism, was a pillar of Polish studies in Wrocław and IBL [Institute of Literary Research] and a reviewer for *Odrodzenie* and *Twórczość*.

93. Central Committee, Polish Workers' Party.

94.   The main hero of Kazimierz Brandys's novel *Samson* (1948), Jakub Gold is standing in for the author here.

95.   As quickly turned out, this was in preparation for getting rid of Borejsza (Bratny also) and linking *Odrodzenie* with *Kuźnica* to pave the way for socialist realism.

96.   In English in the original.—TRANS.

97.   Doubtless at Żółkiewski's prompting—in connection with the tensions existing between *Kuźnica* and the young writers, as evidenced also in the following letter—a *Kuźnica* evening took place at the Klub Młodych [Young People's Club].

98.   Hanna Golde, a student, then a journalist, friend of M. Buczkówna; prototype for the heroine of Rudnicki's *Pałeczki*.

99.   Miłosz's "Traktat moralny" (1947), prophesying the gloomy perspective of Stalinism, managed to appear in *Twórczość* 7 (1948).

100. A writer's evening for T. Różewicz in the Warsaw Klub Młodych Artystów i Naukowców [Young Artists and Scholars Club], which Borowski ran at the time.

101. Jasienica twice spoke on the issue of Borowski's review of Z. Kossak-Szczucka's Auschwitz memoir. The first time he upheld, and even broadened, the accusations of *Dziś i Jutro,* to which the author reacted by sending him two books in a row: *We Were in Auschwitz* and *Farewell to Maria.* After reading them, Jasienica in his article "Spowiedź udreczonych" ["Confession of the Tormented"] (*TP* [*Tygodnik Powszechny*] 40, 1947) not only changed his mind about the review, but generally stood up in defense of Borowski's creative work. His voice, like S. Kisielewski's polemics in *Dziś i Jutro,* had a serious impact on the fate of the controversy about Borowski.

102. Stanisława Sowińska (Barbara), *Lata walki* [*Years of Fighting*], reviewed by Borowski under the title "Małe i wielkie legendy" ["Small and Great Legends"] in *Odrodzenie* 9 (1948).

103. Jerzy Turowicz's attitude toward Borowski was similar. After Borowski's death, he wrote: "He was our avowed opponent; despite that, we say farewell to him today with sorrow, not only as an excellent writer whose parting is an irretrievable loss, but also a man who with all the passion and vehemence of his temperament sought the truth, fought for human issues, believing that that fight would make impossible the return of the 'times of contempt' (reprinted in "Kalendarium," *Tygodnik Powszechny* 6 [1999]).

104. For some reason Borowski replaced Różewicz at the club soiree.

105. The cycle of stories from *Kamienny świat,* rejected by *Kuźnica,* appeared in *Nowiny Literackie* 21–24 (May–June 1948).

106. At the end of the first, title story of *Kamienny świat,* the author announced "I plan to write a great, immortal epic work," and this was not, as will soon be made clear, a complete bluff.

107. Wolność i Niepodległość [Freedom and Independence] was an anti-Soviet and anti-Communist underground organization.—TRANS.

108. ZAiKS was first located in Sobieszów, then quickly liquidated.

109. W. Leopold sent the writer a clipping from *Panorama,* "Najkrótsze nowelki" ["The Shortest Stories"] about a game in the overseas press based on making up stories in a few sentences, and she gave him a sample of eighty-six possible varieties (e.g., gastronomical, political-educational, reviews, on a hunchback, etc.) that were in his area of interest—the possibilities of the "short story."

110. Wyka's review of *Pożegnanie z Marią,* entitled "Gdziekolwiek ziemia jest snem" ["Wherever the World Is a Dream"], *Odrodzenie* 23 (1948), reprinted in *Pogranicze powieście* [*Borders of the Novel*].

111. Story entitled "January Offensive," printed in *Odrodzenie* 45 (1948).

112. I published the unfinished story about Wacław Bojarski, entitled "Zostawcie umarlych w spokoju" ["Leave the Dead in Peace"], in *Polityka* 37 (1965).

113. Russian for "The Russian Question."—TRANS.

114. "Ojczyzna" ["Fatherland"], a story of medium quality (in the author's estimation). Violent conversations in a train between the victors on a German battlefield; the actual words of the awkward fragment read: "they bring up old clothes, ideas, women," *Zeszyty* 3 (1948).

115. Discussion about the text of the libretto to the opera *Janko Muzykant* (based on H. Sienkiewicz's story), cowritten by Borowski and Wygodzki. The world premiere with music by Witold Rudziński took place in 1953 at the Silesian Opera in Bytom.

116. Hieronim E. Michalski, literary critic, publisher; at the time, Director of the Department of Literature and the Book, at MKiS [Ministry of Culture and Art]. Immediately after returning from the sanatorium in Germany in April 1947, Wygodzki became his replacement.

117. The previous secretary of the POP PZPR [Basic Party Organization, Polish United People's Party] writers in Warsaw was Wanda Żółkiewska.

118. Institut Badan Literackich, or Institute of Literary Research.—TRANS.

119. His friend did not take his suggestions. W. Leopold's review (*Kuźnica* 39

[1948])—next to P. Jasienica and W. Szymborska—penetrated most deeply into the author's premises.

120. In the then most prestigious *Odrodzenie* prize, which in 1948 was finally given to Andrzejewski's novel *Popiol i diament* [*Ashes and Diamonds*], *Pożegnanie z Marią* received a mention. On the front page of the journal, next to photographs of Andrzejewski, Adolf Rudnicki, Boguszewski, Pryszyński, and Lucjan Rudnicki appeared a postcamp photograph of Borowski.

121. Wiktor Woroszyłski.

122. In the poem "Na odwrocie nekrologu Wincentego Pstrowskiego" ["On the Other Side of Wincent Pstrowski's Necrology"], Woroszyłski called political poets—Bratny, Gruszczyński, T. Kubiak—into competition ("Dziennik Literacki" ["Literary Daily"], supplement to *Dziennik Polski* [*Polish Daily*] 30 [1948]).

123. T. Borowski, "Redagujemy gazete Kongresu" ["We Edit the Congress Newspaper"], *Zeszyty Wrocławskie* 3 (1948). "Formally, Borowski was then the assistant to the editor in chief," W. Wirpsza adds in *Nowa Kultura*, "actually he was everything: editor in chief, translator, proofreader, night editor, compositor, errand boy."

124. Jerzy Borejsza (1905–52), president of Czytelnik, was the initiator and the head of the Swiatowy Kongres Intelektualistów [World Congress of Intellectuals].

125. The German letters about the trip to Berlin were translated by Anna Krzemińska.

126. Rafael Glucksmann, graphic artist and publisher, was at the time the director of the Biuro Wydawnicze Czytelnik, where Borowski published *Kamienny świat*.

127. At the Polish studies students conference in Łódź (end of October 1948), devoted to the Twenty Years of Independence, Borowski was respondent to a paper and gave a speech against the "dirty war" in Vietnam.

128. Review of Prof. Konrad Górski's *Poezja jako wyraz* [*Poetry as Expression*], *Pamiętnik Literacki* [*Literary Journal*], 1947.

129. Because of the poem "Plemnik w spodniach" ["Spermatazoon in trousers"], S. R. Dobrowolski disqualified Różewicz's second volume *Czerwona rękawiczka* [*The Red Glove*] (*Kronika tygodniowa* [*Weekly Chronicle*] 48 [1948]).

130. From November 18 to 21, Borowski, probably at the invitation of the Klub 13 [!] Muz [Club of the 13 Muses] made several appearances: at the club, in the cultural center of Huta Szczecin, and other workplaces. Out of these activities, and reactions to them, came the journalistic-reportage story "Zabawa z wódką"

["Social with Vodka"] (*Odrodzenie* 50 [1948]), which, apart from offering profiles of three "upholders of civilization," contained two ideas directed at two different targets: the official demand of writers that they eschew elitism and the markedly more indulgent demand that workers renounce "socials with vodka."

131. As a result of finalizing and revising *Rdza*.

132. Jan Kott restricted his "structure of the human fate" at the time to sociology.

133. *Kamienny świat* was neither; it was foremost an extension of "concentration camp reality" into the postwar period.

134. "Puntek" was the nickname of their son, Aleksander Wirpsza. Later a poet and literary critic writing under the pseudonym Leszek Szaruga.

135. Perhaps Elga Gundela Kern, an anti-fascist writer living in Germany before the war. Interested at the time in Poland and feminism. She attempted to get permission for a translation of *Nocy i dni* [*Nights and Days*], which she did not receive; her bibliography included the unpublished translation, *Tage und Nachte* (1934).

136. Lidia Wirpsza.

137. Matuszewki's review—after Sandauer's attack "Sprawa Borowskiego i innych" ["The Case of Borowski and Others"]—carried, in the end, the title "The Art of Minor Forms, or, In the Case of Borowski," *Kuźnica* 3 (1948).

138. Jan Aleksander Król, editor of *Chłopi* [*Peasants*] and *Wsi* [*Villages*]. Despite the passage of time, he continued to conduct himself like a partisan, sporting breeches, thigh boots, a pistol, and, as in the well-known partisan song, he came from "the Góry Świętokrzyskie" [the Świętokrzyskie Mountains].

139. In 1948, Prof. Tadeusz Mikulski received the city's literary prize for *Spotkania wrocławskie* [*Wrocław Meetings*].

140. To Żółkiewski as fighter for realism he dedicated "Opowiadanie z prawdziwego świata" ["Story from the Real World"], to Żukrowski "Lato w miasteczku" ["Summer in a Small Town"], in whose landscape a priest and wits play the main parts.

141. He is talking about S. Wygodzki's *Pamietnik miłosci* (1948). Borowski assisted at its birth in Germany, he did not write the review.

142. For the Kongres Zjednoczeniowy PPR-PPS [Polish Workers' and Polish Socialist Parties Unification Congress], Borowski wrote, probably for PAP [Polish Press Agency] a popular article, "Oddamy kulturę masom ludowym" ["We'll Give Culture Back to the Working Classes"] printed in many papers.

143. Congress of the Polish United Workers' Party.—TRANS.

144. He's alluding to the socialist anthem "Armaty pod Stoczkiem" ["Gunfire near Stoczek"] in which the peasants in the Stoczek area stage an armed revolution while the gentlemen in town smoke cigars and pontificate.—TRANS.

145. Everything points to this being about the secretaryship at the Szczecin Conference (where the main speaker, Minister Sokorski, while not naming him, unambiguously referred to Borowski as "a dangerous phenomenon, sometimes even positively harmful"). If the placement of this letter is on target, Borowski followed the advice of the secretary to the POP writers in this matter: he acted as conference secretary and appeared as secretary in official matters, but said not a word from the rostrum about literature and publicly railed against Sokorski's hypocrisy.

146. By Grzegorz Zaleski.

147. A liberal-democratic literary weekly edited by J. Iwaszkiewicz, published in Warsaw 1947–48.—TRANS.

148. Ministry of Foreign Affairs.—TRANS.

149. A reference to the Szczecin literary conference, of course.

150. Vereinigung der Verfolgten des Naziregimes.—TRANS.

151. See letter 9 in appendix A.—TRANS.

152. Phrase written in English.—TRANS.

153. Phrase written in English.—TRANS.

154. "Sea Horse" was Borowski, Olszewski, and Girs's name for Siedlecki in Munich.—TRANS.

155. Phrase written in English.—TRANS.

156. Russian for "will get there."—TRANS.

157. Anatolij W. Sofronow, poet and dramatist, was a delegate of the Union of Soviet Writers to the Szczecin meeting.

158. Lucjan Rudnicki (1882–1968) was a prose writer, journalist, political activist in the workers' party.

159. Jan Rojewski, an architect; wrote for stage and screen after the war. He emigrated to Israel in 1957.

160. "Elegia prowincjonalna" ["Provincial Elegy"], *Twórczość* (1949, 1).

161. Circa 1465, first Polish vernacular poet.—TRANS.

162. Jan Andrzej Morsztyn (1613–93).—TRANS.

163. *People's News,* a Czech newspaper from Prague.—TRANS.

164. *Słowo* probably reprinted from *Rzeczypospolita* [*The Republic*] Borowski's column

from the cycle "Nasz wiek XX—Our Twentieth Century," which was collected in *Opowiadania z ksiazek i gazet* [*Stories from Books and Papers*] (1949).

165. *We Were in Auschwitz.*

166. The last line of Ignacy Krasicki's poem "Przyjaciele" ["Friends"], meaning that people who seem to be friends really aren't.—TRANS.

167. W. Wirpsza, "Traktat polemiczny" ["Polemical Tract"] in *Polemiki i pieśnie* [*Polemics and Songs*], 1951, with a nod to Miłosz's art. Wirpsza countered his diagnosis—instead of "jądra ciemności" ["the center of darkness"], he prophesied, "I w dniu dzisiejszym ocalenie/I w dniu dzisiejszym jutro błyska" ["And on this day salvation/And on this day tomorrow shines"].

168. In addition to *Kamenneho sveta,* published in a book in 1966, Teigova with her daughter M. Stachova translated *Pożegnanie z Marią* as *Rozlouceni s Marii* (1987).

169. *Ucieczka z Jasnej Polany* (1949) was the second volume of Rudnicki's stories from *Epoka pieców* [*Epoch of Ovens*].

170. T. Borowski, "Szukam prawdy o 'Antygonie' " ["I Seek the Truth About 'Antigone' "], *Odrodzenie* (1949, 16–17).

171. The reference is to "Kłopoty pani Doroty" ["Miss Dorothy's Problems"]; the author published this story only after returning from Berlin, in *Nowa Kultura* 13–14 (1950).

172. Jan Hus (1369–1415), a religious thinker and reformer from Bohemia.—TRANS.

IV. JUNE 1949–JULY 3, 1951

1. Ministerstwo Spraw Zagranicznych, or Ministry of Foreign Affairs.—TRANS.

2. Edmund Jan Osmańczyk (1914–89), a community activist and journalist. Before the war, he was active in Opolszczyzna and served as director of the Press Headquarters of the Union of Poles in Germany. During the war, he worked in the secret Home Army radio, and was a war correspondent during the battle over Berlin, then at the Potsdam Conference and the Nuremberg Trials. As a foreign correspondent, he specialized in the area of Central Europe and America. He served as a two-term Sejm representative and a member of the Rada Panstwowa [State Council] (1979–80), before becoming a senator in 1989. He is the author of *Sprawy Polaków* [*Polish Matters*] (1948), *Rzeczypospolitej Polaków* [*Polish Republic Poles*] (1977), *Polska-Rosja* [*Poland-Russia*] (N.Y., 1989), and foreign encyclopedias. In Germany, he became friends with Borowski, whom he wrote about in *Sprawy Polaków* and in

the brochure "Publicystyka w kraju budujacym socjalizm" ["Journalism in a Country Building Socialism"] (1953).

3. Borowski and Osmanczyk, together with the Polish delegation (Leon Kruczkowski, Aleksander Wat, Adam Ważyk), took part in celebrations for the bicentennial of Goethe's birthday in Weimar.

4. Wiktor Woroszyłski—*Smierci nie ma! Poezje* [*Death Doesn't Exist: Poems*], 1949; *Weekend Mister Smitha* [*Mr. Smith's Weekend*], 1949; *Satires and Epigrams,* 1949; *Noc Komunarda. Poemat* [*Communard's Night*], 1949; *Szkola dwustu milionow* [*School of Two Hundred Million*], 1950; S. Kirsanow—*Niebo nad ojczyzna* [*Night Over the Fatherland*], 1949.

5. From the A. Wat archive at the Beinecke Rare Book Library at Yale University in New Haven, Connecicut.

6. The factory described in *Ucieczka Lotha* [*Loth's Escape*]; an allusion to the continuation of the writing of this novel in Venice?

7. On October 7, 1949, the establishment of the German Democratic Republic was proclaimed. For further observations about the last period of Borowski's life, see the A. Wat biographical notes.

8. In the Polish cultural chronicle, in the report on Szczecin, Stanisław Telega (*Twórcość* 9 [1949]) noted that since the evening at Klub 13 Muz (already renamed Swietlica Artystyczna [Artistic Community Center]) when the writer's opponents were accused of reactionaryism, all literary discussions and altercations ended. Referring to "Zabawa z wódką," he added that no collaboration with workers' community centers had developed either.

9. E. Osmańczyk, "*Niemcy* w Berlinie" ["*The Germans* in Berlin"], *Odrodzenie* (1949, 46); a discussion of Kruczkowski's play against the backdrop of newer German national drama. The added epilogue was wrong, according to Osmańczyk.

10. Komitet Centralny, or Central Committee.—TRANS.

11. At the Third Plenary Assembly of PZPR the newly appointed Marshal Rokossowski was included; Gomułka, Kliszka, and Spychalski, however, were removed. They were accused of employing "old double-dealers" of whom Włodzimierz Lechowicz was supposedly one.

12. Przedsiębiorstwo Państwowe, or State Enterprise.—TRANS.

13. The Third Plenary Session of the Polish United Workers' Party (November 1949) became sensitized to "infiltration of agents."

14. Stefan Żółkiewski.—TRANS.

15. Paweł Hoffman (1903–78) was a KPP [Communist Party of Poland] activist before the war, translator of Marx, and a journalist; after the war, he was director

of the Wydział Kultury [Dept. of Culture] of the KC PZPR and editor of *Nowa Kultura*, from which he was fired in 1955 for publishing "Poemat dla dorosłych" ["Poem for Adults"] by Adam Ważyk.

16. Kuźnica and *Odrodzenie*, however, were closed down at the beginning of 1950, and in the place of the two previous cultural weeklies, *Nowa Kultura* was established under the editorship of Hoffman. It was he who brought in Borowski, who shortly became the journal's leading figure as a columnist ("Mała Kronika" ["Small Chronicle"]) and journalist.

17. Natan Silber was Polish literature editor at PIW.

18. Kajetan Sosnowski was an abstract artist, mainly a geometric-colorist. He received international fame for his artistic design for the main room in the Palais des Nations in Geneva.

19. A reference to *Pałeczka, czyli każdemu to, na czym mu najmniej zależy* [*A Wand, in Other Words, to Each What Matters Least*] (1950), which is called a novel, though it is more a long love story.

20. The story "On the Setting of the Sun" appeared in the weekly *Radio i Świat* [*The Radio and the World*] and, under a different title, expanded, in the volume *Miejsce urodzenia* [*Place of Birth*], PIW [Polski Instytut Wydawniczy, or National Publishing Institute], 1953.

21. Klub Dobrej Książki i Klub *Odrodzenie* [Good Book Club and *Odrodzenie* Club], fashionable at that time and soliciting news—foreign and domestic.

22. T. Borowski, *Opowiadania z książek i gazet* [*Stories from Books and Newspapers*], PIW, 1949.

23. The German means "very important!"—TRANS.

24. "Curiosities of Cultural History."—TRANS.

25. From the time of the seminar for young writers in Nieborów in January 1948, there appeared from time to time in *Odrodzenie* articles about the poetry of the younger generation (A. Słucki, R. Bratny, W. Wirpsza). These articles were so scattered and rare that it's hard to call them a discussion. At this time, Miłosz expressed himself on the same subject—critically, but calmly and without using names.

In *Odrodzenie*, however, on the eve of the conference with Jakub Berman about socialist realism, were published two markedly more general and very polemical texts advocating socialist realism: J. Andrzejewski's "Notatki Wyznania i rozmyślania pisarza" ["The Writer's Confessional and Contemplative Notes"] (urging the authorities to be intolerant with artists) and

W. Woroszyłski's "Baralia o Majakowskiego" ["Mnemonics on Mayakovsky"] (against the poetry of "the old"), both in 1950, no. 5.

26. Reference to a vocal article by Borowski entitled "Rozmowy" ["Conversations"] that *Odrodzenie* published precisely at the time of the conference, in vol. 8, with the headline "Wolna Trybuna" ["Independent Tribune"], containing an unprecedented sectarian attack on many writers (Breza, Kazimierz Brandys, Sandauer, Adolf Rudnicki, Dygat, Czesk, Bocheński) and misguided self-condemnation.

27. T. Borowski, "Mała Kronika," *Nowa Kultura* 4 (1950).

28. Friedrich Wolf (1888–1953), a famous German dramatist, the author of *Cyjankala* and *Professor Mamlock,* was a doctor by profession. An old German Communist, he became an émigré after 1933. Cofounder during the war of ZSRR National Committee's "Free Germany." East German ambassador to Poland 1950–51.

29. A reference to the writing of joint reportage about the Oder-Nyse border, which was never realized.

30. From April 21 to April 24, 1951, Borowski, as a journalist, accompanied B. Bierut on his return visit to East Germany.

31. The young artists' congress also took place in April in Berlin.

32. *Mała kronika wielkich spraw* [*A Small Chronicle About Great Matters*] and *Na przedpolu* [*In the Foreground*].

33. Most probably "Czerwony maj" ["Red May"], a story about F. Dzherzhinsky for a literary anthology on the twenty-fifth anniversary of his death.

34. In connection with the National Peace Plebiscite, the writer made an appeal "Do młodych agitatorów pokóju" ["To Young Agitators for Peace"] in *Sztandar Młodych* [*Banner of Youth*] (1951, 103).

35. The tour of ZLP youth centers in which Borowski took part with J. Putrament lasted from June 5 through June 10.

APPENDIX A

1. Siedlecki's girlfriend in Auschwitz; she appears in the story "Fire Freezes" (*We Were in Auschwitz*).—TRANS.

2. A suburb of Warsaw.—TRANS.

3. In English in the original.—TRANS.

4. In English.—TRANS.

5. *"The Accomplished Senator" of Laurentius Goslicius,* by W. J. Stankiewicz, published by Anatol Girs in Munich in 1946.—TRANS.

APPENDIX B

1. A district of Warsaw.—TRANS.
2. Borowski arrived in Dautmergen on August 23, 1944; on April 7, 1945, he was transported from there to Allach, arriving April 12, 1945.—TRANS.
3. "This Way for the Gas, Ladies and Gentlemen," "A Day at Harmenz," "The People Who Walked On," and "Auschwitz, Our Home (A Letter)."—TRANS.

APPENDIX C

1. Juliusz Kaden-Bandrowski (1885–1944), a novelist and short story writer. —TRANS.
2. The second volume of Brandys's four-volume novel, *Between the Wars* (1948–51).—TRANS.
3. Girs was taken from Warsaw first to Auschwitz; transported August 22, 1944, to Dautmergen; and from there in April 1945 to Dachau-Allach.
4. Jerry Giedroyc (1906–2000), editor of *Polityka* and, in 1947, founder and editor of the Paris-based Polish literary journal *Kultura.*—TRANS.
5. T. Drewnowski's biography of Borowski.—TRANS.
6. POW camp for non-commissioned officers in Nazi Germany.—TRANS.
7. Arts Institute of the Polish Academy of Sciences.—TRANS.
8. Wrocław University was 70 percent destroyed during the Second World War.—TRANS.
9. Also of Schörzingen, subcamp of Natzweiler-Struthof.—TRANS.
10. Cultural Movement.
11. *Cultural Affairs.*
12. Polish Socialist Party (1892–1948).—TRANS.
13. Polish United Workers' Party.
14. "Civitas Christi."
15. Polish expression from Communist days meaning to defect.—TRANS.
16. A Polish Communist literary monthly.—TRANS.
17. Preeminent publisher.
18. Centralna Agencja Fotograficzna (Central Agency of Photography).—TRANS.
19. Antoni Słonimski (1895–1976), preeminent Polish Jewish poet.

20. "Gray Ranks," a cryptonym for the resistance activists within the Polish Boy Scouts Organization.—TRANS.

21. From a Jewish, middle-class family in Łódź, Tuwim was Poland's preeminent poet in the period between the wars and one of the founders of the *Skamander* review. His poems for children, "The Locomotive" and "The Turnip," are classics. When Germany occupied Poland in 1939, Tuwim escaped first to Rio de Janeiro and then New York, returning to Poland at the end of the war.—TRANS.

22. Woroszylski also wrote a biography of Borowski—*O Tadeuszu Borowski, jego życiu i twórczości* [*About Tadeusz Borowski, His Life and Work*], 1955.—TRANS.

23. *Twórczość* published Borowski's "A Day at Harmenz" and, under Olszewski's name, "The Sosnowiec-Będzin Transport" (as "This Way for the Gas, Ladies and Gentlemen" was originally titled) in 1946, dissociating itself from the stories' moral stance.—TRANS.

INDEX OF NAMES

Numbers in boldface refer to biographies.

Kirsanow, Siemion I., 283, 295, 296, 371n4
Kisch, Egon Erwin, 218, 273
Kislelewski, Jan August, 332
Kisielewski, Stefan (Kisiel), 168, 173, 176,
    211–12, 301–2, 325, **332–33,** 362n61,
    365n101
Kisielewski, Zygmunt Jan, 332
Klabund (real name Alfred Henschke), 332
Kleiner, Juliusz, 199
Kleist, Heinrich von, 201
Knuth-Siebenlist, Kurt, 242, **333,** 348n5
Koestler, Arthur, 117, 118, 191, 231, 347n54,
    363n72
Komorowski, Tadeusz Bór, 128, 132
Konopnicka, Maria, 44, 352n37
Konwicki, Tadeusz, 205, 229, 230, 303
Koprowski, Jan, 241
Kornacki, Jerzy, 167
Kossak-Szczucka, Zofia, 55, 162, 174, 178,
    180, 210, 331, 352n35, 362n50, 365n101
Kossobudzka, Pola, 319, 320, 363n64
Kott, Jan, 135, 200, 201, 202, 236, 364n86,
    368n132, 352n28
Kowalewski, Stanisław, 135, 200
Kowalska, Anna, 7, 158, 160, 216, 237, 337,
    361n43
Kowalski, Jerzy, 160, 213, 245, 337, 361n43
Koźniewski, Kazimierz, 136
Krasiński, Zygmunt, 53, 57, 352n28
Kreutz, Edmund, 47, 67
Kreutz, Jerzy, 47, 67, 126, 349n14, 351n17
Kreutz, Piotr, 67
Kreutz, Zofia, née Neugebauer, 351n17
Krleza, Miroslav, 195
Król, Jan Aleksander, 235, 249, 368n138
Kruczkowski, Leon, 43, 278–79, 285, 288,
    333, 351n22, 371n3, 371n9
Krzemińska, Anna, 367n125
Krzyżanowski, Julian, 46, 47, 56, 74, 117,
    127, 161, 273, 340, 341, 351n19
Krzyżanowski, Julian Tadeusz, 341
Kuba. *See* Barthel, Kurt
Kubiak, Tadeusz, 304, 367n122
Kujawski, Edmund, 47, 207, 348n14,
    349n12, 349n14, 350n14
Kulągowska, Hanna, 341, 360n39

Kurecka-Wirpsza, Maria, 232–34, 276–77,
    334
Kurek, Jalu, 124, 136
Kuryluk, Karol, 204, 255, 262, 280, 284
Kuthan, Zbigniew, 125

Lam, Stanisław, 356n36
Laskowska-Szwykowska, Halina, 8, 71–72,
    103, **334,** 353n52
Lasocka, Maria (real name Landau), 117,
    140, 357n55
Lechoń, Jan, 40, 71, 103, 352
Lechowicz, Włodzimierz, 288, 371n11
Lehman, John, 184
Leopold, Stanisław, 335
Leopold, Wanda, xi, 7, 47, 147, 149–50, 155,
    158, 159, 184–85, 188, 192, 194, 195–96,
    198, 199–203, 204–5, 213–14, 219–20,
    281–82, 290–94, 328, **334–35,** 353n57,
    360n31, 366n109, 366n119
Leszczyńska, Barbara, née Rundo, 282,
    355n12
Lewandowska, Bożenna, 303, **335**
Lichański, Stefan, 167
Liebert, Jerzy, 141
Lindsay, Nicholas Vachel, 254, 286
Lipiński, Karol, 47, 359n12
Loebel, Cecil (Cil), 108, 356–57n37
London, Jack, 260
Lukács, György, 282, 285, 288
Lutogniewski, Tadeusz, 361n43

Łobzowska, Ludwik, 113–14, 357n43

Mach, Wilhelm, 168, 171, 172, 173, 175,
    205, 225, 227, 229, 245, **335–36,** 362n62,
    363n62
Machejek, Władysław, 359n15
Mackiewicz, Wincenty, 316, 355n14
Maczek, Stanisław, 338
Malewska, Hanna, 161, 167
Malinowski, Bronisław, 86
Malraux, André, 95, 208
Małek, Felicia. *See* Świdwińska-
    Krzyżanowska, Zofia Maria
Mankiewicz, Czesław, 44, 47, 162, 362n51

Stankiewicz, Władysław, 149, 320, 374n5
Starski, Ludwik, 259, 275
Steinbeck, John, 172, 176, 181
Stempowski, Jerzy, 6, 7
Stępowski, Janusz, 171, 348n4
Stravinsky, Igor, 95
Stroiński, Zdzisław (pseud. Marek
    Chmura), 47, 67, 334
Suchodolski, Witold, 47, 156, 360n34
Szaniawski, Jerzy, 304, 305
Szaruga, Leszek (real name Wirpsza,
    Aleksander), 368n134
Szczęsna, Justyna, 10, 326
Szelążek, Wacław Jerzy, 113
Szelburg-Zarembina, Ewa, 245
Szmydt-Gniewska, Maria, 47, 54
Szor, Dr., 77
Szpalski, Karol, 203
Szulc, Jerzy, 328
Szymborska, Wisława, 359n15, 367n119

Świdwińska-Krzyżanowska, Zofia Maria,
    7, 19, 27, 29, 35, 38, 41, 45, 46, 47, 56,
    62, 70, 78, 79, 83, 93, 99, 110, 146, **341,**
    349n14
Świerzewski, Stefan, 47, 146

Teigova, Helena, née Peszkowa, 224, 247,
    255, **341,** 370n168
Telega, Stanisław, 290, 371n8
Tito (real name Josip Broz), 184, 195
Tolstoy, Aleksey, 181
Tolstoy, Leo, 198
Topornicki, Karol (pseud.). See Gajcy,
    Tadeusz
Trzebińska, Zofia (later Nagabczyńska),
    349n11
Trzebiński, Andrzej (pseud. Stanisław
    Łomień), 38, 45, 47, 67, 70, 72, 334,
    347n2, 363n75
Tucholski, Kurt, 300, 332
Turowicz, Jerzy, 11, 365n103
Tuśka (Maria Berta Rundo). See Borowska,
    Maria Berta, née Rundo
Tuwim, Julian, 95, 141, 176, 177, 245, 298,
    300, **342,** 347n2, 375n21

Valentino, Rudolf, 257
Valery, Paul, 84
Vegas, Carpio Lope Felix de, 208
Verne, Jules, 290
Villon, François, 51, 84
Voranc, 195

Wajda, Andrzej, 327
Wakar, Andrzej, 347n1, 357n1
Walicki, Janusz, 35
Wallace, Henry Agard, 59
Wańkowicz, Melchior, 7, 56
Wat, Aleksander (real name Chwat), 50,
    196, 203, 285, **342–43,** 351n21, 364n83,
    371n3, 371n5, 371n7
Ważyk, Adam, 196, 203, 249, 371n3,
    371–72n16
Wellisz, Leopold, 192
Werfel, Edda, 203
Werner, Andrzej, 326
Wieczorkiewicz, Bronisław, 162
Wierzyński, Kazimierz, 71
Wihan, Bronisław, 38, 47, 49
Wiktor, Jan, 156, 161
Wilczek, Jan, 304
Wilder, Thornton, 58
Wirpsza, Aleksander. See Szaruga, Leszek
Wirpsza, Lidia, 334, 368n136
Wirpsza, Maria, née Kurecka. See Kurecka-
    Wirpsza, Maria
Wirpsza, Witold, 135, 224, 227–28,
    230–31, 232–33, 241, 252, 254, 259,
    283–84, 289–90, 299, **343**
Wiwatowski, Tadeusz, 47, 351n19
Włodek, Adam, 135, 359n15
Wnuk, Włodzimierz, 175
Wójcik, J. B., 331
Wolf, Friedrich, 304, 373n28
Wölfflin, Heinrich, 58
Woroszylski, Wiktor 13, 220, 257–59, 262,
    264, 277, 282–83, 284–85, 286, 287–89,
    295–97, 299, 300, 304, 305, **343–44,**
    358n6, 360n39, 367nn121–22, 371n4,
    372–73n25, 375n22
Wygodzka, Anka, née Dąb, 351n20
Wygodzka, Inka, 351n20

TADEUSZ DREWNOWSKI is Tadeusz Borowski's Polish biographer and the editor of the multivolume *Diaries of Maria Dąbrowska*.

ALICIA NITECKI is the translator of Tadeusz Borowski's *We Were in Auschwitz*, among other works. She is an associate professor of English at Bentley College in Waltham, Massachusetts.